Long recognized as "America's theologian," Jonathan Edwards (1703–58) is seen as instrumental in the Great Awakening of the 1740s that gripped much of New England and that laid the groundwork for an American Protestant religious identity. This *Cambridge Companion* offers a general, comprehensive introduction to Edwards and examines his life and works from various disciplinary perspectives, including history, literature, theology, religious studies, and philosophy. The book consists of sixteen chapters written by leading religious scholars, historians, and literary critics on Edwards's life, work, and legacy. The *Companion* will be an invaluable aid to teachers and scholars and will be readily accessible to those encountering Edwards for the first time.

STEPHEN J. STEIN taught at Indiana University for thirty-five years before retiring in May 2005. He is the editor of three volumes in the Yale Edition of *The Works of Jonathan Edwards: Apocalyptic Writings* (1977), *Notes on Scripture* (1998), and *The "Blank Bible"* (2006). His volume, *The Shaker Experience in America: A History of the United Society of Believers* (1992), was awarded the Philip Schaff Prize by the American Society of Church History.

CAMBRIDGE COMPANIONS TO RELIGION
This is a series of companions to major topics and key figures in theology
and religious studies. Each volume contains specially commissioned
chapters by international scholars that provide an accessible and
stimulating introduction to the subject for new readers and nonspecialists.

Other titles in the series

THE CAMBRIDGE COMPANION TO CHRISTIAN DOCTRINE
edited by Colin Gunton (1997)
ISBN 0 521 47118 4 hardback   ISBN 0 521 47695 8 paperback

THE CAMBRIDGE COMPANION TO BIBLICAL INTERPRETATION
edited by John Barton (1998)
ISBN 0 521 48144 9 hardback   ISBN 0 521 48593 2 paperback

THE CAMBRIDGE COMPANION TO DIETRICH BONHOEFFER
edited by John de Gruchy (1999)
ISBN 0 521 58258 x hardback   ISBN 0 521 58751 6 paperback

THE CAMBRIDGE COMPANION TO LIBERATION THEOLOGY
edited by Chris Rowland (1999)
ISBN 0 521 46144 8 hardback   ISBN 0 521 46707 1 paperback

THE CAMBRIDGE COMPANION TO KARL BARTH
edited by John Webster (2000)
ISBN 0 521 58476 0 hardback   ISBN 0 521 58560 0 paperback

THE CAMBRIDGE COMPANION TO CHRISTIAN ETHICS
edited by Robin Gill (2001)
ISBN 0 521 77070 x hardback   ISBN 0 521 77918 9 paperback

THE CAMBRIDGE COMPANION TO JESUS
edited by Markus Bockmuehl (2001)
ISBN 0 521 79261 4 hardback   ISBN 0 521 79678 4 paperback

THE CAMBRIDGE COMPANION TO FEMINIST THEOLOGY
edited by Susan Frank Parsons (2002)
ISBN 0 521 66327 x hardback   ISBN 0 521 66380 6 paperback

THE CAMBRIDGE COMPANION TO MARTIN LUTHER
edited by Donald K. McKim (2003)
ISBN 0 521 81648 3 hardback   ISBN 0 521 01673 8 paperback

THE CAMBRIDGE COMPANION TO ST. PAUL
edited by James D. G. Dunn (2003)
ISBN 0 521 78155 8 hardback   ISBN 0 521 78694 0 paperback

THE CAMBRIDGE COMPANION TO MEDIEVAL JEWISH PHILOSOPHY
edited by Daniel H. Frank and Oliver Leaman (2003)
ISBN 0 521 65207 3 hardback   ISBN 0 521 65574 9 paperback

THE CAMBRIDGE COMPANION TO POSTMODERN THEOLOGY
edited by Kevin Vanhoozer (2003)
ISBN 0 521 79062 x hardback   ISBN 0 521 79395 5 paperback

Continued after the Index

THE CAMBRIDGE COMPANION TO

JONATHAN EDWARDS

Edited by Stephen J. Stein

CAMBRIDGE
UNIVERSITY PRESS

CAMBRIDGE UNIVERSITY PRESS
Cambridge, New York, Melbourne, Madrid, Cape Town, Singapore, São Paulo

Cambridge University Press
32 Avenue of the Americas, New York, NY 10013-2473, USA

www.cambridge.org
Information on this title: www.cambridge.org/9780521852906

First published 2007

Printed in the United States of America

A catalog record for this publication is available from the British Library.

Library of Congress Cataloging in Publication Data

The Cambridge companion to Jonathan Edwards / [edited by] Stephen J. Stein.
    p.   cm. – (Cambridge companions to religion)
Includes bibliographical references and index.
ISBN 0-521-85290-0 (hardback) – ISBN 0-521-61805-3 (pbk)
1. Edwards, Jonathan, 1703–1758.   I. Stein, Stephen J., 1940 –   II. Title.   III. Series.
BX7260.E3C28   2006
285.8092–dc22   2006012154

ISBN-13   978-0-521-85290-6 hardback
ISBN-10   0-521-85290-0 hardback

ISBN-13   978-0-521-61805-2 paperback
ISBN-10   0-521-61805-3 paperback

Thomas A. Schafer
Selfless mentor and respected friend
With gratitude

Contents

List of Illustrations

Contributors

D. W. Bebbington is Professor of History at the University of Stirling, Scotland. He is the author of *Evangelicalism in Modern Britain: A History from the 1730s to the 1980s* and coeditor of *Evangelicalism: Comparative Studies of Popular Protestantism in North America, the British Isles, and Beyond, 1700–1900*, and *Biographical Dictionary of Evangelicals*.

Ava Chamberlain is Associate Professor of Religion at Wright State University. She is the editor of volume 18 in *The Works of Jonathan Edwards*, entitled *The "Miscellanies" 501–832*. She is the author of numerous essays focusing on Edwards's social views and is at work on a monograph on the same topic.

Stephen D. Crocco is James Lenox Librarian at Princeton Theological Seminary. He is the editor of the *Princeton Seminary Bulletin* and coeditor of *The Essential Paul Ramsey*. He is currently at work on a book dealing with Jonathan Edwards's legacy in twentieth-century theology.

Stephen H. Daniel is Professor of Philosophy at Texas A&M University. He is the author of *The Philosophy of Jonathan Edwards: A Study in Divine Semiotics* and *John Toland: His Methods, Manners, and Mind*. He is the editor of *Current Continental Theory and Modern Philosophy*.

Philip F. Gura is William S. Newman Distinguished Professor of American Literature and Culture at the University of North Carolina, Chapel Hill. He is the author of *Jonathan Edwards: America's Evangelical*; *A Glimpse of Sion's Glory: Puritan Radicalism in New England, 1620–1660*; and *The Wisdom of Words: Language, Theology, and Literature in the New England Renaissance*.

David D. Hall is Bartlett Professor of New England Church History at Harvard Divinity School. He is the editor of volume 12 in *The Works of Jonathan Edwards*, entitled *Ecclesiastical Writings*. He is the author of *The Faithful*

Shepherd: A History of the New England Ministry in the Seventeenth Century and *Worlds of Wonder, Days of Judgment: Popular Religious Belief in Early New England.*

E. Brooks Holifield is C. H. Candler Professor of American Church History at Candler School of Theology, Emory University. He is the author of *Theology in America: Christian Thought from the Age of the Puritans to the Civil War; The Covenant Sealed: The Development of Puritan Sacramental Theology in Old and New England;* and *The Gentlemen Theologians: American Theology in Southern Culture, 1795–1860.*

Wilson H. Kimnach is Professor of English at the University of Bridgeport. He is general editor of the sermon volumes in *The Works of Jonathan Edwards* as well as the editor of volume 10 in the *Works,* entitled *Sermons and Discourses 1720–1723,* and of volume 25, entitled *Sermons and Discourses 1743–1758* (forthcoming). He is coeditor of *The Sermons of Jonathan Edwards: A Reader.*

M. X. Lesser is the author of *Jonathan Edwards* in the Twayne's United States Authors Series and the editor of volume 19 in *The Works of Jonathan Edwards,* entitled *Sermons and Discourses 1734–1738.* He has compiled multiple bibliographies on Edwards, including *Jonathan Edwards: A Reference Guide; Jonathan Edwards: An Annotated Bibliography, 1979–1993;* and *The Printed Writings of Jonathan Edwards, 1703–1758: A Bibliography* (rev. ed.).

George M. Marsden is Francis A. McAnaney Professor of History at the University of Notre Dame. He is the author of *Jonathan Edwards: A Life; The Evangelical Mind and New School Presbyterian Experience; Fundamentalism and American Culture: The Shaping of Twentieth-Century Evangelicalism;* and *Understanding Fundamentalism and Evangelicalism.*

Kenneth P. Minkema is Executive Editor of *The Works of Jonathan Edwards* at Yale University. He is the editor of volume 14 in *The Works of Jonathan Edwards,* entitled *Sermons and Discourses 1723–1729.* He is coeditor of *A Jonathan Edwards Reader* and of *The Sermons of Jonathan Edwards: A Reader.*

Stephen J. Stein is Chancellor's Professor of Religious Studies, Emeritus, at Indiana University, Bloomington. He is the editor of volume 5 in *The Works of Jonathan Edwards,* entitled *Apocalyptic Writings;* volume 15, entitled *Notes on Scripture;* and volume 24, Parts I and II, entitled *The*

"*Blank Bible.*" He is also the editor of *Jonathan Edwards's Writings: Text, Context, Interpretation.*

Harry S. Stout is Jonathan Edwards Professor of American Christianity at Yale University and General Editor of *The Works of Jonathan Edwards.* He is coeditor of volume 22, entitled *Sermons and Discourses 1739–1742* and of *A Jonathan Edwards Reader.* He is the author of *The New England Soul: Preaching and Religious Culture in Colonial New England* and of *The Divine Dramatist: George Whitefield and the Rise of Modern Evangelicalism.*

Douglas A. Sweeney is Associate Professor and Chair of the Department of Church History and the History of Christian Thought at Trinity Evangelical Seminary. He is the editor of volume 23 in *The Works of Jonathan Edwards*, entitled *The "Miscellanies" 1153–1360*, and coeditor of *The Sermons of Jonathan Edwards: A Reader.* He is the author of *Nathaniel Taylor, New Haven Theology, and the Legacy of Jonathan Edwards.*

Rachel M. Wheeler is Assistant Professor of Religious Studies at Indiana University Purdue University, Indianapolis. She holds a Ph.D. from Yale University. She is currently working on a comparative study of Mahican Indian encounters with Congregational and Moravian missionaries in the mid-eighteenth century that explores questions of religious, cultural, and national identities.

Avihu Zakai is Professor of History at Hebrew University of Jerusalem. He is the author of *Jonathan Edwards's Philosophy of History: The Reenchantment of the World in the Age of the Enlightenment*, as well as *Exile and Kingdom: History and Apocalypse in the Puritan Migration to America* and *Theocracy in Massachusetts: Reformation and Separation in Early Puritan New England.*

Chronology of Jonathan Edwards

1703   Born October 5 in East Windsor, Connecticut
1716   Begins undergraduate studies in Wethersfield, Connecticut
1720   Completes baccalaureate and begins graduate studies at Yale
        College
1721   Experiences conversion at East Windsor
        Begins *Natural Philosophy*
1722   Begins "*Miscellanies*"
1722–3 Serves Presbyterian congregation in New York City
1723   Receives M.A. degree
        Begins "The Mind"
1723–4 Serves congregation in Bolton, Connecticut
1724   Begins *Notes on Scripture*
1724–6 Serves as tutor at Yale College
1727   Becomes Assistant Minister in Northampton, Massachusetts
        Marries Sarah Pierpont
1729   Becomes Senior Minister at Northampton
1730   Begins "Blank Bible"
1731   Gives Boston lecture
1734–5 Takes part in Connecticut Valley revivals
1737   Publishes *Faithful Narrative*
1738   Preaches *Charity and Its Fruits* series
1739   Preaches *History of Redemption* series
1740   Meets George Whitefield in Northampton
1740   Writes *Personal Narrative*
1741   Preaches *Sinners in the Hands of an Angry God*
        Presides over awakening in Northampton
        Delivers *Distinguishing Marks* at Yale commencement
1743   Publishes *Some Thoughts Concerning the Revival*
1744   Responds to "Bad Book" controversy in Northampton
1746   Publishes *Religious Affections*
1747   Hosts David Brainerd at Edwards's home

	Publishes *An Humble Attempt*
1749	Publishes *Life of Brainerd*
	Publishes *An Humble Inquiry*
	Engages in controversy with Northampton congregation
1750	Dismissed as minister at Northampton
	Preaches *Farewell Sermon*
1751	Becomes a missionary in Stockbridge, Massachusetts
1752	Publishes *Misrepresentations Corrected*
1754	Takes charge of Indian schools in Stockbridge
	Experiences lengthy period of ill health
	Publishes *Freedom of the Will*
1755	Writes *End of Creation*
	Writes *The Nature of True Virtue*
1757	Receives offer of presidency of the College of New Jersey
1758	Obtains release from Stockbridge ministry
	Becomes president of the College of New Jersey
	Undergoes inoculation against smallpox
	Dies March 22 from complications

Acknowledgments

In a scholarly undertaking of this sort, the editor incurs debts to many who have assisted with one or another aspect of the project. Among the individuals at Cambridge University Press at the top of the list is Andy Beck who has encouraged and supported the enterprise from the initial planning through the various stages of production. He is much appreciated. Others on the staff who have had a hand in this process include Faith Black, Shari Chappell, Andy Saff, and Kristy Tobin. This volume, of course, would have been impossible without the cooperation and contributions of the authors of the chapters. They all are very busy scholars and I am grateful that they included this project on their respective schedules. One of those authors who has aided in additional ways deserves special mention, namely Kenneth Minkema, Executive Editor of *The Works of Jonathan Edwards*. He has shared knowledge and insight repeatedly without complaint. That is quite unusual. One person who has lived through each stage of this project and probably has cause to complain but also has not done so is Devonia Stein. For her I am very grateful. Finally, it seemed to me highly appropriate that this book be dedicated to Thomas A. Schafer because literally every one of the authors in this collection is building on the pioneering scholarship that Tom Schafer shared with all of us.

THE CAMBRIDGE COMPANION TO
JONATHAN EDWARDS

Introduction

STEPHEN J. STEIN

Jonathan Edwards (1703–58) is, indisputably, a significant figure in American history. He emerged on the religious landscape of New England in the opening half of the eighteenth century, but soon achieved an international reputation. Edwards's description of religious revivals and his defense of evangelical Protestantism vaulted him into the public arena at home and abroad. Though his life was cut short prematurely a few months after becoming the president of the College of New Jersey (later Princeton University), his publications and his personal influence on a subsequent generation of religious leaders assured that his theological legacy would continue after his death.

The impact of Edwards's ideas expanded with the passage of time. In the eighteenth century, disciples and members of his extended family, including Samuel Hopkins, Jonathan Edwards, Jr., and Timothy Dwight, were instrumental in the articulation of an Edwardsean theology. The nineteenth century saw the consolidation and expansion of that tradition within evangelical Protestantism. The image of Edwards as a powerful preacher and a sophisticated apologist for traditional Christianity also attracted literary and cultural reflection by authors as diverse as Harriet Beecher Stowe and Oliver Wendell Holmes. Those same years witnessed the publication of collected editions of Edwards's *Works* as well as the frequent republication of his individual titles, including, most notably, *The Life of David Brainerd.* Biographies of Edwards also abounded, some laudatory and uncritical, others adopting partisan and critical viewpoints. During the first half of the twentieth century, favorable reflections on Edwards were published by such distinguished thinkers as William James and Josiah Royce at the same time that negative judgments were recorded by George Santayana and Clarence Darrow.

The second half of the twentieth century witnessed a surge of scholarly interest in Edwards, triggered, in part, by the publication of contrasting biographies by Ola Elizabeth Winslow and Perry Miller.[1] Winslow's work won the Pulitzer Prize; Miller's set off a wave of sophisticated academic scholarship. Miller was also instrumental in launching the publication of *The Works of Jonathan Edwards* begun in 1957 by Yale University Press. That undertaking set out to make available the full range of Edwards's public and private writings in a critical scholarly edition. To date, the Yale Edition has published twenty-four volumes.[2]

The year 2003 marked the tercentenary of Edwards's birth. Numerous gatherings and professional meetings focused on that anniversary. Scholarly conferences took place at such diverse locations as Princeton Theological Seminary, Calvin College, and the Library of Congress. Publications on Edwards abounded in that year. Notre Dame historian George M. Marsden, in a prize-winning biography, declared Edwards "the most acute early American philosopher and the most brilliant of all American theologians."[3] Avihu Zakai, an historian at Hebrew University of Jerusalem, noted that Edwards "is no less celebrated as a prominent philosopher, ethicist, and moralist."[4] E. Brooks Holifield, an historian of Christian thought at Emory University, asserted that "no other theologian in America" was equal to Edwards "in intellectual depth."[5] Cultural historian Richard Wightman Fox observed that Edwards "influenced believers on both sides of the Atlantic."[6]

Edwards rose to prominence in his own day for more than just his theological accomplishments. Family was another reason that he gained attention and public acclaim. Edwards's father, Timothy, was the minister of the Congregational church in East Windsor, Connecticut. Jonathan was the only son in a family of eleven children – one therefore, in his parents' eyes, virtually destined for the cloth. His mother, Esther, was the daughter of Solomon Stoddard, a prominent and powerful minister in Northampton, Massachusetts. He was also related to the Williams clan that included several prominent ministers in the Connecticut River Valley. These family connections virtually guaranteed Edwards a measure of visibility and vocational opportunities that situated him well for rising professional and personal prominence. Ultimately, he succeeded his grandfather Stoddard and took over the pulpit in Northampton. From that noteworthy location, for more than two decades he exercised an expanding sphere of influence.

Edwards was himself a successful preacher and revivalist. His congregation in Northampton, Massachusetts, and other congregations throughout New England were at times deeply moved by his preaching. Edwards's accounts of local religious awakenings and his engagement with other influential revivalists, including the English itinerant preacher George Whitefield, gave him a prominence that attracted both contemporary commentary and the attention of later historians. The revival that Edwards led in his congregation in 1734–5, for example, assumed a kind of definitive quality for the larger American evangelical movement. His subsequent defense of the widespread awakenings in later years confirmed his pivotal role in the emerging evangelical movement.

Edwards enjoyed a regional reputation as a successful preacher. That reputation grew with the publication of a few of his sermons during his lifetime and then even more with the later appearance of collected editions of his writings. Some of his sermons were deeply theological, almost metaphysical; others were graphically and emotionally disturbing. Sometimes his sermons formed the core of subsequent major publications. The medium of the spoken word was one of the most obvious ways that Edwards achieved high reputation during his lifetime and in subsequent generations. His most famous (or infamous) sermon, *Sinners in the Hands of an Angry God*, has achieved a degree of notoriety in the field of American literature almost without precedent for a piece of religious literature.[7] Anthologized extensively, the sermon evokes reflections on human contingency in the face of a demanding and wrathful God. The image of an offended God holding the sinner over the open fiery pit of hell, as one might hold a spider by a thin thread, suggests the rhetorical power of Edwards the preacher and, even more, his willingness to employ rhetoric for religious ends.

The image of Edwards as a terror-evoking preacher contrasts sharply with another element of his reputation that emerged, especially during the last decade of his life. Theological and philosophical insight and precision came to mark the major treatises published during his lifetime and posthumously. *Religious Affections*, for example, defined and distinguished signs of "gracious affections" or authentic Christianity from signs or evidences that were not proof of true spiritual religion. *An Humble Attempt* employed an apocalyptic argument in support of an international proposal for united prayer on behalf of the advancement of the kingdom of God. *An Humble Inquiry* articulated and defended controversial, alternative, and restrictive conditions for admitting persons to the Lord's Supper. *Freedom of the Will* engaged and contributed to contemporary philosophical discourse centering on the analysis of volition, causation, determinism, and moral necessity. *Original Sin* reaffirmed and clarified a traditional judgment on human depravity and its universal transmission in the face of and in opposition to the Enlightenment's increasingly successful assault on that dogma. *The Nature of True Virtue* abstracted and elevated virtuous love, defined as benevolence or consent to "Being in general" or God, above love to "particular beings" or the neighbor. *The End of Creation* asserted and reinforced the centrality of God and the communication of God's glory as the highest purpose informing the creation of the universe.

Side by side with the theological and the metaphysical – and not unrelated in Edwards's mind – is striking evidence of his pastoral preoccupation throughout his professional life. His fixation on the experience of God's grace in the Christian's life led to both occasional and systematic reflection on the life stages and states of mind characteristic of "visible saints," that is, persons who experienced God's grace in their lives and struggled to reflect the divine presence in their daily activities. At times Edwards held up notable Christian examples and models for others to emulate. Abigail Hutchinson was a young woman in Northampton plagued by serious illness whose "lively sense of the excellency of Christ" maintained her resolve to testify to the glory of God in the face of her impending death. Phebe Bartlett was a four-year-old in the congregation whose devotional activities and spirit of charity were a remarkable example for the members of her family and others in Northampton. And then there was Sarah Pierpont Edwards, Jonathan's wife, who was often "swallowed up" for hours in contemplations of Christ's love and whose body sometimes sank under the weight of these religious experiences. She embodied, par excellence, the virtuous Christian life.

But Edwards's life was not without public setbacks. In the course of his ministry, he came into conflict with his own congregation over the issue of admission to the Lord's Supper. He also irritated and alienated members of that Northampton community by his heavy-handed pastoral style and insensitive communication with his parishioners. The conflict with his congregation, which reached a crisis stage in the late 1740s, ultimately resulted in his dismissal and, after some time, a move with his family to western Massachusetts where he assumed responsibility for a mission to the Mahican Indians centered at Stockbridge. On one level, therefore, as a pastor he was strikingly unsuccessful and defeated, turned out by the members of his own congregation. His defeat and rejection in Northampton were a massive personal and professional blow. They also have placed an enduring stamp upon his public image and led to a vastly different pastoral reputation from that which he had enjoyed during the height of the revivals in Northampton.

Edwards's dismissal by his congregation contrasts sharply with his theological and philosophical achievements. The difficulties in Northampton have also fueled a tradition of commentary that depicts Edwards as a stiff and difficult personality, a fact that he himself seems to have recognized. The reputation appears to be quite accurate. He was accustomed to spelling out the truths of God to others, but he was not given to easy acceptance of criticism. His controversies with other clergy and with theological and philosophical opponents reflect an unbending and self-confident perspective. Perhaps his profession as a minister contributed to the cultivation of that sense of righteous cause rather than self-doubt. With those who accepted his judgments, he felt a close relationship. Students, family, and friends formed a religious coalition that looked to him for leadership while he was alive. Their bond

1. Portrait of Jonathan Edwards by Joseph Badger, courtesy of Yale University Art Gallery, bequest of Eugene Phelps Edwards.

with him appears very strong. After his death, family members and disciples played a central role in the establishment and expansion of his reputation and legacy.

Given the two sides of Edwards's career, it is no surprise to discover that he has been the subject of conflicting artistic representations with the passage of time. Edwards's image in the widely disseminated Joseph Badger portrait painted in the mid-eighteenth century can be described as penetrating and searching (see Figure 1). Edwards's face captures all attention of the viewer. The powdered wig, the clerical bands, and the dark robe are

2. Portrait of the Reverend Jonathan Edwards by John Ferguson Weir, Yale University Art Gallery, gift of Arthur Reed Kimball, B.A. 1877.

mere surrounding appointments. Prominent and central are Edwards's high forehead, his piercing eyes, and his firm mouth. Badger's portrait seems to capture the man well; it is the image of a resolute man of God. By contrast, the portrait by John F. Weir painted in 1910 places Edwards at a desk with an open book, a quill pen, and paper (see Figure 2). The same clerical appointments are present, but softened in severity, as is also the prominence of his forehead, eyes, and mouth. A bookshelf in the faint background adds ambiance of a working study to this portrayal of Edwards as a scholar. One can almost imagine Weir's Edwards, though deep in thought, allowing a smile to break forth across his face – an unthinkable prospect on Badger's portrait. A more recent representation, a woodcut by Lance Hidy, which serves as the frontispiece in an Edwards giftbook published in 1974, evokes a sense of both austerity and inflexibility. The rough texture of the carved facial lines dominates the image (see Figure 3). One can perhaps even imagine a sneer coming from the pursed lips of this Edwards. Diverse "portraits" of Edwards

3. Wood-engraving of Jonathan Edwards by Lance Hidy, the frontispiece in *Of Insects by Jonathan Edwards*, edited by Wallace E. Anderson (New Haven, CT: Jonathan Edwards College Press, 1974). Courtesy of Ruth M. Anderson.

have been present for more than two and a half centuries – witness the depictions of Oliver Wendell Holmes and Mark Twain – and have contributed to contrasting judgments of the man and his life.

One measure of Edwards's continuing prominence in the twenty-first century is his presence on the Internet. The number and variety of websites identified by entering "Jonathan Edwards" in a search engine is truly astonishing. (One must, of course, discount references to others by the same name, including the contemporary musician Jonathan Edwards.) Thousands of websites invite perusal. Some identify diverse scholarly resources. At the official website of *The Works of Jonathan Edwards* at Yale University, for example, one can examine scholarly resources, gain access to online archives including materials never before available in printed form, and take part in a beta-testing program that provides feedback to the Yale Edition for its impending launch of *The Works of Jonathan Edwards* online.[8] This site represents the most sophisticated option available to those interested in Edwards. But it is hardly typical of the majority of the entries on the Web. On many sites, one can access the texts of treatises and other writings by Edwards, available in whole or in part. Most of these are drawn from nineteenth-century editions of his *Works*.[9] Sermons by Edwards are present in text, audio, and video on the Web.[10] Devotional readings selected from Edwards's writings appear in different formats. One release, entitled "Day by Day with Jonathan Edwards: Selected Readings," represents itself as [f]eaturing 365 thought-provoking reflections" that offer "a daily measure of penetrating insight and thoughtful encouragement."[11] Another site by John Piper banners its offering under the title "A God-Entranced Vision of All-Things," and subtitles the site, "Why We Need Jonathan Edwards Three Hundred Years Later."[12] If one desires a more material Edwards item, that too is available on the Web. "Reformer Ware" offers for sale the "Jonathan Edwards" coffee mug on the back of which reads, "The enjoyment of God is the only happiness with which our souls can be satisfied."[13] And, of course, there are bloggers who write of their admiration for Edwards. One blog, entitled "Sojourner: Admiring Jonathan Edwards," dated August 19, 2005, was posted by a Baptist minister in "Bayou country," a person who regards Edwards as a "super-genius."[14] It is intriguing to speculate about the kind of website that Edwards would have constructed had he been alive in the age of cyberspace.

This *Companion* seeks to open for you the reader the life and times of Edwards, his religious and professional achievements, and the full range of his reputation in diverse fields. This book includes work by three generations of distinguished scholars whose ground-breaking research has opened new insights on Edwards's background, life, accomplishments, and legacy. The chapters that follow are organized into three parts dealing with Edwards's life and context, his roles and achievements, and his legacy and reputation, respectively. The parts are not exclusive of one another. On the contrary, the three are mutually reinforcing of the ways in which the study of one or another particular aspect of Edwards leads inexorably into other dimensions of his experience. There is no chapter in this book that does not cast distinctive light on his life circumstances. Yet biography qua biography is the specific assignment of only one of the contributors. The other chapters are biographically complementary and expansive. That is also true with respect to the place of Edwards in American history. All of the chapters that follow provide perspective on the professional roles he played during his lifetime and on the subsequent ways that later Americans and persons outside America have viewed him and his accomplishments. However, no single viewpoint or critical perspective on Edwards controls these chapters. The range of judgments expressed by the contributors includes admiration as well as criticism, objective evaluation as well as subjective engagement, scholarly detachment as well as personal opinion. Frankly, it is impossible to read about Edwards and to engage the scholarship that he has elicited without coming to some conflicting judgments regarding him and his place in American history.

The goal of this *Cambridge Companion to Jonathan Edwards* is to provide a wide-ranging interdisciplinary encounter with this significant American figure. In the chapters that follow, Edwards is situated in the exciting world of the eighteenth century. He is examined as a person, theologian, philosopher, preacher, pastor, exegete, missionary, husband, father, observer of nature, British colonial, and resident in both New England and the Atlantic community. He was living in a culture that was changing rapidly. His engagement with the forces of change is, in fact, one subtheme that ties together many of the chapters in this book. The Atlantic community of which he was a part was locked in international tension that broke into open warfare more than once during his lifetime. Political tension was also commonplace in eighteenth-century New England. Religious conflict in the American colonies followed traditional lines stretching back to the Reformation, but it was fueled in new ways by the growth and development of alternative religious movements. Philosophical advances linked to the celebration of reason exalted by the Enlightenment challenged longstanding assumptions about human nature and the world. Yet cultural and racial hierarchies continued to exercise dominance in most aspects of life. These diverse challenges posed by the eighteenth century are very evident in Edwards's life and work.

Edwards is remembered by most nonspecialists as the preacher of a potentially frightening (or disturbing) sermon that pictures the human plight in the face of a stern God. Scholars, by contrast, underscore the pivotal role that Edwards played in articulating an evangelical religious perspective, defending the revivals that were the agency of expansion for evangelicalism, and in establishing the religious framework for a tradition that would grow into one of America's most powerful religious and cultural forces.

Part I of this *Companion*, which focuses on Edwards's life and context, introduces readers to the complexity of Edwards's biography. George M. Marsden, an historian who perhaps has written the definitive modern biography of Edwards, underscores the importance of understanding the diverse contexts in which Edwards lived – one as wide as the transatlantic Western world and another as narrow as the confines of the town of Northampton, Massachusetts. Central to his life, according to Marsden, were a continuing preeminent concern with his own spirituality and a vocational attention to the religious well-being of those around him and those whom he served as a minister. Though a public figure much of his life, Edwards also had a very private sense of self that is revealed in his personal writings. Kenneth P. Minkema, who has written extensively about Edwards's public and private life, explores the documents Edwards wrote for himself and those in which he revealed himself to others. From these there emerges a complex person who has not always been evident in studies of Edwards. Minkema, for example, sheds light on Edwards's ambition, his sense of self, his interpersonal style, his ultimate commitments, as well as his attitudes toward women and slaves.

Edwards was, of course, a product of Puritan New England, and it is that religious and cultural context that David D. Hall, who has invested his career in the historical study of that region, addresses in his chapter. Longstanding controversial issues of central importance for the "Congregational Way" in New England, including the nature of the church and of the ministry, occupied Edwards and shaped the outcome of his career. In his chapter, Hall opens that historical context and the religious background in New England in a most revealing way. But Edwards was also engaged with the intellectual changes occurring in the larger Atlantic community, many of which were the product of the transforming forces associated with the Enlightenment. In his chapter, Avihu Zakai, who has written extensively about the ways that Western thought was refashioned by the Enlightenment, charts Edwards's encounter with modern thought and the manner in which he struggled to respond to the challenges it posed for his theological positions. Zakai evaluates Edwards's engagement with European thinkers who were writing in controversial ways about such topics as revelation, history, natural philosophy, and ethics. Collectively, the chapters in the opening part of this book set the stage for considering the particular ways that Edwards engaged the worlds of which he was a part.

Part II of this *Companion* focuses on the diverse professional roles Edwards filled during his lifetime and his achievements in those roles as well as his limitations with respect to those vocational functions. It may appear that focusing on one professional role at a time artificially divides his activities; in fact, however, all of the professional functions considered in Part II relate to one another in Edwards's experience.

One role Edwards filled throughout his career that invites scholarly attention is his pastoral function as a preacher, the primary public task required of him by definition as a minister. Wilson H. Kimnach, who is the leading authority on Edwards as a preacher, situates him in the homiletical traditions of early New England, describing both the customs and practices Edwards accepted and the distinctive historical stages evident in his preaching career. The changing pastoral contexts in which Edwards found himself during his lifetime, Kimnach demonstrates, shaped his sermons and his reputation as a preacher. Edwards clearly exercised immense influence from the pulpit. Closely linked to his regular preaching responsibilities were the tasks he assumed as an architect and practitioner of revivalism. Harry S. Stout, General Editor of *The Works of Jonathan Edwards*, identifies the theological assumptions that informed Edwards's lifelong desire to promote revivals as the means for implementing what he perceived to be the divine plan for redemption of the world. Stout identifies the diverse roles played by heaven, hell, and earth in the divine schema that Edwards elaborated when he spoke and wrote in support of the revival cause. He also shows how Edwards was influenced by the prominent English revivalist George Whitefield, who visited the American colonies multiple times, and how *Sinners in the Hands of an Angry God* fits into the larger story of Edwards the revivalist.

The theological message that Edwards preached and taught, whether in regular sermons or on occasions when he was trying to promote revivals, is what E. Brooks Holifield, who has published extensively on the history of American theology, examines in his chapter on Edwards as a theologian. Drawing on the full range of Edwards's published treatises and private notebooks, he shows how the traditional theological judgments of the Reformed tradition found new and powerful expression in Edwards's diverse writings and how he utilized a central insight to tie together his views. Holifield also points to the ways in which Edwards's theological positions were informed and reinforced by his philosophical assumptions. In Edwards's case, it is impossible to separate theological ideas from philosophical assumptions. For that reason, therefore, it is important to examine the role Edwards played as a philosopher, a task that Stephen H. Daniel, who has written extensively about modern philosophy and about Edwards's philosophy, undertakes in his chapter on Edwards as a philosopher. He shows how Edwards entered into a number of the debates that European philosophers were engaged in at the time, including such issues as the nature of reality, the problem of knowledge, and the extent of human freedom, as well as a series of aesthetic and moral questions. Daniel provides a compelling argument that it is inappropriate to dismiss Edwards as a philosopher; he demonstrates the ways that Edwards joined the discourse of other "theocentric metaphysicians." It is instructive to note that the judgments of Holifield on Edwards as a theologian and those of Daniel on Edwards as a philosopher intersect strikingly with one another.

Two other professional roles of Edwards are complementary to those already identified and also distinctive in their own right. Edwards invested an immense amount of thought and time in the study of the Bible. My chapter examines his role as an exegete. An editor of the biblical notebooks compiled by Edwards, I note in my chapter his deep and abiding commitment to the authority of Scripture, his creative approaches to the interpretation of the biblical text, and ways in which his diverse private and public writings reflect that exegetical base. My chapter points out how Edwards was at odds with the growing critical approach to the Bible and also how he often put the biblical text to polemical uses. One other professional role is complementary to those mentioned previously and also distinctive. After losing his struggle with and being dismissed by his Northampton congregation, Edwards accepted a position as a missionary to the Mahican Indians and moved with his family to Stockbridge, Massachusetts. His years in that new position and his engagement with the politically and culturally complex situation of Native Americans are the subject of the chapter by Rachel M. Wheeler, who has focused her scholarship on eighteenth-century Indian missions. She shows the diverse and varied functions Edwards fulfilled as an advocate for the Mahicans at Stockbridge and as their pastor and preacher. Wheeler also documents how his experiences at that frontier outpost left an identifiable mark on the theological treatises he wrote during those years. Edwards's experiences both as an exegete and as a missionary intersected with the other public and prominent roles that he carried out in his ministry.

Part III of this *Companion* sets out to assess the legacy and reputation of Edwards in a variety of areas. This part is premised on the major influence he exerted during his lifetime and in subsequent periods of history. The areas chosen for this measurement are diverse and suggestive of the different fields in which scholars, disciples, and critics have engaged Edwards.

The massive impact of Edwards on the world of religion is evident in several of the chapters in Part III. The primary influence of Edwards on the American evangelical tradition, beginning in the generations immediately following his death during the eighteenth and nineteenth centuries and continuing today in America, is the subject of Douglas A. Sweeney's chapter. Sweeney, the editor of a volume of Edwards's "*Miscellanies*" and author of several studies dealing with the Edwardsean tradition, examines the ways in which Edwards's understanding of "true religion" involving a spiritual rebirth has been central to the evangelical movement in the United States from the time of his immediate successors, through advocates of the Christian missionary movement, down to the contemporary Edwardsean renaissance. Interestingly, not all of those sharing his central commitment concerning conversion have accepted Edwards's Calvinism. It was not only among evangelicals in America, however, that Edwards enjoyed reputation and influence; nor is it only in America today. In his chapter, D. W. Bebbington, the author of multiple studies of evangelicalism outside the United States, writing from his professional location in Scotland, describes the ways in which Edwards's writings were published and engaged outside America, first and primarily in the British Isles, then in a few other European locations, and by the end of the twentieth century in other parts of the globe. Again, however, the engagement with Edwards was not only by those who agreed completely with his views. In some instances, criticism and rejection of his philosophical and theological views were the occasion for attention to Edwards's writings.

But it has not only been religious persons of evangelical persuasion who have engaged Edwards and contributed to the construction and expansion of his legacy and reputation. The larger American context in the generations after Edwards's death saw the first assessments of Edwards as a writer in an emerging field of American *literature*, a term used for written expression including all kinds of writing. Edwards's reputation as a writer is the subject that Philip Gura, author of a biography of Edwards as well as works on the history of American literature, addresses in his chapter. Edwards's reputation as a significant literary artist whose writings engaged ideas is complex and controverted, but now well established in the field. His reputation as a writer rests on more than *Sinners in the Hands of an Angry God.* Closely related is the essay by M. X. Lesser, the editor of a volume of Edwards's *Sermons and Discourses* and the leading bibliographer in the field of Edwards studies. In his chapter, Lesser traces the presence of Edwards's writings and his constructed images in all sorts of publications, from reprints of Edwards's own writings to popular novels, from articles in *The New Yorker* to gatherings held on the tercentenary of Edwards's birth. It is this complexity of his reputation and legacy in American culture that still characterizes the contemporary situation.

This greater complexity involved with Edwards's reputation is also the subject of the chapter by Stephen Crocco, who is an historian of twentieth-century Protestant thought. In his chapter, he shows how the period from the Civil War until the 1930s witnessed a variety of ways that Edwards was engaged by persons with diverse interests, including both those of liberal persuasion and Neo-Orthodox religious thinkers. Edwards's observations on nature and his metaphysical reflections were some of the topics attracting attention among these groups. Out of this mixed cultural context emerged Perry Miller, who played a key role in the recovery of Edwards and in the growth of the modern scholarly Edwards enterprise.

The final chapter in this *Companion* carries the issue of Edwards's legacy and reputation into an area where there has been more modest scholarly investment, at best, until relatively recently, namely, his engagement with and views on a variety of social issues. The editor of one of the volumes of Edwards's *"Miscellanies"* and the author of several seminal essays dealing with Edwards's social views, Ava Chamberlain in her chapter describes and evaluates his judgments on age and class, gender and sexuality, and race and slavery. What role, if any, Edwards's judgments on these issues may play in the contemporary culture wars in America remains to be seen because of the increasing politicalization of the contemporary American evangelical movement on both the local and the national levels.

The study of Jonathan Edwards continues today, and it will continue in the future. Only now is the full extent of his writings becoming available in published and/or electronic form. The Yale Edition of *The Works of Jonathan Edwards* will soon publish the last two volumes in the letterpress edition. After that, the Edition will make available online the complete corpus of Edwards's writings, including transcriptions of previously unpublished manuscript notebooks and of previously unpublished manuscript sermons. This massive body of materials will invite examination by persons of all persuasions – scholars of different perspectives and other persons attracted to the study of Edwards either by sharing his religious viewpoint or by rejecting the implications of his judgments – be they theological, philosophical, or social in nature. In other words, the last word has not yet been written regarding Jonathan Edwards, his life and activities, his theology and other ideas, or his reputation and legacy.

Notes

1. Ola Elizabeth Winslow, *Jonathan Edwards, 1703–1758: A Biography* (New York: Macmillan, 1940); Perry Miller, *Jonathan Edwards* (New York: William Sloane Associates, 1949).
2. Most of the references to the writings of Edwards in this *Companion* are to texts contained in volumes that are part of the Yale Edition of *The Works of Jonathan Edwards* (New Haven: Yale University Press, 1957 ff). The endnotes in this book utilize a short reference form for citing that scholarly edition. References will include "WJE," followed by volume and page numbers. See the Appendix for a complete listing of the volumes in the Yale Edition and their editors.
3. George M. Marsden, *Jonathan Edwards: A Life* (New Haven: Yale University Press, 2003), 1.

4. Avihu Zakai, *Jonathan Edwards's Philosophy of History: The Reenchantment of the World in the Age of Enlightenment* (Princeton, NJ: Princeton University Press, 2003), xiii.

5. E. Brooks Holifield, *Theology in America: Christian Thought from the Age of the Puritans to the Civil War* (New Haven: Yale University Press, 2003), 102.

6. Richard Wightman Fox, *Jesus in America: Personal Savior, Cultural Hero, National Obsession* (San Francisco: Harper San Francisco, 2004), 115.

7. WJE, 22:400–35.

8. See http://edwards.yale.edu.

9. See, for example, http://www.jonathanedwards.com.

10. See, for example, http://www.sermonaudio.com, where David Bruce Sonner reads *Sinners in the Hands of an Angry God.*

11. http://www.hendrickson.com/html/product/633881.trade.html.

12. http://www.desiringgod.org/library/topics/edwards/edwards_300.html.

13. See http://www.reformerware.com/edwards.htm.

14. See http://alienman.blogspot.com/2005/08/admiring-jonathan-edwards.html.

Part I

Edwards's life and context

1 Biography

GEORGE M. MARSDEN

If we are to appreciate Jonathan Edwards as a real person and not just as an intellectual or spiritual prodigy who appears out of nowhere in the American wilderness, we must try to get a sense of his contexts. Edwards lived in a time and place very different from our own, and so it takes some acts of imagination to get a good sense of him in his own times.

First, we must think of *when* Edwards lived. Born in 1703 and living until 1758, he came of age almost a full century after the first American Puritan settlements; but he died before there was an inkling of the American Revolution. Even most educated Americans today would be hard pressed to name anything that happened in colonial America between 1703 and 1758, except perhaps the awakening with which Edwards himself was associated and the outbreak of the French and Indian War during Edwards's last years. They might also recall that Benjamin Franklin, born in 1706, was a contemporary of Edwards and thus provides us with some secular glimpses of these largely unknown decades.

Our picture of Edwards's world is helped considerably if we think about Europe during his time. One of the most momentous developments was the intellectual revolution of the Enlightenment, which was growing throughout Edwards's lifetime. Edwards's early thought was shaped by the great English figures of the previous generation, Isaac Newton and John Locke, and he was a contemporary of the Scottish David Hume, whose work he knew well. Edwards's intellectual context was shaped by a host of British and European thinkers who were shepherding Christendom from an age of intense faiths and religious wars into what they hoped would be an age of reason, science, and common sense. Benjamin Franklin's secular outlook is a testimony to the appeal that these impressively formulated British and European Enlightenment views often had for young colonials.

The reminder that Edwards was working in the context of a broader British and European intellectual world is of a piece with a more fundamental observation, that Edwards was not an "American" in the modern sense, but an English colonial loyal to the British crown. The same was true of Franklin in 1758, and in fact the Philadelphian remained a British monarchist well into the 1770s. The British military was essential to colonial security, and American colonials cherished their English constitutional heritage.

In Edwards's case, the bonds of loyalty to the king were greatly strengthened because the British crown was firmly Protestant. One dimension of living in this pre-revolutionary era was that religion and politics were far more closely related than they would later be in the United States. Ever since the Reformation, Christendom had been divided into Protestant and Catholic lands, depending almost always on the disposition of the monarch. England was one of the countries in which the warfare and intrigue between Protestant and Catholic factions had been most long lasting and intense. As recently as the 1680s, a Catholic, James II, had held the English crown. After the "Glorious Revolution" of 1688, the monarchy of Great Britain (including Scotland after 1707) was declared permanently Protestant. Nonetheless, the matter did not rest there. One of the most dramatic political events of Edwards's day was the attempt of "Bonnie Prince Charles" – Catholic claimant to the throne as heir to James II, who invaded Scotland and England in 1745–6 – to recapture the crown.

Edwards lived on the far western frontier of this British world in a region intensely involved in its religious-political conflicts. We can understand him best if we think of him as living near the intersection of three competing civilizations: British Protestant, French Catholic, and Indian. British Protestants had recently settled western New England, displacing most of the Indians. Many of the displaced Indians were just to the north and to the west, and most of them were allied with the French Catholics not far beyond in Upper Canada. Edwards's lifetime was punctuated by various wars, usually of European origin, that typically pitted New Englanders against the French and Indians. Edwards was also deeply interested in missions to the Indians and himself became a missionary for a time. If we notice the constant presence of Indians in his world, we can get a better sense that he lived in exciting and sometimes dangerous times.

Living in New England also placed him in a world deeply influenced by an unusual heritage. New England had been settled by Puritans, or those who in England had been intent on purifying the Church of England according to Calvinistic standards of doctrine and practice. The Puritan settlements of Massachusetts and Connecticut became remarkably successful communities shaped substantially by religious ideals. Calvinism was not just a theological ideal for the church; it also involved a vision of society guided by God's Word in Scripture, so far as that was practical. By Edwards's day, several generations since the first settlements, New England had lost its virtual independence. Nonetheless, the Puritan era had left an indelible imprint on New England's state-supported churches, which were still strongly Calvinist (or Reformed) in theology and an unsettled mix of Congregational and Presbyterian elements in governance. To understand Edwards, it is essential to appreciate that he saw himself as heir to a formidable theological heritage that placed him not only in the context of his seventeenth-century Calvinist predecessors, but also in the larger history of the Christian church.

This heritage left an especially strong impression on him because he was shaped in a close-knit and remarkable family. His father, Timothy Edwards, was pastor from 1694 to 1758 in the village of East Windsor, just across the Connecticut River from Hartford, Connecticut. A conservative Calvinist with zeal for religious awakenings, Timothy was a formidable presence in his own right. He combined rigid principles of theology, morality, and church practice with an affectionate demeanor toward his family. Jonathan was the only son among ten daughters, and Timothy lavished attention on educating and grooming him for the ministry. Esther Stoddard Edwards, Jonathan's mother, may have been at least as important in passing on the heritage. Esther was the daughter of the most famous and influential pastor in the Connecticut River Valley, Solomon Stoddard of Northampton, Massachusetts, and was expert in theology. Young Jonathan was also surrounded by sisters, four older and six younger, which doubtless helped shape his outlook. In his theology he placed special emphasis on religious affections and often pointed to women he knew as models of true spirituality.

Timothy prepared Jonathan in the Greek and Latin necessary for collegiate study, and Jonathan entered the Collegiate School of Connecticut (soon to become Yale College) at age thirteen. At the time the college was being conducted in several locations, and Jonathan spent his first college years in nearby Wethersfield under the tutorship of an impressive cousin, Elisha Williams. Edwards completed his undergraduate study in New Haven just after Yale College settled there, and he gave the class valedictory address. Continuing in M.A. work, typically two years of independent study, Jonathan remained in New Haven the first year and then went to New York City to serve as an interim pastor of a small Presbyterian church from August 1722 to May 1723.

During his late teen years, he underwent intense religious struggles and experiences that would shape the rest of his life. In his senior year, when he was still sixteen, he nearly died from a serious illness, and was terrified about the state of his soul, feeling that God "shook me over the pit of hell."[1] During the next year, he strenuously sought God and moral purity, but he did not find any resolution until the spring of his seventeenth year, when he began to have some remarkable experiences of a sense of joy in the beauty of God's goodness. Yet not all was bliss or a life of ease in the arduous pilgrim's progress that followed. Late in 1722, while he was serving as a fledgling pastor in New York, he set down a lengthy open-ended list of resolutions to discipline his spiritual and moral life[2] and also began a spiritual diary that he continued with some regularity for a couple of years.[3] In the latter it is immediately apparent that he oscillated from day to day and week to week between spiritual depressions and ecstasies. Nonetheless, he later regarded his intense experiences of this era as the beginnings of his genuine spirituality, and he enjoyed throughout his life periodic renewals of the overwhelming sense of God's presence.

What he later regarded as his conversion, which true to the Puritan heritage was normally an arduous process rather than a single moment, also involved a major intellectual component. During his collegiate years in New Haven, Jonathan avidly read the works of Isaac Newton and John Locke. Adapting the revolutionary new science and new philosophy to his own purposes, Jonathan found ways to resolve great objections he formerly had regarding God's sovereignty. At the same time, when he was still ages eighteen and nineteen, as he was enjoying periodically intense ecstatic experiences of God's glory and goodness, he was laying the intellectual foundations for a lifelong project of showing how such an all-powerful loving and good being might operate in the immense, yet fallen, universe. Having felt the power of the objections that the new liberal Christian thought of the early British Enlightenment posed for Calvinist affirmations concerning God's sovereignty, one of his major goals was to show how the old Calvinist faith in which he had been reared could answer the often-skeptical challenges of the Enlightenment. These ideas, which he developed with remarkable philosophical sophistication in private notebooks, became the framework for his thought throughout his life.

To put the matter most simply, Edwards countered the intellectual trends of his day by emphasizing that human understanding of everything must start with the God of Christianity. At the center of reality was the perfectly good and loving being revealed in Scripture as the triune God who created and sustained everything. The reason why a perfect God would create a universe was as an expression of the overflowing love among the persons of the Trinity. The triune God wished to share that love with responsible creatures. So the whole creation was an expression of the beauty of the love of God, ultimately most fully manifested in the most beautiful love imaginable, the sacrificial death of Jesus Christ for undeserving creatures who had contemptuously rebelled against God's love. Impressed by Isaac Newton's work that the universe was one of constantly changing relationships and hence new at every moment, Edwards argued that God's creative activity was not something that just happened long ago but was an ongoing expression of

God's love as God sustained this immense reality at every point in time. Further, in such a universe created and sustained by God, the most important relationship was to God. So spiritual relationships were the most basic dimensions of reality. Physical objects were most essentially means by which God communicated with other created minds.

Edwards was thus countering some of the most prevalent trends in the progressive thought of the era. Most of the fashionable thinkers of the day, impressed by the power of natural law to explain both the natural world and proper human relationships, tended to distance God from reality and to make God superfluous. Deism was the epitome of this trend, but many liberal Christian thinkers tended toward the same direction. In Deism, God was the distant creator of natural laws that worked on their own without direct divine intervention. Edwards, by contrast, stressed God's intimate and ongoing relationship to all reality.

Edwards's theological and philosophical reflections were closely related to his personal religious experience. Throughout his life, Edwards's spiritual labors, which were marked by intense devotional and personal disciplines, were punctuated by ecstatic experiences as he went to the fields or the woods for contemplation and prayer. He would be overwhelmed with a sense of God's glory, beauty, goodness, and love. He would be so overcome by a "sweet delight in God and divine things" that he would break into ecstatic spiritual singing or chanting.[4] Edwards's sense of God's beauty in nature grew out of his philosophical reflections on how God was intimately related to reality at every moment so that everything was a communication from God. So natural objects were part of the language of God, distinct from God but still intimate expressions of the divine character. These views, in turn, related to a typological view of reality. Every natural thing could be seen as pointing to a spiritual principle. Ultimately everything converged in pointing to the wonders of God's beauty and love in the redemptive work of Christ. Edwards kept a notebook on "Images of Divine Things" in which he noted these connections.[5] These meanings, however, would not be intelligible without Scripture, which was the key that unlocked the meaning of all reality. Scripture was to be understood not only as a literal historical record and as an authoritative source of faith and doctrine, but also typologically. Edwards called one of his notebooks "Types of the Messiah," and in it he expounded on how Scripture was filled with types of Christ.[6]

At the same time as young Jonathan was developing the frameworks for his theological and philosophical outlook and searching intensely for spiritual signs of God's grace, he was anxious about his career. In May 1723 he returned to his family home from New York City and prepared for his M.A. oration at Yale, which he delivered in October. By that time prospects for a dearly desired return to New York had fallen through, and in November he reluctantly accepted a pastorate in the village of Bolton, Connecticut, near his home. In June 1724 he secured a release from Bolton to accept a position as tutor at Yale. The college had been severely shaken when its rector, Timothy Cutler, had defected to Anglicanism, and it was still without a rector. With no such senior personage overseeing the college and classes being conducted by a few young tutors, the students were especially rowdy. Edwards, who was somewhat brittle personally, struggled to maintain order and related these difficulties to falling into "a low, sunk estate and condition" spiritually, which lasted several years.[7]

Simultaneously he was distracted by his courtship of young Sarah Pierpont. Sarah was the daughter of the late Reverend James Pierpont, Sr., of New Haven. Jonathan already had his eye on her at least by the fall of 1723, when she was only thirteen and he was almost twenty. Around that time he wrote a prose poem to her praising a "young lady ... who is beloved of that almighty Being, who made and rules the world, and that there are certain seasons in which the great Being ... comes to her and fills her mind with exceeding great delight," and that she "will sometimes go about, singing sweetly, ... and seems to be always full of joy and pleasure."[8] During the next years in New Haven, Jonathan won the heart of this girl who seemed the spiritual counterpart to himself. We know little of their courtship but only that they were married in July 1727, when Jonathan was nearing twenty-four and she was seventeen.

By that time his vocational prospects also took a decisive turn. In 1726 he accepted a call to become assistant to his grandfather, the renowned Solomon Stoddard, in Northampton, Massachusetts. Northampton was a town of about one thousand people with a church of virtually the same size, both among the largest in western Massachusetts. Stoddard was especially known for opening church membership to all who could give a basic profession of faith (rather than an account of being converted) and who were free from notorious scandal in their lives. Jonathan, following his father's views, had reservations about this practice, but he was willing to live with it.

When Solomon Stoddard died early in 1729, Edwards became the sole pastor of the church. The town had already granted him and his young bride funds to purchase a comfortable "mansion house," plus land for a pasture, and forty acres on the edge of town that could be used for income. Jonathan and Sarah soon turned the house into a substantial household. Beginning with their daughter, Sarah, born in 1728, and continuing until 1750, eleven children arrived, eight girls and three boys. Despite her regular pregnancies, Sarah oversaw this ever-expanding household and much of the farming economy that helped support it.

Edwards's position in the town was secured from the beginning by being the beneficiary of the patronage of Colonel John Stoddard, Solomon Stoddard's son and Jonathan's uncle. Solomon Stoddard had been the most influential clergyman in the region, and John Stoddard was the most influential magistrate. John Stoddard was often a representative to the colonial government in Boston, a local judge, the military leader of the region in times of periodic warfare with the Indians, and a leading negotiator with them. Pious and loyal to the orthodoxy of his father, he typically chaired local church councils and firmly supported his nephew's ministry. In the meantime, Jonathan's sister Mary cared for their widowed grandmother, Esther Stoddard, until her death in 1736. In an era when men of elite extended families ran most things, Jonathan's position was strengthened not only by the Stoddard connection, but also by his relation to the clergyman who succeeded Solomon Stoddard as the region's leading cleric, William Williams of nearby Hatfield. Williams was married to Solomon Stoddard's daughter, Christian, a sister of Jonathan's mother and of John Stoddard. The Williams family was one of the region's most influential clans of clergy and magistrates and was intermarried with just about every other family of note.

Edwards recalled the years immediately after Solomon Stoddard's death as a low point for religion in Northampton, especially among the young people. They had known Stoddard only in his later years and had developed their own culture marked by "frolics" and other unregulated youthful activities. After a few years, however, the intense young Edwards began to win a hearing with the young people, and by 1734 a remarkable awakening began among the youth and spread throughout the town. Awakenings were nothing new to Northampton or to the region. Solomon Stoddard had fostered them periodically, as had Timothy Edwards, William Williams, and others. Typically they were regional affairs spreading from town to town.

The awakening in Northampton, which also had many counterparts in the region, differed from its predecessors in two major respects. First, it was, in Edwards's estimation, the most intense and universal awakening that he had seen or heard about in any town. Nearly everyone seemed to be affected, experiencing God's grace, or at least awakened to their need for God's grace. Hundreds made very affecting professions of faith, and Edwards estimated that within a three-month period three hundred, or almost half the adult population, were savingly converted. Virtually everyone else was either already converted or seeking it. For months, especially in the spring of 1735, nobody seemed to talk of anything else. The townspeople, who had previously been perennially contentious, were more openly loving than ever before. Even illnesses virtually disappeared, as Edwards noted by the lack of "prayer bills," or prayer requests for healing, for several months. Visitors came to witness the amazing Northampton spirituality and often carried the infectious enthusiasm back to their own towns.

The other major factor that distinguished the Northampton awakening was that Edwards effectively publicized it. In the new scientific age, philosophers typically reported unusual natural phenomena by corresponding about them to their peers, who would publicize them throughout the intellectual community. Edwards did just that regarding the phenomena of the awakening. As a young pastor, Edwards had traveled to Boston in 1731 to preach a notable public sermon during the week of the Harvard commencement and had established a solid reputation among the orthodox Boston clergy.[9] Building on such connections, in 1735 he penned a lengthy account of the Northampton awakening and sent it to Benjamin Colman, Boston's most influential clergyman, hoping for help in publishing it. Colman immediately appended an abridgement of the account to a Boston publication of some sermons by William Williams (somewhat to the embarrassment of Edwards, who had not said much of the awakenings in neighboring towns). Colman sent the whole of Edwards's account to Isaac Watts in London, who saw to the publication in 1737 of *A Faithful Narrative of the Surprising Work of God*.[10] Edwards and the Northampton awakening soon gained an international reputation among those who hoped for wider awakenings, including John and Charles Wesley and George Whitefield in England, and a number of Scottish admirers.

By the time it was being internationally acclaimed, the Northampton awakening was well in the past. In fact, the event that effectively brought it to an end happened just as Edwards was about to send off his *Faithful Narrative*, so that he had to add to it a grim postscript. On Sunday morning, June 1, 1735, one of Northampton's leading citizens, Joseph Hawley, slit his throat and died. Hawley, Edwards's uncle married to another of Solomon Stoddard's daughters, had been tormented for months by extreme anxieties about the state of his soul. Though Edwards considered Hawley emotionally unstable, he had not relented from including in his preaching the doom of the unconverted. In Edwards's account of the awakening, he interpreted the suicide as just the sort of counterstroke one might expect from Satan, enraged by the spiritual outpouring.[11]

During the next years, after the initial fervor of the awakening had died down, Edwards worked hard to build on the foundation it provided. In 1738, for instance, he preached a series of sermons, *Charity and Its Fruits*, that depicted the long-term loving attitudes that should grow out of true religion.[12] In another long series of sermons, *A History of the Work of*

Redemption, preached in 1739, he emphasized the conflict between God and Satan throughout history.[13] Revivals, of which the Northampton awakening was one of the most notable ever, were God's characteristic way of working in history. Nonetheless, he worried that Northamptonites did not appreciate their historic role and that, rather than being a model for the world, they were reverting to their old not-so-spiritual and not-so-charitable ways.

Edwards's hopes were renewed when he heard of the triumphs of a young English evangelist, George Whitefield. Both in England and then in the colonies in 1739, Whitefield was preaching outdoors to record crowds and sparking awakenings wherever he went. Edwards eagerly wrote to him early in 1740, inviting him to Northampton during a planned New England tour.[14] Whitefield agreed. In New England the itinerant evangelist first spent a month in Boston, where, despite some opposition, his successes were as great as elsewhere. He often preached to crowds of five thousand to eight thousand, immense for a colonial town. By the time Whitefield came to Northampton in mid-October, virtually everyone in New England knew of him, and enthusiastic crowds clamored to hear him as he traversed the countryside. Edwards was duly impressed and saw Whitefield and the awakening he was igniting as an answer to prayer.

The next two years, the peak of the New England phase of the colonialwide revivals that became known as the Great Awakening, were times of intense religious excitement in which Edwards was deeply involved. Whitefield sparked a revolution in New England's religious style. Prior to the Great Awakening, the settled congregational clergy controlled almost all of New England's organized religion, including local awakenings. Whitefield made the itinerant evangelist the new standard and tied the awakenings directly to the emerging transatlantic movement that eventually became known as evangelicalism. The best-known itinerant to follow closely on Whitefield's heels was Gilbert Tennent, a young Presbyterian evangelist who had been closely associated with Whitefield's work in New Jersey. Tennent had already sparked a controversy among the Presbyterians in the Middle Colonies by preaching on *The Danger of an Unconverted Ministry*.[15] Whitefield himself had intimated that some of the settled clergy in New England were unconverted, and the publication of his diary confirming that opinion and criticizing both Harvard and Yale as spiritually dead would help divide the clergy into "New Light" (pro-awakening) and "Old Light" (anti-awakening) camps. The fiery Tennent, preaching in New England early in 1741, fanned the fires both of the awakening and of emerging criticism from some of the Old Lights. Meanwhile, by the summer of 1741, some of New England's own New Light evangelists were itinerating through the region, preaching awakening. Local New Light clergy were also cooperating outside their parishes to promote revivals in neighboring towns.

Edwards preached his most famous sermon in this context. In July 1741 a team of clergy, including Edwards, had gathered in Enfield, Connecticut, for a series of midweek services to promote awakening. Edwards chose a sermon, *Sinners in the Hands of an Angry God*, which he had recently preached in Northampton with no unusual effect. The sermon, on God's restraint in temporarily holding back the wrath that sinners' rebellion against his love deserved, was remarkable among Edwards's sermons in building up vivid images. He depicted a dam ready to burst, an arrow pointed at one's heart and the bow drawn, and (most famously) a spider held over a fire suspended by the most fragile thread.[16] Preaching with his characteristic quiet intensity, Edwards brought the congregation to such an intense emotional pitch that he could not finish the sermon because of the wails and shrieking of those overcome by their terrible plight. Edwards did not preach on dangers of hell any more often than most clergy did within the cycle of biblical doctrines, but he did not shy away from the topic either. Neither was it so unusual for listeners to be overcome by intense emotional and physical reactions to New Light preaching. What was most remarkable about the sermon, which was soon published, was the combination of Edwards's reputation in the awakening and the sermon's rhetorical power that eventually made it a classic of early American literature.

Edwards also became the chief apologist for the awakening. In the early fall of 1741 he preached at the Yale commencement in New Haven. Yale, like the rest of New England, was rapidly becoming sharply divided over the awakening. New Light students were accusing their clergymen teachers of being unconverted; and just prior to Edwards's visit, one of the most extreme of the new itinerants, James Davenport, a Yale graduate himself, had been preaching that the pastor of New Haven's First Church, where students were required to attend, was a "wolf in sheep's clothing."[17]

While Edwards warned strongly against judging the condition of other people's souls, his sermon, soon published as a short treatise, *Distinguishing Marks of the Work of the Spirit of God* (1741), was a ringing endorsement of the awakening.[18] Old Lights, who now included Yale's president, Thomas Clap, were discrediting the awakening on the grounds of its excesses and irregularities, especially the extreme emotional and physical responses of many who supposedly were savingly converted. Edwards explained that some indefensible irregularities were to be expected to be associated with any great work of God since Satan was working more intensely at such times trying to undermine true spiritual experiences by encouraging delusions. Intense emotional and physical responses to awakening preaching, Edwards argued, were neither proofs of the validity of the revivals nor proofs of their invalidity. The distinguishing marks of a true work of God were the same as they always had been: heart-felt love to God and conformity to the doctrines and practices revealed in God's Word.

In a preface to *Distinguishing Marks*, one of Boston's leading pastors, William Cooper of Brattle Street Church, threw down the gauntlet to Old Lights. If, as Edwards, Cooper, and others believed, the awakening was, despite some inevitable excesses, one of the great events in the history of redemption, then to oppose it was to oppose the Spirit of God and "approaches near to the unpardonable sin."[19] Edwards himself expressed his suspicions not only about those clergy who condemned the awakening, but even about those who remained silent concerning it: "such silent ministers stand in the way of God; as Christ said of old, 'He that is not with us is against us.'"[20]

By this time it was clear that the gloves were off, and the Old Light clergy, led by Charles Chauncy of Boston's First Church, opened up an all-out attack on the excesses and irregularities of the awakening. The Old Light case was helped by the extreme eccentricities of the radical New Light itinerant James Davenport. Having helped provoke a ban on uninvited itinerants by the Connecticut General Assembly in May 1742, Davenport was soon arrested and declared out of his mind. Not long after that, he appeared in Boston, as wild as ever, freely announcing that Chauncy and other leading clergy were unregenerate. Chauncy responded in a sermon at the Harvard Commencement in July that religious "enthusiasm" was "properly a disease, a sort of madness," that could spread in epidemic form.[21]

Edwards had just seen close up the very sort of extreme religious intensity that Chauncy diagnosed as madness and had been confirmed in his opposed analysis. Even if in some cases the Devil played on mental instability to mock true religion, there were many other cases in which being overcome was unmistakably associated with true works of the Holy Spirit. Early in 1742 when Edwards was away for a two-week preaching tour and a young evangelist, Samuel Buell, was preaching in Northampton, Sarah Pierpont Edwards went through a most extraordinary religious experience. For more than a week, she enjoyed a "heavenly elysium" in which she felt "entirely swallowed up in God" in a foretaste of eternity.[22] While still managing her household duties, she was often physically overcome by these raptures and ecstasies. Jonathan, knowing his wife's long history of piety, was entirely sure her experiences were manifestations of the Holy Spirit working in a mature Christian, not a temporary aberration induced by the contagion of "enthusiasm." In his second more lengthy defense of the awakenings, *Some Thoughts Concerning the Present Revival of Religion*, published in the fall of 1742, he incorporated Sarah's story, while disguising her identity, as one proof of the authenticity of the Spirit's work for which he could personally vouch.[23]

By 1743 the awakening itself was beginning to abate in New England, but not the controversy. Competing meetings of New England clergy assembling in Boston issued conflicting assessments of the awakening. In September Chauncy's massive attack on the awakening, *Seasonable Thoughts on the State of Religion in New England*, came out with the support of over five hundred prominent subscribers.[24] In part the debate between Chauncy and Edwards reflected an old division in Reformed thinking. Chauncy represented the "intellectualist" school that argued that one's will should follow the best dictates of reason. Edwards was in the Augustinian "voluntarist" camp that held that the affections of the will guided the whole person. By this time, however, the harsh accusations on both sides had carried the debate beyond constructive argument and permanently destroyed any semblance of unity among New England's established clergy.

Edwards made his last major statement on the subject in his *Treatise on Religious Affections*, which appeared in 1746 and eventually became a classic.[25] By 1746 circumstances had changed dramatically, and Edwards was not simply providing another answer to Chauncy. While reiterating his basic positions that the heart of true religion was one's affections or loves, and that heightened emotions and physical reactions did not prove anything one way or the other, he seemed most concerned to address the issue of how to tell genuine religious affections from their imitators. Part of his concern was that the awakening had, indeed, taken some more radical turns beyond what he would have liked. Edwards himself had dealt with some of the continuing excesses of Davenport and others. By 1743 the awakening had pretty much come to an end in New England's established churches, but it was ongoing among groups that had separated from those churches. Some of these separates had become Baptists who dispensed with educated clergy. With such issues only in the background, the focus of Edwards's analysis in *Religious Affections* was to explore how one might distinguish true religious affections from false. Among twelve signs of godly affections he included subjective traits such as self-renunciation, gentleness, humility, and a "lamblike, dovelike spirit," all of which the more extreme New Lights often lacked.[26] The twelfth and culminating sign, which he treated at greatest length, was that true religion must result in true Christian practice.

Edwards was also thinking of the deteriorating situation in Northampton as he enumerated these distinguishing signs of true Godly affections. At the time of Sarah's experience and Buell's guest ministry in the spring of 1742, Northampton went through what proved to be its last intense awakening.

Edwards had already become disillusioned with some of his people for whom he had had such high hopes during the awakening of 1734 to 1735, but who had later reverted to many of their old ways. Although he still could point to many converts from the awakenings, by the time of this second revival he was much more cautious in his estimates of true religion and made an effort to guarantee something more lasting, especially in Christian practice as a community. At the height of the revival, he had the town's people sign a solemn covenant in which the adults promised to continue not to slip back into their old contentiousness and the young people promised to avoid any "familiarities of company" that tend to "stir up or gratify a lust of lasciviousness." All were to devote themselves wholly to religion.[27]

Within two years it had become clear that the revival, despite some long term beneficial effects, would not turn the town into a place of almost monastic rectitude, as Edwards seemed to have hoped. What had been a long romance between Edwards and his Northampton parishioners now turned into petty bickering. The episode that exposed this conflict between Edwards and his parishioners arose when some young women reported that some young men in their twenties were using a slightly disreputable book of physiological information and a midwifery text for prurient purposes and were taunting women about their menstrual cycles. Not primarily because of the books, but because of the public nature of the taunting, Edwards made it a public matter for church discipline. He was outraged, it seemed, because the incident revealed a longstanding lascivious male youth culture and because some of the ringleaders were his supposed converts. They called one of the books "the young folks bible." Edwards handled the incident poorly, at first not distinguishing between those accused and other young people of leading families, who were merely witnesses. In the end, only a few less-reputable ringleaders were forced to make public confessions, and many of the townspeople had turned against Edwards as unduly severe.[28]

Even while relationships between Edwards and many of his parishioners were cooling in Northampton, he was continuing to pour energy into writing projects for promoting international awakening. Edwards's overall view of history was strongly optimistic, and he had a tendency toward hyperbole in describing events that fit his framework. That framework was shaped by his millennial views. Based on his study of the prophetic portions of Scripture and following some schools of interpretation common at the time, Edwards developed what later would be called a postmillennial view of the end times. He believed that the visions in the book of Revelation revealed the contours of history between Christ's first and second comings. Working from the premise, already developed in his sermons on the *History of the Work of Redemption*, that the great turning points in that history were marked by massive religious revivals (Edwards viewed the era after Constantine and the Reformation as the best examples), he expected worldwide awakenings to mark the coming centuries in human history. For a time these ever-advancing revivals would be met with fierce counterattacks by Satan and resulting tribulations for Christians; but eventually – probably beginning around the year 2000 A.D. – the whole world would be virtually Christianized, and there would be a millennial age for a literal one thousand years, after which Christ would return again.

Viewing things in this framework made Edwards see grand historical significance in the outbreak of awakenings, which he regarded as the beginning of the era of great spiritual advances, as well as of struggles and setbacks, leading to the millennium. In 1742 in *Some Thoughts*, he went so far as to suggest that "the dawn of that glorious day" might be evidenced in the awakenings in America.[29] He soon disavowed any implication that the millennium might begin in America, pointing out that he was only talking about signs of the dawn of the preceding era. He also turned his hopes for revival toward international awakenings, especially as he became a correspondent with the promoters of remarkable revivals in Scotland. In 1747 Edwards published *An Humble Attempt*, a book with a lengthy title that announced an international concert of prayer to promote revival.[30] In addition, the Reverend Thomas Prince, Edwards's closest associate in Boston, had instituted a periodical called *The Christian History* to publicize accounts of revival at home and abroad.

The millennial outlooks of Edwards and his pro-revival associates had much to do with their views of international politics. The approach of the millennium, they held, would involve the defeat of the Antichrist, whom they identified as the Pope. Edwards kept notebooks in which he recorded news reports of any defeats or setbacks of Roman Catholic interests or nations. He and his Scottish correspondents rejoiced at the defeat of the Catholic pretender, "Bonnie Prince Charles," in 1746.[31] In Northampton this religious-political outlook had immediate practical implications whenever warfare broke out between the Catholic French with their Indian allies and the British Protestants on the New England frontier. Usually that happened when European wars spilled over to the New World, as had the War of Austrian Succession, known by the colonists as King George's War. From 1744 to 1748, New England was deeply involved in that war against the French in America. Colonel John Stoddard was the head of military operations in vulnerable western New England. Northampton also sent troops in support of what proved New England's greatest military triumph, the capture of the mighty French fortress at Louisbourg on Cape Breton Island. Edwards, like many other New England clergy, attributed this remarkable victory to God's direct intervention, and he also saw the defeat of Catholic forces as another sign of the approach of millennial times.

In this context we can better appreciate the significance of one of the best-known episodes in Edwards's life, the visit to the Edwards home of the ailing young missionary to the Indians, David Brainerd. When Brainerd arrived in Northampton in May 1747, the town was fortified against possible Indian attacks. Brainerd's record of selfless devotion to missions to the Indians, even after he had apparently contracted tuberculosis, provided a striking contrast to the usual white man's attitude of being more ready to kill Indians than to be willing to die on behalf of their eternal souls. In the busy Edwards household (Sarah had just given birth to Elizabeth, their tenth child), the task of caring for Brainerd fell to Jerusha, the Edwards's second daughter, age seventeen. Jerusha was deeply spiritual herself and dedicated herself to serving the sickly missionary. After Brainerd died in October, Jerusha aided her father in editing the missionary's diary. Then in February of 1748, Jerusha herself died suddenly from a mysterious ailment. Edwards had her buried next to Brainerd, thus contributing to the legend of their spiritual romance. As for Edwards, his willingness to drop plans to write a major treatise on the freedom of the will, in order to publish Brainerd's diary, signals his view of the importance of such a model of the selfless saint. Edwards's *Life of David Brainerd* helped inspire the missionary movement of the next century.[32]

Jerusha's death brought to an end twenty years of remarkable well-being in the Edwards household and inaugurated some years of painful trials. The sudden death of the family's patron, Colonel John Stoddard, in June 1748 was another blow, one that had important implications for Jonathan Edwards's standing in the town. Edwards, who was not a great master of diplomacy, soon exacerbated any resentments between the townspeople and himself by announcing late in 1748 his intention to do away with the relatively open standards for communicant church membership that his revered grandfather had instituted several generations earlier. Edwards said that he would now require a credible profession of heartfelt faith, rather than just a profession of faith in the church's teachings and a life without scandal, as the new standard for communicant membership. Further, he would end the "Half-Way Covenant," which allowed grandchildren of believers to be baptized even if the parents were not communicants. Many of the townspeople, who had come to think of church membership and certainly baptism as a sort of right, were outraged and accused Edwards of waiting until his uncle John Stoddard's death to turn thus from his grandfather's ways. Edwards said that he was just implementing a principle that he had already made known to a number of townspeople and that he had only been waiting for an occasion, in spiritually low times, for applicants for membership who could meet his more stringent test.

Most of the townspeople, who themselves saw high principle involved, would have nothing to do with the changes. In the bitter controversy that followed, they had little interest in Edwards's arguments which, character-istically, he provided in a treatise.[33] By the spring of 1750, the majority of church members were resolved to sever their relation with Edwards as their pastor and were granted approval to do so by a council from surrounding churches. Edwards, who was reputed to sit through the council with a remark-able appearance of tranquility, was nonetheless bitter about his rejection by his parishioners. Soon after his dismissal, he preached a farewell sermon in which he suggested that he would be vindicated on the Day of Judgment.[34] To make matters more difficult for him and his beleaguered family, they remained in Northampton for an additional year while he sought another position. Further, on some occasions during that time, he accepted invita-tions to preach to his former parishioners, even though the church leaders always made clear that he was their last option.

After turning down some conventional pastorates, including one in Scotland, Edwards accepted a call to be pastor and missionary to the Indians in the town of Stockbridge, Massachusetts. Edwards moved in the winter of 1751, and the next fall his sizable family made the journey to this outlying frontier village in the Berkshire Mountains in the southwestern corner of the colony. Stockbridge had been founded in the late 1730s to be a model for rebuilding New England's Indian missions, which had been largely in disarray since King Philip's War in the 1670s. In addition to being a settle-ment for a couple hundred Mahican Indians, the town included a number of English families who were to help ease the hoped-for transition of the Indians to European ways, which was thought to be an appropriate complement to conversion to Christianity. The first missionary, John Sergeant, had minis-tered with some success before his death in 1749. Sergeant's wife, Abigail Williams Sergeant, was the daughter of Ephraim Williams, Sr., the head of the leading Stockbridge English family, which was part of the Williams clan to which Edwards was related. Abigail was an impressive young woman of refined tastes and intellectual interests. Although she at first found Edwards of a broader spirit than she expected, she soon became his principal oppo-nent in an intense struggle for control of the mission, particularly its several schools for Indian children that were supported by funds from missions agencies in Boston and London. Abigail's position was greatly strengthened after Edwards brought his friend, Brigadier General Joseph Dwight, to serve as village magistrate and Edwards's patron, only to have Abigail quickly charm and marry the general.

Edwards eventually prevailed in gaining support of the missions agencies for his version of the mission, but the division among the English hurt the overall cause. By the time the matter was settled early in 1754, many of the Mohawks, members of a powerful tribe who had spent time in Stockbridge and sent some children to school there, had left. Edwards seems generally to have enjoyed cordial relations with the Indians, and he reported that they were especially fond of his wife Sarah. Nonetheless, he never reported any awakening in Stockbridge. The circumstances became far more difficult in the summer of 1754, when hostilities broke out in the buildup to the French and Indian War. Edwards had been incapacitated for months by "the longest and most tedious sickness that I ever had" in a lifetime of periodic illnesses.[35] In September of 1754, Stockbridge and its neighboring towns went into a severe panic when Indians killed a few settlers. Predictably, the settlers who assembled to protect the region soon killed some friendly Indians. In that tense setting, Stockbridge became an armed camp, but was also vulnerable should there be any major Indian attack.

Remarkably, during his Stockbridge years Edwards did some of his best writing. After firing off a parting shot on the Northampton communion controversy,[36] he wrote between 1754 and 1758 the four theological/philosophical works for which is he best remembered, *Freedom of the Will, Original Sin, Concerning the End for Which God Created the World,* and *The Nature of True Virtue.*[37] These were all directed against fashionable Enlightenment ideas that emphasized humans' abilities to do good on their own. Edwards considered such "Arminian" views the major threat of the day to the essential doctrine of God's sovereign grace. Edwards was able to produce these finely argued works so quickly because he had been working on these issues in the large notebooks that he kept his whole life. He also kept notebooks for what he hoped would be two great culminating works, a biblical study on "*The Harmony of the Old and New Testaments*" and "*A History of the Work of Redemption,*" in which he hoped to recast theology by putting it in the framework of God's work in history.[38]

By the Stockbridge years, the large Edwards household was changing also. Their last child, Pierpont, was born in 1750 just before Edwards's dismissal. That same year the eldest daughter, Sarah, married Elihu Parsons, and sixteen-year-old Mary married Timothy Dwight, Jr., of a prominent local family that she would help make famous. She remained in Northampton always in a strained relationship with the church that dismissed her father. After the rest of the family had moved to Stockbridge, Aaron Burr, an admirer of Edwards, suddenly appeared in the spring of 1752 to ask for and receive the hand of twenty-year-old Esther. Burr, sixteen years her senior, was president of the College of New Jersey, a key New Light school soon to move to Princeton. Sarah, Sr., accompanied her daughter to New Jersey for the wedding. Fourteen-year-old Timothy came along to enter the college. Jonathan himself visited the Burrs in 1755 and also went with his son-in-law to Philadelphia to attend the meeting of the Presbyterian Synod of New York and New Jersey. Philadelphia was the farthest he ever traveled, and this was the occasion when it is most likely he may have crossed paths with fellow New Englander Benjamin Franklin, who had published a little of his work.

The Edwards household often included students mentored by Edwards, most famously his first biographer, Samuel Hopkins, in the early 1740s, and guests, often ministerial, who appeared at the door needing lodging. Stockbridge was freer from such distractions, but living next to an Indian village had its own demands.

Caring for this household, land, and animals involved hired hands, servants, and usually a woman slave. During Edwards's lifetime the ownership of slaves was seldom debated in the white colonial community. Benjamin Franklin, for instance, who later became an opponent of slavery, owned slaves well after the 1750s. Most New England clergy who could afford it owned a household slave or two. In Edwards's case, family slaves became full church members. Edwards and his contemporaries were aware, however, that the African slavery of their day differed from the biblical precedents used to justify it. In the one case we know, when Edwards was asked his opinion, he acknowledged that there was no justification for enslaving Africans on the basis of race. Nonetheless, he apparently thought there was no practical way to extricate oneself from a trade system so integral to the colonial economy, whether one personally owned slaves or not. Whatever Edwards's shortcoming in this matter, he had high regard for the potential of other peoples and remarked that he believed that in the future there would be great African and American Indian philosophers and theologians.[39] Regarding the Indians, he believed they would benefit not only from conversion to Christianity, but also from learning Christian standards for civilization. He, nonetheless, valued learning Indian ways for missionary purposes. In 1755, during wartime, the Edwards sent their ten-year-old son, Jonathan, Jr., on a lengthy trip with missionary Gideon Hawley to an Indian settlement in northern Pennsylvania so that Jonathan might become truly expert in Indian languages.

In September 1757 Aaron Burr, Sr., died suddenly, and the trustees of the College of New Jersey quickly decided that Edwards would be the ideal replacement as president. In January, upon advice of a local council, Edwards accepted, apparently with some reluctance. He soon left for Princeton and made plans for the family to follow in the spring. At Princeton, Edwards moved into the new president's house with his daughter Esther and her two small children, Sally and Aaron, Jr. (the future Vice President of the United States), and Edwards's seventeen-year-old daughter Lucy, who had been helping her sister. Because of a smallpox epidemic, Edwards persuaded the family to undergo smallpox inoculations in late February. Edwards soon contracted a secondary infection and died on March 22. The family trials only continued. Esther died of a mysterious fever less than two weeks after her father. Sarah Edwards came to Princeton in August and then to Philadelphia to fetch her orphaned grandchildren, but she too died on October 2, 1758. The Edwardses had spent much of their lives cultivating a sense of living in the shadow of eternity, hence to be prepared for adversity and death itself. As he was dying, Jonathan told Lucy to convey to Sarah his belief that their "uncommon union" was spiritual and therefore eternal.[40]

Notes
1. *Personal Narrative*, WJE, 16:791.
2. "Resolutions," WJE, 16:753–9.
3. "Diary," WJE, 16:759–89.
4. WJE, 16:792.
5. Ibid., 11:49–142.
6. Ibid., 187–328.
7. "Diary," WJE, 16:788.
8. "On Sarah Pierpont," WJE, 16:789–90.
9. *God Glorified in Man's Dependence*, WJE, 17:196–216.
10. WJE, 4:97–211.
11. Ibid., 206–7.
12. Ibid., 8:123–397.
13. Ibid., 9:111–528.
14. Feb. 12, 1740, WJE, 16:79–81.
15. Philadelphia, 1740.
16. WJE, 22:400–35.
17. George M. Marsden, *Jonathan Edwards: A Life* (New Haven: Yale University Press, 2003), 232–3.
18. WJE, 4:213–88.
19. Ibid., 223.
20. Ibid., 272–3.
21. Charles Chauncy, *Enthusiasm Described and Cautioned Against. A Sermon Preached . . . the Lord's Day after the Commencement . . .* (Boston, 1742). Available in Alan Heimert and Perry Miller, eds., *The Great Awakening: Documents Illustrating the Crisis and Its Consequences* (Indianapolis, IN: Bobbs-Merrill, 1967), pp. 228–56 (quotation from p. 231).
22. Sarah Edwards, "Narrative" (1742), in Sereno E. Dwight, ed., *The Works of President Edwards with a Memoir of His Life* (10 vols. New York: Converse, 1829), I:178.
23. WJE, 4:331–41.
24. Boston, 1743.
25. WJE, 2:84–461.

26. Ibid., 344.
27. Ibid., 16:121–5.
28. Marsden, *Jonathan Edwards*, 292–302.
29. WJE, 4:358.
30. *An Humble Attempt to Promote Explicit Agreement and Visible Union of God's People in Extraordinary Prayer for the Revival of Religion and the Advancement of Christ's Kingdom on Earth, Pursuant to Scripture-Promises and Prophecies Concerning the Last Time*, WJE, 5:307–436.
31. Letter to John MacLaurin, May 12, 1746, WJE, 16:203–7.
32. WJE, 7:87–476.
33. *An Humble Inquiry into the Rules of the Word of God, Concerning the Qualifications Requisite to a Complete Standing and Full Communion in the Visible Christian Church*, WJE, 12:165–325.
34. *A Farewell Sermon Preached at the First Precinct in Northampton, after the People's Public Rejection of Their Minister . . . on June 22, 1750*, in Wilson H. Kimnach, Kenneth P. Minkema, and Douglas A. Sweeney, eds., *The Sermons of Jonathan Edwards: A Reader* (New Haven, CT: Yale University Press, 1999), 212–41.
35. Letter to John Erskine, WJE, 16:662.
36. The "parting shot" was *Misrepresentations Corrected, and Truth Vindicated*, WJE, 12:349–497.
37. See WJE, 1:129–439; 8:403–536, 537–627; and 3:102–437, respectively.
38. See Letter to the Trustees of the College of New Jersey, WJE, 16:725–30.
39. Marsden, *Jonathan Edwards*, 255–8.
40. William Shippen to Sarah Edwards, March 22, 1758, from Dwight, ed., *Works*, I:578.

2 Personal writings

KENNETH P. MINKEMA

In 1735 Bernard Bartlett, a member of the church of Northampton, Massachusetts, said that his pastor, Jonathan Edwards, "was as Great an Instrument as the Devil Had on this Side [of] Hell to bring Souls to Hell." Seven years later, the Reverend David Hall of Sutton, Massachusetts, after a visit from Edwards, wrote in his diary, "I thought I had not saw in any man for some years so much of the grace of God causing ye face to shine."[1] These two very different estimations from people who were acquainted with Edwards attest to the challenge of understanding Edwards on a personal level. As a man in authority and a widely published author, he was subject to vastly different reactions. How can we, at three centuries' remove, hope to plumb the private occupations of this complicated individual?

Although the autobiographical documents Edwards left are rich and revealing, they are regrettably few in number. But in the face of this dearth, those who want to understand Edwards's sense of self, personal and religious, can define "personal" differently. Strictly speaking, "personal" encompasses documents Edwards composed for himself only, such as the "Resolutions" and "Diary," to track and regulate his religious life. More broadly, we can define "personal" to include documents in which Edwards revealed his sense of self but that were written for other purposes or were addressed to others. This would include "On Sarah Pierpont" and the *Personal Narrative*, along with selected letters (or parts of them), especially those to family members and trusted confidants. Still other documents, such as his "Account Book" and "Last Will and Testament," more social in nature, shed light on Edwards's lifestyle and social network, both of which are key indicators of private selves and public identities. Conceived in this way, our search for the personal Edwards is not so limited as it may seem at first glance.

THE "RESOLUTIONS"

However we define "personal," the "Resolutions" is Edwards's earliest extant personal writing, begun when he was about nineteen. The discipline of making lists of resolutions was fairly common in Edwards's time. William Beveridge, Bishop of St. Asaph, drew up a list of forty resolutions, posthumously published in *Private Thoughts on Religion* (1709–12), a title Edwards inscribed in his "Catalogue of Reading" shortly after starting the "Resolutions." Likewise, as a young man Benjamin Franklin drew up a list of thirteen "virtues," and the teen-aged George Washington copied 110 "Rules of Civility" into his school notebook.[2]

Franklin's and Washington's precepts aimed at cultivating personal morality and becoming socially acceptable. Edwards's "Resolutions," however, were nearly all religious in nature and partook of Puritan self-discipline and self-abasement. In the preamble he entreated God's assistance to fulfill his promises and self-admonitions, and he noted, "Remember to read over these 'Resolutions' once a week." He exhorted himself in separate entries to review his behavior "at the end of every day, week, month, and year, wherein I could possibly in any respect have done better" (nos. 37, 41).[3] The first "Resolution" set the tone:

> Resolved, that I will do whatsoever I think to be most to God's glory, and my own good, profit and pleasure, in the whole of my duration, without any consideration of the time, whether now, or never so many myriads of ages hence. Resolved to do whatever I think to be my duty, and most for the good and advantage of mankind in general. Resolved to do this, whatever difficulties I meet with, how many and how great soever.[4]

As the rest of the "Resolutions" make clear, "my own good," for Edwards, meant the salvation of his soul rather than earthly happiness.

The "Resolutions," while all composed with one goal – heaven – generally fell into several categories. Some dealt with specific habits, such as "improving" time (no. 5), maximizing study (no. 11), controlling diet (nos. 20, 40), reading the Scriptures (no. 28), and combating "listlessness" (no. 61). Others, going deeper into the self, pertained to examining motives, tracing back an action to "the original intention, designs and ends of it" (nos. 23, 24). These included revenge (no. 14), speaking ill of others (nos. 16, 31, 36), profaning the sabbath (no. 38), and dishonoring parents (no. 46).[5]

Deeper still, another category of entries related to being, as Edwards put it in no. 63, "a complete Christian." Glorifying God in every thought, word, and deed, modeling oneself after and "venturing" one's soul upon Christ, were tantamount. "Resolved, to live with all my might, while I do live," he declared in no. 6. This meant living every moment as if it were "the last hour of my life" (no. 7) and committing every act as if he were about to "hear the last trump" (no. 19). Edwards's piety was Puritan in its existentialism, with its dictate, *momento mori*: "Resolved, to think much on all occasions of my own dying, and of the common circumstances which attend death" (no. 9).[6]

Remembering death, however, did not lead to fatalism. Instead, it was a spur to dedicate himself to religion and to God. It entailed guarding against thinking or doing anything that was not agreeable to the cause of religion and the good of his soul – "never to give over, nor in the least to slacken my fight with corruptions, however unsuccessful I may be" (no. 56) – as well as declaring himself through prayer, charity, and self-reflection as a subject of his God.[7]

THE "DIARY"

Edwards began his "Diary" in late 1722, shortly after the "Resolutions." The original manuscripts for neither exist, which makes close dating impossible. With nine entries from 1722, twenty-five from 1724, seven from 1725, and six spanning the years 1726 through 1735, 1723 is the most represented year in the document, with entries for 103 days. Thus, they focus most intently on the period of Edwards's ministry in New York City, the completion of his graduate studies, and the beginning of his brief pastorate at Bolton, trailing off into the Yale tutorship and the Northampton years.

Edwards was not unique among his peers in keeping a spiritual diary. We may have more diaries from colonial New England than any other region per capita in the world during this period. From its origins, the Puritan movement encouraged the keeping of personal diaries as a means of tracking the ebb and flow of one's relationship with God. Diaries by Thomas Shepard and Michael Wigglesworth from the seventeenth century and by Ebenezer Parkman and Hannah Heaton from the eighteenth provide detailed information not only about daily activities but about the constant self-scrutiny to which these individuals subjected themselves.[8] As in earlier diaries, such as that by Shepard, Edwards's has a cyclical nature, reflected in his use of the words "dull," "decayed," and "reviving" to summarize his religious state. Periods of indifference would lead to a sense of having "backslidden," only to be pulled out of his angst by an experience of divine comfort and a desire to press on.

Another feature of Edwards's "Diary" is its clinical nature. Here the young pastor-scientist studied himself the way he had studied spiders and would make a career of studying souls under conversion. If the "Resolutions" were objective guidelines distilled from daily experiences, the "Diary" recorded how the young Edwards formulated them and his attempts to live by them. He cross-referenced the documents, linking them in his quest for spiritual improvement, so that it is helpful to read them together. For example, at the end of a "Resolution" he might append the date of a "Diary" entry, and in a "Diary" entry he might refer to a particular "Resolution." Also, the "Diary" referred in several places to the "Wednesday Resolution," which was "Resolution" no. 16, "Never to speak evil of any one," something with which Edwards apparently struggled.[9] Placing himself in the spiritual balance, he would take a "weekly account" of himself, tallying up pledges kept and broken.

But the "Diary" is by no means a purely dispassionate self-study. Edwards's concerns were ultimate, his commitments intense. If he counted his sins, he also meditated deeply on repenting of them. Already in the first entry of the "Diary," December 18, 1722, he sensed an important difference between himself and the religious culture in which he was raised. Edwards expressed consternation, repeated in later entries, that he did not "experience regeneration, exactly in those steps, in which divines say it is generally wrought." By "steps," Edwards referred to the teaching among New England ministers (including his grandfather, Solomon Stoddard) that conversion occurred in stages in which one utilized the "means of grace" – reading, worship, and prayer – to help "prepare" for regeneration. Edwards feared his experience of "Christian graces" was only superficial, not "wrought into my very nature, as I could wish." He decided "never to leave searching" until he had solved this problem.[10] This was an important moment for Edwards. As he came to realize, and to explore later in the *Personal Narrative*, his experience of grace upset accepted conventions, which opened up to him the importance of reconceiving how God acts in the soul and the role that believers have in that relationship.

Another important moment, marked by the longest entry, came in New York City on January 12, 1723: "I have this day solemnly renewed my baptismal covenant and self-dedication, which I renewed when I was received into communion of the church." This was a private, not a public, act. That Edwards was a fledgling minister anticipating a clerical career played some role in this decision, but his status as a pastor was secondary to the act of giving up his whole self, his talents and body, to the service of God. "I have been before God; and have given myself, all that I am and have to God, so that I am not in any respect my own."[11] No other end but religion would henceforth influence his actions.

From this height, however, Edwards soon descended. The remainder of the entry qualified the terms of his self-dedication, as if he had gone too far, adding that he should be able to take pleasure in friends and good food, and that "too constant a mortification, and too vigorous application to religion, may be prejudicial to health; but nevertheless, I will plainly feel it and experience it, before I cease, on this account."[12] Not surprisingly, at several stressful points in his life – as in 1725, 1729, and 1735 – Edwards suffered what apparently were physical collapses. In 1739, the Reverend Timothy Cutler of Boston, Edwards's former college rector, commented that Edwards continued to apply himself so stringently to his duties and studies, "and in such a degree, that He is very much emaciated, and impair'd in his Hea[lth] and it is doubtful to me whether He will attain to the Age of 40."[13] That may have been wishful thinking on Cutler's part, but for the remainder of his life Edwards did battle illness and fatigue. Edwards himself picturesquely described his condition in 1757: "I have a constitution in many respects peculiar unhappy, attended with flaccid solids, vapid, sizy and scarce fluids, and a low tide of spirits; often occasioning a kind of childish weakness and contemptibleness of speech, presence and demeanor; with a disagreeable dullness and stiffness, much unfitting me for conversation."[14]

Several recurrent themes in the "Diary" suggest much about Edwards's temperament, his self-perception, and the content of his inner spiritual life. One theme was a concern with "enemies." To what extent these opponents were abstract or actual is uncertain, but throughout his life Edwards was preoccupied with personal enemies – the Williamses, for instance – and enemies of the "true" church – Arminians, Deists, and Catholics, for a start. In the entry for January 15, 1723, Edwards acknowledged his weakness, chastising himself for believing that through his own strength he was "ready to triumph over my enemies," when actually it was only Christ's strength that gave him "liberty to smile to see my enemies flee."[15]

In a related vein, he worried in a lengthy entry on August 24, 1723, that he had "not practiced quite right about revenge." Edwards feared he had indulged in a "secret sort of revenge" in the repentance of offenders, which is "taking the matter out of God's hands. . . . Well, therefore, may he leave me to boggle at it."[16] The summer of 1723 was spent at home composing his M.A. oration *Quaestio*, the orthodox theme of which – justification by faith alone – may have caused him to imagine critical reactions from many quarters and to fret over its "public acceptance."[17]

Edwards's concern that his performance be acceptable stemmed from an ambition to be an acclaimed author. In early notes on writing, he tutored himself to have a "modest" style (no. 4), "very moderate in the use of terms of art" (no. 9), so as not to be thought an "upstart." Giving shape to his ambition (yet hiding it in shorthand), he continued, "Before I venture to publish in London, to make some experiment in my own country; to play at small games first, that I may gain some experience in writing. First to write letters to some in England, and to try my [hand at] lesser matters before I venture in great."[18] That Jonathan shared his lofty dreams of notoriety in London, the center of the British world, with his concerned parents is suggested in "Diary" entries (e.g., August 13, 1723), in the "Resolutions" (e.g., no. 46), and in a sermon written in 1724 by his father. Timothy, an habitual doodler, drew a design that revealingly juxtaposed the words "Jonathan," "London," and "Corruption" with the words "humble" and "management" written upside down between them.[19] While Jonathan associated London with fame, Timothy associated the metropolis with "corruption," which called for his son to observe more humility and to be managed by his parents. His parents' disapproval of his aspirations may explain why there were several entries in the "Diary" and "Resolutions" in which Edwards reminded himself not to allow old age to limit his ability to adopt new ideas. This is not to suggest that Edwards was a disobedient son, but that he was driven by his ideals and aspirations.

As indicated in this episode with his parents, Edwards himself may in part have been to blame for the enemies he made. With his serious and capacious mind and a strong streak of self-righteousness, he did not suffer fools gladly. He allowed himself to display humor only when portraying sinners' follies and when skewering his adversaries' logic. Behind the "Wednesday Resolution" lay a certain quickness to criticize, sometimes in a harsh way, a habit which seems to have plagued him. He rebuked himself for speaking badly of others on several occasions. His behavior made him fear he had "lost some friendship." On April 1, 1723, he wrote, "I think it best not to allow myself to laugh at the faults, follies and infirmities of others."[20] Edwards's letters from college, in which he related tensions with other students, echoed in his observation of July 1, 1723, that he needed to "observe rather more of meekness, moderation and temper in disputes." Several days later came a reminder to "offend not in word." Edwards even quotes from the Presbyterian divine Thomas Manton's sermon on evil-speaking, which counseled that "them that either devise or receive reproaches" were both sinful. Reproach and criticism were touchy issues in European culture at this time because of the importance placed upon honor, reputation, and one's good name. The quote from Manton, for example, contained the Shakespearean and scriptural injunction, "He that robs thee of thy name, is the worst kind of thief."[21] When Edwards himself was the brunt of criticism and ridicule, he resolved on July 30, 1723, "to receive slanders and reproaches, as glorious opportunities" to lament times he had slandered and reproached others. The following day, Edwards went even further, instructing himself, "Never in the least to seek to hear sarcastical relations of others' faults."[22]

Yet, reproving or correcting others was a central duty in New England religious culture, and it was a tenet that Edwards taught and his family members practiced. This was not merely Puritans fitting the modern stereotypes of busy-bodies and kill-joys; rather, reproof of others' faults, or "witnessing," was a covenant obligation of church members that was meant to insure the harmony of the community. However righteous the ideal may have been, nevertheless, it was easy for reproof to slide into slander or for sincere admonitions to be taken in the wrong way by individuals who resented invasion of their privacy. Perhaps with this in mind, Edwards cautioned on August 17, 1723, "Let there, in the general, be something of benevolence in all that I speak." On December 12 of that year, he again warned himself to be careful if "forced to tell others of that wherein I think they are something to blame," mindful that people took such reproof as "the effect of little, fretting, angry emotions of mind."[23] Edwards was concerned that reproofs be delivered and taken in the right spirit. "When I reprove for faults," he wrote on May 22, 1725, "whereby I am in any way injured, to defer, 'till the thing is quite over and done with; for that is the way, both to reprove aright, . . . and to have reproofs effectual, and not suspected."[24]

Edwards's attitudes about reproof suggest an inability to take reproof. His self-righteousness, or conviction of his rightness once he had made up his mind, was at once a noble aspect of his character as well as a hubris. When, after prolonged study and soul-searching, Edwards decided that the procedure of admission into the Northampton church had to be changed, he went forward regardless of the cost to himself and his family. He wrote to Thomas Foxcroft in 1749, "I seem as it were to be casting myself off from a precipice; and have no other way, but to go on, as it were blindfold, i.e. shutting my eyes to everything else but the evidences of the mind and will of God, and the path of duty."[25] Edwards's willingness to be a martyr for what he saw as the truth was admirable. Yet, some of his contemporaries observed, a little diplomacy and circumspection would have served Edwards well. Colonel Ephraim Williams of Stockbridge, commenting on Edwards's decision to become a missionary, perhaps said it best: "I am sorry that a head so full of divinity should be so empty of politics." Williams noted in his objections to Edwards that he was "a very great bigot, for he would not admit any person into heaven, but those that agreed fully to his sentiments."[26] It is no coincidence that two subjects Edwards explored in his notebooks and sermons through his entire career were pride and self-righteousness.

Edwards's self-prejudice was a blind spot in his ability to know himself, which led even friends and sympathizers to criticize him. When he tried to be a realist, he earned only the poor opinion of his peers. Gideon Hawley, the Stockbridge schoolteacher, lamented over how Edwards was naïve about the political exploitation of the mission.

> I wont go among Indians in the character of a Christian Missionary, except I can go upon Christian Principles. . . . Mr. Edwards . . . has blind

notions about Things and no Wonder seeing he knows nothing but by hearsay and the half has never been told to him. If he would endeavour to excite me to engage in my mission and use only the Motives which are suggested in Christianity I should like it better. Mr. Edwards is a very good man but capible of being biased.[27]

Commenting on Edwards's constant efforts to find agreement between the opponents and supporters of the revivals, Andrew Croswell wrote, "Mr. Edwards is a Gentleman I have no personal Knowledge of; but yet love him Dearly, and never can think of him (scarcely) without blessing God for him: however I make no Doubt at the Same time but that he is too timerous or *Cowardly* in the Cause of X[t], and that twas Owing to this Infirmity and a Culpable Desire of pleasing both Sides."[28] It is worth noting that Croswell was a radical New Light and so somewhat biased himself, but the observation is nonetheless discerning, especially for someone who had never met Edwards.

Edwards knew he was thought to be stiff and opinionated; his "Diary" entries also exhibited concern over his introversion. He visited parishioners rarely and reproached himself for neglecting "social duties." But within a small circle of family and friends, he could be at ease and intimate. After discussions with Edwards in 1743 over his spiritual state and his career prospects as a minister, the young John Walley, with whom Edwards hiked to the top of Mount Tom and enjoyed a picnic lunch, remarked that his discourse was "pleasant and edifying."[29] Writing in 1754 from Newark to Sally Prince in Boston, Esther Edwards Burr longingly imagined the get-together then occurring in the Prince home, with Edwards at the center of a convivial scene: "I imagine now this Eve Mr Burr is at your house. *Father* is there and some others. You all set in the Middleroom, *Father* has the *talk*, and Mr Burr has the *Laugh*, Mr Prince gets room to stick in a word once in a while. The rest of you set and see, and hear, and make observations to yourselves."[30]

"ON SARAH PIERPONT"

This brief piece, a prose poem for which there is no original manuscript, has traditionally been interpreted as Edwards's apostrophe for the woman he would marry in 1727. If Edwards had not met Sarah Pierpont before coming to study in New Haven, he surely did upon his taking up residence at the college hall in 1719. He was twenty and Sarah thirteen when he apparently presented to the New Haven minister's daughter a book with an inscription on the flyleaf.[31]

Edwards's idea of an epithalamium was not to be witty or elegant. The subject of his meditation was Pierpont's rich communion with the Creator. The opening of the apostrophe reads:

> They say there is a young lady in [New Haven] who is beloved of that almighty Being, who made and rules the world, and that there are certain seasons in which this great Being, in some way or other invisible, comes to her and fills her mind with exceeding sweet delight, and that she hardly cares for anything, except to meditate on him – that she expects after a while to be received up where he is, to be raised out of the world and caught up into heaven; being assured that he loves her too well to let her remain at a distance from him always.[32]

For Edwards, Pierpont was an ethereal, almost angelic being. She had a source of joy that was a mystery to others – though not to him. She had more conversation with the Great Being than with other creatures, and she was content with that. Like Edwards, who in the *Personal Narrative* described his experience of "inward sweetness" as culminating in "a kind of vision . . . of being alone in the mountains, . . . sweetly conversing with Christ," Pierpont loved to "wander in the fields and on the mountains," where she could commune with God.[33] She epitomized Edwards's ideal of godliness: sweetness, virtue, purity, and heavenly-mindedness.

There is in the apostrophe an undercurrent of longing, even envy, for the same access to God that Sarah Pierpont enjoyed. Edwards praised her as a model to emulate for her spiritual virtues. In this sense, the person portrayed was an expression of Edwards's vision of the true saint. Yet Edwards was not the only man to be impressed by Pierpont. George Whitefield prayed that God would send him a wife like Sarah Pierpont Edwards, and Samuel Hopkins, Edwards's most famous disciple, was highly influenced by her self-negating piety in his formulation of "disinterestedness."[34] So Edwards's effort to portray godliness theoretically and in concrete lives began with his future wife, as real believer and ideal saint, as seen in future compositions including his own *Personal Narrative* and other spiritual biographies. One such opportunity presented itself in 1742, at the height of the Great Awakening, when Sarah experienced a series of dramatic religious episodes. Here, she appeared more human than in the apostrophe and bound up in worldly concerns, but they provided the emotional springboard to sustained trances and "transports" to a "heavenly elysium."[35]

If "On Sarah Pierpont" was symbolic, it was also extremely personal. Jonathan and Sarah were married for thirty-one years, raised eleven children, and suffered many hardships together. But those who observed them and their family all remarked on their extraordinary life together. Whitefield could not recall in all his travels a "sweeter couple."[36] John Walley wrote, "Surely there is a ... Union of soul among Believers, a sensible sweetness at some [ti]mes; I think I love Mr. Edwards & his Wife, because I see so much of [the] Image of God in them." Five years later, Joseph Emerson of Concord described the Edwardses as "the most agreable Family I was ever acquainted with. [M]uch of the Presence of God there."[37] On his deathbed, Jonathan spoke of the "uncommon union" that bound him with Sarah, a union that, most importantly for him, was spiritual.[38]

There were, however, less rosy aspects to their relationship. Jonathan's family had a dark past, including a violent relationship between his grandparents that ended in a protracted divorce case.[39] Sarah's transports of 1742 began when she worried that she had incurred Jonathan's "ill-will" over a "point of prudence," and, in an unpublished fragment from her narrative, imagined him "horsewhipping" her out of town. Edwards encouraged his wife to write down the narrative of her experiences, which he used in *Some Thoughts Concerning the Revival*; while commending her highly, he rendered her text in a gender-neutral fashion, effectively "silencing" Sarah's true voice.[40] Regardless, later evangelical literature romanticized Jonathan and Sarah's life together in the interest of creating an idyll of Christian domesticity.[41]

PERSONAL NARRATIVE

Sometime in late 1740, Aaron Burr, pastor of the Presbyterian church of Newark, New Jersey, wrote to Edwards. What he asked for – whether some general guidelines about self-examination or a particular account – we do not know, since his letter does not exist, but Edwards responded carefully and at length. Edwards must have completed the composition by early December, for in March 1741 Burr wrote,

> Your's of Dec[r] 14 Came Safe to hand y[e] 5th of this instant. I received it with Joy & heartily thank you for it. I desire to bless God that he inclined you to write & especialy to write So freely of your own Experiences. I think it has been much blessed to my Spiritual Good: tho I have often heard & read of others Experiences, I neer [met] with'm any thing that had the like Effect upon Me.[42]

Burr, who would eventually become Edwards's son-in-law and predecessor as president of the College of New Jersey, then went on to give a detailed account of his own spiritual experiences.

Edwards's autograph letter is no longer extant, but, as with the "Diary" and "Resolutions," we owe the preservation of the text to Hopkins, who published it in his 1765 memoir of Edwards as "*An Account of his* CONVER-SION, EXPERIENCES, *and* RELIGIOUS EXERCISES, *given by himself.*"[43] Through the nineteenth century, when the text was reprinted and sold in tracts by the hundreds of thousands, it was known as "The Conversion of President Edwards." Not until the early twentieth century did it start to be called a "Narrative," and then a "Personal Narrative." Today the document is anthologized and studied widely. After his sermon *Sinners in the Hands of an Angry God,* it may be the text by which most people know Edwards.

The *Personal Narrative* drew on a long tradition of spiritual autobiography in Puritanism. One of the distinguishing features of Puritan churches founded in the New World was the requirement that individuals presenting themselves for full membership give before the congregation an account of their spiritual experience. The Cambridge Platform of 1648, which codified ecclesiastical practices in Massachusetts Bay, affirmed, "A personall & publick *confession*, & declaring of Gods manner of working upon the soul, is both lawfull, expedient, & usefull."[44] This confession, or "relation," provided an important basis on which to judge whether the narrator was worthy of admission into the church. By the end of the seventeenth century, New Englanders had extended the genre to include narratives of travel, witchcraft, natural catastrophes, and Indian captivity. Edwards's *Personal Narrative* continued the form of the spiritual relation, but, composed in a revival context, employing an original religious epistemology, and utilizing a language of "affections," it also represented a new form of self-disclosure that was formative for modern American evangelicalism.

Structurally, the *Personal Narrative* falls into two parts. The first two-thirds is a chronological review of important phases or events in Edwards's spiritual life, and the last third is thematic, a collection of doctrinal and pietistic loci. Where the "Diary" is nearly a day-by-day account, the *Personal Narrative* is retrospective. Many of the tensions and obsessions of the young Edwards are absent from the older one, almost two decades later.

In the first section, Edwards slowly built narrative intensity as his inner misgivings about religion were resolved and he obtained a "new sense." He recounted his efforts as a boy, once during an awakening in his father's church (when he constructed "a booth in a swamp" for prayer), and another during college. In hindsight, he realized that during his youth he was relying on his own efforts, his seeking "miserable." Gradually, his "cavils" about divine sovereignty were overcome as he was convinced of the justice of God. Indeed, he not only accepted the doctrines of sovereignty and election, but he had a *happy* acceptance of them; he yearned (echoing "On Sarah Pierpont") to be "wrapt up to God in heaven" and "swallowed up in Him" – a loss of self that is more rapturous than his earlier ideas of humility.[45] Similarly, whereas before his new-found convictions he had been "uncommonly terrified with thunder," now "it rejoiced me."[46] Edwards gives us the image of him eagerly going outside to view approaching storms, all the while singing or chanting meditations. (Another type of utterance for Edwards was weeping, which seemed to be an important expression of his piety, whether in contemplating God's magnificence or his own puniness.)

As in the "entertainment" found in thunderstorms, the role of nature as a place of divine inspiration was a constant theme in the *Personal Narrative*. Edwards was but one of many colonial authors, such as William Bradford, Anne Bradstreet, and Edward Taylor, for whom nature played a significant part in their lives and writings.[47] While in New York, Edwards customarily sought out a "solitary place" on the Hudson River "for contemplation on divine things, and secret converse with God." Walking out alone in the fields at Bolton, he had "one special season of uncommon sweetness."[48] The new sense made all nature appear glorious because, to the regenerate eye, it communicated God's glory.

As Edwards recounted how the world of divine things opened itself up to his mind, the experiences he related became more dramatic, his language more expansive, to the point where he strained to find words to convey his full meaning. Nowhere in the *Personal Narrative* is this more evident than in his description of an event in the summer of 1721, following a conversation he had with his father about some of his late "discoveries." Strolling in the family pasture, he had such an overpowering "sweet sense . . . that I know not how to express." In a passage that is often quoted, he used paradox to describe God's majesty and grace: "I seemed to see them both in a sweet conjunction: majesty and meekness joined together: it was a sweet and gentle, and holy majesty; and also a majestic meekness; an awful sweetness; a high, and great, and holy gentleness."[49] Following this episode, Edwards had a thirsting after holiness combined with increasing apprehension of his "feebleness and impotence" to satisfy that thirst. In describing the quest for holiness, Edwards drew on the "Diary" and contemporary compositions, quoting at length from the first entry of the "*Miscellanies*," a meditation on the nature of holiness. Seeking to show how he applied his views of holiness to his life, he cited the "Diary" entry of January 12, 1723 – his solemn dedication of himself to God – aware that he had fallen short of his promises.[50]

Though Edwards dwelt on his inabilities to fulfill his expanding desires for holiness, he did not identify his inability to locate a single moment of conversion as a defect in his experience. Instead, he portrayed conversion as a gradual process of enlightenment and a realization of grace that, like the document itself, was retrospective. He "never could give an account, how, or by what means," he was first convinced of divine sovereignty," nor saw any "extraordinary influence" in it at the time, "nor a long time after." His "delights" were "of a different kind" from before, his "sense of divine things" heightened, but he never gave them the name of conversion.[51] As he had noted in the "Diary," his own experience was different from what "divines" posited, and through that he came to realize that religion was varied.[52] For Edwards, what mattered was not a normative process or an identifiable moment of regeneration, but the cumulative combination of affections and behavior, a formula he would elucidate in *Religious Affections*.

The concluding section of the *Personal Narrative* switched from the episodic to a summary of Edwards's personal religious affections. The "holiness of God," unity with Christ, the advancement of God's kingdom, the "excellent fullness of Christ," the glory of the Holy Ghost, and the excellency of the Word of God were topics that Edwards found "delightful" in contemplation for their own sakes, apart from his own interest or fate. Turning to his own state in comparison, he saw more of his own sinfulness and vileness, his "perfectly ineffable" wickedness (which he lamented was "infinite upon infinite!"), his lack of conviction of sin and a "broken heart" (not in the romantic but in the religious sense of contriteness), his ignorance as a "young Christian," and his dependence on God's grace and strength.[53]

Letters in colonial times, such as the one containing the *Personal Narrative*, were semipublic documents that were shared by immediate and extended family, and sometimes by a wider community. "Scribal publication" complemented typographic publication as an important source of information and of spiritual formation. Edwards could expect that his account would be circulated, which may explain the care he took in composing it. Wittingly or unwittingly, Edwards anticipated a trend. The Great Awakening, for which the Northampton revival of 1734–5 was a precursor, was a fertile context for letter writing. During the 1740s, revival leaders established a transatlantic evangelical network that reported news of awakenings and distributed accounts of conversion.[54]

With Edwards, the purpose of the *Personal Narrative* was didactic – to instruct others. Mindful that many of the supposed conversions during the Connecticut Valley revival had proven false, and hoping for a new spate of revivals, Edwards sought to present a balanced depiction of saintly striving. In this sense, the depiction may be a particular construction, a partial version, of his private self. In *A Faithful Narrative*, he used a young woman, Abigail Hutchinson, and a child, Phebe Bartlett, as models of faith. In the *Personal Narrative*, Edwards turned his scrutiny, as he had in his "Diary" almost two decades earlier, on himself. Though he felt himself wanting in many respects, he had worked out the main points of his view of Christian holiness. In the years to come, he would use his *Personal Narrative* as a basis for presenting other individuals as paragons of experimental piety as he defined it, including Sarah Pierpont Edwards, as first seen in "On Sarah Pierpont" and later in *Some Thoughts*, and, most strikingly and at greatest length, David Brainerd in his *Life of Brainerd*.[55]

THE "ACCOUNT BOOK"

Thus far the focus has been on the classic, well-known documents that deal largely with Edwards's private religiosity, though they also shed light on other aspects of his life and character. Now comes an examination of documents that show Edwards in his daily interactions with others. In his "Account Book," containing entries from 1733 to 1757, Edwards emerges as a family provider, businessman, farmer, pastor, and teacher.

One prevailing image of Edwards is as a person concerned only with metaphysical speculations, with no head for common affairs. But his personal accounts and letters show he was a competent businessman, a skill he learned from his father who kept meticulous records of transactions with his parishioners and was obsessive about stewarding his goods. Clerical salaries were frequently in arrears or fulfilled with "country pay" – undervalued produce. The "Account Book" shows Edwards's struggles to collect his pay from the town constables. Given the collection problem, ministers had to be conscientious about keeping track of receipts and expenditures, overseeing the production and upkeep of crops and livestock at home, and seeking other sources of revenue – Edwards especially so, with his "large and chargeable family." As a means of extra income, Sarah Pierpont Edwards and the daughters constructed fans for sale in Boston. Even after watching every penny, however, Edwards sometimes still came up short. His records show him borrowing large amounts of money, on two occasions as much as £150.[56]

Edwards's workaday world became increasingly busier as he moved up professionally and as his family grew. Documents like the "Account Book" are therefore surrogate records of Edwards's mature personal life in lieu of anything strictly autobiographical. Farming was a time-consuming occupation. He bargained with Northampton factors to till his lands and harvest the crops in return for a portion of the harvest. Livestock were another responsibility. His accounts contained his descriptions of several steer calves and heifers so that he could identify them should they roam – a common problem of the time. Transactions with townspeople included the purchase of staples such as oats and apples, or building materials for his house at Stockbridge. Letters to friends and colleagues contained arrangements for everything from the purchase of sheep and turnips to the large amounts of chocolate the

Edwardses consumed.[57] Using intermediaries or agents – English, Dutch, and Indian – was a customary way of conducting business, as illustrated in the "Account Book," which has frequent mention of sending money by a person traveling to Boston, Rhode Island, or elsewhere for specific household necessities. Through individuals local and distant, Edwards was part of an economic and social network of barter, trade, credit, and representation that was essential to conducting business in a pre-modern society. Together, these relationships show his connectedness with the communities around him and his regular transactions, even with religious and personal opponents such as Springfield pastor Robert Breck, whose 1736 ordination Edwards had opposed, and Abigail Williams Sargeant Dwight of Stockbridge.

As part of his role as a pastor and author, Edwards was a conduit for books and other published materials. His "Account Book" shows that from 1745 to 1757 he lent over a hundred books from his library to more than sixty parishioners, family members, and colleagues. These works dealt with all manner of religious topics. Curiously, the book Edwards lent most often during the Northampton years was Richard Steele's *The Ladies Library* (1714), a collection of essays on manners and style, which he had used himself as a young aspiring author. During the Stockbridge years, Edwards became a distributor of Bibles, perhaps addressing a lack of them along the frontier and among the Indians. He also continued to bring the latest in news and culture, disseminating newspapers and even Samuel Richardson's novels, particularly *Clarissa*. (Interestingly, Sally Prince's nickname for Esther Edwards Burr was "Burrissa."[58])

Edwards was a teacher from a young age, starting as a tutor at Yale College. At Northampton, he had the duty of catechizing the children and young people. A manuscript list of over a hundred questions on arcane biblical facts, accompanied by names of Northampton boys to whom they were assigned, suggests how demanding Edwards could be in this role.[59] He hosted at his house many students preparing for ministry, including Samuel Hopkins and Joseph Bellamy;[60] the "Account Book" mentioned another student, a David Webster.[61] (Not only did he board students, but he also quartered soldiers in his Northampton and Stockbridge homes in times of Indian raids, keeping careful track of their expenses so he could be reimbursed by the province.) At Stockbridge, Edwards helped to teach Indian children and developed a pedagogical strategy for instructing boys and girls in a Socratic method.[62]

"LAST WILL AND TESTAMENT" AND "CHILDREN'S ACCOUNTS"

Edwards's relationship with his family is reflected in selected letters and financial documents. Visitors commented on the moving nature of the family prayer times, and on the musical pastimes of the family, which included singing and lute and violin playing. Edwards regularly spoke with each child individually about his or her soul's concerns. Less pleasant to contemplate, governance within the Edwards family included corporal punishment. Esther Edwards Burr wrote that her ten-month-old Sally had to be "Whip'd once on *Old Adams* account," a method Burr doubtless learned at her parents' hands.[63] Yet, such measures were part of accepted child-rearing practices of the time. Edwards's letters to his children are filled with stark, though tenderly meant, religious advice. To his ten-year-old son Jonathan, Jr., then on the New York frontier among the Mohawks, Edwards recommended trusting in a heavenly Father rather than an earthly one,[64] and to his daughter Esther in 1753, he first advised resignation in affliction and then offered medical remedies (including even a rattlesnake for stomach problems). Three years later, when Esther was visiting Stockbridge, she and her father had a conversation about "soul concerns," and she commented in her journal: "Last eve I had some free discourse with My Father on the great things that concern my best intrest.... He gave me some excellent directions to be observed in secret that tend to keep the soul near to God, as well as others to be observed in a more publick way – What a mercy that I have such a Father! Such a Guide!"[65]

Edwards also provided for his family's worldly needs. Stray receipts from merchants and doctors (since illness was a frequent reality) itemize his efforts to procure bodily necessities as well as the occasional luxury, including a "locket and chaine" for his wife, or "ribbands" and "playthings" for the children. Apparently each child from birth had a sort of allowance, perhaps a dowry or career assets. Remarkably, Edwards kept meticulous track of his "borrowing" from his children at the back of his "Interleaved Bible," a repository of Scripture commentary. Sometimes the amount "owed," never great, was paid off with a gift, such as an enameled ring for Sarah in 1748 or gold buttons for Eunice in 1756.[66]

In his "Last Will and Testament," Edwards, despite economic woes, provided quite amply for his family. His wife was to receive his entire estate, his manuscripts, and a small portion of the library (no doubt her husband knew she had certain favorites). His children each received "ounces of silver" in varying amounts – the boys 638 (approximately £1500 at the time), and the unmarried girls 319.[67] Any of the boys "brought up to learning" would get the bulk of the library, which had grown to over eight hundred books and pamphlets. After Edwards and his wife died, their estate was valued at approximately £1,050, not including parcels of land in several towns and "a right in the Susquehannah Purchase," totaling over five hundred acres.[68] These amounts did not place Edwards in the top economic tier, but they were nonetheless indicative of an upper-class family.

The inventory of Edwards's household goods reveals mostly utilitarian devices needed for home and barn, but the family's refined, cosmopolitan tastes show through in certain items, reflecting an emulation of latest English fashions taking hold in mid-eighteenth-century New England.[69] Edwards himself sported a beaver hat, a fine calamanco vest, silver knee buckles, spectacles, and a cane. His wife owned a silver engraved patch box that contained not items for mending but felt beauty marks that were adhered to the face; even in the wilds of Stockbridge, she retained the literal markings of high European culture. The family had a tea service and ate on china plates and cups, used damask tablecloths and napkins, and decorated the walls with looking glasses and "small pictures" – a version of provincially genteel, though unostentatious, living.

Edwards's sense of status extended to issues surrounding race. Owning slaves was a symbol of social rank, and during his lifetime he owned a succession of African slaves. The inventory of his estate lists "a negro boy named Titus," valued at £30, whom Edwards did not emancipate. In fact, Edwards defended the institution of slavery as ordained by God in Scripture. However, he did come to oppose the slave trade, thereby providing a basis for the abolitionism espoused by his son Jonathan, Jr., and disciples such as Samuel Hopkins. For Edwards, just as white society was ordered vertically, with superiors and "lower sorts," so there were racial hierarchies. He adhered to the accepted wisdom of the time that Africans, Indians, and Jews were inferior to white Christian Europeans. And he subscribed to the doctrines of racism and cultural elitism, though his exposure to Indians at Stockbridge caused him to reevaluate his views on human nature to some degree, and his teachings do contain some democratic implications.[70]

Jonathan and Sarah had their portraits painted around 1750 by Joseph Badger of Boston, commissioned by Edwards's Scottish admirer William Hogg. The subjects' self-presentations give us clues to their characters. Sarah's portrait is not that of a prudish and plain latter-day Puritan, with a hatred of earthly display (see Figure 4). She smiles gently; her hair falls freely about her shoulders rather than tucked under a bonnet, as was expected of married women, and she is dressed in a bright blue dress with a plunging neckline and ruffles. And while she is not wearing a beauty mark, she does have rouge on her cheeks. Jonathan, meanwhile, appears in the trappings of his ministerial calling – Geneva gown, preaching bands, and powdered wig (see Figure 1). That wig tells us much about Edwards. In a time of rising democratic sentiments, it bespoke his adherence to older, commonwealth values. It also reflected his aristocratic attitudes. As a minister and member of a prominent extended family, he expected deference from his "inferiors," and he defended the prerogatives of his profession and class. In the tightly drawn

4. Portrait of Sarah Edwards by Joseph Badger, courtesy of Yale University Art Gallery, bequest of Eugene Phelps Edwards.

lips we can perhaps detect the unsociability and inflexibility that Edwards himself and others saw in him. Timothy Cutler at one time recalled Edwards as "Critical, sa[d] and peculiar.... Always a sober Person withal pretty recluse, austere and rigid," and at another, "a man of much sobriety and gravity, ... but odd in his principles, haughty and stiff and morose."[71] If his flaws render him more human, they also make his accomplishments the more remarkable. Edwards never sought to be an "affable, facecious Gentleman"; he would have placed greater contentment in Samuel Hopkins's estimation: "a life that has been greatly useful."[72]

In formulating guidelines by which to live his life; in closely examining his spiritual state, his motives, and his relationship with God; in his longing for a soul-mate; in reflecting on his life as an older man; in his social, cultural, and economic interactions with a network of far-flung individuals; in his roles as a husband, parent, businessperson, and pastor; and in his attitudes about society, gender, race, and ethnicity, Edwards was in many ways typical of his place and time. But the combination of intelligence and faith in him made him a unique character, one who stands out as truly original. He was Janus-faced, looking backward and forward, with reference points in the Reformed, Puritan heritage and worldview *and* in the era of empire, Enlightenment, and evangelicalism. Edwards's "Personal Writings" provide the best entrée into his intense religious life. They also illuminate how he applied his own experience to change the world in which he lived.

Notes

1. Preserved Clapp, Jan. 1735/36, General Sessions of the Peace, Hampshire County, Connecticut State Library, Mss. Collection, Hartford, Conn.; David Hall, MS Diary, Sutton, Feb. 3, 1742, Massachusetts Historical Society.

2. JE, "Catalogue of Reading," no. 56 (c. 1723), MS, Beinecke Library, Yale University. (Unless otherwise indicated, all MSS referred to are in the Beinecke Collection.) Henry Steele Commager, ed., *The Autobiography of Benjamin Franklin* (New York: Modern Library, 1944), 92–5; Charles Moore, ed., *George Washington's Rules of Civility and Decent Behaviour in Company and Conversation* (Boston: Houghton Mifflin, 1926).

3. References to the "Resolutions" and "Diary" are to entry numbers or dates, in WJE 16:753–89; quotes from "On Sarah Pierpont" and the *Personal Narrative*, ibid., 789–804, are referenced parenthetically in the text.

4. WJE, 16:753.

5. Ibid., 753–6.

6. Ibid., 753–4, 758.

7. Ibid., 757.

8. Michael McGiffert, ed., *God's Plot: Puritan Spirituality in Thomas Shepard's Cambridge* (Amherst: University of Massachusetts Press, 1972), 81–134; Edmund S. Morgan, ed., *The Diary of Michael Wigglesworth, 1653–1657* (New York: Harper Torchbooks, 1946); Francis G. Walett, ed., *The Diary of Ebenezer Parkman, 1703–1782* (Worcester: American Antiquarian Society, 1974); Barbara E. Lacey, ed., *The World of Hannah Heaton: The Diary of an Eighteenth-Century New England Farm Woman* (DeKalb, IL: Northern Illinois University Press, 2003).

9. WJE, 16:754.

10. Ibid., 759.

11. Ibid., 762.

12. Ibid., 762–3.

13. Timothy Cutler to Bp. Edmund Gibson, May 28, 1739, in Kenneth W. Cameron, ed., *The Church of England in Pre-Revolutionary Connecticut* (Hartford: Transcendental, 1976), 54.

14. Letter to Trustees of the College of New Jersey, Oct. 19, 1757, in WJE, 16:726.

15. WJE, 16:764–5.

16. Ibid., 779–80.

17. Ibid., 777.

18. Ibid., 6:192–5.

19. Ibid., 16:779; ibid., 756; Timothy Edwards, MS Sermon Notebook, 1724, Connecticut Historical Society, Hartford.

20. "Diary," WJE, 16:768.

21. WJE, 16:773–4; Letters, ibid., 30–40.

22. WJE, 16:777.

23. Ibid., 779, 782.

24. Ibid., 787.

25. Letter of May 24, WJE, 16:284.

26. Letter to Jonathan Ashley, May 2, 1751, in Wyllis E. Wright, ed., *Colonel Ephraim Williams: A Documentary Life* (Pittsfield, MA: Berkshire County Historical Society, 1970), 61.

27. Quoted in *Sibley's Harvard Graduates*, Vol. 12, 1746–1750 (Boston: Massachusetts Historical Society, 1962), 399.

28. Croswell to Eleazar Wheelock, May 3, 1749, Dartmouth University Library, Wheelock Papers, no. 742303.

29. Walley, MS Diary, 1742–59, Oct. 10, 1743, Ipswich (MA) Historical Society.

30. Carol Karlsen and Laurie Crumpacker, eds., *The Journal of Esther Edwards Burr, 1754–57* (New Haven: Yale University Press, 1984), 54.

31. Sereno E. Dwight, ed., *Works of President Edwards* (10 vols. New York: 1830), I:114; John Stoughton, *Windsor Farmes: A Glimpse of an Old Parish* (Hartford, 1883), 82.

32. WJE, 16:789–90.

33. "On Sarah Pierpont," WJE, 16:790; *Personal Narrative*, WJE, 16:793.

34. *George Whitefield's Journals* (London: Banner of Truth, 1960), 477; Stephen G. Post, *Christian Love and Self-Denial: An Historical and Normative Study of Jonathan Edwards, Samuel Hopkins, and American Theological Ethics* (Lanham, MD, 1987), 28.

35. For Sarah Pierpont Edwards's 1742 narrative, see Dwight, ed., *Works*, 1:171–86. See also Julie Ellison, "The Sociology of 'Holy Indifference': Sarah Edwards's Narrative," *American Quarterly* 56 (1984): 479–95; Amanda Porterfield, *Feminine Spirituality in America: From Sarah Edwards to Martha Graham* (Philadelphia: Temple University Press, 1980), 39–48.

36. *A Continuation of the Reverend Mr. Whitefield's Journal from Savannah, June 25. 1740...* (Boston, 1741), 83.

37. Walley, Diary, Oct. 12, 1743; "Joseph Emerson's Diary, 1748–49," *Massachusetts Historical Society Proceedings* 46 (1910–11): 267.

38. William Shippen to Sarah Edwards, March 22, 1758, Franklin Trask Library, Andover Newton Theological School.

39. Ola Elizabeth Winslow, *Jonathan Edwards 1703–1758* (New York: Macmillan, 1940), 338–9; George M. Marsden, *Jonathan Edwards: A Life* (New Haven: Yale University Press, 2003), 22–3.

40. Sandra M. Gustafson, *Eloquence is Power: Oratory & Performance in Early America* (Chapel Hill: University of North Carolina Press, 2000), 61–74.

41. WJE, 16:746, nn. 1–2.

42. Burr to JE, March 1741, Edwards Papers, f. 1741, #7, Andover Newton Theological School.

43. Samuel Hopkins, *The Life and Character of the Late Reverend Mr. Jonathan Edwards* (Boston, 1765), 23–39.

44. Patricia Caldwell, *The Puritan Conversion Narrative: The Beginnings of American Expression* (Cambridge: Cambridge University Press, 1993); The Cambridge Platform, Ch. XII, ¶ 5, in Williston Walker, *The Creeds and Platforms of Congregationalism* (New York, 1893), 223.

45. WJE, 16:791–2.

46. Ibid., 794.

47. See William Bradford, *A Religion or Journall of the Beginning and Proceedings of the English Plantation at Plimoth in New England...*(London, 1622); Anne Bradstreet, *Tenth Muse Lately Sprung up in America...*(London, 1650); Edward Taylor, *Poems*, ed. Donald E. Stanford (New Haven: Yale University Press, 1960).

48. WJE, 16:797–8.

49. Ibid., 793.

50. Ibid., 762–3, 795–6.

51. Ibid., 792.

52. Ibid., 759.

53. Ibid., 799–804.

54. Harold Love, *Scribal Publication in Seventeenth-Century England*(Oxford: Oxford University Press, 1993); Frank Lambert, *Inventing the "Great Awakening"*(Princeton: Princeton University Press, 1999).

55. Daniel B. Shea Jr., "The Art and Instruction of Jonathan Edwards's *Personal Narrative*," *American Literature* 37 (1965), 17–32; Norman Pettit, "Introduction," WJE, 7:5–10.

56. JE, MS "Account Book."

57. Receipt, 1741, in JE, MS Sermon on Deuteronomy 29:4.

58. Karlsen and Crumpacker, eds., *The Journal of Esther Edwards Burr*, 279, 282.

59. JE, MS "Questions for Young People."

60. Joseph Bellamy, MS Notebook, c. 1736, Special Collections, Yale Divinity School.

61. "Account Book," entry for July 8, 1734, MS, p. 5.

62. JE to Sir William Pepperrell, Nov. 28, 1751, in WJE 16:406–13.

63. Karlsen and Crumpacker, eds., *Journal of Esther Edwards Burr*, 95; Philip J. Greven, *The Protestant Temperament: Patterns of Child-Rearing, Religious Experience, and the Self in Early America* (New York: Knopf, 1977).

64. JE to Jonathan Edwards, Jr., May 27, 1755.

65. JE to Esther Edwards Burr, March 28, 1753, in WJE, 16:666–7, 576–8; Karlsen and Crumpacker, eds., *Journal of Esther Edwards Burr*, 224.

66. JE, "Interleaved Bible," MS, pp. 902–4.

67. Jonathan Edwards' Last Will, and the Inventory of His Estate," *Bibliotheca Sacra* 33 (1876): 438–46.

68. Ibid., 447.

69. Richard L. Bushman, *The Refinement of America: Persons, Houses, Cities* (New York: Knopf, 1992).

70. Kenneth P. Minkema and Harry S. Stout, "The Edwardsean Tradition and Antislavery Debate, 1740–1865," *Journal of American History* 92 (June 2005): 47–74;

Rachel Wheeler, "'Friends to Your Souls': Jonathan Edwards' Indian Pastorate and the Doctrine of Original Sin," *Church History* 72 (Dec. 2003): 736–65.

71. Timothy Cutler to Bp. Edmund Gibson, May 28, 1739, in Kenneth W. Cameron, ed. *The Church of England in Pre-Revolutionary Connecticut,* (Hartford: Transcendental Books, 1976) 54; Timothy Cutler to Thomas Secker, Aug. 28, 1754, in *Documents Relative to the Colonial History of the State of New-York* (Albany, 1855), 6:906.

72. Hopkins, *Life,* [ii], 42.

3 The New England background

DAVID D. HALL

The religious culture of early eighteenth-century New England was recognizably "Puritan" in important respects despite changes in social and political life that resulted in toleration of the once-despised Baptists, Anglicans, and Quakers and a sharp curtailing of the ministers' influence in political affairs. Both were consequences of the colonists' "adjustment to empire."[1] Yet the signs of continuity were many. The *Platform of Discipline* of 1648, familiarly known in New England as the Cambridge Platform, remained a persuasive description of the "Congregational Way" that had been inaugurated in the 1630s. In their everyday preaching, the clergy reiterated the distinction, so important to the generation of John Cotton, Thomas Hooker, and Thomas Shepard, between "vital" or "experimental" religion and religion that was merely external, or a matter of "formality." Simultaneously, the ministers were voicing another Puritan commonplace: the obligation of everyone in a Christian society to practice certain moral duties. No less conventional were complaints that young people were flouting these duties and that civil magistrates were inconsistent in punishing the disorderly. Even so, New England seemed to some contemporaries a society in which social life was penetrated by the work of "reformation" that had meant so much to the Puritan movement.[2] Meanwhile, congregations and ministers were deeply involved with the rituals of fasts and thanksgivings that evoked long-persisting assumptions about a covenanted people's obligations to observe God's will.

As Jonathan Edwards settled into his ministry in Northampton at the beginning of the 1730s, he may well have imagined benefiting from these elements of continuity, including long tenure in his post. Had not Solomon Stoddard, at once his grandfather and predecessor in the pulpit, served as the town's minister for sixty years and, in reputation if not always in reality, acquired remarkable authority in local affairs? A circumstance that would serve Edwards well into the mid-1740s was his participation in an extended network of kinfolk, many of whom were high-status ministers and lay people.[3] Edwards may have supposed that he would be a minister in the mold of Grindal Rawson of Mendon, Massachusetts, commemorated after his many years of service as "a great Peace-Maker; So that in all of Thirty-five Years of his Continuance in the Town, there was no considerable Difference." Or perhaps of Samuel Danforth of Taunton, who at the beginning of the century organized "the greatest Part of the Youth" of his town "into Societies for religious Exercises, ... The good Effect whereof was the putting an End to & utter Banishment of their former disorderly and profane Meetings to drink, &c."[4] For sure, Edwards hoped that he could emulate his grandfather Stoddard, father Timothy, and various of his Williams kin in staging seasons of special fervency, or "harvests" of souls newly saved for Christ.

Yet as Edwards surely knew, some of the elements of continuity with the Puritan and New England past were not so promising. Since the 1660s, when the three oldest churches in Connecticut had each fallen into disarray and dissidents withdrew from Boston First to found Third Church, the noise of "contention" had filled the land as factions disputed the leadership of colonial governments, and, in town after town, people quarreled over policies of church membership, the location of a new meetinghouse, the choice of minister, and whether to allow outlying farmers a church of their own. Northampton had its own history of factionalism that Edwards remarked upon in *A Faithful Narrative of the Surprising Work of God* (1738). Contention was bad news for the clergy, limiting what they could do in public life by making it almost impossible not to become partisans of one side or the other. Such was the fate of Samuel Parris, the fourth person employed as minister in faction-torn Salem Village. Parris never won the support of those who opposed his candidacy at the outset, and the witch-hunt of 1692 added fuel to an already kindled fire. Meanwhile the economics of being a minister, though favorable in some respects, were deteriorating; the downward pressure on ministerial salaries during the troubled 1680s and early 1690s, when war-related expenses forced Massachusetts to issue paper currency that rapidly became worthless, was manifested in the shortfalls that accumulated in many towns. Well before this moment, every installation of a new minister was already requiring extensive negotiations about the level of salary, modes of payment, and access to land and housing.[5] When inflation struck in the 1720s, salaries fixed in calmer times depreciated in value to the point where some ministers fell into financial difficulty.[6]

But of greater consequence for anyone entering the ministry were tensions within the Puritan understanding of the church and ministry. Forged in the context of a national, comprehensive church that admitted everyone to membership, the Puritan movement in Elizabethan England had imagined a church that excluded wayward or uninformed people from the sacraments of baptism and the Lord's Supper. Radicals within the movement, a few of them "Separatists" who denounced the national church as false, called for a "gathered" membership limited to those who covenanted with each other to "walk in the ways" of holiness. More mainstream Puritans struggled to hold together the rival values of exclusivity and comprehensiveness. The movement was also committed to enhancing lay participation in church government, to the point of empowering the laity to elect their local ministers to office. Yet this impulse bothered those of more "Presbyterian" thinking who emphasized the importance of ordination and the independence of the office of ministry. By the early seventeenth century, the reaction against an hierarchical and centralized national church had led some within the movement to question whether councils or synods had any authority over local congregations.

On these matters the immigrants of the 1630s, strongly moved as they were by the Christian primitivist vision of reclaiming the true church from centuries of apostasy, had preferred the more radical possibilities. They did so dramatically by requiring of every candidate for membership "a personall & publick confession, & declaring of Gods manner of working upon the soul," an exercise that became known as making a "relation" of the "work of grace." All church members were also obliged to join in covenant with each other. In practice and in principle, no one entered any of the churches being organized in the colonies merely on the basis of his or her membership in the Church of England, and children could not be baptized unless one of their parents became a member. The "Congregational Way," the name that emerged for the colonists' new system, thus veered toward the sectarian pole of the Puritan spectrum. Not surprisingly, some immigrants complained of being excluded. Other criticism came from mainstream Puritans in England who warned that the colonists were attempting to accomplish the impossible, a church consisting only of "visible saints." Nor did everyone in New England or abroad welcome the empowering of the laity that was another feature of the Congregational Way, or its insistence on the autonomy of each congregation.[7]

Initially the new system worked fairly well, for many of the immigrants were deeply versed in the "practical divinity" and its description of the work of grace. In some communities perhaps as many as 70 percent of the adults passed into membership under the new rules, aided by the generous interpretation of "visible" preferred by ministers such as Thomas Hooker of Hartford or the "judgment of charity" that the Cambridge Platform recommended.[8] Yet in no town did every adult join and in most, it seems, married men lagged behind their wives.[9] Moreover, by the 1650s the situation was changing for the worse. The baptized children of these adult members, now transformed into adults themselves and beginning to have children, were failing to make the "relations" that had come so easily to their parents. These "adult children" were, it seemed, members of the church because of their baptismal covenant, but according to the Cambridge Platform their children were not entitled to be baptized nor they themselves allowed to partake of the Lord's Supper unless, like their parents, they met the criterion of the "work of grace" and became "full" members.

Finding some means of keeping these people in the church and allowing their children to be baptized occupied a conclave of ministers in 1657 and a second in 1662, which reaffirmed the recommendations of the first. These were that the adult children were truly members on the basis of the "external" covenant God had made with Abraham (Genesis 17:7) and all of his descendants, and that the children of these adults, encompassed as they were within the same covenant, could be baptized. Scripturally, these arguments assumed that the Abrahamic covenant of the Old Testament extended into the New, a hermeneutics Baptists rejected on the grounds that the covenant of grace superseded the "national" covenant of old Israel. The ministers also insisted that no one be admitted to the Lord's Table without providing testimony of the work of grace, and that only those in full membership could vote on crucial matters of church business, such as admitting persons to membership and acts of church discipline.[10] The architects of this scheme regarded it as a "middle way between extremes." One extreme would have been to erase the difference between the two sacraments and admit everyone in covenant to all the means of grace. The other would have been to strip "adult children" of their membership or confine them to some probationary status unless they qualified (as adults) for membership by offering a relation of the work of grace. Neither seemed tenable, the first because it would mean giving up a bedrock principle that the "profane" should not be allowed into the church, the second because it would sharply reduce the number of persons in membership.[11]

The group that met in 1657 and again in 1662 persuaded themselves that the new rule linking baptism to family membership had the sanction of the leading architects of the Congregational Way, including Cotton, Shepard, and Richard Mather. Less happily, another of the founders, John Davenport of New Haven, opposed the recommendations of 1662 and quoted Thomas Hooker's opinion that only parents in regular membership could have their children baptized.[12] Lay church members were of several minds, some welcoming the new measures but many others enraged by them. Controversy and schism were the inevitable outcome as churches and ministers attempted to practice the synod's recommendations.[13]

Did the decisions of 1657 and 1662 weaken the place of religion in New England? Some at the time said yes, as have many modern interpreters. Recent interpretations that follow this line owe much to nineteenth-century

Congregational historians who blamed the rules of 1662 for allowing the churches to fill up with "lax" members. These historians also disliked Edwards's grandfather Solomon Stoddard for proposing that every out-wardly moral townsperson be admitted to the Lord's Supper: In their eyes "Stoddardeanism" was laxness carried to an extreme. Together, Stoddard's policy and the "Half-Way Covenant" of 1662 (as the measure regarding bap-tism was eventually nicknamed) were regarded as having placed the New England churches on a downward slope that culminated in the emergence of Unitarianism in the early nineteenth century.[14] In the mid-twentieth cen-tury, this interpretation gained the support of Perry Miller. He regarded the ministers' decision to acknowledge that the merits of "hypocrisy" – that is, shifting to external appearances instead of insisting on conversion – opened the way to a broader erosion of piety and theology. His master term for this process was "declension," a term he borrowed from the colonists themselves. Others shared his point of view and sought to reinforce it, as Edmund S. Mor-gan did in suggesting that the Half-Way Covenant fostered a "tribalism" that isolated the churches from the wider society.[15]

Yet the actual situation was a good deal more complex than the story of decline acknowledges. One circumstance was the age profile of the pop-ulation. Toward the end of the seventeenth century the high birth rate and (for an early modern society) low rate of infant mortality in New England had greatly increased the number of persons who fell into the age range of "young people," and their numbers remained large well into the eighteenth century. Perhaps as many as half of the population were between the ages of sixteen and thirty, and the median age for the colonists as a whole was sixteen. No explicit role existed for these young people in the church or in civil society. Most were below the customary age for joining in full member-ship, and many of those in their teens and early twenties had yet to marry and form families of their own. Curbing the restlessness of these young peo-ple became a principal preoccupation of churches and towns by the 1660s and 1670s, one step being the appointment of tithing men to keep order among the unmarried men who sat in the galleries of the town meeting-house. The "Reforming Synod" of 1679 aimed several of its complaints at the young, noting, for example, that they were "absenting themselves out of the families whereunto they belong in the night, and meeting with corrupt company without leave," and appealing for stronger family governance.[16] The "night-walking" of the young was as irritating to Edwards at the debut of his ministry as it was to the Reforming Synod.[17]

But the real weakness of the case for "declension" is that it ignores pat-terns of behavior writ large in town and church records. The most important of these patterns is the presence of large numbers of adults who seemed indifferent to church membership and to having their children baptized. By the 1660s Anglican or anti-Puritan contemporaries were insisting that substantial numbers of colonists were demonstrating such indifference, which these observers blamed on the rules of the Congregational Way. A hostile witness insisted in 1689 that the ratio of members to nonmembers was one in ten.[18] Other, less biased observers called attention to the same phenomenon, as when the Connecticut General Assembly in 1676 complained that "many Baptized Adult persons [were] neglecting & too many refusing to Own their Baptismal Covenant."[19] Writing in 1671 from Killingworth, Connecticut, the town minister John Woodbridge told Richard Baxter in England of discovering that sixty "men, women, and children" were "unbaptized ... though the whole plantation consist not of above 30 householders."[20] Newly arrived in Salem Village (Danvers) at the beginning of the eighteenth century, Joseph Green noted that "many Persons ... belong to the Congregation who are not baptized," and he made it one of the goals of his ministry to "persuade and incline them (or some of them at least) to seek after that Ordinance of Baptisme."[21] It seemed that every town had its John Horsfield, a large property holder in Windsor, Connecticut, for whom there is "no evidence he presented any of his nine children for baptism or became a full member." Indeed, only about a third of the adult males in Windsor were members in the 1660s.[22]

More light is thrown on the presence of these people by the response of ministers such as Simon Bradstreet, who became minister of New London in 1670, and Joseph Capen, who arrived as the new minister of the Topsfield, Massachusetts, church in 1684. Bradstreet's church had twenty-five full members. By 1683 he had added another forty-four but separately had baptized some 438 persons, "a considerable number [of whom] were adults; some parents baptized themselves, at the time that they owned the covenant, and presented their children for baptism." Joseph Capen counted forty-nine members, twenty-seven of them women, in Topsfield. Within seven years he had baptized two hundred townspeople, some of whom must have been adults; by 1702 the total had reached 572. His records reveal that entire families had neglected to participate, for on a single day in 1697, seven Perleys "entered into Covenant ... on thar fathers account at the same time," and, on the same day, so did eight or nine Averills.[23] In other churches, too, children were being brought to baptism in bunches, like grapes, either the same or following Sunday after one of their parents was baptized for the first time or agreed to renew his or her baptismal covenant.[24]

These alternating rhythms of indifference and affiliation cannot be explained as the response to changes in church policy, for these occur too widely in space and time for this to be the case. Not a newly introduced

"laxness" but marriage and family formation account for some of these decisions to affiliate with the church, though why certain parents waited until
several children had been born before making any effort to have them baptized, while others acted more promptly, is a mystery.

The haste to bring newborn children to the meetinghouse to be baptized
constitutes a second pattern of lay behavior. Here again, church records
provide innumerable examples of children being baptized within a few days,
or at most ten, of their birth. Many congregations contained women like the
wife of James Minot of Dorchester, whose "great desire" it was "to have hier
Children baptized."[25] Sixty percent of the children in those Essex County,
Massachusetts, churches for whom both the dates of birth and baptism are
known were brought to church by the age of ten days. As in the case of
Mrs. Minot, the data also indicate that adults came forward to renew their
baptismal covenant in close proximity to the birth of children as a means of
ensuring their newborns could be baptized. Even though the Puritan theory
of baptism limited it to being a sign of grace, lay people reasoned otherwise,
grieving when a child died before the ordinance could be administered or
finding comfort from having brought their child within the covenant.[26]

A third pattern of lay behavior, noted not only in church records but also
in sermons, was a reluctance among baptized adults to complete their membership by participating in the Lord's Supper. "The so general a neglect [of
the Lord's Table] . . . hath been both a wonder, and grief of heart to me, almost
ever since I have been in the Ministry," Benjamin Wadsworth of Boston testified in 1724. Half a century earlier, the Connecticut General Assembly had
complained of "Many persons not coming to the Lords Supper or So Much as
Seeking ye Enjoyment of such a Gospel priviledge."[27] The extent of the problem is revealed in the discrepancy between the number of adults admitted
as half-way members and those admitted as full, that is, having satisfied the
qualification – still in most congregations some form of relation – for making
that transition. Stoddard estimated in 1708 that the ratio for the churches
in general was four half-way members to each full member. At one extreme,
the number in full membership exceeded those who were not, but in Wren-
tham, Massachusetts, on the eve of the Great Awakening, the church had a
grand total of two persons in full membership.[28] Whatever the exact per-
centages, almost every congregation included several persons who attended
regularly, were deemed Christian in how they behaved, had their children
baptized (early or late), but who never came forward to describe themselves
as converted. The "laxness" interpretation cannot account for these people,
for it was scrupulosity that made them hesitate. Having absorbed the message that the Lord's Supper was reserved for persons who had assurance
of being converted, and hearing too that anyone "unworthy" who partook

of the sacrament was eating and drinking his own damnation (1 Corinthians 11:28–30), these people were (as Stoddard said in his pungent manner) "scared out of Religion."[29]

These overlapping forms of behavior greatly complicated the pastoral and evangelical work of the ministers. Should they reiterate the traditional emphasis upon conversion as a process that required strenuous self-examination and a deep sense of "humiliation" as the necessary prelude to faith? Should they couple this challenging message with the reassurance that, since the visible church had no certain rule (as Stoddard put it) for determining who were true saints and who mere hypocrites, people should partake of the means of grace in order to strengthen their spiritual condition? Should parents be informed that baptism, though never formally efficacious as a means of grace, was rich in blessings for them and their children? Or should those parents and children be told that the "external" covenant was, in the end, entirely different from the covenant of grace? Should half-way members be reminded that God was angry with them for betraying their baptismal covenant by not growing in grace? And should the hyperscrupulous be taught that the smallest measure of assurance – indeed, assurance mixed with doubt – sufficed to qualify them for the Lord's Supper? Or was it more important to emphasize the purity of the Lord's Table and persist in barring anyone who seemed unworthy, unsure, or unconverted from the sacrament?

Collectively, the ministers in late seventeenth- and early eighteenth-century New England voiced all of these themes in their regular preaching. The men who may have influenced Edwards most directly, his grandfather Stoddard, his father Timothy, and the clan of Williamses to whom he was related, emphasized again and again that lay people needed to hear the core truths of the practical divinity: the fallen state of humankind, Christ's offer of mercy, the emptiness of moral behavior, the sinner's dependence on grace provided by a sovereign God. "Man hath destroyed himself, but it is beyond his power to save himself," William Williams declared in *The Great Salvation Revealed and Offered in the Gospel* (1717). In the same breath, he and his allies encouraged each other in the use of terror, meanwhile insisting that sinners prepare themselves through the "law" for the offer of grace.

> The more sensible thou art of thy unworthiness to lay hold
> Upon the promises, the more thou art fitted, and qualified, to
> Lay hold upon them, for the promises are ... the fruits of free Grace.[30]

Preaching centered on these themes was "evangelical" in bringing the gospel message of "new birth" to sinners who were otherwise condemned to suffer God's wrath. It was evangelical, too, in that some Connecticut Valley ministers, anticipating the itinerancy of the 1740s, were preaching to other congregations than their own, the premise being that outsiders could enliven a local situation.

The Williamses and their allies elsewhere in New England knew that other ministers were beginning to emphasize motifs that, by the 1730s, were being broadly characterized as "Arminianism." Converts to Anglicanism in the 1720s were among the first to jettison evangelical Calvinism, but some younger graduates of Harvard and Yale were also preaching sermons flavored with arguments in behalf of natural religion and innate moral righteousness.[31] In the coastal town of Hingham, Massachusetts, Ebenezer Gay was a leading figure in an emerging network of "Catholick" preachers some of whom greatly admired the style and substance of Archbishop John Tillotson's sermons.[32] Yet hindsight should not overly color our understanding of the 1720s, for no one at the time could have foreseen the strength of the liberalizing currents that had already disrupted English Nonconformity and the Church of Scotland. For the moment the required texts in theology at Yale remained William Ames's *Marrow of Sacred Divinity* and Johann Wollebius's *Abridgement of Christian Divinitie,* each dating from the early seventeenth century. The Harvard curriculum was somewhat more up to date, yet in both institutions the Westminster Confession of 1646 (or the "Savoy" version of it) was officially or unofficially the standard of orthodoxy, as it was for the ministry as a whole.[33]

The Williamses had other strings to their bow. Like Increase Mather and Samuel Willard before them, they proclaimed the importance of the "external" covenant and the "advantages" it provided the baptized, advantages that accrued to those who performed the "Duties" of the Christian religion – that is, attending faithfully on the means of grace. As though they had momentarily forgotten the message of divine sovereignty, the Williamses declared that "out of the visible Church the Elect are ordinarily gathered, for which end, God hath established his Ordinances amongst them." This emphasis on the nurturing role of the church and the efficacy of duties in the economy of grace was accompanied by assertions that church members must be active Christians, using the "free Choice" that was theirs to embrace the external covenant.[34] And when William Williams was pleading the importance of infant baptism, his repertory of arguments included the happiness of parents who had brought their children to be baptized and the deep sorrow of those who waited too long to do so, themes the first-generation minister Richard Mather had already employed in the middle of the seventeenth century.[35]

This mixture of motifs had its correlate in how the Williamses and their allies dealt with the nexus of church membership and conversion. In their capacity as fervent evangelicals hoping to overcome the paralysis that affected so many lay people, Stoddard, Timothy Edwards, and several of the Williams clan succeeded from time to time in arousing their congregations to a fresh sense of the age-old question, "What shall I do to be saved?"[36] During such moments – it seems anachronistic to term them "revivals" – some who had been indifferent or overly scrupulous passed into full membership. An earthquake that struck New England in 1727 provoked many to act in this manner. In its immediate aftermath, thousands of people – forty-nine of them in Northampton alone – broke through the psychological barriers that had kept them from full membership. Another device was the ceremony of renewal of covenant that the Reforming Synod of 1679 had endorsed as a means of enlisting adults who had not yet had their children baptized. Some churches resisted the ceremony. But in others it spurred dozens of adults and children to affirm their baptismal covenant – as it did notably in Taunton, Massachusetts, in 1705, when three hundred persons subscribed to the covenant, a ceremony so powerful that (as reported by the minister) the scene included "Parents weeping for Joy, seeing their Children give their names to Christ," and in three Connecticut Valley towns, one of them Northampton, where in 1727 111 persons joined their local congregations after participating in the rite.[37] Less dramatically, many young adults seem to have used the ceremony as a means of gaining a fuller degree of church membership, though perhaps still falling short of "full" membership as defined in 1662. Edwards himself may have been this kind of member, for he resolved in January 1723, "frequently to renew the dedication of myself to God, which was made at my baptism; which I solemnly renewed, when I was received into the communion of the church."[38]

Interspersed as they were with the "harvests" of evangelical preaching, these ceremonies are a forceful reminder that such preaching coexisted with a strong view of the church as means of grace. Moreover, some of the most evangelical ministers in the Connecticut River Valley verged toward Stoddardeanism, suspending the high hurdle of relations and inviting everyone of moral character to participate in the sacraments even as others such as Timothy Edwards continued to insist on protecting the Lord's Supper from those deemed unfit.[39] As always, lay behavior confounded the logic of Stoddardean intentions, for as Stoddard himself had discovered, lay people clung to the very patterns of behavior that made him a critic of the Congregational Way. In 1669 the Northampton church voted to accept the Half-Way Covenant. Within five months after implementing the measure in 1672, 104 adults and children were admitted under its provisions. Despite this initial moment of incorporation and, by the 1680s, Stoddard's rejection of relations of grace, the Northampton congregation continued to include adults who persisted in their scrupulosity as well as others who waited to renew their baptismal covenant until marriage or child-bearing gave them reasons for doing so. Of the 104 who came into membership in 1672, only about 10 percent had passed over into full membership by the end of the decade. Eventually Stoddard abandoned the double bookkeeping called for by the provisions of 1662, and by the early eighteenth century the Northampton congregation was very nearly the same size as the town. Yet it is certain that in 1728, when Stoddard died, nearly half of the congregation was not participating in the Lord's Supper; and in the early years of the ministry of his grandson, many of the townspeople were renewing their baptismal covenants at the moment they were married or began to have children.[40]

Whatever their style of churchmanship, the ministers in early eighteenth-century New England fretted about the state of their authority. From a longer historical perspective, there was nothing new about doing so, for the Congregational Way and, further back in time, the Puritan movement, had never resolved the relationship between the privileges of clerical office and those of the laity to everyone's satisfaction. On the one hand, the immigrants had emphasized the participatory aspects of the church covenant: Every important action required the "consent" of the men who were adult members. As expressed more formally in Congregational theory, the "power of the keys" (Matthew 18:17) in church discipline belonged to the entire community. Because Congregational theory also held that the visible church consisted of autonomous units, the immigrant generation had reasoned that ministers derived their authority from the congregation that elected them to office; out of office, this authority lapsed. The deeper purpose of these measures was to eliminate hierarchies of rank, to ensure that ministers were always resident in their congregations, and to guarantee a role for "consent" in church affairs. In the same breath, however, the founders insisted that ministers were "ambassadors" of God and, in this capacity, had powers distinct from those of ordinary Christians. Ministers were to lead their congregations, not give way to majority rule, a possibility that the Cambridge Platform warded off by assigning a "negative voice," or veto, to the ministers.[41]

Yet as the clergy discovered to their sorrow, few congregations were willing to accept recommendations in matters of church discipline or other church business that ran counter to their own sense of local justice – or self-interest. John Fiske's notebook of debate on matters of church discipline in the Chelmsford, Massachusetts, church reveals that his congregation "grew increasingly uncooperative, disrespectful, and contentious" during the mid-seventeenth century. "Well versed in Congregationalism . . . the laity seemed to relish playing devil's advocate with their minister, calling Fiske's authority into question every step of the way as he attempted to define and defend church procedures." Elsewhere, the recommendations of the Synod of 1662 prompted accusations of ministerial highhandedness in trying to push the measure through their churches. Attempts to do so provoked reprisals or schism; in Boston Second Church, lay opposition prevented the congregation's two ministers, Increase and Cotton Mather, from implementing the new procedures until the early 1690s.[42]

These local skirmishes, together with the strong support among many laity for the participatory provisions of the Cambridge Platform, prompted reflections and proposals among the ministry on how to reinforce their authority. Preventing lay people from participating in the ceremony of ordination in order to enhance the image and idea of ministry as a distinctive office was a step that most congregations were able to concede. Few were willing, however, to relinquish the "power of the keys," an idea that Solomon Stoddard floated in 1724 and that some ministers, such as John Woodbridge in Killingworth, had privately supported since the 1670s.[43] Nor did congregations easily concede more authority to interchurch councils, a measure urged by Stoddard and several others. Despite its "Presbyterian" flavor, this step appealed to some clergy as a means of establishing a counterbalance to local pressures. An intermediate possibility was to gather together in countywide associations. Boston-area ministers organized the first such association in 1690. Other regions followed suit, the ministers of Hampshire County doing so in 1731 after having previously formed a "Council of the Churches of the County" in 1714. In practice, however, the county associations, though useful venues for discussing issues of the day, had little success as counterweights to the laity. Only in Connecticut did measures to strengthen the authority of councils, the so-called "Saybrook Platform" of 1708, have any teeth. A synod summoned by the General Assembly drafted articles calling for the "establishment of consociations in each county with oversight of local congregations, county ministerial associations with the responsibility of advising and examining ministerial candidates, and a general ministerial association" to "meet annually." Four county groupings of ministers ratified these articles, as did the General Assembly, though with the proviso that individual churches could decide not to accept them, as, in time, several did. Similar proposals in Massachusetts never gained the support of the civil state or of all the ministers.[44]

These pressures on a minister's authority are registered in the experience of Timothy Edwards in East Windsor and Stephen Williams in Longmeadow, Massachusetts. Timothy Edwards fell out with his congregation when he tried to prevent people in the town whom he judged immoral from having their children baptized or coming to the Lord's Supper. He claimed a veto power in these matters; in his opinion, "the elders [were] to be rulers and enjoin obedience" to their decisions, a judgment for which he found support in the Saybrook Platform. But in the 1730s, his congregation denied he had such powers, citing in their favor the Cambridge Platform.[45] The diary Stephen Williams kept during his ministry in Longmeadow records his uneasiness as he worried about keeping someone from the Lord's Supper and fell out with a group of kinfolk in his parish over styles of singing and accusations that he was too "Presbyterian." The diary reveals that "few cases" of church discipline "were actually brought out into the open and that most ended in some sort of compromise solution," a sign of Williams's "inability" to act as he would have wished.[46]

The ongoing strength of the laity helps to explain the attractiveness of Anglicanism to a small handful of Congregational ministers in the early eighteenth century, and may also have encouraged a significant number of Yale College graduates to affiliate with presbyteries of the Church of Scotland in New York, New Jersey, and Pennsylvania.[47] The converts to Anglicanism seem to have relished being reordained by bishops who (it was said) owed their sacerdotal powers to the apostolic succession. The pamphlet war that broke out over this issue – Congregationalists and their Presbyterian allies defending their version of ministry, Anglican missionaries ridiculing it – may not have resonated within local congregations, most of whom were more concerned with preserving other parts of the Cambridge Platform. The emergence of genuine Presbyterianism in the Middle Colonies in tandem with the arrival of thousands of immigrants from Scotland and Ulster did, however, open up new possibilities for employment for a cohort of New England–born clergy. Among those drifting southward was Jonathan Edwards, who accepted a call to a newly formed congregation of Scotch Irish in New York City in 1722. The extent of these affiliations is suggested by the fact that nine of the twenty trustees of the College of New Jersey when it was chartered in 1746 were graduates of Yale.

Changes in the relationship between civil society and the churches were also affecting the authority of the clergy. Initially, two of the orthodox colonies, Massachusetts and New Haven, had made participation in political affairs ("freemanship") contingent upon church membership; and in Plymouth and Connecticut, freemen were expected to be supportive of the new church system. But by the 1690s all direct connections between the franchise and church membership had been severed.[48] Initially, too, congregations had taken the lead in choosing their ministers, but by the end of the century town meetings were exerting more influence in such elections, to the dismay of some clergy.[49] Under the new Massachusetts charter of 1691, which incorporated Plymouth into the larger colony, the governor became a royal appointee. Yet the charter left it up to the colony to decide which group or groups would enjoy the legal status of "orthodox" religion, and to no one's surprise, the General Court chose the Congregational Way. Baptists and Anglicans were allowed to have their own ministers and congregations, but they were not released from supporting the Congregational Way, at least in principle, until 1727.

Even though elements of a state-supported single church persisted well into the eighteenth century, as early as the 1670s the ministers were complaining that civil leaders could not be counted upon to pursue the work of "reformation." What had worked (barely) in 1679, when the Massachusetts General Court sanctioned the Reforming Synod, went nowhere in 1725 when the governor and General Court ignored a "Memorial and address" asking for a special synod to consider the reasons that the province was experiencing "a series of various Judgments."[50] The situation in Connecticut was more advantageous, probably because the colony retained a far greater degree of self-governance. When Gurdon Saltonstall passed from the ministry to governorship of the colony in 1707, he and others of his thinking persuaded the General Assembly to summon the Saybrook synod.

Where change was also manifest was in social ethics and enforcement of the rules of Christian community. The burden of punishing premarital sex and the abuse of alcohol had long since passed from the churches to the magistrates and juries of the county courts. By the beginning of the eighteenth century, these courts were ceasing to require young men convicted of illicit sex to make a public confession. Instead, the courts used a simpler and, in some sense, secular system of fines.[51] In the realm of social ethics, the theme of "mutuality" so important to the founders – we are "knit together in the bonds of love," John Winthrop had declared in the "Model of Christian Charity" – still figured in some church covenants and sermons.[52] Yet in the realm of actual charity, the urban poor, suddenly more numerous thanks to the casualties of war and economic downturns, were far more likely to be the subjects of regulation than of local sympathy.[53] Did these changes mark the coming of "individualism" in place of the ethics of community that ministers and lay leaders of the first generation had articulated? So it has seemed to some historians, even though they acknowledge that the process of change was slow and extended well into the eighteenth century. The history of the Winthrop family seems a case in point, for the grandsons and great-grandsons of John Winthrop I appear more "Yankee" than "Puritan."[54] As for political ideology, the most important word after 1690 may have been "liberty" in the singular, a word of fresh significance in the aftermath of the Glorious Revolution as the colonists struggled to align their local ideologies with metropolitan patterns of discourse.

Yet almost to a person the ministers continued to rehearse a tradition of discourse grounded on the parallel between New England and Old Israel as peoples in covenant with God. This covenant promised them God's favor if they remained faithful to its obligations, but God's judgments if they lapsed into "formality" or became "devoted to the World." Invariably, the ministers found much to complain about. Military setbacks at the outset of the eighteenth century prompted Timothy Edwards to label the defeats "a corrective affliction" that required "Sincere Repentance and hearty and Real returning unto God" on the part of a "Sinfull and disobedient people."[55] No minister sounded these themes more than Increase Mather. Along with his son Cotton, he became a self-appointed historian of the "wonders" of God's providence at a time when the scientific revolution was transforming comets, monster births, and other would-be portents into merely natural phenomena. Amid these shifting currents of opinion, the Mathers and most of their colleagues continued to insist on the special relationship between the colonists and the God with whom this people were in covenant.

But could prophecy withstand these currents of intellectual change or Christian primitivism the defeat of the Puritan movement in England? The first-generation ministers had allowed themselves to imagine that God was working in history to restore his kingdom, a process that would eventuate in "godly rule." The collapse of the "Puritan Revolution" in England and the restoration of Charles II in 1660 made a mockery of such predictions. Moreover, after 1660 it was harder to believe that the Congregational Way would serve as a model for other national churches seeking to recover from apostasy. With Episcopacy firmly back in the saddle, historians such as Cotton Mather had to recast the story of why the colonists had left their homeland in the 1630s: not because that church was unlawful but because the policies of a misguided few, such as Archbishop Laud, had deprived some English of liberty of conscience.[56]

Like so many other generalizations about this period, this narrative of prophecy in eclipse cannot encompass on-the-ground complexity. The arrival of Anglican missionaries, together with Catholic power in the person of Louis XIV and the French in Canada, prompted fresh evocations of primitivism and apocalyptic struggle between Antichrist and the saints.[57] Indeed the fortunes of French kings would become a veritable obsession with Jonathan Edwards in the 1740s, as would the ever-contested questions of church membership and ministerial authority.

Notes

1. Richard R. Johnson, *Adjustment to Empire: The New England Colonies, 1675–1715* (New Brunswick, NJ: Rutgers University Press, 1981).
2. Stephen Foster, *The Long Argument: English Puritanism and the Shaping of New England Culture, 1570–1700* (Chapel Hill: University of North Carolina Press, 1991), 220–2.

3. Kevin M. Sweeney, "River Gods and Related Minor Deities: The Williams Family and the Connecticut River Valley, 1637–1790" (Ph.D. dissertation, Yale University, 1986).

4. John L. Sibley, *Biographical Sketches of Graduates of Harvard University* (3 vols. Cambridge, MA, 1873–85), 3:163; *The Christian History Containing Accounts of the Propagation and Revival of Religion in England, Scotland and America, No. 14, June 4, 1743*, 109–12.

5. David D. Hall, *The Faithful Shepherd: A History of the New England Ministry in the Seventeenth Century* (Chapel Hill: University of North Carolina Press, 1972), 190–5. The process of securing a post and being ordained in the early eighteenth century is described in J. William T. Youngs, Jr., *God's Messengers: Religious Leadership in Colonial New England, 1700–1750* (Baltimore: Johns Hopkins University Press, 1976), chap. 2.

6. Sibley, *Biographical Sketches*, 3:274; James W. Schmotter, "Ministerial Careers in Eighteenth-Century New England" *Journal of Social History* 9 (1975–6): 257–60.

7. Williston Walker, *The Creeds and Platforms of Congregationalism* (New York, 1893), 223, chap. 10.

8. Ibid., 222; Baird Tipson, "Invisible Saints: The 'Judgment of Charity' in Early New England Churches," *Church History* 44 (1975): 1–12.

9. Mary McManus Ramsbottom, "Religion, Society and the Family in Charlestown, Massachusetts, 1630–1740" (Ph.D. dissertation, Yale University, 1987).

10. Walker, *Creeds and Platforms*, chap. 11.

11. Cotton Mather, *Magnalia Christi Americana* (1702; reprint, 2 vols. Hartford, CT, 1853–5), 2:98–104.

12. Increase Mather, *The First Principles of New-England* (Cambridge, MA, 1675); Robert G. Pope, *The Half-Way Covenant: Church Membership in Puritan New England* (New Haven: Yale University Press, 1969), chap. 2.

13. These agonies are narrated in ibid.

14. See, e.g., Benjamin Trumbull; *A Complete History of Connecticut Civil and Ecclesiastical* (1797; reprint, 2 vols. New London, CT, 1898); Sereno E. Dwight, ed., *The Works of President Edwards* (10 vols, New York, 1830), *Life of President Edwards*, I. For an overall critique, see Harry S. Stout and Catharine A. Breckus, "Declension, Gender, and the 'New Religious History,'" in Philip R. Vandermere and Richard P. Swierenga, eds., *Belief and Behavior: Essays in the New Religious History* (New Brunswick: Rutgers University Press, 1991), 15–36.

15. Perry Miller, *The New England Mind: From Colony to Province* (Cambridge, MA: Harvard University Press, 1953), chaps. 5, 24, passim; Edmund S. Morgan, *The Puritan Family* (rev. ed., New York: Harper Torchbooks, 1966), chap. 7. Gerald F. Moran demonstrates the expansive capacities of "tribalism" in "Religious Renewal, Puritan Tribalism, and the Family in Seventeenth-Century Milford, Connecticut," *William and Mary Quarterly*, 3d ser., 36 (1979): 36–54.

16. Foster, *Long Argument*, 181–2; Walker; *Creeds and Platforms*, chap. 13; for a local example, Sarah Loring Bailey, *Historical Sketches of Andover* (Boston, 1880), 413.

17. WJE, 4:146. Social historians have argued that young people in the early to mid-eighteenth century were facing an uncertain economic future as the supply of land held by their families diminished. The "deprivation thesis," as this argument may be termed, is not supported by more recent studies of economic development and wealth creation. Gloria L. Main, *Peoples of a Spacious Land:*

Families and Cultures in Colonial New England (Cambridge, MA: Harvard University Press, 2001), chap. 9.

18. Samuel Maverick, "A Brief Discription [sic] of New England and the Severall Townes therein, together with the Present Government thereof " (c. 1661), *Proceedings of the Massachusetts Historical Society*, 2nd ser. 1 (1884–5): 240; W. H. Whitmore, ed., *Andros Tracts* (3 vols. Boston: Prince Society, 1868–74), II: 29, 37.

19. Wyllys Papers, Connecticut Historical Society Collections 21 (1924): 237.

20. Raymond Phineas Stearns, "Correspondence of John Woodbridge, Jr., and Richard Baxter," *New England Quarterly* 10 (1937): 576.

21. "Danvers Church Records," *Essex Institute Historical Collections* 11 (1857): 321.

22. Frank Thistlethwaite, *Dorset Pilgrims: The Story of Westcountry Pilgrims Who Went to New England in the Seventeenth Century* (London: Barrie and Jenkins, 1989), 204, 223.

23. John H. Gould, "Early Records of the Church in Topsfield," *Essex Institute Historical Collections* 24 (1888): 3–27.

24. See, e.g., "Church Records of Farmington in Connecticut," *New England Historical and Genealogical Register* 11 (1857): 323–8.

25. *Records of the First Church at Dorchester in New England 1636–1734* (Boston 1891), 34.

26. The Essex County data are in Anne S. Brown, "'Bound Up in a Bundle of Life': The Social Meaning of Religious Practice in Northeastern Massachusetts, 1700–1765" (Ph.D. dissertation, Boston University, 1995). For the links between marriage and covenant renewal, see ibid., 63, 245; Mather, *Magnalia Christi Americana*, 2: 111; Benjamin Colman, *Reliquiae Turellaie, et Lachrymae Aeternae. Two Sermons Preach'd at Medford* (Boston, 1735), 101.

27. Benjamin Wadsworth, *A Dialogue between a Minister and His Neighbour, about the Lord's Supper* (Boston, 1724), 1–2; Wyllys Papers, *Connecticut Historical Society Collections* 21 (1924): 237.

28. Solomon Stoddard, *The Inexcusableness of Neglecting the Worship of God* (Boston, 1708) 22; *Christian History*, No. 30, Sept. 24, 1743, 238; Sweeney, "River Gods," 192.

29. Stoddard, *Inexcusableness*, 18, 22–3. That such behavior arose out of scrupulosity was suggested by Edmund S. Morgan, "New England Puritanism: Another Approach," *William and Mary Quarterly*, 3rd ser., 18 (1961): 236–42. This argument (with additional evidence) appears in David D. Hall, *Worlds of Wonder, Days of Judgment: Popular Religious Belief in Early New England* (New York: Knopf, 1989), 153–60; James F. Cooper, Jr., *Tenacious of Their Liberties: The Congregationalists in Colonial Massachusetts* (New York: Oxford University Press, 1999), 134–7.

30. James A. Goulding, "The Controversy Between Solomon Stoddard and The Mathers: Western versus Eastern Massachusetts Congregationalism" (Ph.D. thesis, Claremont Graduate School, 1971), chap. 13; Sweeney, "River Gods," 194–5.

31. But see Gerald L. Godwin, "The Myth of 'Arminian-Calvinism' in Eighteenth-Century New England," *New England Quarterly* 41 (1968): 2–19.

32. Robert J. Wilson, *The Benevolent Deity: Ebenezer Gay and the Rise of Rational Religion in New England, 1696–1787* (Philadelphia: University of Pennsylvania Press, 1984); Norman Fiering, "The First American Enlightenment: Tillotson,

Leverett, and Philosophical Anglicanism," *New England Quarterly* 44 (1981): 107–44.

33. Richard Warch, *School of the Prophets: Yale College 1701–1740* (New Haven: Yale University Press, 1973), chaps. 9–10. Cotton Mather, the person Perry Miller and others have regarded as instrument and symbol of a weakening orthodoxy, is thoroughly validated in Richard F. Lovelace, *The American Pietism of Cotton Mather: Origins of American Evangelicalism* (Grand Rapids: Christian University Press, 1979), chaps. 2–3.

34. Sweeney, "River Gods," 215–16.

35. William Williams, *The Duty and Interest of a People, among Whom Religion Has Been Planted, to Continue Steadfast and Sincere in the Profession and Practice of It* (Boston 1736), 102. For earlier preaching along these lines by Samuel Willard, see Mark A. Peterson, *The Price of Redemption: The Spiritual Economy of Puritan New England* (Stanford: Stanford University Press, 1997), 131–3.

36. In a diary entry of Feb. 22, 1716, Stephen Williams recorded "an extraordinary stir among the people at East Windsor – many were crying what shall we do to be saved." Quoted in Kenneth Pieter Minkema, "The Edwardses: A Ministerial Family in Eighteenth-Century New England" (Ph.D. dissertation, University of Connecticut, 1988), 75. The actual number admitted on this occasion to full communion was thirteen. Ibid., 76.

37. Thomas Prince, ed., *The Christian History . . . for the Year 1743* (Boston, 1744), 110–11; Sweeney, "River Gods," 218.

38. WJE, 12:736.

39. Minkema, "The Edwardses," 84. Even the "Stoddardean" ministers did not buy into the entire package of Stoddard's theology, such as the belief that the Lord's Supper was converting or that the true church was national in its nature.

40. Goulding, "Controversy," 339–43; 347–9; WJE, 12:44–5, 52, 59–60.

41. Hall, *Faithful Shepherd*, chaps. 2, 5.

42. Cooper, *Tenacious of their Liberties*, 120–1, chap. 5.

43. Ibid., 181–2. See also Youngs, *God's Messengers*, chaps. 4–5.

44. Warch, *School of the Prophets*, 55–6; Walker, *Creeds and Platforms*, chap. 15; Sweeney, "River Gods," 166–7.

45. Minkema, "The Edwardses," chap 3.

46. Sweeney, "River Gods," 179–83.

47. These affiliations may be followed in Franklin Bowditch Dexter, *Biographical Sketches of the Graduates of Yale College* (6 vols. New York, 1885–1912), vols. 1–2.

48. By the 1680s a sharp decline in the number of freemen prepared the way for this change. See, e.g., Ronald K. Snell, "Freemanship, Office Holding, and the Town Franchise in Seventeenth-Century Springfield, Massachusetts," *New England Historical and Genealogical Register* 138 (1979): 163–79.

49. William G. McLoughlin, *New England Dissent, 1630–1833: The Baptists and the Separation of Church and State* (2 vols. Cambridge, MA: Harvard University Press, 1971), Parts II–III.

50. William Stevens Perry, ed., *Historical Collections Relating to the American Colonial Church* (3 vols. [Hartford, CT], 1870–3), 3:172–3.

51. Cornelia. Hughes Dayton, *Women before the Bar: Gender, Law, and Society in Connecticut, 1639–1789* (Chapel Hill: University of North Carolina Press, 1995).

52. Minkema, "The Edwardses," 34; Lovelace, *American Pietism*, 226–37.

53. Christine L. Heyrmann, "The Fashion among More Superior People: Charity and Social Change in Provincial New England, 1700–1740," *American Quarterly* 34 (1982): 107–24.

54. Richard L. Dunn, *Puritans and Yankees: The Winthrop Dynasty of New England 1630–1717* (Princeton: Princeton University Press, 1962); Cooper, *Tenacious of Their Liberties*.

55. Quoted in Harry S. Stout, *The New England Soul: Preaching and Religious Culture in Colonial New England* (New York: Oxford University Press, 1986), 145.

56. Mather, *Magnalia*, General Introduction.

57. William Williams, *The Great Concern of Christians* (Boston, 1723), 9.

4 The age of Enlightenment
AVIHU ZAKAI

From the second half of the seventeenth till the end of the eighteenth century, Western Christianity underwent a profound intellectual transformation; it went through a prolonged series of critical self-reexaminations of its basic intellectual foundations in many spheres – religion and science, society and politics, morals and manners, gender and race, economy and markets, education and childhood, crime and punishment. This reassessment marked the disenchantment of the world and the beginning of the modern age as we know it today. "Our age is, in special degree, the age of criticism," wrote Immanuel Kant (1724–1804) in *Critique of Pure Reason* (1781), "and to criticism everything must submit. Religion through its sanctity, and law-giving through its majesty, may seek to exempt themselves from it. But they then awaken just suspicion, and cannot claim the sincere respect which reason accords only to that which has been able to sustain the test of free and open examination."[1] The intellectual movement associated with this important ideological and cultural transformation in the history of Western civilization is commonly called the age of Enlightenment.[2]

Instead of accepting traditional religious worldviews at face value or uncritically adopting the values of established authority, Enlightenment thinkers elevated the role of the mind and emphasized the power of reason, thus leading to the abolition of customarily accepted moral and religious absolutes. "In much the same way that the world became the object of scientific inquiry in the sixteenth and seventeenth centuries through a process of desacralisation, so too, religious practices" were "demystified by the imposition of *natural laws*." As "the physical world ceased to be a theatre in which the drama of creation was constantly re-directed by divine interventions,"[3] so too the variety of human experience seemed more and more the outcome of natural and historical processes rather than the work of God. Once considered the sole source and locus for human experience and expectations, religious thought and belief were increasingly pushed out of the realms of nature, politics, ethics, and history.

The "enlightened age" witnessed the replacement of religion by reason as the main agent for providing "objective truths" about the world in
which human life is set. The supremacy and primacy of divine revelation
were attacked. "The role of reason was magnified, that of revelation was
depressed. The scriptures were subjected to intensive and often to unsympa-
thetic scrutiny. Miracles were challenged. Prophecy was reassessed. Christian
thought faced a threat which might have stripped it of all its uniqueness and
authority."[4]

Indeed, religion and morality continued to be of primary concern, but
they became subject to critical examination. The period is marked by the
loss of the unquestioned traditional legitimacy of a divinely instituted order.
Enlightenment thinkers fostered trust in human power and ability, arguing
for the authority of reason rather than the traditional authority of Scripture.
In England most writers, following John Locke (1632–1704), did not substitute reason for Scripture, but called for a more reasonable approach to
Scripture. On the continent, rationality was advocated as a means of establishing authoritative systems of thought based on reason, leading humanity toward progress out of what was termed a long period of irrationality,
superstition, tyranny, and barbarism. This is ultimately what distinguished
Western Christian culture from other civilizations at this period.

To orthodox Christians, such a radical transformation constituted a threat
to traditional religious thought and belief. The New England theologian
Jonathan Edwards recognized and grappled with the challenges posed to
Christian orthodoxy by the emergence of new modes of thought: Deistic
attacks on revealed religion, the physical discoveries of Newton, the development of new narratives of history, and the emergence of new moral theories.
Indeed, much of Edwards's life of the mind can be characterized as a struggle
"against most of the prevailing errors of the present day," which tended to
"the utter subverting of the gospel of Christ."[5] During this time, "every evangelical doctrine is run down," and many "bold attempts are made" against
"Christ, and the religion he taught."[6] What sets Edwards apart from many
contemporary champions of religious orthodoxy is, indeed, his attempt to
provide a serious and systematic alternative to Enlightenment modes of conviction and persuasion. Living in an age of rapid and dramatic intellectual
innovations, he took upon himself the task of refuting them.

DEISM

Edwards's encounter with and reaction to Enlightenment thought is no
more apparent than in his long and constant struggle against Deism, as can

be seen in many of his works. The reason for this is not hard to find: the proponents of this mode of thought denied some of Christianity's essential creeds, and their radical ideas were subversive of revealed religion.

Deism emerged in England at the end of the seventeenth century and in the early eighteenth century. It signified the crisis of Christian culture during the age of Enlightenment, as manifested in the fracturing of doctrinal orthodoxy through attacks on established theological culture and authority, such as the authority of the Bible, the integrity and validity of revelation, the credibility of Old Testament prophecies, and the reliability of New Testament miracles.[7] Deists generally believed in one and only one God who has moral and intellectual virtues in perfection and whose active powers are displayed in the world – a God who created, sustained, and ordered the world by means of divinely sanctioned natural laws, both moral and physical. Emphasizing that God's ordering of events constitutes a general providence but denying special providence, and claiming that miracles or other miraculous divine interventions violate the lawful natural order, the Deists raised the fears that the Jehovah of the Old Testament could hardly be identified with their God and the mechanical God of natural philosophers. Thus in *The Dunciad* (1742), the poet Alexander Pope (1688–1744) denounced the Deist idea of God who is "Wrapt up in Self, a God without a Thought, Regardless of our merit or default."[8]

If Deism was the Enlightenment philosophy of religion, it was above all a religion of reason, a rational religion, or a religion of nature: "there is a Religion of Nature and Reason written in the Hearts of every One of us from the first Creation," claimed Matthew Tindal (1657–1733) in *Christianity as Old as the Creation,* a book considered the "Bible of Deism."[9] Deist writers stressed belief in a God based on reason and experience in contrast to faith and revelation, and most of them believed that the God who created the universe is known by the light of reason. They therefore questioned revealed religion, or religion based on a special revelation of God, emphasizing instead rational, natural religion. Asserting the existence of a God upon the testimony of reason, they therefore argued that human reason alone is sufficient to provide the knowledge necessary to lead a moral and religious life. John Toland (1670–1722) claimed in *Christianity Not Mysterious,* that "by *Reason* we arrive at the certainty of God's own existence."[10] Christianity, then, is neither contrary to reason nor above reason.

Deists denied the traditional Christian view of human corruption as well as the belief that human beings' reason is so corrupted by sin that special revelation is necessary for the conduct of moral life. Instead they argued that reason should be the basis of belief and that it is essential in making moral decisions. Tindal declared that "Our Reason, which gives us a Demonstration of the Divine Perfections," directs us also in regard to ethics and morals "concerning the Nature of those Duties God requires . . . to ourselves, and one another."[11] Dwelling on the notion of "natural religion" – a universal genus of religion based on the light of reason or nature – Deists claimed that reason could look up through nature to nature's God. *"Religion of Nature,"* argued Tindal, is based on "every Thing that is founded on the Reason and Nature of Things," and it "consists in observing those Things, which our Reason, by considering the Nature of God and Man, and the Relation we stand in to him and one another, demonstrates to be our Duty."[12] Deism thus offered a new and optimistic view; no radical, essential evil was allowed within the well-ordered world created by a good God.

Deist writers also attacked the validity of sacred prophecies. Anthony Collins (1676–1729) declared in *A Discourse of the Grounds and Reasons of the Christian Religion* that "to understand the Prophet as having the conception of the Virgin Mary and birth of her son Jesus literally and primarily in view, is a very great *absurdity.*"[13] Whereas Collins rejected the reliability of sacred prophecies, Thomas Woolston (c. 1668–1733) attacked the credibility of the New Testament miracles in *Discourses on the Miracles of Our Saviour,* claiming that they are full of absurdities: "the literal History of many of the Miracles of Jesus, as recorded by the Evangelists, does imply Absurdities, Improbability and Incredibility," and this, in fact, is "very dishonorable to the name of Christ."[14]

Another Deist attack on Christian orthodoxy concerned the "scandal of particularity" – the notion that God revealed himself only to a minute group of people and not to the rest of the world. This view entails, according to Edward, first Lord Herbert of Cherbury (1583–1648), that "the far greatest part of Mankind must be inevitably sentenced to Eternal Punishment," a view he thought "too rigid and severe to be consistent with the Attributes of the *Most Great and Good God.*"[15] Even the poet John Dryden (1631–1700), who attacked Deism in *Religio Laici,* wondered why, before Christ's coming, "the whole world, excepting only the Jewish nation, should lie under inevitable necessity of everlasting punishment, for want of that revelation which was confined to so small a spot of ground as that of Palestine."[16]

Together with most orthodox Christians, Jonathan Edwards believed that Deist views were destroying the foundations of Christianity, and he took upon himself a lifelong mission of refutation.[17] He knew the ideas of the best-known Deists, such as Collins, Tindal, and Toland; besides, he could easily become acquainted with their views through books written by their opponents, such as John Leland, *View of the Principle Deistical Writers* (1745), Philip Skelton, *Deism Revealed* (1749), and Elisha Smith, *The Cure of Deism* (1736).[18]

Edwards rejected the Deists' elevation of reason above revelation as well as their view that reason alone can show humanity basic religious truths: "natural light" is never able to show how sinful humans can be reconciled to their Creator, and "the light of nature alone" cannot prove "that there is a future state." Hence assurance of salvation is impossible to find by reason alone.[19] Indeed, reason is capable of knowing God, but only when the cognitive faculties are correctly disposed. God cannot be known by an "objective" reason that has not been enlivened by spiritual experience. Accordingly, Edwards attacked "Tindal's main argument against the need of any revelation," calling it an "empty, insipid kind of doctrine."[20] While the Deists assumed that reason can unveil the goodness and justice of God, thus inferring that religion is reasonable and nonmysterious, Edwards held that human reason after the Fall is very limited and incapable of possessing the saving knowledge of God, which comes only through knowledge of Christ as presented in scriptural revelation. Only through "the Christian revelation," he wrote, "the world has come to the knowledge of the only one true God."[21] Since the "whole of Christian divinity depends on divine revelation," not only do "we stand in the greatest necessity of a divine revelation," but "it was most fit and proper" that God gave us such a revelation – Christ.[22] Believing that reason is prevented by sin from leading human beings to the true God, Edwards was convinced that revelation is necessary to supply what fallen reason cannot.

Against Deists and other proponents of the "moral sense" inherent in human nature, Edwards insisted on the centrality of revelation to all true systems of morality. "He that sees the beauty of holiness, or true moral good, sees the greatest and most important thing in the world, which is the fullness of all things, without which all the world is empty, no better than nothing, yea, worse than nothing." Theological considerations, then, are inextricable from true morality, for "spiritual understanding primarily consists" in the sense "of the moral beauty of divine things." True morality "consists in the beauty of the moral perfections of God, which wonderfully shines forth in every step" of the "method of salvation": a method of delivering "us from sin and hell," and of bringing us to the "happiness which consists in the possession and enjoyment of moral good, in a way sweetly agreeing with God's moral perfections."[23] There is no such thing as morality without worship; worse, it is blasphemous because it flouts the one who founded and sustains true morality. "True virtue most essentially consists in benevolence to Being in general" or God; it is "that consent, propensity and union of heart to Being in general."[24] In sum, for Edwards the unregenerate reason is incapable of understanding the essence of true religion, and hence the nature and purpose of moral virtue which is inextricable from faith.[25]

In the face of Deistic rejection of the Bible as written revelation, and the argument that God had already revealed in nature and reason all that human beings need to know – hence the special revelation in the Bible was not only unnecessary but patently fraudulent – Edwards declared that if "the New Testament ben't a true revelation of God, then God never has yet given the world any clear revelation of future state." "We must therefore suppose," he continues, "that God did design a further revelation than the Old Testament, because a future state was not clearly revealed by that."[26] In another place he argued that only the Christian revelation had been able to provide true knowledge of God, the world, the nature and destiny of human beings, sin and punishment, and redemption.[27]

In contrast to the Deist claim that religion is not mystery, Edwards argued that even the "wiser heathen were sensible that the things of [the] gods are so high above us."[28] Mystery is to be expected in religion because religion is concerned with spiritual things that are not the objects of our senses. He thus denounced the Deist denial of mystery to religion, and he rejected the claim that morality is the essence of religion, thus subordinating religion to morality. For him morality and justice "are only for the advancement of the *great* business [religion], to assist mutually each other to it."[29]

On the other hand, Edwards accepted the Deist premise that it would be unjust for God to withhold his revelation from the majority of the world – that is, Deists' argument about the "scandal of particularity." Accordingly, he used the notion of *prisca theologia* (ancient theology), an important tradition in apologetic theology that attempted to prove that vestiges of true religion (monotheism, the Trinity, *creatio ex nihilo*) were taught by certain non-Christian traditions, arguing that "the Heathen Philosophers had their notions of the unity of God, of the Trinity."[30] He recalled the claim of the second-century philosopher Numenius of Apamea : "What is Plato but Moses speaking in the Attic Language?"[31] Knowledge of true religion among the heathen, therefore, is based on revelation and not, as the Deists argued, on the light of natural reason.

NATURAL PHILOSOPHY

Together with his attack on Deism, Edwards denounced the dominant scientific culture and imagination of enlightened Europe – mechanical philosophy, the doctrine that all natural phenomena can be explained and understood by the mere mechanics of matter and motion. He attempted to provide a philosophical and theological alternative to the mechanistic explanation of the essential nature of reality, an alternative that would reconstitute the glory of God's absolute sovereignty, power, and will within creation.

This can be seen in a long series of writings on natural philosophy – most notably "Of Being" (1722), "Of Atoms" (1722), and "The Mind" (1724), which reveal Edwards's knowledge of the works of mechanical philosophers such as Robert Boyle (1627–91) and Isaac Newton (1643–1727), and present his attempt to construct a theology or a typology of nature in opposition to mechanical natural philosophy.[32]

The mechanization of the natural world was an important feature of late seventeenth-century science. Its "basic postulate was that nature operates according to mechanical principles, the regularity of which can be expressed in the form of natural laws."[33] Mechanical philosophers conceived of the world as a huge machine running like the work of a clock according to abstract mechanical laws of nature. Boyle said that nature is a "compounded *machine*,"[34] and the "whole universe" is "but a great Automaton, or self-moving engine, wherein all things are performed by the bare motion (or rest), the size, the shape, and the situation, or texture of the parts of the universal matter it consists of."[35] Likewise, Newton believed that a true understanding of the phenomena of nature is based upon "rational mechanics," or "reasoning from mechanical principles" on all "the phenomena of Nature," which are formulated according to "mathematical principles."[36]

The mechanization of the natural world led to the mechanization of God's providential activity in the world. Once set in motion by God, the course of nature and the phenomena of the world are the product of mere mechanical laws and no longer manifest the divine immanence. "[T]he phenomena of the world," wrote Boyle, "are physically produced by the mechanical affections of the part of matter, and what they operate upon one another according to mechanical laws."[37] God's providential scheme was confined mainly to the establishment and maintenance of the general, external laws of nature that regulate the world phenomena. Accordingly, Newton's God is a cosmic legislator, "a Universal Ruler,"[38] who is "an agent acting constantly according to certain laws."[39] With the mechanization of the natural world, the notion of God's relationship to it changed dramatically: "The sovereign Redeemer of Luther and Calvin became," in scientific thought, "the sovereign Ruler of the world machine."[40] Newton's God was first and foremost "the *kosmokrator*, ruler over everything,"[41] or "a 'universal ruler' (*pantokrator*),"[42] and not, as in classical and medieval thought, a God whose symbolic presence was manifested in the nature and harmony of creation. For him, "only a God of true and supreme dominion is a supreme and true God," and this "at the expense of God's love and, apparently, God's intellect."[43]

Fully aware of the ramifications inherent in the premises of mechanical philosophy as they affected the traditional Christian dialectic of God's transcendence and immanence, Edwards recognized that the new scientific interpretation was leading increasingly to a separation between the order of grace and the order of nature, between God and the world, and was thus incompatible with traditional Christian belief. He was alarmed by the mechanistic conception of the world of nature as a self-contained and independent reality, a self-inclusive machine running by itself according to abstract, universal laws of nature, freed from subordination to God's dominion and not affected by his unceasingly watchful eyes. And with great dismay, Edwards observed that mechanical philosophy's notion of a homogeneous, uniform and symmetrical, one-dimensional world of nature not only deprived created order of any teleological ends and purposes, but stipulated that nature could no longer manifest the presence of God.

In response, Edwards constructed his own theology of nature, or typology, interpreting the physical world as a representation or a "shadow" of the spiritual one that celebrates God's glory and sovereignty as they are evidenced in the coherence and beauty, order and harmony, of world phenomena. His goal was to prove God's existence in his majesty and glory within the created world. Hence he attacked mechanical philosophy, claiming "there is no such thing as mechanism" if that word meant that "bodies act each upon other, purely and properly by themselves," because "the very being, and the manner of being, and the whole of bodies depends immediately on the divine power."[44] He appropriated the atomic doctrine of the dominant mechanical philosophy of his time but Christianized it, arguing that God's infinite power is responsible for holding the "atoms together." Hence, the very framework of the material universe is evidence of God's omnipresence, omnipotence, and omniactivity: "the very being, and the manner of being, and the whole of bodies depends immediately on the divine power."[45] Further, claiming that every "atom in the universe is managed by Christ so as to be most to the advantage of the Christian," he reestablished God's direct and intimate relation with the world.[46] Likewise he rejected the mechanistic understanding of the concept of "natural laws," because these laws, setting up a mediating sphere between God and his creation, restricted God's infinite power and limited divine immanence within the phenomena of the world. What "we call the laws of nature" are only "the stated methods of God's acting with respect to bodies."[47] Accordingly, he denounced the mechanical philosophers' claim that God "himself, in common with his creatures," is "subject in his acting to the same laws with inferior beings," thus dethroning God from his place as "the head of the universe" and "the foundation and first spring of all."[48]

In "The Mind," Edwards formulated his idealistic phenomenalism: "the world, i.e. the material universe, exists nowhere but in the mind," and, given that "all material existence is only idea," the "world therefore is an ideal one."[49] His main goal was to show that the essence of reality is a matter of relationship between God and the created order. Accordingly, the principle underlying his theological teleology, the order of being inherent in the structure of the universe, was the concept of "Excellency." Edwards defined this as the "consent of being to being, or being's consent to entity," which in turn defined the relationship within the hierarchy of spirits according to their consent to the supreme being, God. "So far as a thing consents to being in general," Edwards wrote, "so far it consents to him," hence "the more perfect created spirits are, the nearer do they come to their creator in this regard." Seeing that "the more the consent is, and the more extensive, the greater is the excellency," therefore in "the order of beings in the natural world, the more excellent and noble any being is, the more visible and immediate hand of God is there in bringing them into being" with "the most noble of all," the "soul of man."[50]

In undertaking to provide an alternative view of the essence of reality that would lead eventually to the reenchantment of the world, Edwards's ultimate goal was the demonstration of the infinite power of God's absolute sovereignty in both the "order of nature" and the "order of time."[51] His interpretation of natural phenomena therefore constituted a radical departure from the prevalent mechanical philosophy. Believing that "the corporeal world is to no advantage but to the spiritual," he claimed that "to find out the reasons of things in natural philosophy is only to find out the proportion of God's acting."[52] In this venture of the redeifying of the world, Edwards was not alone in the British world, as can be seen in the close affinities between his thought and that of other anti-Newtonians at that time, such as George Berkeley (1685–1753), William Blake (1757–1827), and others, who were opposed to distancing God from the phenomena of nature or detaching the order of grace from the order of nature, as Newton's universal active principles appeared to do.

HISTORY

The same drive to uphold traditional religious belief informs Edwards's contribution to historical thought. His philosophy of history took shape, in part, in opposition to intellectual developments in the early modern European period, and specifically to the new modes of historical thought that were leading to the exclusion of theistic considerations from the realm of history.[53] The view that the course of history is based exclusively on God's redemptive activity was developed by Edwards as a response to the Enlightenment narratives that rejected the Christian sense of time and vision of history. "Shall we prize a history that gives us a clear account of some great earthly prince or mighty warrior, as of Alexander the Great or Julius Caesar, or the duke of Marlborough," asked Edwards, "and shall we not prize the history that God has given us of the glorious kingdom of his son, Jesus Christ, the prince and savior of the world?"[54] Against the de-Christianization and de-divinization of the historical process, Edwards sought the reenthronement of God as the sole author and lord of history.

The "enlightened age" posed grave implications for traditional Christian thought. It signified an entirely new attitude toward history, stressing human autonomy and freedom in determining its course and progress. Enlightenment historians refused "to recognize an absolutely supernatural or an absolutely super-historical sphere," and attempted to free historical thought "from the bonds of Scripture dogmatically interpreted and of the orthodoxy of the preceding centuries."[55] Instead of ordering the structure of history on the dimension of "sacred time," or the operation of divine providence, Enlightenment historical narratives were based on secular, historical time.[56] Henry St. John, Lord Bolingbroke (1678–1751), Voltaire (1694–1778), David Hume (1711–76), and Edward Gibbon (1737–94), to name only a few, strove to "liberate history writing from its subservience to theology" and to free it from the theological view that conceived "the course of human history as the realization of a divine plan."[57] Instead of seeing the historical process as contingent on a metaphysical reality beyond and above it, Enlightenment historians gave their highest attention to human beings' actions and deeds.

No longer considered as the narrative of a God-given providential plan, the historical realm came to be defined as a space of time intended for the realization of the possibilities and abilities inherent in the nature of human beings. Enlightenment historians viewed mankind as "advancing steadily from primitive barbarism to reason and virtue and civilization."[58] In place of the religious vision of history as the drama of human salvation and redemption that would be realized *beyond* history, historical thought in the age of Enlightenment developed the concept of "progress," or the notion of an immanent human advance based on the belief that utopian visions regarding human freedom and happiness could be fulfilled *within* history. *Historia Humana* gradually replaced salvation history in the European mind. This involved not only the detachment of grace from time, redemption from history, and divine agency from temporal events, but ultimately the rejection of the Christian historical worldview.

To Enlightenment historians, the uses of studying history were primarily political, social, and educational, and much less theological and religious. Lord Bolingbroke claimed: "We ought always to keep in mind, that history is philosophy teaching by examples how to conduct ourselves in all the situations of private and public life."[59] Hume argued that history's main use is to reveal the progress of "human society" from "its infancy . . . towards arts and sciences."[60] *Historia Humana*, the annals of human institutions, civil society, laws, manners, nations, and so on, in contrast to the sacred, became the enterprise of Enlightenment historians. The chief use of "history," said Hume, is "to discover the constant and universal principles of human nature, by showing men in all varieties of circumstances and situations," enabling us to "become acquainted with the regular springs of human action and behaviour."[61]

Even more serious for traditional religious thought and belief were the Enlightenment historians' denunciations of the Christian interpretation of history. Hume wrote that religion "has contributed to render CHRISTENDOM the scene of religious wars and divisions. Religions," including Christianity, "arise in ages totally ignorant and barbarous" and "consist mostly of traditional tales and fictions."[62] Also grave for the traditional Christian narrative of history was the threat to the authority of the Bible as an historical source. Bolingbroke directed a major assault on sacred ecclesiastical history. The "historical part" of the "Old Testament," he wrote, "must be reputed insufficient" to the study of history "by every candid and impartial man." Not only is the Bible an insufficient and unreliable source, but "history has been purposely and systematically falsified in all ages" by church historians. Instead of providing historical truths, the Christian interpretation of history has led to the "abuse of history."[63]

Edwards owned and read many works by Enlightenment historians, among them Pierre Bayle's *Historical and Critical Dictionary* (1702), Bolingbroke's *Remarks on the History of England* (1731) and *Letters on the Study and Use of History* (1752), Hume's *Essays Moral, Political and Literary* (1742), and Samuel Pufendorf's *An Introduction to the History of the Principal Kingdoms and States of Europe* (1702). Aware of these modes of European historical thought, and in response to them, Edwards formulated his own philosophy of salvation history; its fullest and most systematic exposition is found in the thirty sermons on the *History of the Work of Redemption* (1739).[64]

Against the Enlightenment historians' new modes of historical, secular time that denied any theistic interpretation of the historical process, Edwards viewed history as lying exclusively in the mind of omniscient God. Taking God as the sole author of history, he argued that divine providence constructed history as a special dimension of sacred, redemptive time designed solely for accomplishing God's work of redemption, the "rise and continued progress of the dispensations of grace towards fallen mankind."[65] The historical process therefore should be understood from the perspective of its maker and author. In this sacred, redemptive context, the "pourings out of the Spirit" and its historical manifestations in the form of revivals and awakenings constitute the ultimate mark of divine agency in the order of time: "from the fall of man to this day wherein we live the Work of Redemption in its effects has mainly been carried on by remarkable pourings out of the Spirit of God" at "special seasons of mercy," or revivals, such as during the age of the apostles or the Protestant Reformation.[66] Religious awakening is the essence of providential history and the main manifestation of divine agency in worldly time.

Edwards's historical narrative therefore deals primarily with the outpouring of the Spirit of God in "dispensations of providence" and, correspondingly, with its historical manifestations in the form of decisive periods of awakenings throughout history.[67] His aim was to demonstrate that the fate of human beings cannot be separated from divine action in time. Given that the whole course and progress of history are based on the effusion of the Spirit as manifested in periods of decisive revivals, history is God's grand "theater" because his transcendent ends determine the drama of human history on earth. Edwards thus defined history as a sacred space of time destined from eternity for God's own self-glorification – the display of the deity's excellence in creation as evidenced in his work of redemption; hence human beings' existence as well as their history are totally dependent on God. Such was Edwards's reply to the exclusion of theistic considerations from the realm of time and history by Enlightenment historians.[68]

ETHICS AND MORALS

Edwards's long involvement with issues of ethics and morals, apparent in his various "ethical writings," such as *Charity and Its Fruits* (1738), *Concerning the End for Which God Created the World* (1755), and *The Nature of True Virtue* (1755), may be understood in the wider ideological context of early modern history and the "Enlightenment project," or its "new science of morals," which presented a contrast to Christian teaching. The first half of the eighteenth century witnessed an attempt on the part of Enlightenment thinkers to establish new concepts of moral theory. Chief among these was the theory of a "moral sense," the *sensus communis* of classical thought. Claiming that the moral sense is the faculty by which we distinguish between right and wrong, writers such as Francis Hutcheson (1694–1746) and David Hume, as well as other members of the British School of Moral Sense, argued that it is possible to have knowledge of good and evil without, and prior to, knowledge of God. The main assumption behind this conception of ethics and morals was the belief that human beings can know from within themselves, without reliance on traditional sources of religious authority, what God intends and expects of them as moral creatures.

The term "moral sense" was first suggested by Anthony Ashley Cooper, third Earl of Shaftesbury (1671–1713), in *An Inquiry Concerning Virtue or Merit* (1699) and in *Characteristics of Men, Manners, Opinions, Times* (1711). In these works he appealed to psychological experience as a foundation for morality, attributing to a moral sense our ability "to be capable of Virtue, and to have a Sense of Right and Wrong," to distinguish between good and evil, virtue and vice.[69] This sense, he believed, along with our common affection for virtue, accounts for the possibility of morality.

Francis Hutcheson, Shaftesbury's principal follower, a professor of moral theology at Glasgow, argued in his *An Inquiry Concerning the Original of Our Ideas of Virtue or Moral Good* (1725) that human beings have disinterested motives, namely, they can act for the sake of the good of others and not merely for their self-advantage. Since "no love to rational Agents can proceed from Self Interest, every action must be disinterested, as far as it flows from Love to rational Agents." This disinterested motive, which he terms " Benevolence, or Love" – the quality of being concerned about others for their own sake – constitutes "the universal Foundation" of the "Moral Sense."[70]

The same endeavor to ground morality exclusively in the benevolence of human nature appears also in Hume's moral philosophy. For him, as with Hutcheson, morality is an entirely human affair based on human nature and not on a divine will. "[M]orality," he claimed, "is nothing in the abstract nature of things, but is entirely relative to the sentiment or mental taste of each particular being."[71] Believing that ethics and religion were separate subjects of inquiry, Hume attempted to provide an analysis of moral principles without connection to religion, defining "virtue as personal merit, or what is useful and agreeable to ourselves and to others."[72]

Edwards knew many works by Enlightenment moral theorists, including Shaftesbury's *Characteristics of Men, Manners, Opinions, Times* (1711), Hutcheson's *An Inquiry into the Original of Our Ideas of Beauty and Virtue* (1725) and *An Essay on the Nature and Conduct of the Passions and Affections with Illustration on the Moral Sense* (1728), as well as Hume's, *A Treatise on Human Nature* (1739), *An Enquiry Concerning Human Understanding* (1748), and *Enquiry Concerning the Principles of Morals* (1751). In these works he could see that the new theories of ethics were leading to the detachment of the moral system from God. The Enlightenment debate on moral philosophy, especially its theory of innate moral sense, thus contained serious implications for Christian ethics. In response, Edwards declared that it is "evident that true virtue must chiefly consist in love to God," and that "all true virtue" is based on "love of Being, and the qualities and acts which arise from it."[73] Since the essence of "true virtue" is "benevolence to being in general," or

God, there is no "true virtue without SUPREME LOVE TO GOD and making God our supreme end."[74]

Edwards devoted much time and energy to refuting the moral sense theory because he would not accept a theory of morals or virtue based exclusively on human nature and independent of God, who exercises "absolute and universal dominion" over the created order: "[T]he whole universe, including all creatures animate and inanimate, in all its actings, proceedings, revolutions, and entire series of events, should proceed from a regard and with a view to *God*, as the supreme and last end of all."[75] Thus in *Charity and Its Fruits,* preached in 1734 and 1735, he asserted that from "love to God springs love to man"; hence without "love to God there can be no true honor," or virtue.[76] Against the attempts by Enlightenment writers to base ethics and morals on secular and naturalistic foundations, Edwards declared that the gracious affections stand above and beyond the natural affections of which all are capable, and true virtue stands above and beyond the disinterested benevolence that marks the ultimate achievement of natural man. He wrote that "what our modern philosophers call natural Moral Taste is a different thing from virtue," because "a supreme regard to the Deity is essential to true virtue."[77]

In *Freedom of the Will* (1754), Edwards attacked the Arminians' and Deists' "grand article concerning *the freedom of the will requisite to moral agency*," the belief that absolute self-determination of the will is necessary for human liberty and moral virtue. Since "every event" in the physical as well as the moral world "must be ordered by God," the "liberty of moral agents does not consist in self-determining power." Accordingly, in this work he wished to demonstrate that "God's moral government over mankind, his treating them as moral agents," is not "inconsistent with a determining disposal of all events." Human beings must do as they will, in accordance with their fallen nature, and they have liberty only in the sense that nothing prevents them from doing what they will in accordance with their nature. But "nothing in the state or acts of the will of man is contingent," for "every event of this kind is necessary." God's foreknowledge eliminates the possibility of contingency in the world, for contingency is the antithesis of God's unlimited prescience. Given that "the power of volition" belongs only to "the man or the soul," there is no such thing as "freedom of the will."[78] That freedom is incompatible with the individual's necessary willing of what he or she can will in accordance with a nature of self already determined. Edwards therefore attacked the "doctrine of self-determining will, as the ground of all moral good and evil," because it "tends to prevent any proper exercise of faith in God and Christ, in the affair of our salvation, as it tends to prevent all dependence upon them."[79]

Likewise, against the Enlightenment notion of human beings as fundamentally rational, moral, and benevolent, Edwards's *Original Sin* (1758) provided "a *general defense* of that great important doctrine" of original sin. This doctrine proclaims both the depravity of the human heart and the imputation of Adam's first sin to his posterity. All of Adam's posterity inherit the existential state of being "exposed, and justly so, to the sorrows of this life, to temporal death, and eternal ruin, unless saved by grace." But corruption of humankind cannot be accounted for by considering the sin of each individual separately. It is essential to the human condition and is based on "the *arbitrary* constitution of the Creator" in creation. Thus, in response to the Enlightenment writers' belief in human moral sense, Edwards declared that "we are by nature, *companions* in a miserable helpless condition," namely, human depravity.[80]

During the eighteenth century, the controversy over human depravity signified an important struggle about the nature of human beings and their potentialities. As a result, the emphasis during the age of Enlightenment on human beings as fundamentally rational, morally and benevolently inclined, endangered the Christian doctrine of original sin. Edwards wrote *Original Sin* against, among others, John Taylor (1694–1761), a Presbyterian minister who published *The Scripture-Doctrine of Original Sin* in 1740, accusing Calvinism of turning God into a monster. Taylor wrote, "[P]ray consider seriously what a God He must be who can be displeased with and curse His innocent creatures even before they have a being."[81] Further, Taylor argued that virtue and holiness result from the free and right choices of human beings. Among respondents to Taylor were John Wesley, who in *The Doctrine of Original Sin* (1757) charged Taylor with overthrowing the foundations of primitive, scriptural Christianity, and Jonathan Edwards, who argued that if we do not posit universal depravity, we cannot explain how every individual does, in fact, freely choose what is evil.

Finally, in *The Nature of True Virtue,* Edwards replied directly to the contemporary "controversies and variety of opinions" about "the nature of true virtue." His aim was to define the disposition that distinguished the godly, claiming that true "virtue most essentially consists in benevolence to Being in general." A true system of morals and ethics is therefore inseparable from religion because the former is grounded on the latter; religion is the true foundation and only source of all virtue. Since "true virtue must chiefly consist in love to God, the Being of beings," continues Edwards, "he that has true virtue, consisting in benevolence to Being in general [or God], and in that complacence in virtue, or moral beauty, and benevolence to virtuous being, must necessarily have a supreme love to God, both of benevolence and complacence." Against Hutcheson's and Hume's separation of morals and religion, Edwards claimed that virtue is by necessity grounded on God since the deity "is the head of the universal system of existence." Hence "nothing is of the nature of true virtue, in which God is not the *first* and the *last.*"[82]

Edwards was fully aware of the grave implications of the Enlightenment's new theories of ethics and morals for the Christian faith. "[U]nless we will be atheists," he declared, "we must allow that true virtue does primarily and most essentially consist in a supreme love to God." Those who oppose this assertion deny that "God maintains a moral kingdom in the world." Morality, then, cannot be separated from God: "a virtuous love in *created* beings, *one to another,* is dependent on, and derived from love to *God.*" Moreover, the foundation of morality cannot be separated from the theological teleology of order inherent in the universe: "they are good moral agents whose temper of mind or propensity of heart is agreeable to the *end* for which God made moral agents." The "last end for which God has made moral agents must be the last end for which God has made all things: it being evident that the moral world is the end of the rest of the world; the inanimate and unintelligent world being made for the rational and moral world."[83]

In the English Enlightenment of the eighteenth century, Edwards's views, strongly opposed to the dominant philosophy of Locke, Newton, Hume, and the Deists, illustrate the expiring power of Calvinism. But in terms of the formation of American culture, his attacks on Enlightenment secular modes of thought helped to create a well-defined American Protestant culture.[84] More specifically, Edwards's rejection of the British school of "moral sense" was incorporated, adopted, and diffused by the New Divinity School in New England and, in fact, was its hallmark during the eighteenth and nineteenth centuries. Likewise, his reaction to the Enlightenment narratives of history led to the development of a singular evangelical historiography, which, by placing revival at the center of salvation history, conditioned many generations of Protestants in America to see religious awakening as the essence of divine agency in time and history.

Notes

1. Immanuel Kant, *Critique of Pure Reason*, ed. Norman K. Smith (New York: Palgrave, 2003), 9.
2. James Schmidt, ed., *What Is Enlightenment? Eighteenth-Century Answers and Twentieth-Century Questions* (Berkeley: University of California Press, 1996).
3. Peter Harrison, *"Religion" and the Religions in the English Enlightenment* (Cambridge: Cambridge University Press, 1990), 5.
4. Gerald R. Cragg, *The Church and the Age of Reason* (London: Penguin, 1990), 13.
5. "Letter to the Trustees of the College of New Jersey" (1757), WJE, 16:727.

6. "Letter to the Reverend Thomas Foxcroft" (1757), WJE, 16:695.

7. Justin Champion, *Republican Learning: John Toland and the Crisis of Christian Culture, 1696–1722* (Manchester: Manchester University Press, 2003), 5–6.

8. Alexander Pope, *The Dunciad* (1742), in *Poetry and Prose of Alexander Pope*, ed. Aubrey William (Boston: Houghton Mifflin, 1969), 372.

9. Matthew Tindal, *Christianity as Old as the Creation* (London, 1730), 70.

10. John Toland, *Christianity Not Mysterious* (London, 1696), 127.

11. Tindal, *Christianity as Old as the Creation*, 16.

12. Ibid., 13–14.

13. Anthony Collins, *A Discourse of the Grounds and Reasons of the Christian Religion* (London, 1724), 42.

14. Thomas Woolston, *A Discourse on the Miracles of Our Savior* (London, 1727), 4, 19.

15. Herbert, Lord of Cherbury, *Antient Religion of the Gentiles* (London, 1711), 1–2.

16. John Dryden, "Religio Laici" (1682), in *John Dryden*, ed. Keith Walker (Oxford: Oxford University Press, 1987), 220.

17. In the following discussion of Edwards's reaction to Deism, I rely on Gerald McDermott's excellent studies, *Jonathan Edwards Confronts the Gods: Christian Theology, Enlightenment Religion, and Non-Christian Faiths* (New York: Oxford University Press, 2000), and "Franklin, Jefferson and Edwards on Religion and the Religions," in Harry S. Stout, Kenneth P. Minkema, and Caleb J. D. Maskell, eds., *Jonathan Edwards at 300: Essays on the Tercentenary of His Birth* (Lanham, MD: University Press of America, 2005), 65–85.

18. Peter J. Thuesen, "Edwards' Intellectual Background," in Sang H. Lee, ed., *Princeton Companion to Jonathan Edwards* (Princeton: Princeton University Press, 2005), 27–8.

19. "Miscell." 1239, WJE, 23:175.

20. "Miscell." 1337, WJE, 23:342.

21. "Miscell." 519, WJE, 18:64.

22. "Miscell." 837, WJE, 20:52–3.

23. *Religious Affections*, WJE, 2:271–4.

24. *The Nature of True Virtue*, WJE, 8:540; "'Controversies' Notebook," WJE, 21:322–3; "Miscell." 1208, WJE 23:139–40.

25. See John E. Smith, "Christian Morality and Common Morality," *Princeton Companion*, 150–1.

26. "Miscell." 582, WJE, 18:118. See also *Notes on Scripture*, WJE, 15:175.

27. "Miscell." 128, WJE, 13:291–2.

28. "Miscell." 964, WJE, 20:248.

29. "Miscell." kk, WJE, 13:186.

30. "Miscell." 953, WJE, 20:222.

31. "Miscell." 1355, WJE, 23:548.

32. WJE, 6:202–7, 208–18, 332–91.

33. John H. Brooke, *Science and Religion* (Cambridge: Cambridge University Press, 1991), 119.

34. Robert Boyle, *A Free Enquiry into the Vulgarly Received Notion of Nature* (1686), in M. A. Stewart, *Selected Philosophical Papers of Robert Boyle* (Indianapolis: Hackett, 1991), 191.

35. Idem, *The Excellency of Theology Compared with Natural Philosophy* (1665), as quoted in Otto Mayr, *Authority, Liberty and Automatic Machinery in Early Modern Europe* (Baltimore: Johns Hopkins University Press, 1986), 56.

36. Sir Isaac Newton, "Newton's Preface to the First Edition," in Florian Cajori, ed., *Sir Isaac Newton's Mathematical Principles of Natural Philosophy and His System of the World* (2 vols. Berkeley: University of California Press, 1934), I:xvii–xviii.

37. *About the Excellency and Grounds of the Mechanical Hypothesis* (1674), in Stewart, ed., *Selected Philosophical Papers of Robert Boyle*, 139.

38. Newton, "General Scholium," in Cajori, ed., *Sir Isaac Newton's Mathematical Principles of Natural Philosophy and His System of the World*, II:544.

39. Idem, "Four Letters to Richard Bentley," Letter III, February 25, 1693, in H. S. Thayer, ed., *Newton's Philosophy of Nature: Selections from His Writings* (New York: Hafner, 1974), 54.

40. Gary B. Deason, "Reformation Theology and the Mechanistic Conception of Nature," in D. C. Lindberg and R. L. Numbers, eds., *God and Nature: Historical Essays on the Encounter between Christianity and Science* (Berkeley: University of California Press, 1986), 187.

41. Amos Funkenstein, *Theology and the Scientific Imagination from the Middle Ages to the Seventeenth Century* (Princeton: Princeton University Press, 1986), 90.

42. J. E. McGuire, "The Fate of the Date: The Theology of Newton's *Principia* Revisited," in Margaret J. Osler, ed., *Rethinking the Scientific Revolution* (Cambridge: Cambridge University Press, 2000), 276.

43. James E. Force, "Newton's God of Dominion: The Unity of Newton's Theological, Scientific, and Political Thought," in James E. Force and Richard H. Popkin, eds., *Essays on the Context, Nature, and Influence of Isaac Newton's Theology* (Dordrecht: Kluwer, 1990), 79, 83. See also Scott Mandelbrote, "Newton and Eighteenth-Century Christianity," in I. B. Cohen et al., *The Cambridge Companion to Newton* (Cambridge: Cambridge University Press, 2002), 409–30.

44. "Of Atoms," WJE, 6:216; "Things to Be Considered an[d] Written Fully about," WJE, 6:235.

45. "Of Atoms," WJE, 6:214; "Things to Be Considered," WJE, 6:235.

46. "Miscell." ff, WJE, 13:184.

47. "Of Atoms," WJE, 6:216.

48. "Miscell." 1263, WJE, 23:212. See also *Notes on Scripture*, WJE, 15:373, 388.

49. "The Mind," WJE, 6:350–6.

50. Ibid., 336–7; "Miscell." 541, WJE, 18:89.

51. "Miscell." 704, WJE, 18:320; *Freedom of the Will*, WJE, 1:177.

52. "The Mind," WJE, 6:353–5.

53. The development of the various Enlightenment narratives of history is discussed, among others, in Karen O'Brien, *Narratives of Enlightenment: Cosmopolitan History from Voltaire to Gibbon* (Cambridge: Cambridge University Press, 1997); Philip Hicks, *Neoclassical History and English Culture: From Clarendon to Hume* (London: Macmillan, 1996), J. G. A. Pocock, *Barbarism and Religion: The Enlightenments of Edward Gibbon, 1737–1764* (Cambridge: Cambridge University Press, 1999); idem, *Barbarism and Religion: Narratives of Civil Government* (Cambridge: Cambridge University Press, 1999).

54. *A History of the Work of Redemption*, WJE, 9:291.

55. Ernst Cassirer, *The Philosophy of the Enlightenment* (Boston: Beacon Press, 1962), 199.

56. J. G. E. Pocock, "Modes of Action and their Pasts in Tudor and Stuart England," in Orest Ranum, ed., *National Consciousness, History and Political Culture in Early Modern Europe* (Baltimore: Johns Hopkins University Press, 1975), 98–117.

57. Peter Gay, *The Enlightenment: The Science of Freedom* (New York: W. W. Norton, 1977), 372–3.

58. G. Barraclough, "Universal History," 1962, as quoted in Sidney Pollard, *The Idea of Progress* (Harmondsworth: Penguin, 1971), 33.

59. Henry St. John, Lord Bolingbroke, *Letters on the Study and Use of History* (1735), *The Works of . . . Henry St. John, Lord Viscount Bolingbroke* (8 vols. London, 1809), III:349–50.

60. David Hume, *Essays, Moral Political and Literary*, ed. T. H. Green (2 vols. London, 1882), II:389.

61. Idem. "History as Guide," in Isaac Kramnick, ed., *The Portable Enlightenment Reader* (New York: Penguin, 1995), 359.

62. Idem, "Of Parties in General" (1741), in Eugene F. Miller, ed., *David Hume: Essays Moral Political and Literary* (Indianapolis: Liberty Classics, 1985), 62–3.

63. Henry St. John, Lord Bolingbroke, "Letters on the Study and Use of History," in Isaac Kramnick, ed., *Lord Bolingbroke: Historical Writings* (Chicago: University of Chicago Press, 1972), 35–6, 51, 53–5.

64. WJE, 9:111–528.

65. *History of the Work of Redemption*, WJE, 9:285.

66. Ibid., 143, 376–81, 438–40.

67. Ibid., 511; *Notes of Scripture*, WJE, 15:385.

68. See Avihu Zakai, *Jonathan Edwards's Philosophy of History: The Reenchantment of the World in the Age of Enlightenment* (Princeton: Princeton University Press, 2003).

69. Francis Hutcheson, *An Inquiry Concerning Virtue or Merit* (1699), in L. A. Selby-Bigge, ed., *British Moralists: Selections from Writers Principally of the Eighteenth Century* (2 vols. Oxford: Clarendon Press, 1897), I:23, 33.

70. Idem, *An Inquiry Concerning the Original of Our Ideas of Virtue or Moral Good*, 2nd edition (1726) in Selby-Bigge, ed., *British Moralists*. I:87, 99, 118.

71. David Hume, *Philosophical Essays Concerning Human Understanding* (London: A. Miller, 1748), 14; Thomas Mautner, ed., *Francis Hutcheson: On Human Nature* (New York: Cambridge University Press, 1993), 152.

72. Isabel Rivers, *Reason, Grace, and Sentiment: A Study of the Language of Religion and Ethics in England 1660–1780* (2 vols. Cambridge: Cambridge University Press, 2000), *Shaftesbury to Hume*, II:288.

73. *The Nature of True Virtue*, WJE, 8:550, 548.

74. "'Controversies' Notebook," WJE, 21:322, 314.

75. *Concerning the End for Which God Created the World*, WJE, 8:424.

76. *Charity and Its Fruits*, WJE, 8:137, 142.

77. "'Controversies' Notebook," WJE, 21:314; "Miscell." 1208, WJE, 23:139.

78. *Freedom of the Will*, WJE, 1:431–3; *Notes on Scripture*, WJE, 15:388.

79. "To the Reverend John Erskine," Aug. 3, 1757, WJE, 16:721. See also Allen C. Guelzo, "Freedom of the Will," *Princeton Companion*, 115–29.

80. *Original Sin*, 3:102, 395, 403, 424.

81. John Taylor, *The Scripture-Doctrine of Original Sin* (London, 1740), 151.
82. *The Nature of True Virtue*, WJE 8:539–51, 560.
83. Ibid., 554, 556–67.
84. Avihu Zakai, "Jonathan Edwards, the Enlightenment, and the Formation of Protestant Tradition in America," in Elizabeth Mancke et al., eds., *The Creation of the British Atlantic World* (Baltimore: Johns Hopkins University Press, 2005), 182–209.

Part II

Edwards's roles and achievements

5 Edwards as preacher

WILSON H. KIMNACH

The great preachers of English-speaking civilization have ranked with the greatest creative writers as shapers of the language, and the literature of the printed sermon is voluminous by any standard; yet the sermon has always labored under certain ambiguities peculiar to its genre. Most obvious is the question of exactly what the text of a sermon represents. Is it what was preached, or a literary correlative, or a separate work altogether? To assert that one is discussing the performance or speech act that is preaching when referring only to a printed text is literally untrue; rather, what is being considered is inevitably a form of literature, the author of which must be considered a literary artist as much as anyone working in the various genres of prose and verse.

The critic Edmund Gosse once observed of the seventeenth-century English preacher Jeremy Taylor that his reputation "has been injured among general readers by the fact that he is a divine, and among divines by the fact that he is an artist."[1] Indeed, the relationship between sermon-making and artistic endeavor involves ambiguities that are probably even more troublesome in America than in England, given the American insistence upon the separateness of the sacred and the secular. For different reasons, perhaps, American clergy and the general public have mutually assumed that sermons are somehow not really "literature" and that the authors of great sermons are not really "artists." The preacher is often seen as a practitioner in the tradition of the ancient Hebrew prophets who speaks as inspired by God, and it is at least implied that recognition of artifice in the communication of that inspiration would call too much attention to the medium – both person and expression – and thus derogate from the authenticity of the source. Certainly some sermons have been incorporated into the national literature, but usually for reasons other than their specific literary merit as sermons.

Edwards himself was probably familiar with the practical implications of these issues at an early age, for he was scion of clerical families on both paternal and maternal sides. His father, the Reverend Timothy Edwards, was respected as a leader of several revivals of religion in his small East Windsor,

Connecticut, parish, though he published only one sermon, an election sermon. On the maternal side, Edwards was grandson of the clerical leader of
the Connecticut Valley, the Reverend Solomon Stoddard of Northampton,
Massachusetts. Stoddard was not only a leader of great local influence but a
powerful writer who had jousted with the Mathers in print and published
a number of sermons and treatises widely circulated in New England and
beyond. Edwards himself seems to have entertained high literary ambitions
in his youth, perhaps inspired by the achievements of his grandfather's controversial publications. In any case, both his father and grandfather were
skilled practitioners in the art of the sermon, and his grandfather Stoddard
had achieved a considerable reputation through the medium of the printed
sermon or sermon/treatise.

   Thus Jonathan Edwards was heir to a notable New England craft long
before his formal training in rhetoric at the nascent Yale College. His early
training would have been that of all young persons in his community who
regularly listened to sermons preached and later recited the "heads" of the
sermons back to the minister. The heads were numbered main points of the
sermon, arranged according to the scheme of Peter Ramus into categories
and subcategories under three primary divisions. The sermon of Edwards's
youth was essentially the seventeenth-century Puritan sermon, as busy in
its formal structure as the music of Johann Sebastian Bach. His father's
baroque sermons could have well over fifty numbered heads (not to mention
subheads), though the language was indeed plain. The argument of such
sermons was a structure of "proofs" made by the preacher and recorded easily
in notebooks by the listeners. If the material carried emotional force because
of the issues involved, the main literary emphasis was upon instruction
through clear, systematic exposition.

   To the sound, if unimaginative, foundation of his father's practice,
Edwards may well have added a few hints from his grandfather Stoddard.
His mother may have suggested that her father had a very outspoken, commanding way of preaching, and the young Edwards doubtless read some of
Stoddard's printed sermons. In them he found the same general form his
father used but much more rhetorical development, and a new emphasis
upon the significance of personal experience in religion. Stoddard had a
practical politician's knowledge of men, and while he appreciated the "scripture proofs" and "rational proofs" of traditional preaching, he appreciated
more than most ministers that sinners needed not only to be convinced of
the truth of the doctrine but of its materiality in their lives: "If they were
thoroughly scared, they would be more earnest in their Endeavours; Sense-
lessness begets Slightiness."[2] Stoddard urged preachers to deal "roundly"

with their congregations and often employed violent imagery when describing effective preaching. All this was not lost on the young Jonathan Edwards,
who ultimately combined the ideals of rigorous logical argument and sensa-
tional impact, resulting in his distinctive idiom of *experienced* ideas.

Like his father and grandfather, Edwards understood the sermon to be
primarily a vehicle of power rather than of reason or beauty. Homiletics was
not philosophy or poetry, though it might utilize both arts in the pursuit of
its ends. In some of his early musings upon preaching, Edwards observed,
"if it was plain to all the world of Christians that I was under the infallible
guidance of Christ, and [that] I was sent forth to teach the world the will of
Christ, then I should have power in all the world."[3] The sermon of such a
messenger would indeed be transcendent, fixing the historical moment of
the sermon's occasion within the eternal reality of the divine presence. Of
course, these were musings, not Edwards's early self-evaluation.

But the sermon form inherited by Edwards from his forbears dramatized
the mediation of the divine in its very formal structure. As preached (or
written), it moves systematically from the divine to the human, but at each
stage of its development places its subject in the divine context. The divine
context is represented by the words of the Scripture, and they are used at
key points throughout the sermon, so many lynchpins known as "Scripture
proofs." But the tripartite structure of the sermon itself is also a dramatic
gesture of mediation. The first stage of the sermon is the Text, consisting
of a passage from Scripture accompanied by a page or two of exegesis. This
division introduces the theme of the sermon in the context of the Word of
God, the eternal truth and reality by which all human reality is evaluated. The
theme is not often so precise or explicit in its statement as human philosophy
would require of a thesis; therefore, the second division of the sermon, the
Doctrine, begins with a statement of doctrine that functions in the sermon as
a thesis in a formal essay. The statement of doctrine is analyzed, explained,
and confirmed in a series of numbered heads known collectively as "reasons."
Finally, the third division of the sermon, the Application (or Improvement),
offers explicit numbered directions, known collectively as "uses," for human
thought and conduct that are inferred from the Doctrine. The Doctrine and
Application divisions each constitute roughly 50 percent of the sermon.

The drama of mediation results from the close argumentative linkage
within the sermon as the preacher moves from the Word of God (Text) to
human understanding (Doctrine) to human conduct (Application), or from
the eternal to the temporal to the moment of experience. Handled properly,
the sermon's progress suggests the drama of Moses' descent from the moun-
tain with the law in hand. (Of course, Edwards and all other preachers had

to keep in mind the cautionary tale of Moses' frustration during that first dramatic effort in literary mediation.)

That Jonathan Edwards was intensely interested in the dramatic potential of the traditional sermon form is apparent from his initial efforts in the sermon. Immediately, it seems, he simplified the form used by his father, reducing the heads to fourteen (only three of them subheads) in his earliest extant sermon. This reduction of heads increased the opportunity for development within each head while it accentuated the drama of the formal unfolding of the sermon's three divisions. During the remainder of his career, Edwards would keep the simpler form, though his long sermons and sermon series can seem very complex to a modern reader. (Of course, even a brief sermon by Edwards may contain very subtle and complex *thought*, but that is another matter.) Thus Edwards accepted and pursued traditional homiletical practices much as he did the ministerial calling itself, not uncritically or without certain doubts and reservations, but according to his own taste after study and reflection.[4]

Edwards's career as a writer of sermons can be understood as an evolution of technique, but it is also divisible into historical phases that derive from his view of the sermon in relation to his calling as one of "Christ's ambassadors" to a fallen world. While there is little evidence of any diminution of his commitment to the Christian ministry over time, there is evidence that the role of the sermon in his ministry did change. In the earliest phase of his work, including that in New York, Bolton, and indeed in all of his posts before he assumed sole leadership of the Northampton congregation in 1729, Edwards is largely concerned with mastering the sermon as a vehicle of religious expression. During the next phase, extending from 1729 through 1742, he is preoccupied with the sermon as an instrument of awakening and pastoral leadership. A final phase, complex but essentially coherent, from 1743 until Edwards's leaving the pastorate to assume the presidency of the College of New Jersey in 1758, shows Edwards investing less of himself in regular pastoral preaching while exploring the limits of the sermon form, whether in the printed discourse (or treatise) or the mission sermon to Indians.

During the first phase, Edwards was initially employed by a splinter congregation in New York City for a few months during the fall, winter, and spring of 1722–3. Working with a small group that had separated from the English Presbyterian church in the city, Edwards apparently found an encouraging audience and something approaching an ideal religious community. His hours of meditation in the rural environs of eighteenth-century Manhattan and his sense of religious fellowship with members of his congregation are celebrated in the *Personal Narrative* as some of the most memorable events of his spiritual life and inevitably constituted formative influences upon him.[5] His preaching – that of a nineteen-year-old – attempted a comprehensive definition of the Christian life in experiential terms, as Edwards seemingly worked out his own spiritual priorities while instructing his congregation. Perhaps *The Way of Holiness* is the seminal document of this early phase of his homiletics. In it Edwards insists that "Holiness is a most beautiful, lovely thing. . . . 'Tis the highest beauty and amiableness . . . 'tis of a sweet, lovely, delightful, serene, calm, and still nature. . . . What a sweet calmness, what a calm ecstacy, doth it bring to the soul!"[6] Edwards used these phrases, along with much of their context from the conclusion of the sermon, to form the first meditation of what would become his vast "*Miscellanies*" notebooks of theological speculation.[7] The language is reflected likewise in his "apostrophe" to Sarah Pierpont and is recalled some sixteen years later in the *Personal Narrative*.[8]

Other sermons from New York, such as *Dedication to God* and *The Nakedness of Job,* stress Edwards's early preoccupation with authenticity, or what he called "reality." "All the world knows the truth of this doctrine perfectly well, but though they know, yet it don't seem at all real to them. . . ."[9] And for the next twenty years, Edwards was to pursue the homiletical challenge of authentic realization of the spiritual. Meanwhile, Edwards habitually appealed to his New York congregation in the idiom of his enlightened age, as in *Christian Happiness*, where he argues that "God always deals with men as reasonable creatures, and every [word] in the Scriptures speaks to us as such."[10] The optimism of such a posture complements his spiritual exaltation in sermons such as *Glorious Grace* and *True Love to God.* Perhaps the greatest achievement of these early efforts in New York is *Christ, the Light of the World,* a sermon in which Edwards's technique is adequate to his argument, and the concept of God's communication of himself through Christ is represented through an ambitious exploration of the traditional metaphor of light.[11]

Even after his return home to East Windsor in the spring of 1723, Edwards's elevated spiritual state continued. Now, with no preaching to preoccupy him, Edwards turned to his notebooks and private writings with renewed energy, resulting in an intellectual flowering to match the spiritual flowering of the previous two years. As he prepared his Latin oration for delivery at the September commencement of Yale College to complete the M.A. degree, Edwards aligned the evangelical mood of New York with an academic milieu by choosing to defend the Calvinist doctrine of justification by faith alone – the first of his many deployments of that doctrine in opposition to the increasingly liberal spirit of the age.[12]

At about the same time, in the fall of 1723, Edwards began preaching to a congregation in nearby Bolton, Connecticut. He there led a newly formed church in a newly formed town, assuming a more formal pastoral role in a more conventional church than he had ministered to in New York. This more "settled" community was troubled by internal dissension, provoking late in 1723 the sermon *Living Peaceably One with Another*.[13] Ironically, Edwards himself may have been one of the factors contributing to the dissension, as some of the congregation had recently departed from his father's congregation and may not have desired an extension of the Edwards ministry into their new community. In addition to repreaching New York sermons, Edwards composed several new sermons for Bolton, such as *A Spiritual Understanding of Divine Things Denied to the Unregenerate* and *The Pleasantness of Religion*.[14] In these, Edwards continued to develop seminal concepts first touched upon in New York and subsequently given new speculative depth in his notebooks, such as "excellency" (the first entry in "The Mind") or the new sense of beauty and harmony experienced by the saints. In the Bolton sermons, Edwards often couches ideas in more objective, pastoral statements that represent a further stage in the development of his homiletical art.

In May 1724, Edwards was rescued from his Bolton pastorate by being elected tutor at Yale College. Given his problematic situation at Bolton and his high ambitions for intellectual achievement, the appointment must have been an answered prayer, if not a plot. Edwards did not preach during most of this period, and when he took on some supply preaching in Glastonbury, Connecticut, near the end of the tutorship, he relied mainly upon old New York sermons. The period of the tutorship was thus one of intellectual investment that would pay rich dividends, but one that temporarily suspended homiletics and, for that matter, religion itself.

The final stage in this first phase of Edwards's preaching career was entered when he was summoned to return to the pastoral ministry. The time was August 1726, and the invitation was from the Northampton church, asking Edwards to assist his aged and ailing grandfather, Solomon Stoddard. The Northampton church was one of the plums of the colony, rivaled only by the great Boston churches. Moreover, Stoddard had made it a center of ecclesiastical power and theological debate, the leading church of the West on the Connecticut River. Edwards must have seen the Northampton pulpit as his most plausible step to early eminence as well.

After he arrived in Northampton on October 26, 1726, Edwards spent a few months as a probationer, usually preaching slightly revised versions of his New York and Bolton sermons as he assisted his grandfather. By the end of the year he had clearly passed muster and was ordained minister in Northampton on February 15, 1727. By July he had married his love and lifelong inspiration, Sarah Pierpont, and settled in as clerical heir apparent. From the beginning, though, there were potential homiletical tensions between Edwards and Stoddard, not least because Stoddard's last publication, *The Defects of Preachers Reproved*, openly inveighed against the reading of sermons in the pulpit, and Edwards was incapable of preaching without his manuscript. On a deeper level, this seemingly trivial issue points to the essential difference between Stoddard, who, though a powerful and even entertaining writer, was essentially a "hands-on" orator and politician, and Edwards, a natural *isolato* and literary man, who won a reputation as a "deep preacher" despite entirely lacking those physical graces that usually mark the successful orator and politician.

While Edwards was at first able to exploit his little library of sermons in assisting Stoddard, it was not long before they were all used. Edwards was always artful in reworking old sermon materials, but he had to be very circumspect because no New England congregation wanted to hear a warmed-over sermon. By the end of the summer of 1728, he was inexorably absorbed into the endless homiletical labor of the settled minister. As Edwards watched and worked beside Stoddard, he inevitably learned many things, but of all the lessons Stoddard may have inculcated, perhaps the most significant – for better or worse – was that of the efficacy of hellfire preaching. Of course the concept of the eternal punishment of the damned was no news to Edwards; indeed, his father had often preached about it, particularly in sermons calculated to get the attention of otherwise comfortably unrepentant sinners. But Stoddard elevated the role of such homiletical intimidation philosophically; indeed, he went so far as to claim, "When men don't Preach much about the danger of Damnation, there is want of good Preaching."[15] Of course, nothing was better calculated to provoke a sudden psychological alteration than good hellfire preaching, and one could also argue that this rough-and-ready approach was part of the frontier culture, where people had little time to sit around taking their spiritual temperature. For Edwards, all this may have been cause for some consternation; but he was an astute observer and he knew that Stoddard's congregation expected Stoddardean preaching.

During the fall of 1728, Edwards demonstrated his ability to preach hellfire with the best, composing what is probably his most thoroughgoing hellfire sermon, *The Torments of Hell Are Exceeding Great*. In it he points out that the biblical imagery of fire and torment used by preachers is of course metaphorical, and that metaphorical language tends to exaggerate when applied to earthly events.

> But when metaphors are used in Scripture about spiritual things, the things of another world, they fall short of the literal truth: for these things are the ultimum, the very highest things that are aimed at by all metaphors and similitudes.... So that we may very rationally conclude

that the similitudes that are used in Scripture about hell don't go beyond the truth, that metaphors of fire will probably be no metaphors after the resurrection.[16]

Directing his genius for exhaustive logical exposition to the service of terror, Edwards then explores the terms and conditions of damnation, intimates the unimaginable sufferings of the damned, and ridicules the obtuseness of mankind when asked to rise above the shadow life called "reality" to confront the authentic reality of God. Stoddard must have been impressed.

On February 11, 1729, "Pope" Stoddard died in his eighty-sixth year, leaving his people in the hands of his twenty-six-year-old assistant. Edwards had had two years to adjust to the peculiar culture of Northampton; now he either had to try to become another Solomon Stoddard or learn to motivate the people in new ways. The evidence of his sermon manuscripts indicates the pressures he experienced as well as the resourcefulness with which he met them. Although he had previous experience with high occasions such as fast days and sacrament sermons, now he had to be ready for all occasions: fasts and thanksgivings, weekly lectures and quarterly lectures, ordinations and funerals, and so on. However, responding to special occasions was probably not as challenging as the regular pastoral preaching, with the necessity of awakening and consoling, instructing and correcting, challenging and uplifting, week in and week out, for each sermon, no matter how comprehensive it may sound, is focused upon a specific local issue in some way.

The second phase of Edwards's preaching career, 1729–42, during which he began to employ the sermon primarily as an instrument of awakening and pastoral leadership, is the period of his most sustained and intensive homiletical effort. Faced with the responsibility of leading a community that had become casual about its religious beliefs and increasingly divided into warring parties identified with class and economic power, Edwards had to pull the community into some kind of manageable unity and revitalize its faith. He now directed his sermons to a particular people, shifting the focus from his own religious meditations and beliefs to the beliefs and conduct of his congregation. This implies no less emphasis upon what he actually believed, but it implies a new objectivism in the expression of those beliefs. He now had to enter the psychological and social milieu of the Northampton community and express his thought in the idiom of the people.

Inevitably during the early 1730s, Edwards was preoccupied with issues of social morality and moral agency. He observed that the young people of the town were morally reckless and indifferent to traditional religious sanctions, while their elders were engaged in business practices similarly reckless. Indeed, he seems to have felt that breaches of honor and trust in business were more in need of correction than the various lusts of youth, according to the proportionate emphasis in his sermons. And when it came to the reformation of conduct, Edwards directly engaged one of the national, or international, issues of the day: whether or not mankind's moral character was corrigible or naturally amenable to human effort. The age of the Enlightenment had made much of human potential, and throughout Edwards's life he had heard of and even read Christian authors who argued for a natural capacity to improve one's spiritual condition through one's own efforts. Such liberal leanings were identified by the term "Arminian" – a term no minister of Puritan New England applied to himself, only to others. But even Edwards himself acknowledged that as a youth he had once thought the opposing Calvinist position of one's essential helplessness a "horrible doctrine."[17]

Given his role as minister to the people of Northampton and his mature commitment to the Calvinist doctrine of justification by faith alone, Edwards opted for a radical theological assessment of Northampton's complex problems: they were all manifestations of sin. Because he believed that all human civilization culminated in theology and that all natural laws were congruent with the laws of God, Edwards could easily perceive all aspects of the human condition as directly dependent upon that central issue of Christian doctrine, salvation from sin. If the people of Northampton could be awakened and, through God's free grace, saved, then the multitudinous issues of church and state might also be rectified in a true Christian community.

Near the outset of his ministry, Edwards had stated his foundational position to the people in the fall of 1730, and when the Boston clergy invited Stoddard's young successor to address them the following summer, he selected that very sermon for his first venture into the colonial "world," preaching what would be printed as *God Glorified in the Work of Redemption, by the Greatness of Man's Dependence upon Him, in the Whole of It* (1731). In what would become a hallmark of his ministry, Edwards had broadcast to the world, through the medium of print, the major issues he deliberated with his congregation, making the parochial pastorate a threshold to the international arena of religious polemics. *God Glorified* is an important sermon because it is the second installment, after the *Quaestio*, of Edwards's anti-Arminian argument validating man's absolute helplessness before a sovereign God. The sermon is also stylistically impressive as an example of Edwards's most metaphysical preaching, where he plays ingeniously upon the prepositions "of," "by," "through," and "in," to dramatize the completeness of man's dependence. The sermon's rhetoric and message were attention-getting, and the Boston clergy voted to have it published – something they did not always do.[18]

Back in Northampton, weekly sermons had to address various issues related to the reform of daily life, and the fact that every sermon was very sharply focused resulted in arguments that might seem to stray from the confines of thoroughgoing Calvinism. Thus, *The Duty of Charity to the Poor* emphasizes the necessity of practical moral effort to please God,[19] while *The Pure in Heart Blessed* celebrates the happiness of those who simply sit back to appreciate the glory of God.[20] Edwards is attempting to clarify specific aspects of conduct and religious experience while motivating his flock to pursue a subtle and even paradoxical agenda. Moral conduct and striving after faith do not save anyone, he insists, but he hints that a sense of "fitness" encourages the pursuit of such instruments, or secondary causes, as they are *associated* with the reception of saving grace. But the issue of salvation from sin – the key issue – had to be handled in a way that made it both clear and tangible as a whole. Somehow, Edwards had to demonstrate that all his people's failings were one, and that the solution was also one; then, perhaps, there would be a way of holiness that was apparent to all.

Christ, the Light of the World, written during Edwards's New York pastorate, first enunciated his enthusiasm for the "most excellent and glorious similitude" of light, and in it he explores the ways in which the metaphor represents the new sensibility of the regenerate person.[21] Subsequently he composed *A Spiritual Understanding of Divine Things Denied to the Unregenerate* (1723), in which he attempts to specify more objectively and abstractly the concepts implied in light imagery,[22] and a sermon on James 1:17, "God is the Father of Lights" (1728, unpublished manuscript), in which he alternatively considers the poetry of light imagery, materially and spiritually, here and hereafter.

Finally, in 1733, Edwards delivered to the people of Northampton a lecture in which he brought together material from his previous sermons, as well as related notebook ruminations, in a definitive interpretation of divine light, published at the request of the hearers in 1734 as *A Divine and Supernatural Light, Immediately Imparted to the Soul by the Spirit of God, Shown to Be Both a Scriptural, and Rational Doctrine*.[23] This is Edwards's most perfectly crafted sermon in lecture format (or perhaps any other), a definition of the manner in which one is saved from sin through *experiential* knowledge of Christ, or a taste of the divine. If sin was the root of all Northampton's problems, then Edwards herein offered a vivid model of the solution: not fear and trembling in the face of hellfire, but hope for a new sense of the divine beauty of Scripture's general revelation and a conviction of its truth and reality imparted by God as directly as a beam of light. Of course, Edwards preached hellfire sermons during this period, if only because that was the Northampton idiom, but it is no fluke that his first publication from Northampton is a vivid delineation of joy in the beauty of holiness and a corresponding code of conduct that is available to the simple as well as the learned. He turned the people's heads, and they seemed to have a new seriousness and curiosity about religious matters.

Shortly thereafter, Edwards noticed signs of an awakening within the congregation that far overshadowed anything he had previously observed, including reaction to the 1727 earthquake. Even the reckless youth of the town seemed to respond; indeed, the youth seemed to lead the way, and Edwards appealed directly to them with *Youth and the Pleasures of Piety* in May 1734.[24] In other sermons he continued to hector the adult congregation for their laxity. Finally, Edwards framed a new external threat to the religious culture of the community of which he at least had long been aware, but which was just now being talked about in the Connecticut Valley: Arminianism. In November he once more took up his anti-Arminian theme of complete dependence upon God in two public lectures on Romans 4:5, having the doctrine, "We are justified only by faith in Christ, and not by any manner of virtue or goodness of our own." This argument seemed to stimulate queries among the people, as if addressing long-forgotten issues, and soon the town was in a religious ferment that would be the most intense Northampton had ever experienced – even under Solomon Stoddard – although it lasted for only about five months during the winter and spring of 1734–5. Edwards wrote to one of his friends in Boston, the Reverend Benjamin Colman, describing the events, and before long he was renowned as an authority on awakenings because of an expanded account, published in London as *A Faithful Narrative of the Surprizing Work of God in the Conversion of Many Hundred Souls in Northampton, and the Neighbouring Towns and Villages of [Hampshire] in New-England* (1737). Homiletically, this episode is equally noteworthy, for it occasioned Edwards's only publication of a volume of collected sermons, *Discourses on Various Important Subjects, Nearly Concerning the Great Affair of the Soul's Eternal Salvation* (Boston, 1738). The volume, underwritten by the people of Northampton even while facing the expense of building a new meetinghouse, was a memorial of the awakening as well as a tribute to the preaching of their pastor.

For his part, Edwards did not allow this homiletical opportunity to pass without making a full improvement of it. Most obvious in the volume is the first discourse, *Justification by Faith Alone*, Edwards's lectures that were believed to have occasioned the awakening. However, the "discourse" is much longer than any that Edwards could have preached in two installments; indeed, it is between four and five preaching units long and actually comprises about half the pages of the volume. In fact, it is his first published treatise, and an example of Edwards's ability to radically expand sermon materials into full-blown treatises, as he was to do most famously in *A Treatise Concerning Religious Affections* (1746). Three other sermons in the volume, also requested by the people, embody the minatory and hortatory elements of awakening preaching, while the concluding sermon, *The Excellency of Jesus Christ*, was selected by Edwards himself because "a discourse on such an evangelical subject, would properly follow others that were chiefly legal and awakening, and . . . something of the excellency of the Savior, was proper to succeed those things that were to show the necessity of salvation."

Not the least fascinating piece in this volume, however, is the "Preface," Edwards's most substantial public statement concerning his own literary style.²⁵ As an introduction to the five discourses, it is appropriately defensive in strategy, for Edwards assumes that his Calvinistic theological posture is the traditional or "standard" one that is being challenged by a new post-Enlightenment, human-centered, Arminian faction. He states his argument in five substantial paragraphs, constituting the body of the "Preface," wherein he takes up the allegation of obscurantism through "speculative niceties, and subtle distinctions" that the Arminians have made against his Calvinistic doctrine. Edwards argues that such distinctions are necessary and rational if the Scripture's mysteries require them, and the "method" (formal organization) of his traditional sermon is implicitly justified by the necessity of making such complexities clear to lay people. He quips that St. Paul's epistles also contain such fine distinctions but go unchallenged because they happen to be canonical. Finally, he notes that the successful revival occasioned by his preaching seems to give empirical proof of God's approval of his doctrine. So the Arminians were left facing off against a triumvirate of Edwards, St. Paul, and God.

Edwards's argument embodies a truism of homiletics: that style is a badge of ecclesiastical and even doctrinal allegiance. The old Puritan plain style was not merely easy to understand; it stood in aesthetic opposition to that of the Anglican Lancelot Andrewes and other high-churchmen. Similarly, in several introductory and concluding paragraphs, Edwards assumes the posture of one whom the people of the frontier have insisted upon elevating into the international arena of print, who is dubious of his public reception there and certain that his style is not "modish" or even "polite" (that is, urban) – characteristics Edwards attributes to the Arminians. Indeed, he goes so far as to insist that the pastoral sermons "now appear in that very plain and unpolished dress, in which they were first prepared and delivered," a claim belied by the evidence of the extant manuscripts. Edwards was a conscious stylist and a meticulous craftsman of verbal nuance in his revisions, but his "Preface" is a propagandistic shot across the bow of his opponents. He represents himself and his western congregation as preservers of the traditional, pure faith in defiance of eastern, urban corruptions.

The publication of Edwards's five discourses in 1738 marked the high point of his pastoral preaching, and the sermons of the 1730s, taken as a whole, have a technical mastery and consistency of finish unmatched elsewhere in his career. Of course, Edwards did not have this historical perspective, but he knew by 1738 that all was not well with the revival; indeed, his "Preface" concludes by asking his people to "lament our declensions." Other sermons preached at the time were more to the point. As early as the summer of 1736, Edwards had preached *A City on a Hill*,[26] cautioning his people against various abuses and insisting that habitual Christian practice was the only thing that would validate the revival. By 1738, in an unpublished manuscript sermon on Nehemiah 2:20, he was even appealing to civic pride, querying,

> Was there ever a town in New England so much set up to public view in religious aspects – as a city that can't be hid – and was there ever a town in the country on whose holy and Christian conversation, [the] honor and influence of religion did so much depend, and whose good behavior would tend so much to build up the city of God, and that ill behavior tend so much to pull it down?[27]

But the town did not respond, at least not to the extent of Edwards's original hopes and expectations, and the experience forever liberated him from any innocent preconceptions he may have entertained about the transformative power of Stoddardean-style awakenings.

The end of the decade shows Edwards experiencing a kind of homiletical restlessness. He had preached sermons and lectures previously in multiple preaching units in order to accommodate more complex or comprehensive arguments to the pulpit. However, after about 1735 this activity increased markedly, culminating (for the time being) in a series of sixteen sermons on I Corinthians 13:1–10 in 1738 and a series of thirty sermons on Isaiah 51:8 in 1739, both published after Edwards's death as *Charity and Its Fruits* and *A History of the Work of Redemption*, respectively.[28] The latter effort amounted to preaching a full-blown treatise in the pulpit. Just what his congregation thought of this new thematic concentration for weeks at a time is unclear. What is clear is Edwards's effort to place personal religious experience in larger social and historical contexts through these sermon series, undoubtedly in an attempt to lift the conversion experience beyond the transitory self-absorption that often characterized it.

Whether or not Edwards had intended to move beyond revivalism, the year 1740 swept him back into it with the arrival of George Whitefield in New England and the eruption of what has come to be called the Great Awakening. Edwards supported the evangelism of the English itinerant, even inviting him to preach in Northampton, but as the new revival spread with frightening and socially destabilizing energy through the activities of persons such as James Davenport and his impolite cohort, Edwards again exerted his leadership through preaching. However, this time he attempted to advance the cause of revival in a new critical spirit, providing the intellectual heft necessary to disarm opponents and destructive supporters alike. He left the pastoral context to preach "nationally," as it were, preaching the commencement sermon at Yale College on September 10, 1741. This sermon enumerated and critically analyzed the most-debated epiphenomena of the Great Awakening while supporting the revivals generally. Enlarged and printed as *The Distinguishing Marks of a Work of the Spirit of God*,[29] the sermon represents the first installment of Edwards's great critique of religious experience, followed by *Some Thoughts Concerning the Present Revival of Religion in New-England* and *A Treatise Concerning Religious Affections*.

Edwards was an active participant in the Great Awakening in a more conventional sense, too, exhorting his weary congregation and even participating in the definitive activity of the 1740s revivals, itineration. The great homiletical memorial of this period is his superb awakening sermon, *Sinners in the Hands of an Angry God*.[30] The modern reader is likely to be more familiar with this work than with any other by Edwards, for his enemies and friends have jointly made it the Edwards icon. It needs no apology, but a few points are worth noting. First, Edwards preached it in June 1741 to his own congregation to no particular effect. A couple of weeks later the pastor of Enfield invited Edwards to preach there because the Enfield congregants had seemed intractable, and the Great Awakening repeatedly demonstrated the Whitefield lesson, that nothing was more efficacious than a visiting exhorter. Edwards selected his used *Sinners* manuscript (his invariable practice when preaching pastoral sermons away from home) and preached with great efficacy. As happened many times during the Great Awakening, the congregation virtually rioted when the preacher had hardly begun, so it is impossible to say that they actually heard the sermon. In any case, Edwards published the sermon as a memorial of his proficiency as an awakening preacher, and *Sinners* is the last sermon he published, excepting ones for ordination, funeral, farewell, or other such special occasions. After Enfield, Edwards apparently preached the sermon a number of times while itinerating, though there were no more explosions as in Enfield.

One further aspect of *Sinners* worth consideration is that it is not actually a hellfire sermon, though it is an awakening sermon. The element of terror in the sermon is not so much the fear of torment as it is the fear of sudden death. Edwards hit upon the true issue separating most believers from fear of judgment: time. All know they will die and be judged, *but not now*. Sometime later they will deal with this. But Edwards inculcates with draconian persistence the obvious fact that no one knows how or when he or she will die, and that death and judgment may happen in a moment. This is eschatological realism, not the hellfire of conventional awakening sermons – even Edwards's.

The Great Awakening, like the earlier surprising conversions, began to evanesce before many months had passed. Edwards had preached to great effect, intellectually and sensationally, but the transformation of society still remained to be accomplished. He led his congregation through a renewal of the church covenant in 1742, an attempt to consolidate the gains of the recent awakening, though subsequent events suggest that his hopes may again have been misplaced.

The final phase of Edwards's preaching career, extending from 1743 to 1758, was inaugurated when he preached a series of sermons – how many is uncertain, the original manuscripts being lost – in which he attempted to differentiate definitively between the signs of authentic religious experience and the many false impressions of it that had arisen during the recent awakenings. The outcome of these sermons or lectures was published in 1746 as *A Treatise Concerning Religious Affections*.[31] The treatise is one of Edwards's greatest, perhaps *the* greatest, and it was preached in Northampton, at least in part. Could this learned and laborious work ever have been efficacious pastoral preaching? Certainly there is a great difference between *Justification by Faith Alone* and *Religious Affections*, even allowing for varying amplification of the sermon texts in preparing the treatises. But the trend is clear enough: Edwards had moved from sharing a pastoral concern with the larger world to sharing a message for the larger world with his congregation as pastoral preaching. By 1743, it seems, the literary Edwards was beginning to dominate the pastoral Edwards, and given what is known about his new use of radical outlining in regular sermons, sermons of the more routine sort cannot have had the polish or depth that the sermon-sophisticated Northampton congregation had learned over the years to expect.

If Edwards's pastoral sermons were perceptibly less fully prepared and his preaching thus less compelling to his congregation, Edwards did not otherwise relent as a shepherd. Indeed, the post-awakening 1740s were the most turbulent years in his Northampton pastorate. Having concluded in the aftermath of the Great Awakening that the best indicator of grace was daily conduct or characteristic behavior, Edwards addressed the various age, gender, and social subdivisions of his parish with a new directness concerning conduct, and when complaints came to him concerning lewd talk and sexual harassment by certain lively young bumpkins, he joined the cause of reform in all earnestness. The result was the "bad book" episode, an essentially trivial event that apparently seriously undermined his reputation in a community that expected its pastor to be an astute politician as well as a profound thinker. But this episode was soon eclipsed by Edwards's decision, in December 1748, to require a formal profession by candidates for church membership, flying in the face of Northampton's traditional "Stoddardean way" of virtually open admission. Thus the decade of the 1740s was a time of tension between pastor and flock that seemed only to increase as Edwards attempted to resolve issues through decisive acts of pastoral leadership.

Meanwhile, Edwards's regional preaching activities continued to expand in the light of his renown as a leader of the Great Awakening, and he was frequently asked to deliver ordination sermons. He preached most of his printed ordination sermons between 1743 and 1750, sermons such as *The Great Concern of a Watchman for Souls* for Jonathan Judd in 1743, *The True Excellency of a Minister of the Gospel* for Robert Abercrombie in 1744, *The Church's Marriage to Her Sons, and to Her God* for Samuel Buell in 1746, *Sons of Oil, Heavenly Lights* for Joseph Ashley in 1747, and *Christ the Great Example of Gospel Ministers* for Job Strong in 1749.[32] Different ordination sermons emphasized such themes as the minister's role as protector of his people, the need for balance between intellect and affection, the importance of rich imaginative resources for explication of the Scripture, and warnings against lay exhortation, separatism, and other abuses of the recent revivals. However, a common thread connecting all of them, even intensifying as the decade wore on, is that of the heroic ministry. Traditionally, Puritans had called ministers "ambassadors of Christ," but they had also stressed that ministers were in themselves "earthen vessels," and thus as weak as other persons. However, in his ordination sermons, Edwards asked ministers to rise as individuals to heroic, even self-sacrificial roles as ministers, and thus living embodiments of Christ's dying love. His effort was evidently an attempt to insulate ordinary pastors from charges of laxity, as had been made by itinerants during the Great Awakening, as well as guarding against opportunities for separatist motions such as had divided a number of churches after the Great Awakening.

In a more programmatic effort to redirect post-revival energies, Edwards joined an international movement to invoke the millennium. In 1744 he had preached *Approaching the End of God's Grand Design* to instill in his congregation a sense of the larger context of all earthly spiritual movements.[33] In 1747 he preached a fast day sermon making a concrete proposal to realize God's universal design in earthly activity of a new kind: an international union in extraordinary prayer. Taking up the proposal of some Scottish clerical correspondents, Edwards strove to lead his congregation and, ultimately, the Christian world in a new, perhaps less disruptive movement of religious renewal. He enlarged his sermon and published it in 1747 as *An Humble*

Attempt to Promote Explicit Agreement and Visible Union of God's People in Extraordinary Prayer.[34] In this instance, Edwards's effort to reassert religious leadership met with a tepid response both at home and abroad.

By the end of the decade, the more immediate issue of qualifications for church membership had crowded out all others in Northampton. Edwards clung to his position absolutely, arguing that it was the only one justifiable by Scripture, and the majority of church members clung to the "Stoddardean way" absolutely. There have been numerous interpretations of this extraordinary breach, and whether reverence for Stoddard's precedent, the "bad book" episode, changing social and economic conditions in the community, or other factors played the larger role will continue to be debated. But it should not be forgotten that for several years Edwards had ceased to put the same literary effort into his pastoral sermons that he had up through the Great Awakening, and that his congregation undoubtedly would have noticed this "laxness" on his part, especially as he continued to demand new strictness and commitment from them. In any event, the church requested a separation, an ecclesiastical council of the Hampshire Association backed its request, and Jonathan Edwards was effectively fired. In July 1750 he preached his *Farewell Sermon,* one of his most perfectly crafted sermons. This is not to say that it would ever be anyone's favorite by Edwards, but it does what it was meant to do brilliantly. It is not quite a farewell, for its thesis is that only Christ dissolves the bond between ministers and their people, or resolves their controversies, and that only at the day of judgment. The sermon is an *apologia,* but its tone embodies the steady gaze of a sheriff confronting a lynch mob, while the argument minutely analyzes the respective actions of minister and people with a detective's detachment. Indeed, the sermon has a pervasive sense of finality, but not a jot of self-pity – only the sense that Edwards sincerely believes that he has done as well as his Master could have expected of a mere mortal, even a Christian hero. His summation characterizes his Northampton ministry as an effort to instill "the high, mysterious, evangelical doctrines of the religion of Jesus Christ, and their genuine effects in true experimental religion."[35] Perhaps that was not what the Northampton elders had really wanted.

With his dismissal from Northampton, Edwards entered upon the final episode of his preaching career, the Stockbridge Indian mission. He had been given alternatives – offers of positions from Scotland to Virginia – and he had made candidating appearances in several New England churches, but perhaps because of the example of his personal hero, the Indian missionary David Brainerd, he chose a post that would seem the least appropriate for a leading intellectual and sophisticated preacher. After a trial period in the winter and spring of 1751, when Edwards went out to Stockbridge alone and attempted to work up a sermon format that would be effective during simultaneous translation, he finally moved his family and his papers to the Stockbridge settlement in October 1751. The remainder of his pastoral career would be spent serving the needs of a small English congregation of about twelve families and preaching to a shifting population of Mahican (Stockbridge) and Mohawk Indians who were long before his arrival accustomed to the abuse and deceit of their supposed English friends.

Edwards's Stockbridge sermons are not great sermons, but they do illustrate a great mind at work, addressing the cause of Christ in the wilderness. He preached mostly Northampton sermons to the English congregation, often the good old ones from the 1730s. He did compose some new ones for them, however, such as *Sacramental Union in Christ* (1751), a reassertion of his position on qualifications for communion in case anyone imagined that his mind had been changed by his ordeal in Northampton.[36] But it is the earlier Indian sermons that represent the most imaginative homiletical effort by Edwards. He modified his customary form by removing numbered heads and division titles while preserving the form's aesthetic and logical structure. Sermons for the Native Americans had to be much shorter than sermons to the English congregation, but his early Indian sermons are well written out in single columns in large booklets – as if Edwards saw himself beginning a new preaching career.

Beneath the external form of the sermon, however, Edwards made even greater innovations. His first sermon to the Indians, *The Things That Belong to True Religion* (1751), begins with the usual biblical text, but instead of his customary analysis of the text for its theological implications, Edwards rehearses it as a story.[37] In this case it is the story of Peter's converting Cornelius, the first non-Jewish convert to Christianity. Edwards encouragingly identifies Cornelius as a "warrior." He then narrates the history of the westward spread of Christianity, concluding with his own standing before the Indians. This substitution of narration for exegesis was the pattern to be followed in his Indian sermons generally, as if Edwards had concluded that a good story or vivid picture would be more memorable and persuasive to the Indians than the most powerful logical analysis. Significantly, Edwards continued to use his personal religious vocabulary, emphasizing "excellency," "sweetness," the heart, and the loveliness of Christ. Many of these new Indian sermons were, in fact, based on Northampton sermons, some even synthesizing the material of a whole sermon series.

Perhaps the most important alteration of the sermon for Indian consumption is a radical shift from analysis to synthesis as the vehicle of exposition. As a result, his sermons to Native Americans are often like primers of Edwards's thought. His theology is not altered or simplified, but simple, comprehensive statements replace the analytical meditations of his former sermons, and some sermons, such as *He That Believeth Shall Be Saved* (1751), offer a grand synthesis of Edwardsean Christianity in a few pages.[38] The simple diction and sentence structure in the Indian sermons may lead a reader to suspect that the message is simple, but a sermon such as *God Is Infinitely Strong* (1753), based on the book of Job, presents a very intellectual conception of God, including Edwards's occasionalist concept of continuous creation and some of the latest scientific thought on the universe.[39] Edwards displays in these sermons a genius for compressing his philosophical theology into a brief talk without simplifying his ideas much, however simple the diction.

Finally, perhaps the most important new thematic emphasis in this last phase of Edwards's sermon composition is that on warfare. Just after the end of the Great Awakening, Edwards had preached a sermon on the English expedition against the French fortification of Louisburg on Cape Breton Island, *The Duties of Christians in a Time of War* (1745). Over the next decade, his preoccupation with war gained in intensity along with the French and Indian War of the Stockbridge period. He preached to the Mahican Indians *In the Name of the Lord of Hosts* (1755), a reminder that the English, like the French, depended on the Indians to do much of their fighting. The climax of Edwards's war preaching came soon after when, in the light of Braddock's defeat, he wrote *God's People Tried by a Battle Lost* (1755), wherein he observes, "the affair of war is one of the most important of all the affairs of the universe: the state of the world of mankind principally depends upon it."[40] The English had had their greatest setback of the French and Indian Wars, but before offering comfort, Edwards explicitly analyzes the moral failures and weaknesses of the English. The war sermons demonstrate Edwards's familiarity with many aspects of political, economic, and military affairs, but they also provide a concrete context for his millenarian speculations. Indeed, the cause of the Protestant English against the Catholic French represented a new public venue for the people's religious commitment in the years after the waning of the Great Awakening.

In the various phases of his preaching career, then, Edwards adjusted homiletical form and practice to meet his needs as a thinker, pastor, and author. Whether perfecting the expression of his unique religious sensibility in the first phase, taking up the practical authority of pastoral leadership in the second, or exploring beyond the limits of conventional pastoral preaching in the third, Edwards fully exploited the sermon genre, the essential medium through which he first published his thought throughout his life.

During the eighteenth century, Jonathan Edwards and his clerical contemporaries lived – like all persons in all ages – in a time of transition. In the homiletical arena there were two broad trends, one of which Edwards espoused and one he resisted. The trend he espoused resulted from the rapid growth of the domestic press during the century, and it involved a media translation of the sermon from oratory to literature. The vast majority of sermons remained oratorical events, but increasingly leading preachers sought the wider circulation and permanence of print for their most important statements. The literary Edwards was a natural proponent of print, and even when living on the frontier he increasingly exploited the medium of print, employing the aid of friends, such as Thomas Foxcroft in Boston, to see his works through the press. As a result, Edwards has long been recognized as America's greatest preacher (read "author of sermons") and theologian.

The trend that Edwards resisted was a transition from the traditional sermon form with its Ramist exoskeleton of numbered heads to the newer form of the essay-sermon. He exploited the aura of logic in the traditional sermon's formal structure to provide openings for the arbitrary exegesis of Scripture and the imaginative utilization of imagery and metaphor through which he developed the argumentative mosaics characteristic of his sermons. He seems to have appreciated that the complexity of his argumentative strategies would have been less easily accommodated within the "line of argument" of the rational discourses favored by the liberals and proto-Unitarians. Politically, of course, Edwards had no desire to wear the rhetorical dress of the opposing camp. Nevertheless, especially during the second half of his ministry, Edwards did tend to downplay the statement of doctrine – the keystone of the traditional sermon – by integrating it as merely a "proposition" or "thing to be considered" in the course of argument, making at least a gesture of accommodation to the trend of the times.

On the local level, however, Edwards initiated what may have been his most radical adjustment when in 1747 he preached the hellfire sermon, *Yield to God's Word, or Be Broken by His Hand.* After a recapitulation of his customary hellfire rhetoric, Edwards observed in concluding the sermon, "when I went about preparing this discourse, it was with considerable discouragement . . . so many had been offered with so little apparent effect that I thought with myself, I know not what to say further."[41] And for the remainder of his career in Northampton and Stockbridge, Edwards was not to return to full-blown hellfire preaching. The revivalist had seen the limitations of revival preaching, and while a fear of damnation was only rational in the context of his faith, it seems Edwards no longer saw the Stoddardean emphasis upon fear as a positive dimension of preaching.

In sermons such as *The Way of Holiness* (1722) and "Heaven Is a World of Love" (the conclusion of the sermon series *Charity and Its Fruits* [1738]), Jonathan Edwards sketched the lineaments of his commanding vision.

Between such exalted moments, Edwards inculcated the intricate structure of Christian doctrine and strove to represent the authentic experience of realization that would validate the presence of saving grace. He stirred up the indifferent and attempted to convince hardy frontiersmen of the reality of a spiritual world sustaining a shadow they knew as the "real" world. As a result of his genius and unremitting hard work, Edwards left a literary legacy unequaled in the literature of the American sermon for its depth of thought and power of expression.

Notes

1. Edwin C. Dargan, *A History of Preaching* (New York: Hodder and Stoughton, Doran, 1905–12), 2:158.
2. Solomon Stoddard, *The Benefit of the Gospel, to Those That Are Wounded in Spirit* (Boston, 1713), 181.
3. "Miscell." 40, WJE, 13:222.
4. For an extensive consideration of Edwards's homiletical practices, see my "Introduction" to WJE, 10:3–258.
5. See *Personal Narrative*, WJE, 16:795–8.
6. WJE, 10:478–9.
7. Ibid., 13:163–4.
8. Ibid., 789–90, 796.
9. WJE, 10:406.
10. Ibid., 296.
11. Ibid., 535–46.
12. The oration, or *Quaestio*, is printed and translated in WJE, 14:55–66.
13. WJE, 14:116–33.
14. Ibid., 67–115.
15. Jonathan Edwards, *The Defects of Preachers Reproved* (Boston, 1724), 13.
16. WJE, 14:312–13.
17. Ibid., 16:792.
18. Ibid., 17:200–16.
19. Ibid., 371–404.
20. Ibid., 59–86.
21. WJE, 10:535–46.
22. Ibid., 14:70–96.
23. Ibid., 17:408–26.
24. Ibid., 19:81–90.
25. Ibid., 794–8.
26. Ibid., 539–59.
27. Edwards's sermon manuscript, Beinecke Rare Book and Manuscript Library, Yale University, August 1738.
28. See WJE, 8:129, and 9:111–528.
29. See WJE, 4:226–88.
30. See WJE, 22:404–18.
31. WJE, 2:84–461.
32. All are in WJE, 25 (forthcoming).

33. Ibid.
34. Ibid., and WJE, 5:309–436.
35. Ibid.
36. Ibid.
37. Ibid.
38. See Wilson H. Kimnach, Kenneth P. Minkema, and Douglas A. Sweeney, eds., *The Sermons of Jonathan Edwards: A Reader,* (New Haven, CT: Yale University Press, 1999), 111–20.
39. WJE, 25.
40. Ibid. The other war sermons previously mentioned are also in WJE, 25.
41. WJE, 25.

6 Edwards as revivalist

HARRY S. STOUT

In a profound sense, revivals were in Jonathan Edwards's genes. Were there to be a spiritual genome, "revival" and "Jonathan Edwards" would make a perfect match. From his father, Timothy Edwards, he would acquire the tools and ambition to be America's greatest preacher and theologian. And from his maternal grandfather, Solomon Stoddard, he would inherit a revivalist role model without peer. When Edwards succeeded Stoddard in the wealthy and powerful Northampton, Massachusetts, pulpit, he succeeded an evangelistic legend. Under Stoddard's impassioned and terrifying preaching, Northampton residents went through five "harvests" of mass conversions marked by sudden jumps in church membership. The challenge for young Edwards was to replicate his grandfather's achievement.

Like his grandfather, Edwards would strategize for revival, and always at the center of that strategizing would be the young people. In April 1734, the death of a young person in the congregation set off a general concern among the youth, and in the months that followed, Edwards saw "soul concerns" spread through the town. Soon revivals spread from the youth to the adults. In all, Edwards noted, over three hundred people were savingly converted; well over two hundred were admitted into church membership in the two-year period – at one point as many as one hundred in one day. Equally pleasing to Edwards was the atmosphere of harmony and Christian behavior that prevailed in notoriously contentious Northampton. Even more encouraging were reports from nearly thirty communities up and down the Connecticut River Valley attesting to the revival spirit in their churches.

As reports of the revivals in Northampton spread, religious leaders throughout Anglo-America began to inquire into the truth and nature of the phenomena. To satisfy their curiosity, Edwards wrote what would become a best seller: *A Faithful Narrative of the Surprising Work of God in the Conversion of Many Hundred Souls in Northampton*.[1] The pamphlet was published in London in 1737 and in Boston a year later. Subsequent translations soon appeared in German and Dutch, putting Edwards and his church before the eyes of an international audience.

Like the incipient scientist he was, Edwards presented readers with an astute social and demographic profile of the town of Northampton, followed by a sophisticated portrait of the religious psychology that he observed among his parishioners. In particular, he made famous two of his converts, the dying Abigail Hutchinson and the four-year-old Phebe Bartlett, whose religious experiences he described almost clinically in psychological terms. *A Faithful Narrative* became nothing less than the model for conducting and monitoring future revivals worldwide.

Tragically for Edwards, at the very time his triumphalist account appeared in print, his "Little Awakening" was coming to an ignominious end. In June 1735, Edwards's uncle Joseph Hawley, certain that he was damned and incapable of conversion, killed himself by slitting his throat. The tragedy cast a pall over the town, and from that point on the revival waned precipitously. A disconsolate Edwards watched as his congregation, including many of those who were supposedly converted, returned to their "vicious habits" and general indifference to religion.

Though disappointed in the failure of his revival to promote lasting peace and piety, Edwards never gave up hope. The reason is to be found in a sermon series of no less than thirty installments preached in 1739 and later published as *A History of the Work of Redemption.*[2] Though primarily concerned with critical historical problems regarding the biblical narratives, the original sermon series, which Edwards intended (but did not live long enough) to turn into a major treatise, had as its immediate inspiration the Northampton revivals he shepherded five years earlier. In these sermons, Edwards depicted revivals as the operational vehicle that God would employ to accomplish his magisterial plan of cosmic redemption.

In seeking a form to describe God's plan of redemption and the revivals' central place in it, Edwards bypassed systematic theology in favor of cosmic narrative. For Christian faith to survive and lead the way into a new heaven and a new earth, it would need to don new garments. By 1739 and even earlier, Edwards began to suspect that "history" was, in fact, larger than the antiquarian terms by which it was then known; indeed, it was larger than theology itself. In his evolving thought, carefully recorded and organized in reams of notebooks, commentaries, and sermons, history was emerging as nothing less than a container for the synthetic whole of theology, and indeed of God's innermost self-revelation.[3] Gone were parochial notions of history as genealogy or the simple chronicle of human achievements and sequential events. Gone, even, was the larger but still theologically restrained notion, familiar to Puritans always, of history as the chronicle of "God's Wonder-Working Providence" on earth. Edwards had an even grander conception of history, capacious enough to contain all these ideas – and more.

Earlier Protestant thinkers such as Philip Melanchthon, John Calvin, and William Ames had thought of theology as the ultimate canvas on which to record the being of God and his relationship to his creation. Whatever distance the reformers may have traveled from Rome, they had still retained a medieval sense of systematic theology as the queen of the sciences. Edwards would substitute history. Edwards's history was not the history of William Bradford or Cotton Mather, a mere recording of New England towns and their ministers under the nationalistic gloss of *Magnalia Christi Americana*. Nor, as historian John Wilson convincingly demonstrates, was it history in the emerging Enlightenment sense, the "scientific" history of politics and great men based strictly on empirical observation with no recourse to supernatural revelation. By comparison, Edwards's history was, in Wilson's terms, a "profoundly unhistoriographical [method] in any modern sense."[4]

Alongside these modern senses of history, however, lies another, more mythic sense of history that is best labeled "metanarrative." The modern model of history, that we might label "ordinary" or "historiographical," or in Edwards's term, "actual" time, is simple chronology – history measured in minutes and years and recorded in written records. But as anthropologists and biblical scholars remind us, it is also possible to order and understand history in what we might term mythic or, in Edwards's terms, "divine" or "virtual" time – history as seen from God's time-transcending eternal perspective. Central to this model would be separate but overlapping senses of time, as in the creation myths common to all religions. But, as we shall see, Edwards had an even larger story in mind – a narrative of "redemption." To frame the metanarrative of redemption, Edwards would employ historiographical time from every source he could lay his hands on, both sacred and profane. But he would also subject it to the most important time in the narrative – divine time. For all of his piety, perhaps *because* of his piety, Edwards was not afraid to see time from God's vantage point. He would take his narrative where others before him were afraid to tread. If a majestic enough story could be constructed, Edwards speculated, it could contain all the doctrines and philosophical underpinnings of systematic theology in a more compelling – and popularly accessible – format. In other words, a metanarrative method could do all that systematic theology, and for that matter historiography, could do and more.

Edwards's history incorporated philosophy, theology, and narrative as a synthetic whole. Earlier he had established the proposition that "heaven is a world of love," a metaphysical state infused with the innermost being and character of the Trinity. So too, he proposed, earth was a world of pulsating divine energy, and hell a perversion of love that set in motion the intergalactic supernatural conflict between God and Satan with earth as the prize. What if the history of all three – heaven, earth, and hell – were integrated into one narrative, a narrative superior to systematic theology for its drama, and to earthbound historiography for its prophetic inspiration?

At the same time that Edwards discovered his true artistic genre, he located the organizing theme for this history as "salvation" or "redemption," the most sublime theme of all, grander even than creation. If Edwards's vision bore a close similarity to Scripture itself, that should not be surprising to modern scholars. Scripture narratives, as Erich Auerbach and Hans Frei have shown, represented a new literary form, a "realistic narrative."[5]

By 1757, on the eve of his premature death, the grand vision had formally matured into nothing less than a Descartes-like new "method" for conceiving religion and thinking about God. When, in 1757, the trustees of the College of New Jersey invited Edwards to be their new president, he hesitated primarily because his history was not completed. In a sense, all of his great treatises, written in six-month bursts between 1750 and 1757, were ingredients to be pasteurized and refitted into the triworld narrative. Those who see "the end" of Edwards's scholarly career as his all-fronts assault on Arminianism and Deism miss the larger goal. Those treatises were intended only to remove so much heterodox debris from the highway so that the way would be cleared to his true destination: the narrative history of redemption. In his often-cited letter to the Princeton trustees, he revealed his ambition:

> I have had on my mind and heart, (which I long ago began, not with any view to publication,) a great work, which I call *History of the Work of Redemption*, a body of divinity in an entire new method, being thrown into the form of a history; considering the affair of Christian Theology, as the whole of it, in each part, stands in reference to the great work of redemption by Jesus Christ; which I suppose to be, of all others, the grand design of God, and the *summum* and *ultimum* of all the divine operations and decrees; particularly considering all parts of the grand scheme, in their historical order.[6]

As he continued to describe his project to the trustees, Edwards made plain how his new history would differ from prevailing notions in several particulars. First, it would be a history in which theology was subordinated to history rather than vice versa. Second, and more shocking, Edwards went on in his letter to observe that his new history would be one that transcended space and recorded time, a history telling the simultaneous stories of "three worlds"– heaven, earth, and hell.

> This history will be carried on with regard to all three worlds, heaven, earth and hell; considering the connected, successive events and

alterations in each, so far as the scriptures give any light; introducing all parts of divinity in that order which is most scriptural and most natural; a method which appears to me the most beautiful and entertaining, wherein every divine doctrine will appear to the greatest advantage, in the brightest light, in the most striking manner, showing the admirable contexture and harmony of the whole.[7]

The word "method" carried with it steep claims, indeed the highest claims.

For redemptive history – and the worlds it described – Edwards's primary source was, of course, Scripture. But even here Scripture would be augmented by the history of heaven and hell as it evolved from the Church Fathers, through the Reformers and the Puritans, right down to his own Northampton revivals. Heaven and hell no less than earth had their histories, as did their citizens: angels and demons. For Edwards, each of these worlds was equally real and dynamic, a constantly evolving protean force that emanated ultimately from the mind of God. Each, moreover, was equally knowable through creation and the revelation of nature, and through the Scriptures, the revealed self-disclosure of God in his diverse created worlds. Each, therefore, required a history. These histories would not be independent of one another, but interconnected and whole, like a finely spun tapestry. Instead of connecting doctrines, Edwards would weave a story – a story that introduced all the major doctrines and philosophical underpinnings of Christian theology – but in the process, he would introduce a different, dramatic form, one that he identified as the history of redemption.

Edwards's doctrine of redemption as the central thread of his great project would not have been well suited to a systematic theology. To be grasped in all its completeness, it had to move out of the polemical confines of the schoolmen and theologians and present itself as a narrative story – indeed, the greatest story ever told. It is precisely the epic quality of *A History of Redemption* in its posthumously printed form in the nineteenth century that gave it its "enormous influence" on "popular culture."[8]

The "scheme" of redemption perfectly fitted Edwards's ambitions to move through two times with the overt goal of promoting revivals worldwide. At the outset he observed that "the work [of redemption] itself and all that pertained to it, was virtually done [i.e., in divine time] and finished [before creation], but not actually [in historiographical time]." In "virtual" time – God's time – an indivisible divine "present" engulfs earthly past and future. God's time – and only God's time – is eternal. Even heaven, though a world without end, is finite. In *A History of Heaven,* Jeffrey Burton Russell makes this important distinction: "Endless life is one thing, but God's ability to comprehend and embrace all time in one moment is another. Endlessness is perpetual, but only the existence of the entire space and time of the cosmos in one moment is eternal."9 In similar terms, Edwards pointed out that in God's time, every event merges with every other event, not in successive chronological sequence, but "several parts of one scheme . . . in which all the persons of the Trinity do conspire and all the various dispensations that belong to it are united, as the several wheels in one machine, to answer an end, and produce one effect."10

Conscious of heaven and eternity, Edwards made clear that redemption *required* the fact of sin to generate the need for salvation (hence the Fall, and not creation, marked the starting point for his narrative in "actual" time), and the "scheme" or divine plan was, in fact, eternal and "virtual." Before creation, "The persons of the Trinity were as it were confederated in a design and covenant of redemption." Indeed, "the world itself seems to have been created in order to it."11 With the historical metanarrative in mind, he prompted his congregation to expect a personally riveting narrative of the purpose for which God created them. It was, Edwards stated, a far more important history than that of creation, for creation was the means to a greater end. Since God created the world as his stage to dramatize redemption, the "end" of creation could not possibly be the happiness of his creatures, as "rationalists" and "Deists" were claiming. It had to be God's own self-glorification.12

Edwards would use the history of earth and earthly time as the spine of his narrative and interleave the worlds of heaven and hell as they intersected, so that the whole resembled "an house or temple that is building, first the workmen are sent forth, then the materials are gathered, then the ground fitted, then the foundation is laid, then the superstructure erected one part after another, till at length the topstone is laid. And all is finished."13 In these terms, earth was the foundation, heaven and hell the superstructure. And all existed, in one way or another, to promote revival. While he never lived to complete the project, we can infer key aspects of the tri-world history, starting with heaven.

HEAVEN

Though earth grounded his narrative project, Edwards would begin with heaven: the creation of the angels and the eternal communications of the deity. Few systematic theologies dwelt excessively on heaven and its citizens, which was one more reason that Edwards could not frame his life's ambition in a formal theology. Heaven could only exist in narrative form communicated to the church through a series of stories and histories. Heaven transcended formal theology and abstract categories and placed the ordinary person on a level with the most advanced academic.[14] Heaven, no less than earth, was created and not eternal, and it was created for the same end: the work of redemption. Earlier, in his *"Miscellanies,"* Edwards ruminated over invisible worlds: "Heaven is a part of the universe that, in the first creation and the disposition of things that was made in the beginning, was appropriated to God to be that part of the universe that should be his residence, while other parts were destined to other uses."[15]

The entree into this divine residence was love. In a sermon series on *Charity and Its Fruits* preached in 1738, Edwards described heaven as "a world of love," created "to be the place of [God's] glorious presence.... There dwells God the Father, and so the Son, who are united in infinitely dear and incomprehensible mutual love.... There is the Holy Spirit, the spirit of divine love, in whom the very essence of God, as it were, all flows out or is breathed forth in love.... There in heaven this fountain of love, this eternal three in one, is set open without any obstacle to hinder access to it."[16]

Though not eternal, heaven was older than earth. Like earth, heaven was a place with a physical, social, and spiritual topography. There were gardens, cities, temples, and fountains. If streets were not made of gold (Edwards was ready to concede the metaphoric power of gold), there were nonetheless streets. Likewise heaven had a spiritual architecture as the abode of the elect, the crown of the martyrs, and the fount of enlightenment. Heaven also had clouds on which Christ would one day descend; heaven radiated a physicality with material and moral landscapes of inexpressible beauty. At the center of Edwards's Dantean vision of heaven is supernatural light not unlike the "blazing point" of *Paradiso*, with angels spinning a ring of light.

Heaven embraced saints, angels, and, of course, the persons of the Trinity. Between them, the three constituents formed a divine "society." Heaven, Edwards believed, is "the only way that ever has been contrived for the gathering together angels and men into one society and one place of habitation."[17] The best human analogy to this heavenly society was the church community in worship.

Modern readers – even Christian readers accustomed to the discourse of theology – might be surprised at how frequently angels appear as central characters in Edwards's tri-world narrative. Edwards repeated themes he first recorded privately in his *"Miscellanies,"* reminding his hearers, "The creating heaven was in order to the Work of Redemption; it was to be an habitation for the redeemed and the Redeemer. Angels [were created to be] ministering spirits [to the inhabitants of the] lower world [that is] to be the stage of the wonderful work [of redemption]."[18] Some angels had names, such as Michael the warrior, the archangel identified principally with ancient Israel, who later at Armageddon will command the celestial armies in battle against Satan and his demons. In contrast, the archangel Gabriel appears as the messenger of mercy and promise in Daniel and Luke. In Luke, it is Gabriel who informs the Virgin Mary of her coming glory. A hierarchy of powers and angels existed among angels, from archangels and angels at the top, whose activities embraced heaven and earth, to cherubim and seraphim, whose sole residence is heaven surrounding the heavenly throne (Isaiah 6:1– 6). Satan himself was formerly an archangel and, in popular church teaching, second only to God. With his banishment for rebellion, along with "hundreds" of other rebel angels, the ranks of remaining angels were purified so that, Edwards concluded, "they never will sin, and they are out of any danger of it." While only a handful of angelic names were known, and while most were invisible to human eyes, they numbered in the legions.[19]

Saints and angels interacted with the Trinity. In an early sermon, Edwards pointed out that "God is a spirit and is not to be seen with bodily [eyes]. . . . 'Tis not any sight with the bodily eyes. For [the] souls of the saints [in heaven], they see God, and the angels [also, who are] spirit and never were united to bodies. . . ."[20]

Though citizens of heaven, angels spent considerable time on earth as ministering spirits. Indeed, they exist all around true believers in invisible armies. Though rejecting the Roman Catholic belief in "guardian angels" for children commissioned at baptism, Edwards frequently reminded his young listeners that angels were particularly attentive to them. In his sermon *Children Ought to Love the Lord*, delivered in August 1740, Edwards consoled his young listeners with these words:

> If you truly love Christ, all the glorious angels of heaven will love you. For they delight in those that love Christ; they love to see such a sight as children giving their hearts to Christ. There will be joy in heaven among the angels that day that you begin to love Christ. And they will be your angels; they will take care of you while you sleep, and God will give 'em charge to keep you in all your ways.[21]

But angels were neither childish nor limited to children. As ever-present realities, they represented for Edwards a possibility in human nature to become like angels; they lent an intensification of being and becoming unavailable to fallen human mortals.

Although peaceful after Satan's expulsion, heaven was never static. Indeed, it was a theater of dramas every bit as consuming as earth's. And unlike those on earth, heaven's inhabitants could participate in their own heavenly dramas and conflicts and, at the same time, could view and even participate in the dramas on earth. Heaven no less than earth remained incomplete, in need of "newness," so that "with respect to the saints and angels, all things in heaven and earth and throughout the universe are in a state of preparation for the state of consummation; all the wheels are going, none of them stop, and all are moving in a direction to the last and most perfect state."[22]

EARTH

Since redemption and revival lay at the center of actual history, the hinge dates of earth's history were not tied to the rise and fall of the great empires, but to the outworking of redemption: in individuals such as Abraham, David, Christ, the apostles, and Constantine; in movements such as the Reformation, and the Puritan migration; and – quite soon, again – in places such as Northampton. In like manner, the triggering mechanism for these turning points in actual history would not be wars and conquests, but revivals of true religion.

Throughout the history of fallen mankind, interaction among heaven, hell, and earth never ceased, according to Edwards, although it varied in intensity and immediacy. The form of that interaction he frequently likened to a journey or progress. In the artistic manner of Bunyan, Dante, Milton, or, later, C. S. Lewis, Edwards's history portrayed a dramatic contest between good and evil, with confederations within the Trinity itself playing the triumphant role.

Edwards divided his earth history into three major epochs: from the Fall of humankind to the incarnation of Christ, the god-man; from the incarnation to the bodily resurrection of Christ; and from the resurrection to the end of time. The briefest yet most important period of interaction between heaven, hell, and earth came during the life, death, and resurrection of Christ. At Christ's birth, the minions of Satan trembled even as the response in heaven was ecstatic: "This appears by their joyful songs on this occasion, heard by the shepherds in the night. This was the greatest event of providence that ever the angels beheld."[23]

Following the resurrection, "Christ entered into heaven in order to the obtaining the success of his purchase.... And as he ascended into heaven, God the Father did in a visible manner set him on the throne as king of the universe. He then put the angels all under him, and he subjected heaven and earth under him, that he might govern them for the good of the people that he had died for...."[24] Throughout his preaching, Edwards drew on church history and profane history to integrate the postresurrection history of earth into one divine "conspiracy."

HELL

Of hell, Edwards had no less detail for his history. In contrast to modern avoidance of hell, seventeenth- and eighteenth-century religious culture and art were more attuned to hell than to heaven.[25] If Edwards was more balanced in his preaching, hell was hardly neglected and formed a central component in his redemption narrative. Soon after the world was created, "evil entered into the world in the fall of the angels and man.... Satan rose up against God, endeavoring to frustrate his design in the creation of this lower world."[26] Satan's rebellion would introduce the narrative of hell – a place as real and palpable as heaven and earth. Modern readers miss Edwards entirely if they cannot understand the immediacy of Satan in his thought. Removed or glossed over, Satan, Christ, the Trinity, and heaven and hell become abstractions, and the whole narrative scheme of Edwards's history is lost.

Edwards did not hesitate to introduce young listeners to the horrors of hell at the earliest moments. In a 1740 sermon directed to young children, Edwards spared no detail in describing the evils of hell and Satan, but then went on to assure them that they were safe in Christ.

> If you love Christ, you will be safe from the devil, that roaring lion that goes about seeking whom he may devour. He will not be able to hurt; you shall be out of his reach. If the devil should appear to you, you need not be afraid of him, but might triumph over him. The devil knows that Christ will subdue him under the feet of such as love him. Christ will bring down that dreadful giant and cause all holy children that love him to come and set their feet upon his neck.[27]

Satan's kingdom was hell, a place without goodness or God, a physicality of pain and suffering where flames licked at sinners with relentless ferocity. Where many medieval writers favored images of hell that played on infinite darkness, Edwards preferred images of furnaces and fire. In a *"Miscellanies"* entry he wrote, "Hell is represented by fire and brimstone.... Lightning is a string of brimstone; and if that stream of brimstone which we are told kindles hell be as hot as streams of lightning, it will be vehement beyond conception."[28] What made this infinite stream of fire even more agonizing was the fact that God permitted the damned to view the alternative paradise of the saints in heaven. And as with Calvin, Edwards's God would allow for no second chances after death. Hell was eternal and irreversible. With relentless logic he would insist that because God hates sin, "it is suitable that he should execute an infinite punishment."[29] Soon, Edwards would discover that nothing would promote revival better than the haunting specter of "infinite punishment."

Like heaven, hell's history was intimately connected to earth's, and necessary to engage the drama of redemption. In a *"Miscellanies"* entry dating from 1740, Edwards noted, "God hath so ordered it that all the great concerns and events of the universe should be some way concerning of this work [of redemption], that the occasion of the fall of some of the angels should be something about this." Indeed, he continued, redemption was "why the fall of man was so soon permitted." When the Israelites were enslaved in Egypt, "Hell was as much and much more engaged [than Egypt]. The pride and cruelty of Satan, that old serpent was more concerned in it than Pharaoh's."[30] With deliverance, Israel enjoyed a victory as much over hell as over Egypt.

When earth history, at last, was to come to an end in the final climactic battles with Antichrist and Satan, all three worlds would come together, with heaven especially enlisted for the conflict: "At the day of judgment, the Sun of righteousness shall appear in its greatest glory; Christ shall then come in the glory of his Father, and all the holy angels with him." In a sermon on *Christ the Spiritual Sun*, Edwards cautioned that the destruction to accompany this day of judgment would exceed the persecutions of the Jews at Christ's death.

> Soon after [the resurrection], he brought the amazing destruction of the unbelieving Jews, terribly destroying their city and country by the Romans. So when he will come in a spiritual sense at the beginning of the expected glorious times of the church, he will come [not only] for the deliverance and healing and rejoicing of his church, but for the amazing destruction of Antichrist and other enemies of his church.[31]

With the toppling of Antichrist, Satan's earthly kingdoms would be utterly abolished. Satan would be banished from earth as he was from heaven. There would be a "new heaven" no less than a "new earth." Indeed, from *"Miscellanies"* entries it is clear that Edwards believed the "new heavens and new earth" would strictly be located in heaven: "The NEW HEAVENS AND NEW EARTH, so far as a place of habitation, is meant by 'em, are heaven and not the lower world." While the old heaven was corruptible, as evidenced by Satan's fall, the new heaven would be pure and incorruptible, a paradise without end. With Christ's Second Coming, the saints already in heaven and those joining them would see glories that were previously unavailable even in heaven. Human minds would see universes inside an atom. "'Tis only for want of sufficient accurateness, strength and comprehension of mind, that from the motion of any one particular atom we can't tell all that ever has been, [all] that now is in the whole extent of creation ... and everything that ever shall be. Corol. What room for improvement of reason is there [in heaven] for angels and glorified minds."[32]

REVIVALS AS MILLENNIAL HARBINGERS

In seeking signs of the triumph of Christ the redeemer, revivals assumed central importance. They were simultaneously tangible events, prophetic signs, and portents of coming triumphs.

Even as he read voraciously in the history of heaven, earth, and hell and sketched their interconnected histories, Edwards eagerly scanned the horizons of his own world for signs of revival and regeneration that would presage the new heavens and the new earth. In a letter to Josiah Willard, a widely connected evangelical and secretary of the Massachusetts Province, Edwards inquired after the state of revivals worldwide. Familiar with the itinerant phenomenon George Whitefield and the British Isles, he extended his inquiry to Prussia, and in particular to the city of Halle, where a Dr. August Hermann Francke was rumored to have promoted revivals. He also expressed curiosity about the East Indies and Moscovy, adding that "I cannot but hope that God is about to accomplish glorious things for his church, which makes me the more desirous of knowing as fully as may be the present state of religion in the world."[33]

From his reading and correspondence, Edwards was able to apprise his congregation of recent events and set them in historical context. At a "private meeting" in December 1739, Edwards reported on "God's Grace Carried On in Other Places." In particular, he singled out "a remarkable work of God's grace that has of late appeared in some parts of the British dominions." Even more surprising was the fact that this movement grew out of the Church of England which, though "sound in its principles, in the beginning of the Reformation," fell prey to heresy and corruption "especially [during] King Charles the Second's reign." With mounting excitement, recalling Northampton's great revival of 1734, he informed his listeners that "God has raised up in England a number of younger ministers . . . [c]alled, by way of derision, the New Methodists."[34] Soon, this British revival would land on colonial shores with hurricane force.

On October 17, Whitefield arrived in Northampton and preached to Edwards's congregation and in the parsonage later that evening. The next day he preached twice more. All correspondents agreed that something dramatic had happened. Whitefield himself reported great movings, including "Mr. Edwards," who "wept during the whole time of the exercise."[35] Edwards reported that "the congregation was extraordinarily melted by each sermon, almost the whole assembly being in tears for a great part of the time."[36]

NORTHAMPTON AFTER WHITEFIELD

Following Whitefield's visit, Edwards sought to fan the flames by preaching a sermon series on the parable of the sower, enjoining his listeners to be planted in the Word. While pleased that a revival spirit seemed to be thriving, Edwards was careful not to gloat. Recalling the earlier revival, he asked: "Was there too much of an appearance of a public pride, if I may so call it? Were we not lifted up with the honor that God had put upon us as a people, beyond most other people?"[37]

In December, Edwards wrote to Whitefield describing the state of religion in Northampton as having "been gradually reviving and prevailing more and more, ever since you was here." He noted of special importance "a considerable number of our young people, some of them children, have already been savingly brought home to Christ." Among these young converts were "one, if not more, of my children." In a later account, first written as a letter to Boston's Thomas Prince and later published in Prince's magazine *Christian History*, Edwards happily reported:

> In about a month or six weeks there was a great alteration in the town, both as to the revivals of professors, and awakenings of others. By the middle of December a very considerable work of God appeared among those that were very young, and the revival of religion continued to increase; so that in the spring, an engagedness of spirit about things of religion was become very general amongst young people and children.... [38]

Edwards had good reason to focus on the young people. From a demographic analysis of Northampton church membership lists, historian Kenneth P. Minkema has shown how large a majority of the recalcitrant members who criticized Edwards and eventually dismissed him were older members who had entered the church under the ministry of his grandfather and predecessor, Solomon Stoddard. Many of these members resented Edwards's fame at the expense of their beloved Mr. Stoddard and his criticism of Stoddard's lax admission policies. But by then, Edwards was not innocent. In retaliation, he berated the aged as too old for conversion and held the youth up as role models of faith.[39]

The youth were Edwards's best hope and the ones he would especially cultivate for conversion. Signs of "young people" and even "children" converting appeared throughout his reports as a special providence. Following the drowning of a young man named Billy Sheldon in February 1741, Edwards pressed home the mortality of youth. The lesson he enjoined was familiar: "Don't set your heart on youthful pleasures and other vain enjoyments of this world...." Instead, prepare for eternity. Even now, Edwards warned, another youth was presently dying of consumption and "upon the brink of eternity.... Therefore lose no more time."[40]

In another sermon, delivered in July 1740, Edwards again directed his young listeners' attention to a different world, but this time to heaven rather than hell. He was particularly concerned about the consequences of conversion in respect to youthful conversation. In place of mundane or vulgar conversation, he enjoined his young listeners to move their thoughts and communications toward "the great things of another world." Such a subject matter would be infinitely rewarding and encouraging in contrast to the sorrows of life in this world. Young people everywhere, but especially in Northampton, "should be much in speaking of the saints' happiness and glory in heaven, where they will be perfectly holy and happy in the full enjoyment of God and Christ, and in perfect love and friendship one with another, forever and ever."[41]

At about the same time that Edwards wrote to Whitefield in December, he penned his *Personal Narrative*. In reading it, one sees how the revivals buoyed his sagging spirits and uplifted his soul. He recalled his earlier yearnings with startling immediacy. He now recalled how "My mind was very much taken up with contemplations on heaven, and the enjoyments of those there; and living there in perfect holiness, humility and love."[42] How much of this description pertained to Edwards's youthful experience and how much to his renewed hope in 1739 is unclear, but certainly these words expressed Edwards's present state.

EDWARDS THE AWAKENER

Given Edwards's tri-world perspective, we can see why Whitefield's revivals loomed large in his thinking. Indeed, Edwards was obsessed with Whitefield. In his own way he would imitate him. By December 1740, unmistakable evidences appear in Edwards's manuscript sermons that he had begun to experiment and to perfect his own revival rhetoric in Whitefield-like directions. If Edwards's greatest growth as a preacher occurred earlier in the 1730s, his growth as a revivalist specializing in the New Birth or conversion came now. Edwards's sermon "Notebook 45," begun in 1739, is the largest of three and marks a shift in style that reflects both the effect of Whitefield's revivals and his own turbulent relationship with his congregation.[43] By this time Edwards had adopted the duodecimo sermon books that could be "palmed" in the pulpit, allowing for greater freedom and the appearance of extemporaneity.

Edwards knew he was no orator. His voice, gestures, and memory could not equal Whitefield's dramaturgical style. But he also knew he had one advantage that he intended to exploit for his own glory and the glory of God: rhetoric. Edwards was a genius with words, and he set himself to compose the "perfect idea" of an awakening sermon. To aid in that process, he would modify not only his delivery and gestures, but the balance of ideas and the very structure of the composition in ways that are easily uncovered.

Besides altering the form of his manuscript notes, Edwards shifted his content decisively from heaven to hell. While the history of heaven communicated love, the essence of "the new sense of the heart," Edwards believed, for a moment anyway, that one could get to life eternal only after first being scared to death.[44] This rhetorical need demanded the change in emphasis from the history of heaven to the history of hell. In earlier years, sermonic invocations of heaven had easily surpassed hell. But in the 1740s, hell, in all its fury and torture, would have to be enlisted if heaven were ever to be gained. Edwards knew that the indispensable emotional appeal in an awakening sermon was fear, even terror, and it knew no age limits. Children needed to absorb horror no less than adults. Just as children must be taught to fear fire at the earliest age, so also must they be taught to fear the fires of hell. In a later defense of revival preaching, Edwards would observe: "'Tis no argument that a work is not from the Spirit of God, that it seems to be promoted by ministers insisting very much on the terrors of God's holy law, and that with a great deal of pathos and earnestness."[45]

Edwards's first deliberate attempt to shape a new awakening sermon appeared in his sermon entitled *Sinners in Zion* (December 1740). In examining the composition of *Sinners in Zion*, it becomes clear that Edwards was already at work perfecting the style for a Whitefield-like revival sermon. The form would have to promote and encourage extemporaneous delivery, and the content must shift from heaven to hell, from the joys of redemption to the horrors of the damned.[46] In a further step toward freeing up his speech, Edwards began to include large white-space breaks in his notes as a signal to extemporize. In place of fully written-out sentences, he began supplying rhetorical cues: "You are warned by it," and "You are invited by it."

A SECOND *SINNERS*

Two weeks after preaching *Sinners in Zion*, Edwards preached another *Sinners* sermon: *Sinners in the Hands of an Angry God.* It is not clear what effect the second *Sinners* had on his own congregation. Probably not much. They, after all, had heard its substance only two weeks before. Awakening sermons require unfamiliar audiences and spontaneous delivery. Certainly no reports exist of exceptional responses. But in one of his repreachings at Enfield, Massachusetts, on July 8, the effects were extraordinary. The

Reverend Stephen Williams of nearby Longmeadow attended and recorded the event in his diary.

> Went over to Enfield, where we met Dear Mr. Edwards of Northampton who preached a most awakening Sermon from those words Deut 32:35 – and before ye Sermon was done there was a great moaning and crying out throughout ye whole House. What shall I do to be saved – oh I am going to Hell – oh what shall I do for a christ etc. etc. – so that ye minister was obliged to desist. [The] shrieks and crys were piercing and Amazing. After some time of waiting the congregation were still so that a prayer was made by Mr. W – and after that we descended from the pulpit and discoursed with the people – some in one place and some in another. And Amazing and Astonishing [was] ye power. God was seen and several souls were hopefully wrought upon that night and oh ye cheerfulness and pleasantness of their countenances – that received comfort. Oh that God would strengthen and confirm etc. We sung an hymn and prayed and dispersed ye Assembly.

Such was the power – and the fear – generated by this sermon that Edwards apparently never finished preaching it, possibly the only time this had happened. Reflecting on the sermon, Williams wrote that Edwards "seemed affected and moved – ready to dissolve in Tears etc. – but cant well tell why."[47]

Sinners in the Hands of an Angry God is arguably America's greatest sermon. It has been analyzed extensively both in the Yale Edition and in other works.[48] But what is interesting for our purposes here is not the final text as it appeared in print, or even the handwritten full text preserved in Yale's Beinecke Rare Book and Manuscript Library, but an accompanying two-page outline that Edwards prepared at the time of composition for multiple deliveries with minimal notes or prompts.[49] The outline would compel him to preach extemporaneously and connect personally with his listeners. When reading the fragment text as opposed to the fully written-out text, one can discern an almost perfect awakening sermon.

> [Humankind] alwaies exposed to fall
> suddenly fall
> by their own weight
> nothing that tis G. that holds em up
> no want of power in G.
> They deserve it.
> They are Condemned to it [hell]
> Tis the place they belong to

God is angry enough with them

The devil if not Restrained would Immediately fly upon them & seize
    them as his own

They have those Hellish principles in them that if G. should take off his
    Restraints

Tis no security that there are no visible means of death at hand.

Their own care & prudence to preserve their own lives.

The schemes they Lay out for Escaping damnation

There is no promise[50]

For all the attention paid to *Sinners*, no one has appreciated the significance of this fragment version. It confirms the novelty of the sermon, not
only on the level of content and rhetoric in print, but of its extemporaneous
abbreviation. Assuming that Edwards delivered this sermon on more than
two occasions, we can see this two-page fragment text as the real *Sinners*
sermon: the highly portable and powerful cue card allowing multiple deliveries – and unprecedented terror. Contained in these two pages was rhetorical
dynamite.

CONCLUSION

As effective as Edwards's notes were in conveying the reality of hell's
torments, and as powerful as they were in putting terrified listeners in grave
concern for their souls, revival would once again disappoint Edwards. Rue-
fully, he recognized that unrelented terror could not work indefinitely, nor
would his parishioners respond with the "affections" he demanded. By 1745
the evangelical campaign for the trans-Atlantic world became derailed in
the face of renewed war with France, and Edwards would become derailed
by his own congregation who dismissed him with rancor on both sides.
Edwards would not live to see another awakening, and he went to his grave
disappointed and a failure.

But as preacher and chronicler of revivals, Edwards's words would out-
live him, and elevate him to center stage in the now long Anglo-American
history of revivals, awakenings, and "crusades." Even the great Whitefield
would fade, as Edwards's imprint remained fixed in the "evangelical" tradition. Would Edwards have been surprised to know that he was the premier
American revivalist? Probably not. To the end, Edwards believed passionately that he had history on his side, and with it the certainty that God
would make his manual for revival the engine of cosmic transformation and
millennial triumph.

Notes

1. WJE, 4:128–211.
2. Ibid., 9:111–528.
3. Based on his reading of Edwards's "regulatory notebooks," composed in the 1720s, Wilson H. Kimnach concludes that Edwards "conceived of his life's work at a fairly early age." WJE, 10:10, 56.
4. WJE, 9:73.
5. Erich Auerbach, *Mimesis: The Representation of Reality in Western Literature*, trans. Willard R. Trask (Princeton, NJ: Princeton University Press, 1953); Hans W. Frei, *The Eclipse of Biblical Narrative: A Study in Eighteenth and Nineteenth Century Hermeneutics* (New Haven: Yale University Press, 1974).
6. WJE, 16:727–8.
7. Ibid.
8. Ibid., 10:82.
9. Jeffrey Burton Russell, *A History of Heaven: The Singing Silence* (Princeton: Princeton University Press, 1997), 10–11.
10. WJE, 9:118.
11. Ibid.
12. Edwards treated this theme most fully in his *Dissertation Concerning the End for Which God Created the World*, WJE, 8:401–536.
13. WJE, 8:121.
14. Russell, *History of Heaven*, 16–17.
15. "Miscell." 743, WJE, 18:379–80.
16. WJE, 8:369–70.
17. "Miscell." 809, WJE, 18:515.
18. WJE, 9:118–19.
19. "Miscell." 442, WJE, 8:490.
20. "The Pure in Heart Blessed," WJE, 17:62.
21. See WJE, 22:178.
22. "Miscell." 779, WJE, 18:435.
23. WJE, 9:301.
24. Ibid., 361.
25. As with other Puritan preachers, Edwards's thinking about hell and Satan was influenced heavily by medieval glosses on Scripture as well as Scripture itself. See Edward K. Trefz, "Satan as the Prince of Evil: The Preaching of the New England Puritans," *Boston Public Library Quarterly*, 7 (1955), 3. On the gradual minimalization of hell and Satan outside of the Puritans, see D. P. Walker, *The Decline of Hell: Seventeenth-Century Discussions of Eternal Torment* (Chicago: University of Chicago Press, 1964).
26. See WJE, 22:303.
27. See ibid., 169.
28. "Miscell." 275, WJE, 13:376.
29. For a fuller elaboration of Edwards's sense of hell, see Norman Fiering, *Jonathan Edwards's Moral Thought and Its British Context* (Chapel Hill: University of North Carolina Press, 1981), 61–2; Philip C. Almond, *Heaven and Hell in Enlightenment England* (New York: Cambridge University Press, 1994), 98, 151.
30. "Miscell." 702, WJE, 18:303.
31. WJE, 22:61.

32. "Miscell." 809, WJE, 18:516; "Miscell." 272, WJE, 13:374.
33. WJE, 16:83.
34. Ibid., 22, 105–8.
35. Quoted in Arnold A. Dallimore, *George Whitefield: The Life and Times of the Great Evangelist of the Eighteenth-Century Revival* (Westchester, IL: Cornerstone, 1980), I: 539.
36. Letter to Thomas Prince, December 12, 1743, WJE, 16: 116.
37. WJE, 22:255.
38. Ibid., 16:87, 116–17.
39. Kenneth P. Minkema, "Old Age and Religion in the Writings and Life of Jonathan Edwards," *Church History* 70 (Dec. 2001), 674–704.
40. WJE, 22:336, 328. In fact, Edwards exaggerated the numbers of youthful converts. See Minkema, "Old Age and Religion."
41. WJE, 22:163.
42. Ibid., 16:795. The case for dating the composition of the *Personal Narrative* to December 1740 is made by George S. Claghorn in WJE, 16:747.
43. Wilson H. Kimnach describes these shifts in WJE, 10:62–3.
44. The best treatment of Edwards and hell appears in Fiering, *Jonathan Edwards's Moral Thought*, 200–60.
45. WJE, 4:246.
46. Ibid., 22:265–84.
47. Stephen Williams, "Diary," Storrs Library, Longmeadow, MA, typescript, vol. 3, pp. 375–s6.
48. See, especially, Kimnach, ed., WJE, 10:113–15, 175–8; J. A. Leo Lemay, "Rhetorical Strategies in *Sinners in the Hands of an Angry God* and *Narrative of the Late Massacres in Lancaster County*," in Barbara B. Oberg and Harry S. Stout, eds., *Benjamin Franklin, Jonathan Edwards, and the Representation of American Culture* (New York: Oxford University Press, 1993), 186–203. See also Edward J. Gallagher, "*Sinners in the Hands of an Angry God*: Some Unfinished Business," *New England Quarterly* 73 (2000): 202–21.
49. The dating of the fragment is uncertain. See Kimnach's "Introduction," WJE, 10:145. But whatever the date, it is clear that this outline was intended to promote "spontaneous" rhetoric, leading Kimnach to speculate, "The thought arises that JE, under the influence of Whitefield, might have made an outline of his Northampton sermon for the Enfield performance."
50. WJE, 22:434.

7 Edwards as theologian

E. BROOKS HOLIFIELD

As a theologian, Jonathan Edwards stood within the Reformed tradition that emerged from the Protestant Reformation in the Swiss and southern German cities of sixteenth-century Europe. Like other Reformed – or Calvinist – theologians, he accentuated the glory and sovereignty of a triune God, the original sin and depravity of humankind, and the gracious act by which God conferred eternal salvation on a determinate and predestined number of "elect" souls. He shared the standard Reformed belief in salvation by grace through faith, the power of grace to transform the sinful heart, and the value of divine law as a guide for the gradual sanctification that marked the true Christian life. He concurred in the familiar Reformed view that saving truth came solely through the divine revelation in the Christian Bible. Yet Edwards also immersed himself in the philosophy, ethical theory, and natural science of his own era; and his theology manifested a blending of traditional, biblical, and philosophical themes that inaugurated a discrete Edwardsean theological tradition in America. For his admirers, Edwards was the genius who proved that Reformed theology could overcome – and even appropriate for its own purposes – the challenge of the Enlightenment. For his critics, he became the source of errors that threatened the integrity of Calvinist orthodoxy.

Edwards drew on a tradition that defined theology as an eminently practical and not merely theoretical discipline. Since the twelfth century, theologians had argued that theology was a theoretical enterprise insofar as its aim was the beholding of God as an end in itself, an intrinsic good. They had defined it as also practical insofar as it consisted of knowledge that led to a good beyond itself, specifically to the end of blessedness and union with God. Most theologians had contended that theology was both speculative and practical. Edwards agreed, defining theology as "*the doctrine of living to God by Christ.*"[1] As a theoretical enterprise, he added, theology derived from the exercise of the understanding. As a practical discipline, it required a "sense of the heart," an inclination of both the understanding and the will. Edwards insisted that a "speculative knowledge" was of "infinite importance," but he always defined the deeper aim of theology as practical. It nurtured a "sense" of divine things that informed Christian "practice" and drew the believer into a saving knowledge of God.[2]

While some have read Edwards chiefly as a philosophical theologian, framing his thoughts through his engagement with John Locke, Nicolas Malebranche, the Cambridge Platonists, or the British moralists, others, like his disciple Samuel Hopkins, emphasized that he "studied the Bible more than all other books" and that he depended heavily on such works of biblical criticism as Matthew Poole's *Synopsis Criticorum* (1669–76) and Matthew Henry's *Exposition of the Old and New Testaments* (1708–10). Spurred partly by the Deist controversies, he devoted substantial energy to the topics of inspiration, the scope of the canon, the authorship of biblical texts, the historicity of biblical reports, and the biblical depictions of the end times. His works abounded in biblical allusions and proof texts. One task for the interpreter of Edwards as a theologian is to discern the style of thinking or the pattern of his thought that manifested itself in both the philosophical and the biblical reflection and informed a distinctive Edwardsean rendering of traditional themes. The argument of this chapter is that Edwards's attraction to the theme of "excellency" reflected an angle of vision that found expression in almost everything he wrote.[3]

EXCELLENCY, REASON, AND REVELATION

Edwards first analyzed the idea of excellency in his notes on "The Mind," which he probably began in 1723 after completing his theology degree at Yale. He began the notes with the observation that he found himself "more concerned" with excellency than with any other theme. "Yea, we are concerned," he said, "with nothing else." Theologians and philosophers – from Calvinist scholastics to the Cambridge Platonists and British moral philosophers – had long used the term, and Edwards was familiar with definitions of it as harmony, symmetry, fittingness, or proportion. As a young theologian, he concluded that the human mind found the experience of harmony pleasing for the profound reason that proportion defined being itself. "[I]f we examine narrowly," he wrote, being is "nothing else but proportion." Reality consisted of a web of relations constituted by "the consent of being to being," and people found disharmony jarring because they experienced it as contrary to being. Eventually, Edwards qualified his definition of being as proportion, but he never abandoned his understanding of excellency as the consent of being to being or his conviction that it had its grounding in the nature of being.[4]

Edwards found testimonies to the world's deeper spiritual harmonies both in the discoveries of reason and in the truths of revelation. He always insisted that valid reason could not conflict with revealed truth. He followed a tradition known as the *prisca theologia* (ancient theology), which affirmed that all rational philosophical truth embodied remnants of divine revelation to Adam and the ancient Jews. The Deists, who claimed that they could ground theology on reason alone, had merely inherited, unwittingly, traces of the ancient revelation transmitted through cultural traditions. In accord with Calvinist tradition, however, Edwards thought that the unassisted fallen reason, unaided by biblical revelation, could never avoid idolatry. In religious matters, reason required illumination from both Scripture and the Spirit. He spoke therefore of three levels of religious knowledge.[5]

At the first level, reason, or the "light of nature" – the source of natural theology – could discover multiple truths about God. Edwards used familiar rational arguments for God's existence: the order of the world suggested an orderer; the creation required a sufficient cause; the complex human mind could not have resulted from chance; and the yearnings and habits innate in the mind – as well as the mind's inclination toward excellence – required God for their fulfillment. In 1721, as a graduate student at Yale, he began writing the essay "Of Being," which probably had its origins in his reading of the Cambridge Platonist Henry More, though it had parallels in earlier Catholic and Reformed thought. He observed that it was impossible for the mind to conceive of "a state of perfect nothing," for to conceive of nothingness was implicitly to assign to it a form of being. To avoid self-contradiction, therefore, one must concede that "some being should eternally be." And since even empty space was a form of being, this "necessary, eternal being" had to be conceived as "infinite." He knew that the argument did not attain to a Christian conception of God, but it helped prepare the mind to affirm the eternal personal being of Christian theology.[6]

Reason could confirm other religious truths: that human beings were fallen; that some mediation between God and humanity was necessary; that it was plausible to expect God to reveal the means of this mediation; and that the mediation must be "like that of Christ." At the same time, Edwards insisted that in a fallen world the truths of salvation – the truths that counted above all others – had to be matters of "pure revelation above the light of natural reason."[7]

This revealed knowledge – the second level of religious truth – came through the Bible. It was "fit and requisite," Edwards thought, that a gracious God would reveal his design in the world, and both "external" and "internal" arguments showed that the Bible was such a revelation. The traditional "external" proofs included the credibility of the biblical miracles and the fulfillment of Old Testament prophecies. Edwards was especially attracted to the argument that the prophecies of a coming Messiah found their fulfillment

in Christ and that the Old Testament overflowed with "types," or foreshad-
owings, that pointed toward New Testament events. The "internal" proof
clinched the case: The gospel carried its own "light and goodness with it,"
both in the grandeur of its contents and in its internal "harmony," "consistency," and "concurrence." The Bible contained a "vast variety of parts"
connected in "one grand system." Toward the end of his career, Edwards told
the trustees of the College of New Jersey that he was writing a "great work,
which I call *The Harmony of the Old and New Testaments.*" This harmony –
as well as the inner consistency of biblical truths – illustrated for him the
Bible's "excellency."[8]

Edwards's admiration for biblical harmonies accounted for his immense
interest in typology. He prepared extensive biblical commentaries – including especially his *Notes on Scripture* (1724 ff.) and his "Miscellaneous Observations on the Holy Scriptures," known as his "Blank Bible" (1730 ff.) – and
the greater part of them explored Old Testament types and New Testament
antitypes that underscored the harmony of the Bible. He was so attracted to
typology that he found types not only in Scripture but also throughout the
natural world, though he never elevated nature to a level of authority coequal
with Scripture. The listing of natural types that he began to assemble in 1728
as "Images of Divine Things" rather found nature filled with types of biblical
truths. This project, like much of his biblical interpretation, was about excellency; the images showed the "excellent agreement" between nature and the
Bible.[9]

Edwards's main concern, however, was that the reader grasp the "spiritual sense" of the text, the third and deepest level of religious knowledge.
This spiritual apprehension depended on the movement of the Spirit within
the heart, allowing the reader to have "a true sense of the divine excellency
of the things revealed" and to grasp their "truth and reality." Such a grasp of
truth embodied a threefold apprehension of the excellency of God and Christ:
it apprehended their intrinsic beauty; it imbued the heart with a "sense" of
that beauty; and it elicited a consent that the natural reason could never have
given, since reason alone could never discover "the beauty and loveliness"
of spiritual things. Protestants frequently distinguished intellectual assent
from a heartfelt consent made possible by the Spirit. Edwards linked the
distinction to his idea of excellency.[10]

THE EXCELLENCY OF GOD

As a Reformed theologian, Edwards celebrated the glory of God, a glory
manifest especially in divine sovereignty. As a young man, he objected to
the thought of a divine sovereignty exercised in decrees of election and

reprobation, but gradually this thought became "pleasant, bright, and sweet" to him because he gained a "new sense" of the "excellency" of a Being who united both "majesty and grace." While a graduate student at Yale, he found that he could express the glory and sovereignty of God by tracing the implications of a form of philosophical idealism. In his essay "Of Atoms and Perfectly Solid Bodies," which probably reflected his revisions of ideas drawn from the Cambridge Platonist Henry More, Edwards defined the atoms constituting the world as expressions of infinite power – an immaterial force – and in another essay, "Of Being," he asserted that it was impossible to imagine that anything "has any existence ... but either in created or uncreated consciousness" and that a universe devoid of "created intelligence" could exist only in "the divine consciousness." His arguments had affinities with those of the philosophers George Berkeley and Samuel Johnson, but Edwards moved in his own directions, as when he argued that the world continued to exist because a divine "determination," manifested in fixed laws through which God exercised a continual power of creation, maintained the world's existence. Like Berkeley and Johnson, however, he wanted to evoke a sense of divine presence by showing that the world depended, at each moment, on God's creative power.[11]

The idealistic metaphysic provided Edwards a way to argue that God was "the sum of all being," the substance of all that was. It underlay his assertions in 1755 that God was "Being in General," or "the Being of Beings," and that "His existence, being infinite, must be equivalent to universal existence." Some of the Neoplatonic language of his later writing intensified the seeming identity of God with the world. In his *Dissertation Concerning the End for Which God Created the World* (1755), he spoke of creation as an emanation from God, an enlarging of the divine being through communication. But while he thought that God "included" all things, he protected the distinction between God and the world. As utterly dependent on God, the world remained separate from God. The world of created spirits, especially, retained a separate identity, for even the elect saints, chosen for "an infinitely perfect union" with God in eternity, would never attain a perfect oneness. Even more, the reprobate in hell would eternally remain separate from the divine being.[12]

What most clearly marked the distinction between God and the world was God's trinitarian character. Edwards began in 1723 to derive the triunity of God from God's reflection on and delight in his own excellency. He believed that "one alone cannot be excellent, inasmuch as, in such case, there can be no consent." Divine excellency required a divine plurality, and reason alone could recognize that God must have an idea of himself, since otherwise God would lack self-awareness. But God's ideas were perfect, so that God's idea of himself was also God – God the Son. And because the Son and the Father delighted in one another, the begetting of the Son issued in a perfect act of mutual love – or Spirit – which was distinct from and yet one with the Son and Father. Edwards believed that his doctrine improved on earlier Reformed theology that discussed the Spirit mainly as the agent who applied Christ's benefits.[13]

God created the world so that this divine excellency could be expressed, known, and admired. In Edwards's discussion of God's aim in creation, he described it as "fit and suitable in itself" that the divine beauty should express and reveal itself. The ultimate end of creation was not human happiness but the diffusion of God's "excellent fullness" for its own sake. The happiness of the creation was an appropriate secondary aim of God's creative activity, but it was "good in itself" that supreme excellency should emanate in a manner that expanded the circle of consent to itself.[14]

Edwards found the definitive expression of the divine beauty in Christ. The second person of the Trinity became incarnate in Jesus because only a divine-human mediator, united to both alienated parties, could suffer a punishment proportional to the offense of sin against God's infinite excellency. Edwards's disciples appealed to some of his language when they expounded a "governmental" view of the atonement as an act designed to maintain the integrity of the divine moral government, but he still thought of the atonement as an act of "satisfaction," appeasing God's wrath and paying the infinite debt owed by a sinful humanity. The "fitness" and "excellent congruity" of this act – its "suitableness" – provided evidence of the divine wisdom. In dealing with other Christological topics, Edwards often returned to the motif of excellency. Christ revealed the divine beauty because he embodied "an admirable conjunction of diverse excellencies" – glory and humiliation, majesty and meekness, obedience and dominion, sovereignty and resignation. The gospel accounts impressed Edwards as narratives about how Jesus brought opposites into harmonious unity.[15]

THE EXCELLENCY OF GRACE

Edwards cherished the Calvinist doctrine of the sovereignty of grace. He agreed that Christ died only for the elect and that they alone would experience the supernatural and sovereign "divine influence and operation, by which saving virtue is obtained." To explain the fate of the non-elect, or the reprobate, and to magnify the grace that rescued the elect, Edwards thought it important to defend the doctrine of original sin, which had come under attack by liberals such as the English dissenting divine John Taylor. In the last book he wrote during his lifetime, *The Great Christian Doctrine of Original Sin Defended*, which was published posthumously in 1758, he appealed to biblical and secular history to show the universal human tendency to sin, but he also thought that the doctrine would stand even if innocent actions outnumbered crimes. God deserved infinite love, and the creature stood under an infinite debt to the Creator, so any sinful propensity brought a guilt that outweighed all the good. Fallen human beings never loved God in the proper "proportion," since this would require loving God as "infinitely excellent in himself," and not for any self-serving purpose. Since no person, without divine grace, could evince such a love, all displayed the crippling effects of original sin.[16]

In explaining how Adam's successors bore the guilt of his sin, Edwards diverged from Reformed orthodoxy. In his idealist ontology, the continuing identity of anything depended on an "arbitrary divine constitution." The identity of humanity with Adam was merely one instance of this general truth; Adam and humanity were one because God treated them as one. When Adam broke covenant with God, he lost the "supernatural" principle that enabled him to love God in proper proportion, leaving only "natural" principles, such as self-love. Because God constituted all humanity as one with Adam, all humanity shared in the sin and suffered the loss. The argument allowed Edwards to show the reasonableness of the increasingly unfashionable doctrine of the imputation of sin. Seventeenth-century Calvinist theologians typically argued that God imputed Adam's guilt to his posterity because Adam was their legal representative. Edwards, however, argued that God imputed Adam's guilt to men and women because they were truly guilty of it as a result of their divinely constituted unity with Adam. Later, conservative Calvinists saw his proposal, which resembled the doctrine of "mediate imputation" taught by some European Reformed divines, as a lamentable error.[17]

The doctrine of original sin confirmed for Edwards that salvation required a "supernatural and sovereign operation of the Spirit of God." Saving grace had to be "infused." In saying this, Edwards aligned himself with Catholic Thomists and earlier Calvinists who contended that grace moved the will "physically," that is, immediately rather than through moral suasion directed at the intellect. The Calvinist Petrus van Mastricht had argued for infusion in his *Theoretico-Practica Theologia*, the book that Edwards once described as better than "any other Book in the world, excepting the Bible." The word "infusion" emphasized that the new "sense" of divine things came not merely by the Spirit's assisting the natural principles of the mind but by its imparting a "new supernatural principle of life and action."[18]

While Edwards usually drew philosophically from some variant of Christian Platonism, he explicated the idea of infused grace by building on themes derived from seventeenth-century revisions of Aristotelian themes.

He pushed to the forefront such concepts as habit, disposition, and principle to describe the operation of grace. Like the Puritan Thomas Shepard,
whom he often cited, Edwards thought of saving grace as the indwelling and
activity of the Spirit issuing in the formation of a new habit or disposition.
This new disposition, an inherent "excellency," transformed the principle of
human action even before it found public expression in "gracious exercises."
Edwards sometimes spoke of the disposition as prior to conscious awareness, as when he speculated that some infants might have a "regenerated"
disposition before their later conversion.[19]

The new disposition was the foundation of all Christian virtues. The
prime virtue was love. Edwards could speak of love as not only the "chief"
affection but also as the "fountain" of all other Christian affections. In 1738
he delivered a series of sermons titled *Charity and Its Fruits*, which should
be read in part as an effort to evaluate the revivals of the previous four
years. Their central theme was that all saving virtue, which distinguished
true Christians from others, was "summed up" in love. Twenty years later,
he made the same claim that religion "summarily consists in love." The
prominence of the theme exemplified the importance for him of harmony –
he referred repeatedly to the "excellency" of love – but it also allied him with
other eighteenth-century tendencies to move the theme of love closer to the
center of theology.[20]

This impulse found further expression in Edwards's insistence that "all
grace leads to practice." During the Great Awakening, he produced a flurry of
writings designed to state the criteria for discerning the "gracious operations
of God's Spirit." They included not only *Charity and Its Fruits* but also *The
Distinguishing Marks of a Work of the Spirit of God* (1741), *Some Thoughts
Concerning the Present Revival of Religion in New England* (1742), and *A
Treatise Concerning Religious Affections* (1746). Their main purpose was to
defend the revivals while disassociating them from the New Light separatists
who seemed to depreciate good works by resting assurance of salvation
solely on the immediate witness of the Spirit. Edwards argued that gracious
affections enabled the Christian to love the "excellent and amiable nature
of divine things as they are in themselves" and to emulate God's "spiritual
beauty" through holiness of life. He listed numerous signs of grace, but "the
chief of all the signs" was holiness of life as shown forth in the keeping of
Christ's commandments and the doing of good works.[21]

Some of Edwards's disciples would later conclude that his views of
infused grace and the necessity for love in the regenerate heart implied
that love must precede both faith and justification in the order of salvation.
They were willing to redefine what had been the cardinal Protestant doctrine of justification through faith alone. Edwards himself suggested, more

than once, that justification followed upon the conversion in which the Spirit infused the saving disposition of love for God. He argued explicitly, from time to time, that Christian graces were so closely linked that they implied one another and that love was "the most essential ingredient in a saving faith," an argument suggesting that justification might require both faith and love. He avoided, however, the revisions that his disciples found necessary.[22]

Edwards continued to insist on the doctrine of justification through faith. One of the sparks for the revival of 1734 in Northampton was his sermon on *Justification by Faith Alone*, in which Edwards argued, on the basis of Romans 4:5, that God justified the "ungodly." In justification, God accepted the guilty as "free from the guilt of sin" on the grounds of their faith. He defended the idea by recourse to his themes of fittingness and symmetry. Faith did not produce justification but merely made it "fitting." God looked upon it as "fit by a natural fitness" that a faithful relation to Christ should be "agreeable" to justification. It was agreeable to "reason and the nature of things" that God would impute the righteousness of Christ to the faithful since a relation of "union" between a patron and a client made it "fit" to impute the entire merit of one to the other. Christ, moreover, initiated the relation, and the justification resulted from the excellency of the relation, not of the faith. And although he always thought that a genuine faith was united with love, he could still say that faith alone made justification suitable. He opposed New England liberals who contended that faith justified because it included moral obedience in its essence.[23]

In *The Nature of True Virtue*, which Edwards began to write around 1753, he brought his conceptions of love into conversation with British moral philosophy. The argument of the treatise was that true virtue required a consent of the heart to the divine beauty. He believed that the British moralists – Samuel Clarke, Francis Hutcheson, George Turnbull, William Wollaston, and others – had accurately described some features of the natural conscience, or moral sense, but failed to see that it could never attain to the level of true virtue. It could affirm the secondary beauty found in the order, symmetry, and proportion of natural objects or social relations, but it could not discern and love the excellency of being in general. Apart from grace, the natural conscience would always adhere to one or another "private system," and the limited love that ensued would always be opposed to true virtue. Only a consent to "Being in general" – or God – made possible a "general good will," a "disinterested benevolence," a love for God and the neighbor motivated not by a desire for private gain or a provincial loyalty to family and tribe but by the sheer excellency of God as the "Being of beings." In this claim that moral philosophy was misleading without theology, Edwards spoke as a conservative voice, harking back to the earlier beliefs of seventeenth-century Puritans.[24]

Edwards's interest in ethics moved him to write the book that, above all others, would evoke spirited rebuttals and revisions throughout the nineteenth century. To answer critics who believed that Calvinist theology made it impossible to assign moral blame and praise, he published in 1754 *A Careful and Strict Enquiry into the Modern Prevailing Notions of That Freedom of Will, Which Is Supposed to Be Essential to Moral Agency, Virtue, and Vice, Reward and Punishment, Praise and Blame.*[25] Written from the Stockbridge frontier, the book was designed to defend an understanding of human freedom compatible with Calvinist theology and yet also consistent with the language of moral praise and blame.

Edwards understood the critics of Calvinism, among whom he included especially the English writers Thomas Chubb, Samuel Clarke, and Daniel Whitby, to be insisting that the will had to be self-determining or else there could be no moral agency. He accused the critics of contradictions. If the will were self-determining, every free act of the will, including its first free act, had to be freely chosen, and this led either to an infinite regress of free choices or to the self-contradictory notion of a free choice prior to the first free choice. Nor could willing be "indifferent," since willing was by its nature a preference or inclination. And it was also wrong to call the will "contingent," for this implied that it made its choices for no reason whatsoever. Edwards's view was that the will responded always to the strongest motive – defined as the agent's perception of the greatest apparent good as determined by the nature of the object, the liveliness of the perception, the likelihood of attaining it, and the agent's state of mind. The motive operated as the cause of the volition in the sense that any act of the will was an inclination toward one motive or another. But human beings were still free moral agents, for they could do as they pleased or act as they willed. "Let the person come by his volition or choice how he will," Edwards wrote, "yet, if he is able, and there is nothing in the way to hinder his pursuing and executing his will, the man is perfectly free, according to the primary and common notion of freedom." Men and women could not indifferently select their volitions or determine what they would will, but they were free if they could act as they were moved to act. They did what they wanted to do, and they did it willingly.[26]

In making the point, Edwards employed a distinction that had long been common in Reformed circles, among both traditionalists such as Francis Turretin in seventeenth-century Geneva or Cotton Mather in eighteenth-century New England and revisionists such as Moïse Amyraut at Saumur in seventeenth-century France. He distinguished between natural necessity and moral necessity. He conceded the absence of freedom, and of moral accountability, when a "natural necessity," a natural impediment external to the will, made it impossible for people to do what they willed. Moral necessity, however, meant only that the will could not defy its own inclination or disposition. Agents could not will, in a single act of volition, other than as they willed in that act. But this moral necessity offered no impediment to freedom in its "plain and obvious sense" for it assumed the fact of choice and the natural ability to act.[27]

THE BEAUTY OF HISTORY

In addition to his passion for ethics, Edwards had a special interest in God's "moral government" of history, and his speculations on the course of history provided yet another occasion for him to display the "excellence" of God's works. He found in the Bible the clues to the "Grand design" that would bring all the world's diversity into a final unity. All history exhibited the "beauty" of providence as God ordered all events toward a common end. This historical sense fed into Edwards's passionate interest in millennialism, and throughout his career he occupied himself with attempts to map the course of history toward the millennium and the creation of the "new heaven and new earth."[28]

In 1723 he began writing his *Notes on the Apocalypse*, or exegetical comments on the book of Revelation, which he continued to expand until the end of his life. As an interpreter of the apocalyptic prophecies, Edwards carried forward a long-established project. He drew heavily from Whitby, the Cambridge don Joseph Mede, and Moses Lowman, a dissenting English pastor. Like them, Edwards found the clue to the course of history in the machinations of the Antichrist, which he assumed to be the Roman papacy. Like numerous other Protestant predecessors, he correlated the prophetic forty-two months, or 1,260 days of Revelation 11:2–3, each of which he assumed to be a year, with the events of Western history. He decided that the forty-two-month period began in 606, when the Pope became the universal bishop, calculated that the year 1866 would bring the dethroning of the papacy, and concluded, in agreement with Lowman, that the millennium would begin around the year 2000.[29]

Between his own time and the beginning of the millennium, Edwards anticipated years of struggle, marked by revivals and declensions, which he understood in accord with the "afflictive model of progress" that was common among eighteenth-century writers on eschatology. Progress would always alternate with adversity until the millennial era finally arrived. The revival in Northampton intensified his expectation, and his reading of Lowman's *Paraphrase and Notes on the Revelation* (1737) led Edwards to preach in 1739 a series of thirty sermons that were published long after his death as

A History of the Work of Redemption (1774). He would later express an ambition to expand the sermons into a "body of divinity in an entire new method, being thrown into the form of history," but he died before he could complete the project. Nonetheless, the sermons traced the work of redemption through three periods of history – from the fall of Adam to the incarnation of Christ, from the incarnation to the resurrection, and from the resurrection to the end of the world – and showed that the pattern of adversity and deliverance had remained constant as the kingdom of Christ gradually prevailed. He interpreted the third period as a time of "the church's suffering state," but he felt that the world was now near the time of "the glorious work of God's Spirit" that would slowly begin to overthrow "Satan's kingdom" and end the reign of the Antichrist. Through revivals and the conversion of all the peoples of the world, this "glorious work" would eventually lead to "the prosperous state of the church," an era of peace and love that would last for a thousand years.[30]

In 1742 when he published *Some Thoughts Concerning the Present Revival of Religion in New England*, he even thought it "probable" that the "work of God's Spirit," which he seems to have associated with the long period preceding the millennium, might begin soon with events in America, a view that invited ridicule from his Boston critic Charles Chauncy and others, who reminded Edwards of Joseph Mede's prediction that America would become the kingdom of Satan. Edwards complained that his critics misread him, and indeed he typically assigned no special place to America in the events of the last times. In any case, he expected at least another two and a half centuries of struggle before the millennial era began. In 1743, he joined with ministers in Scotland to promote a concert of prayer for the advancement of God's kingdom, and in 1747 he contributed to the cause *An Humble Attempt to Promote Explicit Agreement and Visible Union of God's People in Extraordinary Prayer*. There he speculated that it might be plausible to expect 250 years of "commotions, tumults, and calamities" before the millennium.[31]

When he described the millennial era, Edwards employed the images of excellence, proportion, and beauty that pervaded the rest of his theology. One thing that Edwards found most exciting about the prospect of the millennium was that it would display the unity hidden behind the diversity of history. When he wrote that "all the motions of the whole system of wheels and movements" in history tended toward one "appointed time," he was thinking of the consent of the many to the one, and in the millennial age "all the world" would be "as one church, one orderly, regular, beautiful society, one body, all the members in beautiful proportion." The church itself would be "beautiful," marked by an "excellent order," and all the nations would unite in "sweet harmony." For a thousand years, the peoples of the world would live in prosperity, increasing knowledge, vital religion, and happiness. All would "agree in the sure, great, and important doctrines of the gospel." It would be a time when "this whole great society shall appear in glorious beauty, in genuine amiable Christianity, and excellent order . . . , 'the perfection of beauty' [Psalms 50:2], 'an eternal excellency' [Isaiah 60:15]."[32]

Edwards differed from his New England predecessors Increase and Cotton Mather by virtue of his insistence that the millennial era would precede the final return of Christ. He thought that at the end of the millennium, Satan would be released from bondage, most of the world would fall into apostasy, and Christ would return "in flaming fire to take vengeance." He would judge the nations, descending with the angels as the dead arose, the Spirit transformed the living, and the souls of the departed reunited with their bodies. The saints would ascend to the "new heaven and new earth," which would be located at some "glorious place" in the universe, at an immense distance from the solar system. The wicked would be cast into fire, and the saints would rejoice, for they would see only the glory of God, and God's glory would "in their esteem be of greater consequence, than the welfare of thousands and millions of souls." Edwards thought that this final judgment was "entirely agreeable to reason" because it was "suitable" that God's righteousness be displayed, that injustice be rectified, and that the godly be honored. The final judgment would be one more instance of "due proportion."[33]

Both Edwards's millennial vision and his descriptions of the last things could function as criticisms of Northampton's church and society, and by the mid-1740s he was becoming more critical. Anxious about the waning of revivalist zeal after 1742, irritated by a dispute over salary, embroiled in a controversy over church discipline, and rebuked by parishioners who refused to allow him to decide who could join the church, Edwards began, probably by the end of 1743, to rethink the criteria for church membership that he had inherited from his grandfather Solomon Stoddard. The signs of change were present in his *Religious Affections* (1746), but it was not until 1749 that Edwards was ready to defend, in *An Humble Inquiry into the Rules of the Word of God, Concerning the Qualifications Requisite to a Compleat Standing and Full Communion in the Visible Christian Church*, the conclusion that adults must make a confession of "hearty consent to the terms of the gospel covenant" before they could join the church, receive the Lord's Supper, or present their children for baptism. Edwards was repudiating the Half-Way Covenant that had permitted unconverted parents, baptized as infants, to present their children for baptism. He refused to accept the separatist view that membership should require the public relation of a conversion experience, but he tightened the standards, and the congregation rebelled.[34]

The controversy over admission revealed Edwards's lingering attraction to the covenant theology that had proven so compelling to his Puritan predecessors in seventeenth-century New England. Throughout his career, especially in his *"Miscellanies,"* Edwards still wrote on the covenant of redemption between the Son and the Father, the covenant of works between God and Adam, and the covenant of grace between the believer and Christ. In the covenant of works, God had promised life to Adam if he obeyed the divine law. When Adam failed, God graciously inaugurated a covenant of grace, which stipulated that not obedience but rather faith in Christ alone could suffice for salvation. In most of Edwards's writings, this covenant theology no longer provided the guiding themes, though it appeared occasionally in his sermons. Edwards could employ the familiar sermonic hyperbole declaring that salvation was an "absolute debt to the believer from God" because God had made a covenant to save the faithful, though in other sermons he reversed himself on this claim. The covenant theme remained in the background until 1749, when it reappeared in the *Humble Inquiry.* In that work he argued that to own the covenant was to profess "the consent of our *hearts* to it," and that covenant privileges, such as baptism or church admission, required such consent.[35]

Edwards's position required that he repudiate Stoddard's view of the Lord's Supper as a converting ordinance. It required as well that he soft-pedal the efficacy of baptism. Edwards defended infant baptism on familiar covenantal grounds – the sacrament sealed the covenant of grace to elect infants – but he viewed adult baptism as a token of regeneration, a position that aligned him more closely with Baptists than he would have wanted to acknowledge. Although Edwards thought that God used outward means of grace, he had always been cautious about saying that the means functioned as causes of faith: "There are not truly any secondary causes of it; but it is produced by God immediately." In fact, he taught that when the unregenerate prayed, sang, and listened to sermons and yet remained unregenerate, they intensified the guilt of their sin. A minor point in Edwards's theology, this idea would later produce intense debate between his followers and their opponents.[36]

Edwards's disciples, especially his students Joseph Bellamy and Samuel Hopkins, retained much of his language about the importance of loving God solely for the sake of God's intrinsic excellency, and they shared his interest in virtue, his admiration for selflessness, his understanding of human freedom and bondage, his distinction between moral and natural ability, and his millennial fervor. Nonetheless, Edwards's disciples carried his ideas in directions that he did not travel. They resolved a tension in Edwards's doctrine of salvation by openly affirming that justification required not merely faith but also love, and they emphasized more than Edwards that love represented obedience to divine law. To accentuate the sinner's responsibility to repent immediately, some of them rejected the notion that human guilt resulted from any divine imputation of Adam's culpability, and others defined sin as a matter solely of human choices – not of a sinful nature inherited from Adam. They used the distinction between moral and natural ability as a way to press home the guilt and responsibility of the sinner. Some of the Edwardseans moved away also from Edwards's traditional understanding of the atonement, insisting that Christ died not to satisfy the wrath of God by paying a debt owed by humanity, but rather to maintain the integrity of the cosmic moral government. By drawing out the implications of the demand for a selfless love for God's excellence, they altered Calvinist theology in ways that traditionalists found deeply troubling.[37]

For traditional Calvinists, Edwards was a problem. They had to admire his genius and celebrate his attacks on the critics of Calvinist theology, but they found multiple errors in his thought. They disliked the idealist philosophy that permeated his thought. They regretted his attempt to explain the doctrine of imputation with a theory of human unity with Adam. They believed that he failed to make it clear that God justified the ungodly and therefore that he opened the door for his followers to define love as a condition of justification. They deplored his distinction between moral and natural ability and insisted that the sinful lacked even a natural ability to love God without the assistance of sovereign divine grace. They rejected his definition of true virtue as disinterested benevolence, claiming that it reduced the whole of duty to the love of being in general. The conservative Presbyterian Samuel J. Baird saw Edwards as the source of the doctrinal divisions that split nineteenth-century Calvinists into warring parties. The disharmony occurred, he charged, because "the teachings of Edwards were, in their consequences, fatal to the gospel."[38]

The opponents of Calvinism, on the other hand, found Edwards equally troublesome for entirely different reasons. They, too, criticized him as too "metaphysical," but they deplored his adherence to the doctrine of divine sovereignty and predestination. They believed that his definition of freedom actually supported a determinism that undermined moral responsibility, and they charged repeatedly that it rested on a false understanding of motivation. They insisted that his theory of true virtue unduly depreciated the ordinary human virtues. They believed that his doctrine of original sin either neglected human goodness or unduly limited the grace of God.[39]

The critics neglected the themes of excellence, beauty, and proportion that gave unity and force to Edwards's theology. They criticized discrete doctrines but failed to assess the underlying aesthetic vision that drew the respectful attention of later generations. Edwards attempted to discern patterns of harmony in divine activity, "fit" congruities among doctrines, correspondences within the diverse books of Scripture, and symmetries between the natural and the supernatural. In his metaphysics, he found that beauty, proportion, and relationships served as clues to the nature of reality. In his ethics, he affirmed the striving for self-consistency manifested by the natural conscience, but he insisted that true virtue required moving beyond this merely natural consistency toward the consent to divine beauty attained only by the regenerate saint. In his biblical criticism, he looked for the typological unities that connected the Old and New Testaments, and he sought the "grand design" hidden within the scriptural accounts of history. He found Christ a figure of awe because of the way he brought opposites into harmonious unity. He exalted the virtue of love because it generated social harmony and pious consent to God. He looked for the ways in which things fit together, and when he found them, he discerned signs of God's harmonious intent for the world.

Notes

1. "The Importance and Advantage of a Thorough Knowledge of Divine Truth," WJE, 22:86. For a fuller version of this essay, see E. Brooks Holifield, *Theology in America: Christian Thought from the Age of the Puritans to the Civil War* (New Haven: Yale University Press, 2003), 102–26. I am grateful to Yale University Press for allowing me to present here a compressed and modified version of my chapter on Edwards in that volume.

2. WJE, 22:87; "The Unreasonableness of Indetermination in Religion," WJE, 19:96 ff; William Sparkes Morris, *The Young Jonathan Edwards: A Reconstruction* (Brooklyn: Carlson, 1991), 247.

3. Samuel Hopkins, *The Life and Character of the Late Reverend Mr. Jonathan Edwards, President of the College of New Jersey* (Boston: S. Kneeland, 1765), 40; Stephen J. Stein, "The Spirit and the Word: Jonathan Edwards and Scriptural Exegesis," in Nathan O. Hatch and Harry S. Stout, eds., *Jonathan Edwards and the American Experience* (New York: Oxford University Press, 1988), 120–3; Roland Andre Delattre, *Beauty and Sensibility in the Thought of Jonathan Edwards* (New Haven: Yale University Press, 1968; Robert E. Brown, *Jonathan Edwards and the Bible* (Bloomington: Indiana University Press, 2002), 88–128.

4. "Personal Narrative," WJE, 16:791–9; "The Mind," WJE, 6:332, 336, 362; Thomas A. Schafer, "Introduction" to "*The 'Miscellanies,'*" WJE, 13:14–15.

5. "Miscellaneous Observations on Important Theological Subjects," *The Works of Jonathan Edwards in Eight Volumes,* John Erskine, ed. (Leeds: Edward Baines, 1811) [hereafter "Leeds edition"], 8:155, 157, 209; Gerald R. McDermott, "A Possibility of Reconciliation: Jonathan Edwards and the Salvation of Non-Christians," in Sang Hyun Lee and Allen C. Guelzo, eds., *Edwards in Our Time: Jonathan Edwards and the Shaping of American Religion* (Grand Rapids: William B. Eerdmans, 1999), 179–82; idem, *Jonathan Edwards Confronts the Gods: Christian Theology, Enlightenment Religion, and Non-Christian Faiths* (New York: Oxford

University Press, 2000), 6–10; *Dissertation Concerning the End for Which God Created the World*, WJE, 8:419–24.

6. "Miscell." 91, 149, 199–200, 268, WJE, 13:254–6, 301, 337–8, 373; Morris, *Young Jonathan Edwards*, 313–14; "Of Being," WJE, 6:202; Schafer, "Introduction" to "*The 'Miscellanies'* " WJE, 13:40–1.

7. "Miscell." 94, WJE, 13:256–63; "Miscellaneous Observations," Leeds edition, 8:284; "Importance and Advantage," WJE, 22:86; "Man's Natural Blindness in the Things of Religion," *Sermons on Various Important Subjects* (Boston: S. Kneeland, 1765), 61; "Justification by Faith Alone," WJE, 19:159 ff.; Morris, *Young Jonathan Edwards*, 476, 478; Norman Fiering, *Jonathan Edwards's Moral Thought and Its British Context* (Chapel Hill: University of North Carolina Press, 1981), 83.

8. "Wisdom of God Displayed in the Way of Salvation," *Sermons on Various Important Subjects*, 234; "Miscellaneous Observations," Leeds edition, 8:154; *History of the Work of Redemption*, Leeds edition, 5:133; "Miscell." 1340, WJE, 23:373–4; Letter "To the Trustees of the College of New Jersey," WJE, 16:728–9.

9. *Images of Divine Things*, WJE, 11:59, 63, 74, 106.

10. *A Divine and Supernatural Light*, WJE, 17:413, 422.

11. "Personal Narrative," WJE, 16:790–804; "The Mind," WJE, 332, 344, 350–1; "Miscell." 18, WJE, 13:210; "Of Being," WJE, 6:204; "Of Atoms," WJE:6:216–18; Sang Hyun Lee, *The Philosophical Theology of Jonathan Edwards* (Princeton: Princeton University Press, 1988), 62; *Original Sin*, WJE, 3:400–1.

12. "Miscell." 27a, 94, WJE, 13:213, 256–63; "Miscell." 697, WJE 18:281–2; "Miscell." 880, WJE, 20:121–39; *End of Creation*, WJE, 8:436–8, 455–6, 460–2, 536.

13. "Miscell." 94, 402, WJE, 13:256–63, 466–7; Schafer, "Introduction" to "*The 'Miscellanies,'*" 28–9.

14. *End of Creation*, WJE, 8:421–2, 425, 432–3, 531.

15. "Miscellaneous Observations," Leeds edition, 8:507, 533; "When the Wicked Shall Have Filled Up the Measure of Their Sin," Leeds edition, 6:529; *History of the Work of Redemption*, Leeds edition, 5:150; "God Glorified in Man's Dependence," WJE, 17:214–16, 205–14; "Wisdom of God Displayed," *Sermons on Various Important Subjects*, 178.

16. "Miscellaneous Observations," Leeds edition, 8:416–18, 427; *Original Sin*, WJE, 3:128, 130, 143–4.

17. *Original Sin*, WJE, 3:381, 392, 397, 399, 408. See also Clyde A. Holbrook, "Introduction" to *Original Sin*, WJE, 3:23.

18. "Miscellaneous Observations," Leeds edition, 8:427, 445; *Divine and Supernatural Light*, WJE, 17:411; Anri Morimoto, *Jonathan Edwards and the Catholic Vision of Salvation* (University Park: Pennsylvania State University Press, 1995), 18–19; Conrad Cherry, *The Theology of Jonathan Edwards: A Reappraisal* (Bloomington: Indiana University Press, 1990), 36.

19. Lee, *Philosophical Theology of Jonathan Edwards*, 3–46; Morimoto, *Jonathan Edwards and the Catholic Vision*, 31, 32–59; John Smith, "Introduction" to *Religious Affections*, WJE, 2:56.

20. *Religious Affections*, WJE, 2:111; *Charity and Its Fruits*, WJE, 8:129, 131; *Original Sin*, WJE, 3:168.

21. *Charity and Its Fruits*, WJE, 8:294; *Religious Affections*, WJE, 2:240, 421; David D. Hall, "Introduction" to *Ecclesiastical Writings*, WJE, 12:49.

22. Nathanael Emmons, *A System of Divinity*, ed. Jacob Ide (2 vols. Boston: Crocker and Brewster, 1842), 2:159, 165; Samuel Hopkins, *Two Discourses* (Boston: William McAlpine, 1768), 16; *Charity and Its Fruits*, WJE, 8:329.

23. *Justification by Faith Alone*, WJE, 19:163, 168–77, 180; 232; "Miscellaneous Observations," Leeds edition, 8:517, 524.

24. *The Nature of True Virtue*, WJE, 8:540, 557.

25. *Freedom of the Will*, WJE, 1:129–439.

26. Ibid., 144–5, 164, 191, 197, 226, 270–3, 427.

27. Ibid., 159.

28. *History of the Work of Redemption*, Leeds edition, 5:18, 294, 297; "Miscellaneous Observations," Leeds edition, 8:334.

29. *Notes on the Apocalypse*, WJE, 5:107, 129.

30. James West Davidson, *The Logic of Millennial Thought: Eighteenth-Century New England* (New Haven: Yale University Press, 1977), 129–32; *History of Redemption*, WJE, 9:354, 372, 456, 479, 486; John F. Wilson, "Introduction" to *History of Redemption*, WJE, 9:13.

31. *Some Thoughts*, WJE, 4:353–4; *Humble Attempt*, WJE, 5:411, 533; Stephen J. Stein, "Introduction," WJE, 5:28; Gerald R. McDermott, *One Holy and Happy Society: The Public Theology of Jonathan Edwards* (University Park: Pennsylvania State University Press, 1992), 77–90.

32. *Humble Attempt*, WJE, 5:339, 346; *History of Redemption*, WJE, 9:467, 483–4.

33. *Notes on the Apocalypse*, WJE, 5:129, 141, 177, 183–4; *History of Redemption*, WJE, 9:490; "End of the Wicked Contemplated," Leeds edition, 4:510; "The Day of Judgment," WJE, 14:532, 533–41.

34. Hall, "Introduction," WJE, 12:51–62.

35. "Miscellaneous Observations," Leeds edition, 8:477; "Wisdom of God Displayed," *Sermons on Various Important Subjects*, 207; *Humble Inquiry*, WJE, 12:205.

36. *Humble Inquiry*, WJE, 12:196; *Divine and Supernatural Light*, WJE, 17:417; "Wisdom of God Displayed," *Sermons on Various Important Subjects*, 246.

37. Holifield, *Theology in America*, 127–56.

38. Samuel J. Baird, *History of the New School and of the Questions Involved in the Disruption of the Presbyterian Church in 1838* (Philadelphia: Claxton, Remsen, Haffelfinger, 1868), 175.

39. Holifield, *Theology in America*, 128–35, 264–8.

8 Edwards as philosopher

STEPHEN H. DANIEL

Rarely do accounts of early modern European philosophy mention Jonathan Edwards. His philosophical reflections are typically dismissed as inconsequential because, in the view of many historians of seventeenth- and eighteenth-century philosophy, he does not play a significant role in the discussion of issues raised by his contemporaries. His arguments seem to be so dominated by concerns with Calvinist doctrinal disputes that he is usually understood as an outsider commenting on discussions thematized by Descartes, Locke, and others. Even when he is juxtaposed with thinkers such as Samuel Clarke, Anthony Ashley Cooper (third earl of Shaftesbury), or Francis Hutcheson, he is portrayed as espousing views that are hopelessly immersed in Puritan theology.

Such a marginalizing treatment of Edwards is unfortunate, especially considering how he develops an alternative approach to the way that much of modern philosophy is practiced. He is not alone in pursuing that alternative, for he shares with the Cambridge Platonist Henry More, Nicolas Malebranche, G. W. Leibniz, George Berkeley, and other "theocentric metaphysicians" the view that questions about existence, knowledge, moral judgments, and beauty can be resolved only by understanding things in terms of their place in the universe and their relation to God.[1] For such thinkers, Cartesian minds and simple natures, Hobbesian bodies, and Lockean simple ideas simply cannot be the starting points for a legitimate philosophy, because such insular entities are unintelligible apart from the network of relations that identifies them in the first place.

The key to appreciating the significance of Edwards's philosophy thus lies in noting how he treats all existence as relational. Even God's existence, in terms of which all other existence is intelligible, must be understood as an "agreement" or "consent" that Edwards calls *excellency*. By posing the fundamental concept of philosophy in terms of differentiation and association, Edwards reorients the ways in which traditional questions about reality, God, freedom, personal identity, morality, and beauty are framed.

GOD AND EXCELLENCY

On the surface, Edwards's way of thinking does not seem to be substantially different from the Neoplatonism with which it is often associated in that it locates the source of existence and intelligibility in God. But as is made clear in the case of Spinoza, if God is understood as a substance from which creation emanates, then all things other than God are related to him merely as modes or expressions. That, for many moderns, is not enough of a separation to explain how either God or human beings can be understood in moral terms. So the task faced by Edwards and others like him is to show how God and creation can be ontologically distinct even if creatures are unintelligible apart from God and one another.

To do this, Edwards shifts away from the traditional view of God (*ens entium*) as a being who is somewhat analogous to other beings toward a view of God as the activity of differentiation and association by which all beings are constituted in the first place. Following the Spanish Jesuit Francisco Suárez, Edwards interprets the *ens* of *ens entium* (the being of beings) not as *a* being (a noun) but as the activity of being (a participle) whereby beings become beings.[2] This shift incorporates features of More's claim that God is the space in which everything exists and Malebranche's claim that God is the place of minds.[3] Edwards is especially intrigued by More's claim that, apart from such a space, minds cannot be differentiated from one another. For More, this space cannot be corporeal because it is the principle of corporeal differentiation. Since space itself cannot be differentiated from anything, it is the necessary, eternally existing principle for all else and thus must be God. Edwards agrees: "It is self-evident, I believe, to every man, that space is necessary, eternal, infinite and omnipresent. But I had as good speak plain: I have already said as much as that space is God."[4] Even to try to imagine God's non-existence is to imagine his not being in this space; but this simply affirms his existence by affirming the space in which he is identified in the very attempt to doubt his existence. That is why Edwards opens his early essay "Of Being" (1721) with the proclamation, "That there should absolutely be nothing at all is utterly impossible."[5] To say that "nothing exists" is to utter the "greatest contradiction" and "horrid nonsense," for even *nothing* is intelligible only in relation to something. "Here," Edwards declares, "we are run up to our first principle," in that the divine activity of differentiation and association is the foundation of all intelligibility and existence.

In contrast to More and Malebranche, however, Edwards does not describe God as a substance that can be thought of as logically prior to its activities or relations. Instead, for Edwards, the identity or existence of God (as well as any other thing) consists in his actions and relations and is determined by his nature for all eternity to be what he is in acting exactly as he does. The relations and actions in terms of which all things (including God) exist are not simply predicated of them as subjects, for their being subjects or substances (even as substrata of qualities) is unintelligible apart from the relational properties that define them or the predicates that describe them.[6] So even God must be understood in relational terms; and that, Edwards recognizes, requires a new approach to how we understand existence.

The basis of this new strategy for defining all identity and intelligibility is the "consent of being to being, being's consent to entity."[7] Such consent constitutes what Edwards calls excellency, the inherent agreeableness, harmony, equality, and proportionality of things with one another. Drawing on a similar point made by Malebranche, Edwards acknowledges that the more extensively a being agrees with "being in general" (God and nature together) by plugging into the divine network of ideas, the greater is its excellency and the more firmly established is its existence. But in contrast to Malebranche's doctrine of "seeing all things in God" (where God is still considered a subject distinct from the vision), Edwards's doctrine of excellency assumes that God is the principle whereby the vision's differentiations and associations occur. Any moral or aesthetic harmony that we perceive in the world is thus not accidental, for our perception of nature itself is part of its inherent, divinely established intricacy and order.

This focus on what seems to be an aesthetic basis for existence has some resonance with Shaftesbury's thought as well. But in contrast to the author of the *Characteristics*, Edwards proposes that things can be "agreeable" only if existence itself is understood relationally. Such an insight, he recognizes, marks his account as truly novel. As he proclaims at the beginning of "The Mind," "There has nothing been more without a definition than excellency, although it be what we are more concerned with than anything else whatsoever. Yea, we are concerned with nothing else."[8] Our engagement with the world, he explains, is centrally concerned with excellency because it is not simply a moral or aesthetic gloss on experience. Instead, it is the principle by which things are differentiated from and associated with one another in our consciousness, in their relations with other things in nature, and in their ultimate dependence on God. It is in this sense that the identity and existence of everything is defined by its necessary agreement with an other. When Edwards later writes, then, that "Being or existence is what is necessarily agreeable to being," he reinforces the point that the existence of a thing (like its excellency) is intelligible only in terms of its relations.[9]

This doctrine of excellency is Edwards's most important contribution to modern philosophy, because it – unlike even Leibniz's monadology, to which it is strikingly similar – not only characterizes all relations as intrinsic, but also reveals why all things must be linked to everything else. By emphasizing how identity itself is based on the activity of differentiation and association, Edwards replaces efforts to ground philosophy on doubt, simplicity, and atomistic individualism with a new "sense of the heart" regarding the harmonious unity of nature and experience.

To come up with such an insight, Edwards draws on a variety of figures.[10] From the seventeenth-century followers of the Renaissance logician Peter Ramus (such as William Ames and Alexander Richardson), Edwards retrieves resources for treating ontological consent as an activity best described by noting how terms (subjects and predicates) are unintelligible apart from how they function in propositions.[11] Puritan divines (for example, Richard Baxter) and the Dutch Calvinists (Franco Burgersdyck and Adrian Heereboord) provide Edwards with an explanation of how the loss of an innate appreciation of the integrity of nature (in original sin) is schematized in Scholastic metaphysics.[12] From More and Malebranche's English expositor John Norris, Edwards learns how to adapt the fashionable terminology of Locke, Newton, and Hutcheson to expose the fragmented character of the world they describe and their consequent marginalization of God.[13]

However, by reinstating God at the heart of philosophical reflection, Edwards does not simply repeat the standard claim that all things depend on God. Rather, by characterizing existence in terms of excellence and describing God in plural terms, he shifts the focus of the doctrine of divine sovereignty away from an account of how a transcendent God relates to autonomous creatures to an account of the meaning of existence as relational.[14] It is thus crucial, he argues, to begin with the recognition that "in a being that is absolutely without any plurality, there cannot be excellency, for there can be no such thing as consent or agreement."[15] Accordingly, the identity and unity of God require the harmony or agreement of the persons of the Trinity, because for something to be identical to or one with something else, there must already be a plurality. Identity cannot be understood merely in terms of an isolated subject or predicate, for to say of something that it is identical to or one with itself (for example, X is X) is already to place it in a propositional relation. The first X is said to be identical to or one with the second X in virtue of their differentiation and association in the proposition. Apart from its place in the proposition (and thus in a network of relations), X by itself is unintelligible. Indeed, apart from that place, "it" would not even be seen as an it.

This distinctive privileging of a logic of propositions over a logic of predicates is a legacy of Edwards's training in Ramism.[16] It explains how his characterizations of God and nature as intrinsically communicative are modeled on a view of language in which terms are meaningful not as independently intelligible elements that combine to form a language but as functions whose meanings are determined only because of their differences from and associations with one another. As such, the Trinity and the Book of Nature are not *comprised* of entities; rather, the persons of the Trinity, things in the world, and creation as a whole are entities in virtue of their trinitarian and communicative character. Unlike his contemporaries who attempt to describe nature apart from God or reduce it to simple components, Edwards thus proposes that perceived regularities in the physical world are ultimately due to the divinely established connections among things.

Divine sovereignty – God's intimate involvement in every detail of existence – must then be understood not as the control of one entity by another but as the activity in terms of which entities (God and creatures alike) become intelligible. Such an understanding is central in Edwards's doctrines about the nature of reality, God's ongoing role in creation, human freedom, personal identity, and moral responsibility. To assume, as many commentators do, that Edwards confronts such issues from the same perspective as Malebranche, Locke, and others who do not have a relational ontology is to miss Edwards's creative resolutions of those issues. For even when he adopts the vocabulary of those with whom he differs, he transforms the questions at hand, often concluding that the problems are simply the result of having assumed a non-relational perspective in the first place.

IDEALISM, OCCASIONALISM

In another early essay, "Of Atoms" (1721), Edwards proposes that for something to be a body means that it is solid, and to be solid means to be resistant to division or displacement.[17] The existence of a particular body is thus a certain, determinate resistance to division or displacement. But the resistance of a particular body cannot be explained by saying that it is of the essence of matter or bodies in general to resist division or displacement, for that would not explain how matter acquires such power or why this particular body exists. If matter is understood (as with Hobbes) as its own source of power and motion, then "no matter is, in the most proper sense, matter," because the determination to resist or move in one way or another cannot be resistance or motion itself.[18] A similar objection can be raised against the Cartesian account of extension, for something must account for the resistance and motion of determinate bodies. As More points out, that cause is not extension itself but rather God.[19] To this, Edwards adds the point that if solidity or resistance is "from the immediate exercise of God's power," then solidity is "nothing but the Deity acting in that particular manner in those parts of space where he thinks fit."[20] Since parts of space become identified as parts in virtue of God's exercise of power, the "very substance of the body itself" must be "nothing but the divine power, or the constant exertion of it."[21] The existence of determinate bodies thus consists in nothing other than God's constant exercise of differentiation and association.

This position repudiates Locke's claim that some "unknown" substance supports solidity and other qualities, for as Edwards remarks, "there is no such thing as material substance truly and properly distinct from all those that are called sensible qualities."[22] If, as Locke says,[23] sensible qualities are powers in substances to cause in us certain sensations, then we have to ask why a substance would have such powers in the first place and why those powers would affect us as they do. Edwards answers such questions by his doctrine of a creating and coordinating God whose activity makes the existence of material substances superfluous. Indeed, if all sensible qualities are the direct result of divine activity, then we can justly say that "there is no proper substance but God himself" (with regard to bodies at least).[24] In creating and maintaining all things according to the patterns of his continuous activity (that is, laws of nature), God is literally the substance of all things and "as it were the only substance, or rather, the perfection and steadfastness of his knowledge, wisdom, power and will."[25] In fact, this is why God, as the *space* in which all things are differentiated and associated, is "as it were" the "common substance or subject" of all bodies.[26]

To be sure, Edwards's identification of God with space might strike us as highly unorthodox – at least until we realize that the space to which he refers is not some identifiable thing but rather that which substantiates identification itself through the positing of such identities in relation. As he encapsulates it,

> The secret lies here: that which truly is the substance of all bodies is the infinitely exact and precise and perfectly stable idea in God's mind, together with his stable will that the same shall gradually be communicated to us, and to other minds, according to certain fixed and exact established methods and laws: or in somewhat different language, the infinitely exact, precise and stable will with respect to correspondent communications to created minds, and effects on their minds.[27]

God is the substance of all bodies precisely because he is the will that there be a stable order of communicated resistance. In willing the resistance (that is, identification) of any body, God simultaneously wills the whole network of bodies in the world. Furthermore, this differentiation of bodies occurs in terms of *perceived* differences in resistance and thus must depend on an activity of mind; otherwise neither individual bodies nor the whole corporeal order of the world would be *identifiable* at all. To think of a body's existing apart from such relations would be to imagine it apart from the (mental) differentiations and associations that determine it as this or that entity; and that, Edwards suggests, is simply unintelligible. Accordingly, "[t]he world exists only mentally, so that the very being of the world implies its being perceived or discovered."[28] Apart from its identification as this or that world, there is no "it" to exist. Since the things in that world are identified in the very act of their being differentiated from and associated with other things, their existence as *those* things depends on their being perceived in that specific way. Identity *and* existence are thus products of the same differentiating act of consciousness.

This way of framing Edwards's idealism indicates how he avoids occasionalism. To be sure, he (like Malebranche) proposes that all natural events depend immediately on God as the cause of their existence. He further argues that, even though the existence of a particular thing is intelligible in terms of its relations to other things (for example, as effects), only God can be said to cause the thing to exist. "In natural things," he writes, "means of effects in metaphysical strictness are not the proper causes of the effects, but only occasions."[29] And even as "occasions," prior events have no causal effect on subsequent events, since "the universe is created out of nothing in every moment."[30] But things are not "conserved" by God, nor does he "concur" in their existence, for that would imply that things have some (if only minimal) autonomy in virtue of having identities apart from God's activity. Rather, God simultaneously wills both the identities and existence of things by differentiating and associating them with one another according to the "fixed, determinate, and unchangeable rules" that we call laws of nature.

Edwards's idealism thus differs from Neoplatonism in that it does not assume that Unity or the One is the source of all being and that Mind (*nous*) is an emanation of the One. Instead, it treats identity as the product of differentiation and association (that is, of consciousness) even as it refuses to assume that there is some distinct subject or substance that engages in such activity. So when Edwards writes "nothing has any existence anywhere else but in consciousness," or "[i]t is manifest that there can be nothing like those things we call by the name of bodies out of the mind, unless it be in some other mind or minds," he (like Berkeley) does not mean that perception merely bestows existence on an already possible being.[31] Because a being is possible only in virtue of its differential place in a network of actually perceived relations, it has no merely possible existence. Rather, its actual existence depends on its being supposed as a feature of the order of things, even if it is not perceived by any created mind.

> It may be asked, how do those things exist which have an actual existence, but of which no created mind is conscious – for instance the

furniture of this room when we are absent and the room is shut up and no created mind perceives it – how do these things exist? I answer, there has been in times past such a course and succession of existences that these things must be supposed to make the series complete, according to divine appointment of the order of things; and there will be innumerable things consequential which will be out of joint – out of their constituted series – without the supposition of these.[32]

To think of a being as different than it is (even in the smallest detail) would not be to think of *that* thing nor the universe in which it exists: "yea, the whole universe would be otherwise."[33] It could exist in no other universe, because its identity depends on its relations with other things in its universe. Those relations are perceived within a series of ideas communicated by God to created minds. Speaking "more strictly and metaphysically," then the identities of things depend not only on their being perceived by minds but also on their being perceived "according to [God's] own settled order and that harmony of things which he has appointed." That is, the perception of a certain thing is the perception of the thing as it relates to "the whole system and series of ideas in all created minds."[34] To the extent that a created mind perceives something without understanding how it fits within the divine economy, it does not really perceive that thing at all. To the extent that a mind fails to appreciate the order and harmony of things – and therefore the ways in which things are differentiated and associated – it fails even to be a mind.

This surprising way of speaking about minds indicates how, by saying that God communicates ideas to created minds, Edwards does not suggest that created minds are substances that exist independently of the communication. Indeed, Edwards carefully avoids describing even God as *a* substance; rather, God is *the* substance of the communication. As with Leibniz, Edwards claims that spirits may "more properly" be called beings and are "more substantial" than bodies (which "have no substance of their own").[35] But spirits are no less dependent on God for their existence than bodies, for "what we call spirit is nothing but a composition and series of perceptions, or an universe of coexisting and successive perceptions connected by such wonderful methods and laws."[36] However, a spirit or mind is not a Humean bundle of discrete perceptions, because the very differentiation of perceptions is itself merely the patterning of relations whereby things are identified. Rather, the spirit or substance of a thing – that in terms of which the thing exists – is the space or "universe" in which it is thought. That is why "those beings which have knowledge and consciousness are the only proper and real and substantial beings, inasmuch as the being of other things is only by these."[37]

To be a thing at all is to be an object of mind. "All existence is perception," for apart from a thing's identification, "it" has no existence.[38]

When Edwards concludes, then, that "spirits only are properly substance,"[39] he means that the substance of things consists in their mental or spiritual differentiation and association, not that the principle of differentiation itself is an already differentiated and identifiable substance. Since the substance of things is what is responsible for their identity, it makes no sense to inquire into the identity of the principle of identity. That is why no thought can be explained in terms of the activity or "substance" of a created soul, for the creation of a thought is nothing other than the differentiation of properties that constitute the soul in the first place. The substance of the soul must therefore be explained in terms of the principle of differentiation itself, namely, God.

> The mere exertion of a new thought is a certain proof of God. For certainly there is something that immediately produces and upholds that thought; here is a new thing, and there is a necessity of a cause. It is not antecedent thoughts, for they are vanished and gone; they are past, and what is past is not. But if we say 'tis the substance of the soul (if we mean that there is some substance besides that thought, that brings that thought forth), if it be God, I acknowledge; but if there be meant something else that has no properties, it seems to me absurd. If the removal of all properties, such as extendedness, solidity, thought, etc. leaves nothing, it seems to me that no substance is anything but them.[40]

Because a created spirit has no properties other than its activities, and because those activities are the immediate expressions of God's differentiation and association of objects, created spirits are immediate expressions of God's activity. Unlike in Spinoza's metaphysics, however, spirits are substantial and express God's creative activity to the extent that they are the principles by which their objects are differentiated and related to one another (for example, in terms of resistance). In this way, spirits are more real and substantial than bodies because they express the will to uniform differentiation – something precluded by Spinoza's concept of substance as conceived only through itself.[41]

PERSONAL IDENTITY, FREEDOM, KNOWLEDGE

Edwards's account of mental substance as an expression of God's will presents a problem for explaining the continuity of the self and the legitimacy of moral responsibility. For if, as he says, "we are anew created every moment" and "all created identity is arbitrary," then the personal identity or continuity of the self is due to relations of memory and consciousness that God establishes "entirely at his will and pleasure."[42] But if God wills anything at all, it must be a certain thing that he wills. And if he wills that there be a certain self, he creates the basis for knowing with certainty all that can be said of it.

> There must be a certainty in things themselves, before they are certainly known, or (which is the same thing) known to be certain. For certainty of knowledge is nothing else but knowing or discerning the certainty there is in the things themselves which are known. Therefore there must be a certainty in things to be a ground of the certainty of knowledge, and to render things capable of being known to be certain. And this is nothing but the necessity of the truth known; or its being impossible but that it should be true; or, in other words, the firm and infallible connection between the subject and predicate of the proposition that contains that truth. All certainty of knowledge consists in the view of the firmness of that connection. So God's certain foreknowledge of the future existence of any event, is his view of the firm and indissoluble connection of the subject and predicate of the proposition that affirms its future existence. The subject is that possible event; the predicate is its future existing; but if the future existence be firmly and indissolubly connected with that event, then the future existence of that event is necessary.[43]

A person's identity as a certain being is determined (that is, made certain) by his or her actions and relations to other things in the world. Those predications are not "imposed on" the self, for there is no self apart from the relations or predications that identify it. To the extent that nothing restricts someone from acting in accord with his or her own personality, character, or desires, he or she is free. Edwards dismisses as absolutely incoherent the objection that this does not allow someone the freedom to choose which desires he or she has, for that would mean that someone could desire what he or she does not desire.[44]

Like Hobbes and Locke, Edwards proposes that freedom consists in being able to do what one wants.[45] This rejects the Arminian view that free will requires self-determination and the spontaneity of "indifference," for as Edwards argues, such a view suggests that either our acts of will are caused by other acts of will (and thus generate an infinite regress) or are uncaused and arbitrary (and are thus not acts for which we are responsible). Our actions, he maintains, are not distinct from our choices or volitions because "we are *in them*, i.e. our wills are in them; not so much because they are from some *property* of ours, as because they are our *properties*."[46] In willing that there be a certain arrangement of objects in the world, we situate ourselves in relation to those objects and define ourselves in terms of our actions. As such, our actions are our properties. Through them, we passionately and affectively differentiate and associate things in the world. But the will that there be such a will to differentiation and association – that is, the will that we exist – simply is not ours but rather God's.

This seems to imply that God determines us to will as we do and makes it impossible for us to will otherwise. But to speak this way is to assume that "we" could exist otherwise than we do or that we are constrained to act in a certain way. Edwards insists, however, that there is no "us" to be constrained or necessitated prior to the actions that differentiate us from or associate us with one another and the world. Of course, as things in the world, we are determined by natural causes; and in that sense, it makes sense to talk about "natural necessity." We can even speak of the "moral necessity" of choosing to act in a certain way, if by that term we mean acting in a certain way based on our motives or inclinations.[47] But the fact that we have such inclinations in the first place is intelligible only because of the "philosophical" or "metaphysical" necessity that we have determinate identities that embody our specific actions and relations. To will other than we do would mean to *be* other than who God has determined us to be. For were it not for that determination, we would have no identities at all. So to be free means to be able to do what we are determined to do, namely, differentiate and relate things in the world in a way that is consistent with comparable acts of others.

In short, our actions are determined by God because we are determinate beings, and for all eternity God knows our thoughts and actions with certainty because he knows and wills that we be the *certain* beings that we are. This does not undermine our freedom, because it does not constrain our ability to act as we want in the world. In fact, it highlights our participation in God's creative process, in that we are determined to be who we are in virtue of willing that things in the world be related in determinate ways.

For Edwards, those actions and relations are our basis for being able to justify our claims to have knowledge of the world. Apart from such a basis, we would open up the possibility for skepticism by assuming that things we know might be intelligible apart from the ideas by which they are known. That is why Edwards rejects Locke's definition of knowledge by claiming that "knowledge is not the perception of the agreement or disagreement of ideas, but rather the perception of the union or disunion of ideas."[48] When we know something, we do not first perceive an idea and subsequently associate or dissociate it with another; rather, we perceive the idea in terms of its association with another. In other words, in knowing something, we perceive not only *that* it is associated with something else but also *why* and *how* it is associated in virtue of God's determination of reality in and through us. We thus have access to truth by understanding the fixed sequence of our ideas as existence itself: "In things that are supposed to be without us, 'tis the determination and fixed mode of God's exciting ideas in us. So that truth in these things is an agreement of our ideas with that series in God. 'Tis existence, and that is all that we can say."[49] Truth, in short, is the agreement of our ideas with existence; and the knowledge of truth is possible precisely because existence is a divinely willed series of determinately communicated ideas, not a collection of disconnected facts that exist apart from the expressions of God's will that constitute our minds.

Therefore, far from being alienated or disinterested intellects whose contacts with the world are limited to "speculative knowledge," we are – or at least can be, if we would simply reject our penchant for experiencing things as autonomous and fragmented – intimately engaged in the determination of the objects of our knowledge. That is why the "sense of the heart" thematized in Edwards's metaphysical idealism extends "to all the knowledge we have of all objects whatsoever. For there is no kind of thing that we know but what may be considered as in some respect or other concerning the wills or hearts of spiritual beings."[50] For fallen humanity, objects seem to be intelligible apart from their being perceived. But the regenerate recognize all things as necessarily mental or spiritual because, for them, all things are perceived in terms of the will that they be understood as *those objects in those relations*. In virtue of God's will that we have the ideas we have, we are linked intrinsically to the objects we perceive as their principles of differentiation and association. To the extent that our actions embody the harmony of objects of our experience with one another, we express the integrity and beauty of creation. In this way, our very existence as expressions of God's will is the basis for moral and aesthetic judgments.

MORALITY, AESTHETICS, PHILOSOPHY OF HISTORY

Edwards's theories of morality and aesthetics, like other aspects of his thought, depend on his doctrine that the excellency of existence consists in the agreeableness or "consent" of things to one another. Along with Shaftesbury and Hutcheson, Edwards seizes on the analogy between virtue and beauty, and like Berkeley he argues that our actions are useful and promote happiness because of their harmony with the divinely established order of nature.[51] Like them, he defines virtue not in terms of pleasure or utility but in terms of benevolence. In his view, however, benevolence does not mean sympathizing with another's plight or even simply following our conscience, for by placing ourselves sympathetically in the situation of others, we engage in a form of self-love and validate the propriety of thinking of others apart from their place in the order of creation. Apart from that order, no individual is intelligible, so the will to identify with an individual is a misdirected effort that reinforces the presumed autonomy of individuals.

Even in the case of "natural virtue" – where our conscience allows us to judge things not in terms of how they relate solely to ourselves but in terms of their fitness in the order of nature – nothing truly justifies following our conscience, because there is no guarantee of the uniformity of nature. Apart from such a guarantee, dictates of conscience or moral sense can provide only practical guidelines for behavior, but they do not have any real moral authority because they cannot provide a rationale for the moral order.

> Approbation of conscience is the more readily mistaken for a truly virtuous approbation, because by the wise constitution of the great Governor of the world (as was observed) when conscience is well informed, and thoroughly awakened, it agrees with the latter fully and exactly, as to the object approved, though not as to the ground and reason of approving.... And indeed natural conscience is implanted in all mankind, there to be as it were in God's stead, and to be an internal judge or rule to all, whereby to distinguish right and wrong.... The present state of the world is so ordered and constituted by the wisdom and goodness of its supreme Ruler, that these natural principles for the most part tend to the good of the world of mankind.... But this is no proof that these natural principles have the nature of true virtue. For self-love is a principle that is exceeding useful and necessary in the world of mankind. So are the natural appetites of hunger and thirst, etc. But yet nobody will assert that these have the nature of true virtue.[52]

Conscience relates the self to nature in a way that makes it easier to distinguish right and wrong, but it is not based on an account of why things are related as they are. Natural virtue merely expresses the will that all things be in harmony, but it does not presume or express a concurrent belief that God is the reason for such harmony.

By contrast, in true virtue we will that the objects of our actions be in harmony with one another as expressions of God's will. We act in a truly virtuous way when we are motivated by the love of God, not by concerns for ourselves or others except insofar as we intend all creation (including ourselves and others) to be expressions of God's will. True virtue is thus informed by "benevolence to being in general," the will to make the objects of our actions products of the integrating activity of God. In this way, true virtue is "that consent, propensity and union of heart to Being in general, that is immediately exercised in a general good will," for the truly good will is always concerned with harmonizing all.[53]

In both true and natural virtue, then, the focus is on the effective will that the objects of nature be differentiated and associated in harmony. But in identifying things in relation to other things, conscience – *con-science*, the knowing of things in relation to others – opens up the possibility of shifting attention away from the *activity* by which things come to have identities to the assumption that their identities are intelligible solely in virtue of their place in nature. Even though this shift in attention from act to object is not part of conscientious behavior, it sets the stage for what becomes over time the temptation to ignore the spiritual character of all objects. Such a temptation never occurs in true virtue, for the object of true virtue (being in general) cannot be differentiated from anything else. That is why the principles on which natural virtue and true virtue are based are completely different.

No wonder that by a long continued worldly and sensual life men more and more lose all sense of the deity, who is a spiritual and invisible Being. The mind, being long involved in and engrossed by sensitive objects, becomes sensual in all its operations, excludes all views and impressions of spiritual objects, and is unfit for their contemplation. Thus the conscience and general benevolence are entirely different principles, and the sense of conscience differs from the holy complacence of a benevolent and truly virtuous heart.[54]

Once disconnected from the spiritual principle of their initial identification and considered intelligible in themselves (for example, as substances), natural objects can be reassociated either by appealing to natural relations (as in Newtonian science, Lockean or Humean epistemology, or Hutchesonian ethics) or by invoking God as the cause of the arbitrary arrangement of natural things (as in Malebranchean occasionalism). But both strategies of reassociation ignore the initial integrity of all created things because they start with the things produced by the exercise of power rather than with the original exercise of power (*virtus*) that produces those things as intrinsically related to one another.

By contrast, in Edwards's moral ontology, we and all that we do are expressions of God's activity. In willing that all that we do and perceive be in harmony with everything else, we consent to being in general. If we simply follow our conscience, we can act in ways that just might promote harmony among things. But only when we act for the love of God can we justify our willing as we do, because we recognize how our willing to perceive things in a certain order is part of God's will that those things be perceived in that order.

This means that true virtue depends not only on our willing that things be in harmony but also on the fact that such things actually are in harmony. This requires Edwards to distinguish three senses of consent. First, according to his doctrine of excellence, no thing can be in harmony apart from its ontological consent to other things in virtue of the divine activity that posits differences and associations in the order of things. Second, moral consent refers to the will that things be harmonized with one another in virtue of our actions. In moral consent we affirm our own act of being (and thus our freedom and responsibility) by acknowledging our role in the determination of the intentional objects of our actions. This "sense of the heart" is the basis for true virtue or benevolence (that is, willing the best for the things we perceive by recognizing their inherently spiritual character) because it identifies minds as the principles of the moral or "primary" beauty of those things. Third, the aesthetic sense of consent refers to "secondary" beauty, the order and proportionality of things in nature. This "love of complacence" in perceiving the intricate symmetries and regularities of nature is pleasing and inspiring and reveals a correspondence between the operations of the mind and the world. But because the aesthetic experience of beauty provides no grounds for explaining how such a correspondence is possible, it is at best a shadow or copy of the kind of beauty that enacts the principles on which the mutual consent of beings is based. Just as we feel a certain rightness in following our conscience, so we also experience delight in natural beauty. But in our experience of secondary beauty, just as in natural virtue, we fail to see how the objects we contemplate depend on the mental or spiritual activity that constitutes their harmonies or order.[55]

For Edwards, the idea that the ontological, moral, or aesthetic excellency of something is based on the apprehension of its differentiation from (and completion in) something else applies also to his philosophy of history. Even though his death prevented him from completing his *History of the Work of Redemption*, it is apparent from the materials he prepared for the project that his discussion is couched in the same terms as those found in the other areas of his thought. History in general he explains in terms of divine providence; specific historical events he explains in terms of a biblical eschatology. As in the cases of true versus natural virtue, and spiritual versus natural beauty, he proposes that a particular event can be understood in terms of either its spiritual character or its natural character. In terms of its spiritual character, he writes, an event is properly interpreted typologically, because such an analysis provides the rationale or "substance and consummation" for otherwise disconnected events.[56] In terms of its natural character, an event is merely one of a series that might seem to exhibit a pattern, but its lack of necessary or intrinsic connections to other events precludes any ultimate chance of finding a rationale for it. Regardless, however, of whether we are speaking of history in general or specific events in particular, we need to keep in mind the fact that the meaning of whatever we are talking about is to be found in its transcendence.

In sum, Edwards's forays into the debates in modern philosophy about the nature of reality, the problem of knowledge, human freedom, morality, beauty, and history challenge the naturalistic and humanistic premises on which those debates are founded. Instead of assuming that the natural world is composed of individuated things and minds that are only subsequently related, he recommends a "new sense of the heart" to replace the fallen mentality of isolated minds, bodies, and ideas with a regenerate appreciation of the harmony of things. On the surface, this shift looks merely like Malebranchean occasionalism or Berkeleyan idealism. But instead of invoking God as a corrective to the already presumed fragmentation of experience, Edwards bases the possibility for existence itself on God's will that things be differentiated from and related to one another. When we acknowledge this fact, Edwards observes, we align ourselves with both God and nature, and by means of such a consent, our actions become free and virtuous.

Framed in those terms, Edwards's philosophy is less like that of Hutcheson, Locke, and Shaftesbury than that of Berkeley, Leibniz, Malebranche, and More.[57] However, in contrast to these latter thinkers, Edwards explicitly thematizes the intrinsically relational character of existence in his doctrine of excellency. In doing so, he combines insights from Ramist logicians, Puritan divines, and Scholastic metaphysicians to create strategies for resolving philosophical questions by rejecting the reductionist, naturalistic, and antimetaphysical assumptions of modern philosophy. To some, that might sound like a repudiation of modernity and a return to an earlier mindset. But for Edwards, it is an attempt to locate the issues of modern philosophy within a context that promises more fruitful results.

Notes

1. See Norman Fiering, "The Rationalist Foundations of Jonathan Edwards's Metaphysics," in Nathan O. Hatch and Harry S. Stout, eds., *Jonathan Edwards and the American Experience* (New York: Oxford University Press, 1988), 73–8; Charles J. McCracken, *Malebranche and British Philosophy* (Oxford: Clarendon Press, 1983), 330–40. The expression "theocentric metaphysicians" comes from Louis E. Loeb, *From Descartes to Hume: Continental Metaphysics and the Development of Modern Philosophy* (Ithaca, NY: Cornell University Press, 1981), 29–30.

2. See "Things to Be Considered and Written Fully About," WJE, 6:238; Francisco Suárez, *Disputationes Metaphysicae* 2.4.3, in idem, *Opera* (26 vols. Paris: Vives, 1856–66), 25: 87–92. Cf. William Sparkes Morris, *The Young Jonathan Edwards: A Reconstruction* (Brooklyn: Carlson, 1991), 393–8; Stephen H. Daniel, "Berkeley,

Suárez, and the *Esse–Existere* Distinction," *American Catholic Philosophical Quarterly* 74 (2000): 621–36.

3. Cf. Henry More, *An Appendix to the Foregoing Antidote against Atheism*, VII.6 (London: William Morden, 1662), 165; idem, *Divine Dialogues* (London: James Flesher, 1668), 125; Nicolas Malebranche, *The Search after Truth*, III.2.6, in *The Search after Truth and the Elucidations of the Search after Truth*, trans. Thomas M. Lennon and Paul J. Olscamp (Columbus: Ohio State University Press, 1980), 235. See Wallace E. Anderson, "Introduction" to *Scientific and Philosophical Writings*, WJE, 6:57–61; Stephen H. Daniel, "Berkeley's Pantheistic Discourse," *International Journal for Philosophy of Religion* 49 (2001): 183–7, 190.

4. "Of Being," WJE, 6:203.

5. Ibid., 6:202. Also see the 1732 addition to ibid., 6:207.

6. See Edwards, "Of Atoms," WJE, 6:215; "Miscell." 267, WJE,13:373; "Notes on Knowledge and Existence," WJE, 6:398. Cf. Anderson, "Introduction," WJE, 6:84.

7. "The Mind," 1, WJE, 6:336.

8. Ibid., 332.

9. Ibid., 62; WJE, 6:381. See also "Miscell." 117, WJE, 13:283; Norman Fiering, *Jonathan Edwards's Moral Thought and Its British Context* (Chapel Hill: University of North Carolina Press, 1981), 326.

10. The most helpful studies of the sources of Edwards's philosophy are Morris, *Young Jonathan Edwards*; Fiering, *Jonathan Edwards's Moral Thought*; Anderson, "Introduction," WJE, 6.

11. See Stephen H. Daniel, *The Philosophy of Jonathan Edwards* (Bloomington: Indiana University Press, 1994), 69–83.

12. See Morris, *Young Jonathan Edwards*, 80–128, 270–80.

13. See Allen C. Guelzo, "Learning Is the Handmaid of the Lord: Jonathan Edwards, Reason, and the Life of the Mind," *Midwest Studies in Philosophy* 28 (2004): 4–8; Morris, *Young Jonathan Edwards*, 427; Fiering, *Jonathan Edwards's Moral Thought*, 37.

14. "The Mind," 62, WJE, 6:381.

15. Ibid., 1, WJE, 6:337. See also "Miscell." 117, WJE, 13:284.

16. See Stephen H. Daniel, "Edwards, Berkeley, and Ramist Logic," *Idealistic Studies* 31 (2001): 60–8; idem, "The Ramist Context of Berkeley's Philosophy," *British Journal of the History of Philosophy* 9 (2001): 487–505.

17. "Of Atoms," WJE, 6:211.

18. "Things to Be Considered and Written Fully About," WJE, 6:235. See also WJE, 6:238.

19. See Anderson, "Introduction," WJE, 6:64–5; "Miscell." 383, WJE, 13:451–2.

20. "Of Atoms," WJE, 6:215.

21. "The Mind," 27, WJE, 6:350–1.

22. See "Of Atoms," WJE, 6:215; "Things to Be Considered," WJE, 6:238; "Notes on Knowledge and Existence," WJE, 6:398.

23. See John Locke, *Essay Concerning Human Understanding*, ed. Peter H. Nidditch (Oxford: Clarendon Press, 1975), Bk. II, ch. 8, paragraphs 8–10, pp. 134–5.

24. "Of Atoms," WJE, 6:215. As Anderson observes, this view diverges sharply from the traditional concept of substance as assumed in materialist and dualist theories (WJE, 6:66).

25. Edwards, "Notes on Knowledge and Existence," WJE, 6:398.
26. The Mind," 9, WJE, 6:341.
27. Ibid., 13, WJE, 6:344.
28. "Miscell." 247, WJE, 13:360. See also "Notes on Knowledge and Existence," WJE, 6:398. By saying that the world is "discovered," Edwards does not mean that it was first "out there" and then perceived. In Ramist logic, the discovery or "finding" of a thing refers to its placement as a topic (*topos*) within intelligible discourse.
29. "Miscell." 629, WJE, 18:157.
30. "Things to Be Considered," 47, WJE, 6:241.
31. "Of Being," WJE, 6:204; "The Mind," 13, WJE, 6:344. Similarities with Berkeley abound here, but it seems that Edwards came to these ideas independently of Berkeley.
32. "The Mind," 40, WJE, 6:356–7. See also "The Mind," 36, WJE, 6:355.
33. Ibid., 40, WJE, 6:357.
34. Ibid.
35. "Things to Be Considered," 44, WJE, 6:238. See G. W. Leibniz, "Discourse on Metaphysics," § 35, in *Philosophical Texts*, trans. R. S. Woolhouse and Richard Francks (Oxford: Oxford University Press, 1998), 87.
36. "Notes on Knowledge and Existence," WJE, 6:398.
37. "Of Being," WJE, 6:206.
38. "Notes on Knowledge and Existence," WJE, 6:398.
39. "Of Being," WJE, 6:206.
40. "Miscell." 267, WJE, 13:373.
41. Baruch Spinoza, *Ethics*, I, def. 3, in Edwin Curley, ed., *The Collective Works of Spinoza* (Princeton: Princeton University Press, 1985), 408.
42. "Miscell." 18, WJE, 13:210; "Notes on Knowledge" WJE, 6:398.
43. *Freedom of the Will*, WJE, 1:264–65; see also 152–6. Even though Edwards does not seem to have drawn on Leibniz for his understanding of how all predicates are contained in the complete notion of a substance, there are notable similarities in their views. See Leibniz's "Discourse on Metaphysics," §§ 8, 32–3, in *Philosophical Texts*, 59–64, 84–5, and Leibniz to Arnauld, July 14, 1686, ibid., 109–12.
44. Edwards, *Freedom of the Will*, WJE, 1:156–9.
45. Ibid., 163.
46. Ibid., 428.
47. Ibid., 157. See Fiering, *Jonathan Edwards's Moral Thought*, 305–13.
48. "The Mind," 71, WJE, 6:385.
49. Ibid., 15, WJE, 6:345.
50. "Miscell." 782, WJE, 18:460. See *Original Sin*, WJE, 3:399–404. See also Daniel, *Philosophy of Edwards*, 145–9, 187–96.
51. For the sources of Edwards's moral theory, see Paul Ramsey's introduction, notes, and appendix 2 ("Jonathan Edwards on Moral Sense, and the Sentimentalists") in WJE, 8; Fiering, *Jonathan Edwards's Moral Thought*.
52. *The Nature of True Virtue*, WJE, 8:612–13, 616. See Daniel, *Philosophy of Edwards*, 174–6.
53. *The Nature of True Virtue*, WJE, 8:540, 559.
54. Ibid., 614.

55. See ibid., 544, 550–1, 561–5; "Miscell." 782, WJE, 18:459, 561–77. See also Daniel, *Philosophy of Edwards*, 178–87.

56. "Miscell." 1069 ("Types of the Messiah"), WJE, 11:91. See also *Images of Divine Things*, WJE, 11:53, 69–70; *The Nature of True Virtue*, WJE, 8:564–7; Daniel, *Philosophy of Edwards*, 48–61.

57. See Fiering, "Rationalist Foundations," 77, 92.

9 Edwards as biblical exegete

STEPHEN J. STEIN

In 1740, looking back on earlier years, Jonathan Edwards penned the following statement concerning the central place of the Bible in his personal and professional life. "I had then, and at other times," he wrote, "the greatest delight in the holy Scriptures, of any book whatsoever." His was an apt summary that, in fact, applied to his entire life. In his statement he also sounded a note of unambiguous spiritual pleasure that he derived from the study of the biblical text. "Oftentimes in reading it, every word seemed to touch my heart. I felt an harmony between something in my heart, and those sweet and powerful words." Edwards recollected that the force and power of "every sentence" was such that often he "could not get along in reading." He found himself dwelling "long on one sentence, to see the wonders contained in it." In his judgment, "almost every sentence seemed to be full of wonders."[1]

By the time that he wrote those reflections, Edwards had a well-developed program of private study of the Bible evident in the notebooks and commentaries that he was compiling. Early in his ministerial career, while serving as a supply minister in New York City, he had "Resolved, to study the Scriptures so steadily, constantly, and frequently, as that I may find, and plainly perceive myself to grow in the knowledge of the same."[2] Although from time to time he acknowledged difficulty maintaining that high resolve, he never abandoned the goal of steady, constant, and frequent study of the Bible. The evidence of that lifelong commitment is the massive body of exegetical reflections from his hand.

Samuel Hopkins (1721–1803), Edwards's close friend and first biographer, early on recognized the central role that the Bible played in Edwards's life and ministry. In 1765 he asserted that his mentor "had studied the Bible more than all other books." Hopkins noted his "unwearied study" of the biblical text, and he declared that Edwards was "one of the *greatest of divines*" in considerable measure because of his commitment to the "study and knowledge of the Bible."[3] Sereno E. Dwight (1786–1850), Edwards's great-grandson and editor of the third edition of his *Works*, which included one of Edwards's biblical commentaries, also featured his great-grandfather's "regular and diligent study of the Sacred Scriptures," as well as his high "veneration" of the text and his determination to discover the "true meaning" of even its most difficult passages.[4] Despite this early recognition of the centrality of the Bible in Edwards's life and thought, subsequent disciples and scholars focused more attention on other aspects of his biography and theology. Only in recent decades has this oversight begun to be corrected as more of Edwards's commentaries have been published and as interest in this dimension of his theology has increased.[5]

This chapter will describe and evaluate the variety of Edwards's exegetical writings as well as the hermeneutical principles he employed in his interpretation of the biblical texts. It will also examine the diverse locations in which he wrote about the Bible and situate his commentary within the larger tradition of Western biblical scholarship.

The documentary evidence of Edwards's lifelong preoccupation with Scripture is overwhelming. Over the course of his lifetime he compiled two major biblical commentaries in manuscript that spanned all books of the Bible. The two were *Notes on Scripture*, begun in 1724, and "Miscellaneous Observations on the Holy Scriptures," which he referred to as his "Blank Bible," begun in 1730.[6] Dwight's ten-volume edition of Edwards's *Works* includes a heavily edited, abridged, and reorganized version of the *Notes on Scripture*, which in manuscript consists of more than five hundred separate entries.[7] A critical scholarly edition of the entire commentary first appeared in 1998.[8] The "Blank Bible," which contains more than 5,500 notes and entries on all sections of Scripture, is first appearing in a critical scholarly edition in 2006.[9] Prior to this, 324 entries from the "Blank Bible" appeared in an 1865 publication edited by Alexander B. Grosart, a Scottish editor who carried the commentary to Scotland without the permission of the family in the middle of the nineteenth century.[10] Eventually, late in the century, the Edwards family succeeded in securing the return of the manuscript to America. In addition to these two major commentaries, Edwards compiled a separate notebook on the book of Revelation, entitled *Notes on the Apocalypse*.[11] In 1723 he began that document, which contains diverse materials including Edwards's own reflections as well as notes he compiled from various publications and from newspapers. That commentary appeared for a first and only time in a critical scholarly edition in 1977.[12]

But these biblical commentaries are not the only exegetical reflections by Edwards. Many scriptural observations are part of his *"Miscellanies,"* a series of theological notebooks launched in November 1722 when he was only nineteen years old. The *"Miscellanies"* is the most diverse and perhaps the most important of his private notebooks. The entries range across the full spectrum of theological, philosophical, personal, and pastoral concerns.[13] Many also focus directly on the interpretation of the Bible. The importance and diversity of the *"Miscellanies"* account for the fact that selections from the series have been published at different times by persons with varying interests, including, for example, Jonathan Edwards, Jr., Sereno E. Dwight, and Harvey G. Townsend, a twentieth-century historian of American philosophy.[14]

Some of Edwards's earliest recorded scriptural observations occur in the *"Miscellanies."* Among them, for example, is an exposition of Psalms 96:13 in which he interpreted the prophecy of God's coming into the world as a reference to a visible incarnation.[15] Edwards wrote another early scriptural entry on Revelation 5:10, a text which describes a reign of the saints on earth; he used it to reflect on two resurrections, one spiritual and one natural.[16] His earliest observations also engage hermeneutical questions concerning how to interpret the Bible. In an entry entitled "Scripture," he noted, "Some may ask why the Scripture expresses things so unintelligibly. . . . Why doth it not call these things directly by the intelligible names of those things that lie hid under these expressions?" His answer involves a judgment about efficiency. Simple expressions or "similitudes," the "lively pictures" that fill the pages of the Bible, in his judgment, would require "a hundred pages" to explain.[17] In the *"Miscellanies,"* he introduced the interpretive category that occupied him throughout his lifetime, namely, "Types." He asserted that in typology God used "innumerable things" – both natural and human – to represent and depict "things divine and spiritual."[18]

During the first years that Edwards served as the pastor in Northampton, he began another notebook to which he referred variously, but which is known today by the title *Images of Divine Things*. In this collection of notes he reflected on nature and the surrounding world, finding spiritual and religious meaning therein.[19] Often his entries were linked explicitly with biblical references. For example, in no. 15 which contains reflections about rivers and the trees adjacent to them, Edwards referenced Jeremiah 17:8, Psalms 1:3, and Numbers 24:6, all of which describe both rivers and trees.[20] Some of the entries are explicit exegetical notes. No. 95 is an explanation of the phrase in Genesis 3:14, "upon thy belly shalt thou go, and dust shalt thou eat." Edwards concluded that the serpent's manner of crawling represented a curse "on the devil," and proved the relationship between "outward things" and "spiritual things."[21] In no. 192 he used the experience of "ripe fruit" being "easily gathered" to conclude, "So is a saint that is ripe for heaven: he easily quits this world (Job 5:26)."[22]

Edwards also kept a much smaller notebook on "Types," in which most of the entries were triggered by biblical passages.[23] He opened that notebook with a general affirmation concerning the "typical" quality of the Old Testament experience, whether it be a ceremony, history, or the circumstances

of ancient Israel. The "pool of Siloam" (John 9:7), for example, he declared
typical of the "fount of grace and mercy that is in Christ."[24] The manna
that fed the Israelites in the desert he linked with "the true bread from
heaven" (John 6:31–2) referenced by Jesus.[25] But Edwards's notebook was
premised on the judgment that it was not only Old Testament types that were
instructive. Human nature disposed types to be "a fit method of instruction"
as is evident "in painting, poetry, fables, metaphorical language [and] dramatic performances." That typological assumption was the basis for his long
entry in the *"Miscellanies,"* no. 1069, wherein he expounded on the critical
link between "things" in the Old Testament and assertions regarding "THE
MESSIAH AND HIS KINGDOM AND SALVATION."[26]

Edwards's most explicit and sustained engagement with the Bible as a
commentator, however, occurs in the entries contained in his two major commentaries, the *Notes on Scripture* and the "Blank Bible." He wrote comments
on the interpretation of specific passages in the Bible as he encountered those
passages in the course of his study or as he saw a reason to use them in his
personal or professional life. For that reason the entries must be described
as occasional rather than systematic. In these two commentaries, Edwards
engaged in the full range of tasks that occupy the biblical commentator.

Edwards studied the text of the Bible very closely, sometimes turning
initially to the Hebrew and Greek for a firsthand examination of the ancient
texts. He recognized the linguistic importance of studying the biblical text in
the original languages. But he also knew his own limitations with respect to
the biblical languages. In 1757 he acknowledged that one of the side benefits
involved with accepting the invitation to become the president of the College
of New Jersey was the opportunity it provided to develop more fully his language facility in Hebrew because he would be teaching it to students at the
college.[27] There are many examples of Edwards's drawing insight from the
use of the original biblical languages. For instance, he used his knowledge of
Hebrew in the interpretation of Exodus 12:38 to argue that the translation
of עֵרֶב רַב in the King James Version, "a mixed multitude," should read
"a great mixture," because the persons spoken of included "a great number of hypocrites" who later caused problems for Israel.[28] In his comments
on I Peter 1:14, he noted that the Greek ὑπακοή in the New Testament
is "often put for that compliance and yielding to the gospel that appertains
to true faith." He then cited locations in other epistles where the word is
so used.[29]

Edwards spent a lifetime becoming acquainted with and acquiring aids
for the study of the Bible. Some were publications that shed light on the geography, chronology, and history of the ancient Near East, on Jewish life and
religious practice, on the context of the Greek and Roman worlds that shaped

the culture of the West, and on the development of emergent Christian traditions. For example, he knew and used the work of Herman Moll (d. 1732), a Dutch geographer and mapmaker who published *Atlas Geographus: Or, a Compleat System of Geography, Ancient and Modern*.[30] He relied heavily on Humphrey Prideaux's *The Old and New Testament Connected in the History of the Jews and Neighbouring Nations*.[31] He found very useful the study by Theophilus Gale, *Court of the Gentiles: Or a Discourse Touching the Original of Human Literature, Both Philologie and Philosophie, From Scripture & Jewish Church*.[32] He used Archibald Bower's *The History of the Popes, from the Foundation of the See of Rome to the Present Time*.[33] He read and examined closely these and scores of other works shedding light on the biblical text.

Edwards was preoccupied with obtaining access to scriptural commentaries that allowed him to enter the interpretive discourse of Jewish and Christian thinkers. He took note of such resources in his "Catalogue of Reading" and in his "Account Book."[34] In *Notes on Scripture* and in the "Blank Bible," the most frequently cited works are the massive biblical commentaries by Matthew Poole, *Synopsis Criticorum Aliorumque Sacrae Scripturae Interpretum*, by Matthew Henry, *Exposition of the Old and New Testaments*, and by Philip Doddridge, *The Family Expositor: Or, A Paraphrase and Version of the New Testament: with Critical Notes; and a Practical Improvement of Each Section*.[35] These commentators ranged widely across the entire Bible or, in Doddridge's case, across the entire New Testament. Edwards also used more focused volumes, some dealing with only one book of the Bible, others with particular themes developed throughout Scripture. In his exposition of the Apocalypse, for example, he took extensive notes from the commentary by Moses Lowman, *A Paraphrase and Notes on the Revelation of St. John*.[36] In his entries on the book of Hebrews, Edwards drew heavily on commentaries dealing with that epistle by John Owen, including *A Continuation of the Exposition of the Epistle of Paul the Apostle to the Hebrews: (viz) On the Eleventh, Twelfth & Thirteenth Chapters, Compleating That Elaborate Work*.[37] He cited favorably John Locke's *A Paraphrase and Notes on the Epistle of St. Paul to the Galatians*.[38] Edwards also knew and used extensively Nathaniel Lardner's *The Credibility of the Gospel History, Part II, or the Principal Facts of the New Testament Confirmed by Passages of Ancient Authors, Who Were Contemporary with Our Saviour or His Apostles, or Lived Near Their Time*.[39] These and many other volumes enriched his study and interpretation of Scripture. Often his own exegetical judgments were formed in conversation with opinions expressed in the works he was reading. Throughout his professional life he engaged this Christian tradition of commentarial discourse.

Edwards was constantly watching for additional aids for scriptural study – lexicons, concordances, and dictionaries. He knew and used, for example, the *Lexicon Hebraicum et Chaldaicum* by the Swiss Orientalist Johann Buxtorf (1564–1629)[40] and the *Concordantiae Graecae Versionis Vulgo Dictae LXX Interpretum* by the Dutch scholar Abraham Trommius (1633–1719).[41] He made extensive use of *A Complete Concordance to the Holy Scriptures of the Old and New Testament* by the Scot commentator Alexander Cruden (1701–70).[42] That work, Edwards noted, was said to be "more useful than any book of this kind hitherto published."[43] He employed dictionaries that focused on biblical materials, including *A Complete Christian Dictionary: Wherein the Significations and Several Acceptations of All the Words Mentioned in the Holy Scriptures of the Old and New-Testament, Are Fully Opened, Expressed, Explained* by the Anglican Thomas Wilson (1563–1622)[44] and the *Cyclopaedia, or an Universal Dictionary of Art and Sciences* by Ephraim Chambers (d. 1740).[45] Edwards never abandoned his search for additional scriptural aids.

Edwards's study habits are evident from entries on "Justification" in his "Controversies" notebook where he engaged the judgments of John Taylor's commentary on the book of Romans.[46] Edwards carried out a word study and planned other close textual work. He wrote:

> In an answerable manner, the words "unjust" and "unrighteous" are used in the New Testament, where the word in the Greek is from the same root.
>
> (Note these things above were observed before I received my Greek Concordance. Remember, and when leisure allows, examine the Greek Testament more fully by the Concordance.
>
> Look also in Trommius' Concordance of the Septuagint.
>
> Look also [at] the word *Tzaddik* and other words from the same root in the Hebrew Concordance. Also the word Διμη, and all its derivations, in my Greek Concordance.)[47]

This is the context in which Edwards came to know the rising tradition of innovative critical scholarship that was gaining attention in Europe and raising new challenges to the authority and interpretation of the Bible. His "Catalogue of Reading" includes works whose authors were questioning traditional approaches to the Bible. Among the sources he was reading were *De Veritate Religionis Christianae* by the Dutch theologian Hugo Grotius (1583–1645)[48] and *Christianity as Old as the Creation, or the Gospel a Republication of the Religion of Nature* by the English Deist Matthew Tindal (1655–1733).[49] He also worked through histories such as *The Sacred and Profane History of the World Connected* by Samuel Shuckford (1693/4–1754)[50] and *A Critical and Chronological History of Knowledge* by Henry Winder (1693–1752).[51]

In his commentaries, Edwards engaged a number of the controversial issues of that day. The longest entry in *Notes on Scripture*, no. 416, is entitled "Whether the PENTATEUCH was written by Moses." In it Edwards rebutes the emerging theory of the Pentateuch's multiple authorship. His opening paragraph asserts, "That it was so is the voice of all antiquity, and it has been all along, even to this day, the received opinion, both of Jews and Christians, that Moses, being commanded and inspired by God, wrote those books that are called the Pentateuch. . . ."[52] In the "Blank Bible," at the start of the entries on I Chronicles, Edwards wrote, "Concerning the chronological difficulties and seeming inconsistencies in numbers in the books of Kings and Chronicles, see Bedford's *Scripture Chronology*," a source he used extensively.[53] The key word in his statement is "seeming"; he did not accept the judgment that there were inconsistencies in the scriptural historical accounts. He was equally, if not even more, assertive when addressing differences in details among the synoptic gospels. In both *Notes on Scripture* and the "Blank Bible," Edwards addressed the "seeming inconsistence" among the accounts of Jesus' journey passing through Jericho on the way to Jerusalem. He resolved the conflict in the texts by positing that Jesus lodged for a night in the "suburbs of Jericho" rather than in the "main city," thus making it possible to reconcile conflicting accounts and thus preserve harmony among the gospels.[54] Edwards addressed the question of the "canonical authority" of the book of Revelation in a variety of locations. He argued that both the testimonies of many early Christian writers and the fact that the Apocalypse generated "so many spurious pieces" with similar names in the following centuries prove that the book of Revelation was "received as of great value and authority."[55] In all of these challenges posed by critics, Edwards adopted and defended traditional views.

Edwards was very aware of the growing critical approach to the interpretation of Scripture. He gained that knowledge from his wide reading and study. He adopted a defensive posture over against the biblical text, affirming its historical integrity in the face of new challenges and continuing to assert its relevance for life and thought. His knowledge of the critical challenges reinforced his determination to defend the authority of Scripture. To that end, he invested heavily in his exegetical writings.

Edwards's scriptural preoccupation is apparent in other ways, too. From the time that he began serving the congregation in New York City at the age of nineteen until he assumed responsibilities as president of the college in Princeton, his most persistent, demanding, pastoral responsibility was preaching weekly. His sermons followed the classic Puritan pattern – text, doctrine, and application. Edwards's approach to homiletics rested on the notion that the biblical text was the foundation for the sermon;

from the text the doctrinal statement derived. That observation, however, does not imply that Edwards always constructed his sermons in the same fashion. Sermons, no doubt, sometimes arose from the circumstances in which he found himself. In practice, selection of a biblical text might or might not precede determination of the point of the sermon. Even so, there was no doubt in his mind that the Bible provided the authoritative grounds for asserting the doctrine. Sermons were dependent upon Scripture rather than logic or other human authority. It is impossible to overstate the significance of Edwards's study of the Bible for his preaching. The more than twelve hundred extant sermons by Edwards document that judgment. Two specific examples here will illustrate the role of Scripture in his sermons.

In a sermon on Haggai 1:5 preached in New York City sometime in 1722–1723, Edwards's doctrinal statement, "'Tis our most important duty to consider our ways," echoes the passage in Haggai which reads, "Now therefore thus saith the Lord of hosts; Consider your ways." His exposition of the text contrasts beasts, which have only natural instincts and appetites, with the situation of humans, who have been given "a higher faculty, even reason and understanding." The Israelites, whom the prophet Haggai addressed, were not accepting their responsibility to rebuild the temple, and for that failure they were making excuses. But the prophet proclaimed it their duty as commanded by the Lord. Similarly, Edwards argued that his auditors must consider their ways and do what they must do. They, too, were neglecting their duty. They had chosen sinful pleasures and "earthly things" over "heavenly objects." Therefore they, like ancient Israel, must consider their ways – their thoughts, words, and actions. They must hearken to the text and consider the danger they were in and the steps they must take to avoid tormenting eternal consequences.[56]

Edwards's sermon on Job 14:2, "He cometh forth like a flower, and is cut down," is another graphic example of his effective use of a biblical text. He chose the Job text when addressing a private gathering of young people in February 1741 following the death of Billy Sheldon, a young man in Northampton. In his exposition he compared the life of a human being and the life of a flower with respect to their beginnings and endings. The flower comes forth quickly, but soon, while blooming, is cut down. Edwards dwelt at length on the comparison, speaking of the flowering stage of life – the time of youth – as most promising. But the flower is the part of a plant that is "so short-lived." Young people, he warned, similarly often die without warning. In his application he exhorted the youthful members at the gathering to "get ready for death." Billy Sheldon's death provided him an occasion to counsel his youthful auditors that they now had "an opportunity to prepare for death." This was a warning, Edwards declared, to "get into Christ, that so you may be ready for death."[57]

But preaching was only one pastoral challenge that Edwards addressed scripturally. Early in his ministry he began to publish his judgments regarding contemporary religious developments. During the following decades he addressed a variety of circumstances and controversies that touched his life. Sometimes he published his sermons. His first two publications in the early 1730s, for example, were sermons: *God Glorified in the Work of Redemption* in 1731 and *A Divine and Supernatural Light* in 1734.[58] By 1736, however, Edwards appeared in print in another mode when his reflections concerning the local revival in Northampton beginning in 1734 were published as an addendum to a volume of sermons by William Williams. Subsequently, in 1737 a separate edition of *A Faithful Narrative of the Surprising Work of God in the Conversion of Many Hundred Souls in Northampton* appeared, vaulting Edwards and Northampton into the public eye in a new way. Edwards's description of the Northampton revival was not sermonic, but it made explicit use of the language of the Bible. In describing his own role in the awakening, he spoke of his pastoral duty to "assist and instruct persons in applying Scripture rules" to their lives. He noted how frequently persons experiencing conversion had "many texts of Scripture brought to their minds" and thereby were convinced of the "truth of the Gospel." Citing II Corinthians 5:17, he declared that conversion was "a great change, wherein old things are done away, and all things become new."[59] When describing the conversion of several persons in Northampton, he repeatedly used biblical phrases to summarize the dramatic effects on their lives. Conversion changed the subjects. Their hearts were transformed by God's Spirit, Edwards wrote, and they possessed "groanings that cannot be uttered," a phrase he cited directly from Romans 8:26.[60]

Edwards spent his entire ministry describing and defending the evangelical revivals. His fullest and most important defense of the awakenings, *A Treatise Concerning Religious Affections*, appeared in 1746. In this work he defined and described gracious affections. After setting aside false evidences of grace, he devoted the major portion of the treatise to identifying twelve "distinguishing signs" of gracious affections, or true religion. Many commentators have argued that the twelfth sign is the culmination of his argument. In it Edwards stated, "Gracious and holy affections have their exercise and fruit in Christian practice." To put this another way, true religion for Edwards was evident in "holy practice" and behavior, what he called the "business of religion." He declared that this judgment concerning the practical side of Christianity is clearly taught in the Word of God."[61] Countless biblical citations are part of the treatise. Frequently he cited passages verbatim or paraphrased them as he mined the Scriptures, drawing on Mosaic legislation, the counsel of the Hebrew prophets, the teachings of Christ, and the ethical counsel in the epistles, especially the epistle of James. He wrote,

> Another thing which makes it evident that holy practice is the principal evidence that we ought to make use of in judging both of our own and others' sincerity, is, that this evidence is above all others insisted on in Scripture. A common acquaintance with the Scripture, together with a little attention and observation, will be sufficient to show to anyone, that this is ten times more insisted on as a note of true piety, throughout the Scripture, from the beginning of Genesis to the end of Revelations, than anything else.[62]

When the New England revivals began to fade in the mid-1740s, Edwards and other evangelicals looked for ways to reinvigorate the religious situation. One proposal that attracted his attention came from ministers in Scotland with whom he corresponded. They proposed and Edwards accepted their plan for a "concert of prayer." They called for the establishment of prayer societies on both sides of the Atlantic to pray for the advancement of the kingdom of God. They agreed to unite in prayer at designated times, confident that God would pour out his Spirit on those so engaged. The result would be times of renewed revival. In 1747 Edwards published *An Humble Attempt to Promote Explicit Agreement and Visible Union of God's People in Extraordinary Prayer for the Revival of Religion and the Advancement of Christ's Kingdom on Earth, Pursuant to Scripture-Promises and Prophecies Concerning the Last Time.* His treatise argued for the concert of prayer at the same time that it placed the undertaking in an eschatological framework. Edwards used the *Humble Attempt* to describe the forces of evil opposed to renewed revivals. At the center of the opposing coalition he placed the Antichrist and antichristian forces that he equated with the Pope and the Roman Catholic Church. He spared no words in his condemnation of Catholicism. He spoke confidently about a future "destruction of the Church of Rome" as well as the "entire extirpation of all infidelity, heresies, superstitions and schisms, throughout all Christendom," which he linked with the "gradual progress of religion" described in the Bible.[63] In this case Edwards used the Bible for polemical purposes – to support his deep and virulent opposition to Catholicism.

In the mid-1740s Edwards also became embroiled in controversy with his Northampton congregation. At the heart of the dispute was his changed judgment concerning access to the Lord's Supper. He moved away from a more liberal practice of admission to the sacrament exercised by his grandfather Solomon Stoddard, raising the bar for participation. The controversy evoked by his decision led him to publish a defense of his position in 1749.

In *An Humble Inquiry into the Rules of the Word of God*, Edwards argued for stricter admission requirements, a position that ultimately led to his dismissal by the Northampton congregation. In his treatise he dealt with a variety of biblical passages that were interpreted differently by the parties to the controversy. One of the most interesting involves his reflections on the possible presence of Judas, the disciple who betrayed Jesus, at the institution of the Lord's Supper after the Passover meal. All four New Testament gospels contain an account that bears on the occasion. Edwards's judgment, based on his reading of the gospel of John, was that Judas was present for the Passover, but not for the institution of the Lord's Supper. The *Humble Inquiry* contains an elaborate set of textual reflections and theological rationalizations to support his view.[64] But the treatise in 1749 was not the last word that Edwards wrote about Judas. In *Misrepresentations Corrected* published in 1752, a second defense of his position in the controversy, he responded to the judgments of his opponent, Solomon Williams, who had asserted that Judas was present for the Lord's Supper. Edwards devoted section 13 in Part III of this second treatise to the question of Judas's participation in the sacrament. The crucial passage for him was John 13:27–30, which speaks of Judas leaving "immediately" after "having received the sop."[65] Edwards used the gospel pericopes to support his position in the communion controversy.

Edwards's theological writings reflect his lifelong commitment to the study and authority of the Bible. The last published treatise from his hand, which appeared posthumously in 1758, was *The Great Christian Doctrine of Original Sin*. Written in part as a response to the assault on the doctrine of original sin by the English theologian John Taylor (1694–1761), *Original Sin* is perhaps the most explicitly scriptural treatise from Edwards's hand. It is devoted to examining evidences for and against the doctrine. Taylor's volume laid claim to a biblical basis; his treatise was entitled *The Scripture-Doctrine of Original Sin, Proposed to Free and Candid Examination*.[66] Edwards accepted the challenge implicit in Taylor's work, and he set out to defend the doctrine by considering the "representations and testimonies of holy scripture" with respect to original sin as well as more general observations concerning human experience. Part Two of the treatise, which consists of more than 120 pages in the modern critical edition, contains "observations on particular parts of the holy Scripture, which prove the doctrine of original sin." In this section Edwards dealt at length with the opening three chapters of Genesis as well as with select passages elsewhere in the New Testament. For example, when dealing with Romans 7 and 8, he argued his case by stating that the "terms 'flesh' and 'spirit' (σὰρξ and πνεῦμα) are abundantly repeated and clearly set in opposition."[67] That opposition was fundamental to the theological position he supported, a view of human nature that affirmed the doctrine of original sin using a variety of biblical texts.

The Bible was the foundation for much of Edwards's pastoral activity and his theological publications. There is little ambiguity about that fact. But one additional piece of important biographical evidence confirms the centrality of the Bible in his professional life. Edwards was planning at least two more major publications, both of which rested directly on his lifelong study of the Bible. These plans were cut short by his premature death in 1758 two months after he assumed responsibilities as president at the college in Princeton. He described the plans in his now-famous letter to the trustees of the College of New Jersey written in October 1757 in response to their invitation. In that communication he sketched his personal situation with disarming candor, addressing both his limitations and his plans for the future.

In the letter Edwards described his lifelong method of study which involved an intensive program of reading and writing. He credited that routine and the attendant discipline with the success he had enjoyed in his publications. Then he went on to sketch the two projects on which he was working. One he called *"A History of the Work of Redemption*, a body of divinity in an entire new method, being thrown into the form of an history, considering the affair of Christian theology, as the whole of it, in each part, stands in reference to the great work of redemption by Jesus Christ." This history potentially would embrace all of time, starting from eternity and extending to eternity. It was to include "three worlds, heaven, earth, and hell: considering the connected, successive events and alterations, in each so far as the Scriptures give any light; introducing all parts of divinity in that order which is most scriptural and most natural."[68] In other words, the Bible was to be foundational for this new and all-inclusive historical body of divinity.

A second "great work," on which he had also already invested much, he tentatively entitled *"The Harmony of the Old and New Testament."* It was to have three parts. The first would address prophecies of the Messiah, focusing on both the predictions and the fulfillments. The second would consider Old Testament "types" as well as their agreement with the antitypes evident in the gospel of Christ. The third would examine the harmony between the Old and New Testaments. Edwards confidently stated that this work would explain "a very great part of the holy Scripture." He saw it leading to a "view of the true spirit, design, life and soul of the Scriptures, as well as their proper use and interpretation."[69]

If ever there was ambiguity regarding Edwards's sense of himself as an exegete, the letter to the trustees ends it. He clearly viewed himself in some primary sense as an exegete, an interpreter of Scripture, and on that foundation rested many of his theological accomplishments. These projected "great works" were never written, but Edwards's manuscript notes and notebooks anticipate possible contents of the projected treatises.[70]

In sum, collectively a massive body of Edwards's exegetical writings remains. His biblical reflections – located in notebooks and commentaries, sermons and treatises – beg for closer examination than they have received to date. Much research remains to be done. There is reason to believe that someday a fuller understanding of Edwards the exegete will take its place alongside the established depictions of Edwards as the astute observer of nature, the brilliant philosopher, the powerful preacher, and the creative theologian.

Notes

1. *Personal Narrative*, WJE, 16:797.
2. "Resolutions," WJE, 16:755.
3. Samuel Hopkins, *The Life and Character of the Late Reverend Mr. Jonathan Edwards, President of the College of New Jersey* (Boston, 1765), 40, 47, 51.
4. Dwight, ed., *The Works of President Edwards: With a Memoir of His Life* (10 vols. New York, S. Converse, 1829–30), 1:57.
5. For example, see Stephen J. Stein, "The Quest for the Spiritual Sense: The Biblical Hermeneutics of Jonathan Edwards," *Harvard Theological Review*, 70:1–2 (1977): 99–113; John H. Gerstner, *The Rational Biblical Theology of Jonathan Edwards* (3 vols. Powhatan, VA: Berea, 1991–3); Robert E. Brown, *Jonathan Edwards and the Bible* (Bloomington: Indiana University Press, 2002); Douglas A. Sweeney, "'Longing for More and More of It'? The Strange Career of Jonathan Edwards's Exegetical Exertions," in Harry S. Stout, Kenneth P. Minkema, and Caleb J. D. Maskell, eds., *Jonathan Edwards at 300: Essays on the Tercentenary of His Birth* (Lanham, MD: University Press of America, 2005), 25–37.
6. Both of these manuscripts are in the Beinecke Rare Book and Manuscript Library, Yale University, New Haven, Connecticut.
7. Dwight, ed., *Works*, 9:113–563.
8. WJE, 15:49–613.
9. WJE, 24: Parts 1 and 2.
10. See Grosart, ed., *Selections from the Unpublished Writings of Jonathan Edwards of America* (Edinburgh, 1865).
11. This manuscript is in the Beinecke Rare Book and Manuscript Library.
12. WJE, 5:95–305.
13. See WJE, 13:163–541; 18:51–547; 20:43–525; 23:39–716.
14. See *Miscellaneous Observations on Important Theological Subjects* (Edinburgh, 1793); *Remarks on Important Theological Controversies* (Edinburgh, 1796); *Miscellaneous Remarks on Important Theological Subjects*, Dwight, ed., *Works*, 7:197–572; Harvey G. Townsend, ed., *Philosophy of Jonathan Edwards from His Private Notebooks* (Eugene: University of Oregon Press, 1955).
15. WJE, 13:166.
16. Ibid., 167–8.
17. Ibid., 181.

18. Ibid., 284.
19. This manuscript is in the Beinecke Rare Book and Manuscript Library.
20. WJE, 11:54–5.
21. Ibid., 88.
22. Ibid., 123.
23. This manuscript is in the Trask Library at Andover-Newton Theological School, Newton Centre, Massachusetts.
24. WJE, 11:146.
25. Ibid., 150.
26. Ibid., 191.
27. Letter to the Trustees of the College of New Jersey, Oct. 19, 1757, WJE, 16:729.
28. "Blank Bible," entry on Exodus 12:38, WJE, 24, Part 1, 223.
29. "Blank Bible," entry on I Peter 1:14, WJE, 24, Part 2, 1177–8.
30. Five vols. [London] In the Savoy, 1711–17.
31. Four vols. London, 10th ed., 1719.
32. Four vols. in 2 parts, Oxford, 2nd ed., 1672–8.
33. Seven vols., London, 1748–66.
34. Both of these manuscripts are in the Beinecke Rare Book and Manuscript Library. For more on these important notebooks, which are forthcoming in the Yale Edition of Edwards's *Works*, see Peter J. Thuesen, "Edwards' Intellectual Background," in Sang Hyun Lee, ed., *The Princeton Companion to Jonathan Edwards* (Princeton: Princeton University Press, 2005), 23–7.
35. Four parts in 5 vols. (London, 1669–76); 6 vols. (London, 1708–10); and 6 vols. (London, 1739–56).
36. London, 1737.
37. London, 1684.
38. Third ed., London, 1708.
39. Seventeen vols. (London, 1727–57).
40. Sixth ed., London, 1646.
41. Two vols. (Amstelodami et Trajecti ad Rhenum, 1718).
42. London, 1738.
43. "Catalogue of Reading," 8.
44. 6th ed., London, 1655.
45. Two vols. London, 2nd ed., 1738.
46. *A Paraphrase with Notes on the Epistle to the Romans* (London, 1745).
47. WJE, 21:335.
48. Oxonii, 1650.
49. London, 1730.
50. Four vols. London, 2nd ed., 1731.
51. Two vols. (London, 1745–6).
52. WJE, 15:423.
53. "Blank Bible," WJE, 24, Part 1, 403. See also Arthur Bedford, *Scripture Chronology Demonstrated by Astronomical Calculations, and also by the Year of Jubilee, and the Sabbatical Year among the Jews: or, An Account of Time, from the Creation of the World, to the Destruction of Jerusalem; as It May Be Proved from the Writings of the Old and New Testament* (London, 1730).
54. WJE, 15:182–5; "Blank Bible," WJE, 24, Part 2, 914.
55. WJE, 15:249–251; and "Blank Bible," WJE, 24, Part 2, 1203–4.

56. WJE, 10:480–92.
57. Ibid., 22:319–38.
58. Ibid., 17:200–16, 408–26.
59. Ibid., 4:176–9.
60. Ibid., 4:208.
61. Ibid., 2:383–4.
62. Ibid., 436.
63. Ibid., 5:410–11.
64. Ibid., 12:288–90.
65. Ibid., 478–9.
66. London, 1740.
67. WJE, 3:275.
68. Ibid., 16:727–8.
69. Ibid.
70. See, for example, Kenneth P. Minkema, "The Other Unfinished 'Great Work': Jonathan Edwards, Messianic Prophecy, and 'The Harmony of the Old and New Testament," in *Jonathan Edwards's Writings: Text, Context, Interpretation*, ed. Stephen J. Stein (Bloomington, Indiana University Press, 1996), 52–65.

10 Edwards as missionary

RACHEL M. WHEELER

Jonathan Edwards is rarely remembered for his work as missionary to the Indians. Until recent decades, scholars were interested in Edwards first and foremost as a towering figure in America's intellectual history, while evangelicals have long nurtured an interest in Edwards the revivalist and critic of modern rationalism.[1] The seven years he spent at the mission outpost in Stockbridge at the end of his life are ambivalently remembered at best as a period of productive exile following his dismissal from his Northampton pulpit in 1750. The turn toward the "new social history" in the early 1970s, however, opened new avenues of inquiry into Edwards's life, including his family life, his role as pastor, and, more recently, his years as a missionary.[2]

This chapter begins with a brief overview of Edwards's involvement in Indian mission work prior to his removal from Northampton and his acceptance of the Stockbridge post. In addition, a brief review of the history of the Stockbridge mission before Edwards's arrival sets the stage for a consideration of his years as missionary, during which time he served as defender, pastor, and preacher to the Stockbridge Indians. This chapter also considers what traces Edwards's experiences as a missionary may have left on the philosophical and theological treatises written during his Stockbridge tenure. A final section evaluates the legacy of Edwards's missionary work in relation to the impact of colonial missionary work in general as well as his particular legacy among the Stockbridge Indians.

Long before taking up the post of missionary at the frontier settlement of Stockbridge, Massachusetts, Edwards's life was intimately linked with Indian affairs. A number of Edwards's kin were killed or captured in the 1704 raid on the frontier outpost of Deerfield, Massachusetts, by French-allied Indians. Although Edwards was only four months old (and safely in Windsor, Connecticut) at the time of the raid, the event had a profound and lasting influence on the extended family. Edwards's uncle, John Stoddard, was the only one to escape from the Williams household that day. Stoddard's firsthand experience of the vulnerability of frontier settlements and his futile efforts to reclaim his cousin Eunice Williams from captivity among the Catholic Mohawks of Caughnawaga in Canada arguably shaped Stoddard's career as one of the emerging generation of "River Gods."[3] He would devote his career to strengthening colonial defenses and securing the loyalties of Indians on the Massachusetts frontier. No doubt reflecting the influence of his father, Solomon Stoddard, John Stoddard believed mission work would be an important component of this project. It was largely through his efforts that the Stockbridge mission was founded in 1734, marking the renewal of missionary work on the Massachusetts frontier more than a half-century after King Philip's War.[4] Solomon Stoddard, Edwards's grandfather, was a towering figure in the Connecticut Valley. When the senior Stoddard asked in a 1723 sermon *Whether God Is Not Angry with the Country for Doing So Little toward the Conversion of the Indians?*, it was not simply a rhetorical question. Stoddard believed colonial wars and other trials, such as the raid on Deerfield, were God's punishment for neglecting the colony's commitment to bring the gospel to the Indians as spelled out in the 1629 Massachusetts Bay charter.[5]

Edwards would certainly have been closely attuned to the progress of colonial mission efforts in general, and at Stockbridge in particular, given the close involvement of his kinsmen and his constant searching for signs of the progress of God's redemptive work. But Edwards's closest involvement in missionary work before his Stockbridge tenure involved his work in editing David Brainerd's diary for publication in 1749. Brainerd (1718–47) served for about four years as a missionary, first to the Mahican Indians of Kaunaumeek (near Stockbridge) and later to the Delaware Indians at the Forks of the Delaware, in Pennsylvania, and at Crossweeksung, New Jersey, generally meeting with little success.[6] Brainerd suffered from what Edwards termed melancholy, and his writings from his time as missionary alternate between lamenting his own unworthiness and excoriating his Indian subjects for their stubborn attachment to heathen ways. Brainerd relied on the standard New England catechetical practices, combining doctrinal instruction with study of Scripture, often using the Shorter Catechism, and seeking first to convince hearers of their sinful state as the necessary precondition to receiving God's grace. Brainerd discovered during his work that fire and brimstone preaching did not have the desired effect, but he seems not to have translated this insight into regular practice. Instead, he complained to his sponsors that the Indians were "not only brutishly stupid and ignorant of divine Things, but many of them are obstinately set against Christianity."[7]

The tubercular Brainerd spent the last months of his life in the Edwards household under the nursing care of Jerusha Edwards, no doubt providing ample opportunity for Edwards to discuss mission work with Brainerd. At the time, Edwards was embroiled in the controversy that ultimately cost him his Northampton pulpit. Brainerd's willingness to subject himself to physical and social deprivations and dangers in order to tend to the eternal well-being of a population that was often less than grateful must have provided both inspiration and consolation for Edwards. Brainerd's ministry likely seemed simply a more extreme example of the pastoral challenges that Edwards faced with his English congregation.[8] Edwards admired not so much Brainerd's missionary method, but his example as a model of Christian virtue. In his *Life of Brainerd*, Edwards subtly affirmed his own devotion to the cause of Christ.[9]

At the time that the *Life of Brainerd* was published in 1749, Edwards likely had never contemplated becoming a missionary himself. But it had been painfully clear for some time that he would not continue in the Northampton pulpit as long as his grandfather Solomon Stoddard had.[10] As early as 1744, Edwards began to have doubts about Stoddard's policy of open communion, which required only that an individual give the appearance of being a morally upstanding Christian, but it did not require a public account of conversion for admission to the communion table. The controversy that ensued when he resolved to require a profession of faith for admission to communion struck Edwards in a deeply personal way, leaving him feeling monumentally unappreciated and fearful that his parishioners, with his own Williams relations at the forefront, had willfully turned their backs on the gospel. When a vote was called among church members, only nineteen of six hundred voted in Edwards's favor; and so on June 22, 1750, Edwards found himself without a job. His perceived betrayal in the communion controversy lurks behind much of Edwards's subsequent experiences with his English and Indian congregations at Stockbridge.[11]

In 1750, at what he considered the advanced age of forty-six and with a "chargeable" family of ten children, Edwards felt his professional options were limited, although he did receive at least a few offers, one in Scotland and others in New England.[12] The post at Stockbridge had been vacant since July of 1749 when the first missionary, John Sergeant, died of a fever. Charged by the Massachusetts General Court to head a committee to find a replacement was Ephraim Williams, head of one of the four English families brought to Stockbridge as a living example of English civilization. He was the father of the widow Abigail Sergeant and kin of Edwards's chief opponents in the communion controversy. Williams and his family, especially Abigail, favored Ezra Stiles for the position, but Stiles begged off when he realized that his theological leanings would come under close scrutiny.[13] Much to the dismay of the Williams family, Edwards soon became the front-runner, pushed by the inveterate enemy of the Williamses, Timothy Woodbridge, schoolmaster of the mission school. Ephraim Williams, Jr., summed up his family's objections: Edwards was unsociable and thus not likely to be an effective teacher, he was too old to learn the Indians' native tongue, and "he was a very great Bigot, for he would not admit any person into heaven, but those that agreed fully to his sentiments." Williams did, however, see one advantage to Edwards's presence: the value of his property was sure to rise with the presence of the noted Edwards.[14]

In early 1751 Edwards made several trips to Stockbridge to audition for the pulpit. Given his frustrations with a congregation that had had the benefit of fine gospel teaching, Edwards found an appeal in serving "where the gospel has been little understood or attended to."[15] That April, the Indian and white members of the Stockbridge church voted in favor of Edwards's installation as minister, despite the objections of the Williams family.[16] When Edwards was officially installed as minister at Stockbridge in August of 1751, the mission was quite simply a mess.

The mission was largely the brainchild of Edwards's uncle and benefactor, John Stoddard, who found several reasons to recommend a mission to the Housatonic Indians on the province's border.[17] The mission would make good on the colony's original charter, while freeing more land for English settlers. This, in turn, would cement Massachusetts's claims to the disputed border with New York. And finally, a mission would be one good means of securing friendly Indians on the colony's borders who would act as a buffer from French and Indian attacks should hostilities between the imperial rivals resume. The mission was to follow the longstanding missionary logic of "civilization" before Christianization that had animated all Anglo-Protestant missionary efforts, beginning with "the Apostle to the Indians," John Eliot, who had established more than a dozen "praying towns" before King Philip's War.[18]

The Stockbridge mission had gotten off to a promising start. New residents from nearby villages steadily joined the growing community, drawn by the promise of secure land and an education in the English cultural ways that would help them navigate a future in an increasingly white world. Students at the school made progress in learning their letters, which tribal leaders hoped would not only open the mysteries of the Bible but also protect against fraudulent land deals. Early indications seemed to be that some traditional ways would continue alongside the new. Residents continued to disperse to their sugaring huts in the early spring, and Sergeant raised no objections when a "kientikaw," a mourning ceremony, was planned. English-style houses went up alongside traditional bark wigwams. Fields of wheat and corn grew side by side; and Konkapot, one of the village leaders, built a shingled barn to house his pair of oxen.[19]

But the original design of the mission ensured later tensions. John Sergeant had proposed, and Governor Jonathan Belcher heartily agreed, that the missionary should have the comfort of English neighbors and that the Indians should have the benefit of models of "civilization." Therefore the initial patent for the mission town reserved land for the missionary, schoolteacher, and four English families. Ephraim Williams arrived from Newton in June 1738 as head of one of the model families, which included the charming and indomitable seventeen-year-old Abigail. With the move, Williams substantially improved his lot in life: Before long, Williams had amassed over eleven hundred acres of Stockbridge Indian lands.[20] The new arrivals did much to improve Sergeant's life. Any grieving over his failed courtship of Hannah Edwards, sister of Jonathan, was soon put to an end. Sergeant and Abigail Williams were wed in August 1739 in a ceremony performed by her father and witnessed by ninety Stockbridge Indians.[21] Edwards would later report that the Indians thought that "Mr. Sergeant did very well till he married her; but that afterwards there was a great alteration in him and he became quite another man."[22]

The presence of the English families, as a simple matter of demographics, posed a significant threat to the Stockbridge Indians. The disparity in birthrates between English and Indian families meant that the Indian population quickly would be outnumbered. Moreover, although the Stockbridge Indians were assured they would be granted the same protections as the English, this promise was rarely honored. Petition after petition from the Indians to the provincial government (which more often than not included a Williams family member) protesting unfair land dealings was met with some affirmation of their reasonableness, but rarely with justice.[23]

The tensions caused by the structure of the mission town were only exacerbated by the complex funding sources that supported the Stockbridge mission.[24] New England Puritanism was ill-equipped to church the unchurched. Congregational polity presumed the existence of independently gathered churches whose members would issue a call for a minister and willingly, so it was hoped, furnish his salary.[25] Missions posed a particular conundrum: there could be no gathered churches of Indian Christians before there were missionaries to bring the gospel to the Indians. Further, colonial governments generally saw missionary work as good public policy, motivated in large part out of the legitimate fear that Catholic successes in New France posed a major threat to New England security, but they rarely made it a priority. Attempts by New England clergy to raise funds for mission work from among the laity generally met with closed purses: Indians were seen more as potential threats than as souls to be redeemed.[26]

At Stockbridge, these theoretical problems became all too real. The minister and schoolteacher were funded by the London-based missionary society, the New England Company, of which Elisha Williams was a commissioner. A separate boarding school, begun under John Sergeant's tenure with initial funds from an English benefactor, Isaac Hollis, and completed under the oversight of Ephraim Williams with funds from the Province, was staffed by the ineffective Martin Kellogg, survivor of the 1704 raid on Deerfield and a longtime friend of the Williams family. During his lifetime, Sergeant had courted the Mohawks, hoping to attract members of the powerful Iroquois confederacy to the mission. Soon after his arrival, Edwards brought in Gideon Hawley to serve as schoolteacher to the recently arrived Mohawks, but Kellogg refused to surrender his post. Meanwhile, Abigail, now married to Brigadier Joseph Dwight, was appointed headmistress of a new girls boarding school, also funded by Hollis.[27] Edwards was appalled by the marriage – he had recommended Dwight be appointed as resident overseer of mission affairs, counting him as a friend and ally. Edwards rightly believed the marriage would turn Dwight against him.[28]

Edwards was deeply distraught by the state of the mission. "It is enough," he confessed, "to make one sick." There was no doubt in Edwards's mind that the root of the problem was the Williams family. The Indians shared Edwards's contempt of the Williamses, harboring, he wrote, "a very ill opinion" and "the deepest prejudice" toward Ephraim Williams, "he having often molested 'em with respect to their lands and other affairs, and, as they think, done very unjustly to 'em."[29] Edwards complained to the commissioners about Williams's increasingly erratic and antagonistic behavior, reporting that Williams had embarked on a campaign to set the Indian children against him by telling them that Edwards's previous congregation "had thrown him away" and the "poor Stockbridge Indians" had been willing to take him, but they had best send him away in exchange for a "good minister." According to Edwards, Williams went so far as to ply the children with wine in an unsuccessful effort to get them to sign a petition against him.[30] And indeed the wrangling over mission affairs took a toll on the Indian residents: Mahicans and Mohawks alike were threatening to leave if the schools were not put under better management.[31]

With a campaign of endless letters to the Boston commissioners, wealthy benefactors across the Atlantic, and important New England civic and religious leaders, Edwards sought to bring the mission under better management and to protect the interests of the Stockbridge Indians. Eventually, those who controlled the diverse funding sources – Isaac Hollis, the commissioners of the New England Company, and the legislature – endorsed Edwards's assessment and his leadership. But by this time significant damage had already been done. The simmering conflict between England and France would soon erupt on American shores as the French and Indian War, further straining relations between the English and Indian residents of Stockbridge.[32]

Surprisingly, despite the near constant struggles with the Williams family in Stockbridge, in ministering to the Indian congregation Edwards seems finally to have found a degree of satisfaction and gratification that had eluded him at Northampton. In a note to his father, Edwards remarked with a sense of relief, "the Indians seem much pleased with my family.... Here, at present," he declared, "we live in peace; which has of long time been an unusual thing with us."[33]

The fact that the Stockbridge Indian congregation was increasingly antagonized by the same family that had led the charge against Edwards in Northampton most certainly served to strengthen Edwards's sympathy for the Indians and his commitment to protect their interests, though this sympathy was never manifested as an interest in individuals or in Indian culture. Edwards was not an especially warm person, and the regular duties of a minister to comfort, console, and counsel his flock did not come easily to him.[34] In the case of his Indian congregation, the barriers to personal communication were even greater: Edwards did not speak Mahican, and he believed Indian culture to be in need of fundamental reformation.

Edwards brought with him fairly standard views of Indians and mission work. Like his grandfather Stoddard and other New England divines, Edwards attached temporal and providential significance to the relative successes and failures of mission work, which he understood to be a key element in the struggle between true religion, as embodied by Protestant England, and false religion, as practiced by Catholic France. He lamented, for example, the paltry mission efforts in New England; and he speculated that God "will make them [the Indians] a sore scourge to us as a just punishment of our cruelty to their souls and bodies, by our withholding the Gospel from 'em, defrauding them of their goods, prejudicing them against Christianity by our wickedness; and killing of multitudes of them, and easily diminishing their numbers with strong drink."[35] Edwards devoted much time and effort to trying to persuade officials in Boston of the importance of securing Mohawk allegiance to the English, and to persuading the Mohawks of the falsity of French religion, such as when he warned them that "true religion don't consist in praying to the Virgin Mary and to Saints and Angels as the Popish French do. It don't consist in crossing themselves, in confessing sins to the Priest and worshipping Images of Christ and of the Saints."[36]

Edwards differed little from his contemporaries in his views of Indian culture, and he found in Indian society proof of the truth of Calvinist doctrine against Arminian challenges. When he looked at America's Indian population, he found confirmation of the absolute necessity of regenerating grace. Pointing to the "multitudes of nations" of North and South America, Edwards asked in his treatise on *Original Sin*, "What appearance was there when the Europeans first came hither, of their being recovered, or recovering, in any degree from the grossest ignorance, delusions, and most stupid paganism?"[37] Edwards believed that the Indians suffered not only from "those corruptions of Heart which are naturally in the Hearts of all mankind," but also from the "heathenish barbarous brutish Education" that resulted from "those opinions and customs which they have long lived in."[38] The heathen world, believed Edwards, was held captive by Satan, and missionaries were Christ's army, sent to liberate those held under Satan's sway. It was, Edwards believed, "a special and glorious work of God to open the way for the propagation of the Gospel among the Heathen."[39]

Edwards, like most English proponents of mission work, believed that "civilization" and Christianity were inseparable and that a thorough reformation of Indian culture was necessary in order for Christianity to take root.[40] Along with the gospel, mission residents would be taught the basics of reading, writing, and arithmetic, together with English husbandry and domestic arts. To accomplish this, Edwards reported to the commissioners, "I preach constantly to 'em once every Sabbath and go once a week to instruct their children."[41] Proper instruction in basic verbal and mathematical literacy would serve, Edwards believed, "the more speedily and effectually, to change the taste of Indians, and to bring them off from their barbarism and brutality, to a relish for those things, which belong to civilization and refinement." Edwards quickly discovered, however, that "the ordinary method of teaching among the English" contained "gross defects," which were only magnified when catechizing Indian pupils. By emphasizing rote learning, standard educational practices failed to ensure that "the ideas properly signified by the words" would be "naturally excited in their minds." Edwards's proposed solution bore the marks of Lockean psychology: Biblical stories were to be featured prominently because he believed narrative would serve better to ensure that the proper ideas were evoked by the words.[42] While Edwards was entirely conventional in his conviction that the Indians were in need of a "civilized" education, his methods proved innovative.

It is nearly impossible to assess the impact of Edwards's methods on the mission residents, as his own writings and other mission sources are frustratingly silent on this question. Edwards rarely mentioned individual Indians in his writings, and what few mentions there are do little to illuminate the nature of the relationship between pastor and congregant. One set of sources, however, is particularly intriguing: several professions of faith in Edwards's hand, one of them signed with the names Cornelius and

Mary Munneweaunummuck. In almost all respects, this profession of faith, along with the others, all unsigned, is entirely unexceptional.[43] Given that Edwards was willing to lose his job for his insistence on a profession of faith for admission to full membership, we can safely assume Edwards did not treat these professions as merely pro forma recitations. He must have been persuaded that Cornelius and Mary's testimony, though scripted, was an apt reconstruction of their inner lives.

Whatever the profession meant to the Munneweanummucks, which we have no way of knowing, it does suggest that there had been significant exchange between the candidates and Edwards on the subject of Christian belief and practice. Even while he participated both in the paternalism and the chauvinism that had long been part of English missionary ideology, Edwards believed Indians fully capable of apprehending Christian truths, and as their minister he saw it as his duty to convey the essentials of "true religion" from the pulpit.

Common wisdom holds that Edwards was far too busy in his Stockbridge study to devote much time to preaching to the Indians. But, in fact, week after week Edwards ascended the pulpit to preach to his Indian congregation, averaging three appearances per month in the pulpit throughout his Stockbridge years. The vast majority of these sermons to the Stockbridge Indians were new compositions, though he likely drew on his vast body of notes and prior sermons in writing them.[44] Although the English and Indian members of the town technically belonged to the same congregation, the sermon manuscripts suggest that Edwards preached separately to the two groups.[45]

Indeed, Edwards's engagement with his Indian congregation is visible in the distinctive style of the sermons. In the pulpit, Edwards attempted to adapt his preaching style and message to his new audience, believing "there are not many good philosophers" among the American Indians.[46] Stockbridge schoolmaster Gideon Hawley recalled that Edwards was "a plain and practical preacher" whose delivery was "grave and natural." He refrained from displaying "any metaphysical knowledge in the pulpit" and took care to use sentences that were "concise and full of meaning."[47] Hawley's observations are borne out by the manuscripts.

When Edwards's Indian sermons are compared to those preached to his English congregations, both at Northampton and Stockbridge, their distinctiveness is immediately apparent.[48] For his Indian sermons, Edwards drew most often upon the New Testament with a heavy reliance on the gospels of Matthew and Luke.[49] The content of these sermons suggests why Edwards may have found New Testament texts particularly appealing in preaching to the Indians. Drawing on the parables of the New Testament, Edwards preached of sowers of seed, of fishermen, of ground too dry for a seed to take, of trees fed by rivers that never ran dry, and of briars and thorns that impeded a traveler's way. It is clear in his earlier Northampton sermons that Edwards understood the power of story and imagery; yet in his Indian sermons, this imagery becomes all the more pronounced as he radically simplified the syntax of his sermons.[50] The distinctive style of the Stockbridge sermons thus may be attributed both to pragmatic and philosophical concerns. Given that Edwards had to rely on a translator to convey his message, he no doubt attempted to simplify his delivery and to avoid complex constructions that he believed would be difficult to render in Mahican. Yet his preaching seems also to have been an effort to employ the same Lockean philosophy apparent in his teaching methods, namely, allowing the power of imagery and narrative to carry the weight of his message.

What is most intriguing about Edwards's Stockbridge sermons is not their style or their doctrine, but the application of doctrine. Edwards's experience among the Stockbridge Indians led him to emphasize the encouraging aspects of Calvinist doctrine more in his sermons to the Indians than to the English of Stockbridge.[51] He preached standard Calvinist fare, but he balanced the exhortations to abandon sin with assurances that Christ was ready to serve as shelter for all who came to him, of whatever nation or rank. And so when Edwards preached to his Indian congregation on the total depravity of humanity, he often taught that they were no worse than the English. Similarly, when he preached unconditional election, he emphasized that Christ died for members of all nations and all social ranks. Edwards affirmed English cultural superiority, but he rejected any idea that this superiority was innate. Rather, he affirmed, the English had simply benefited from longer exposure to the gospel; and so, Edwards informed the Indians, "we do no more than our duty in it for it was once with our Forefathers as 'tis with you." God had shown his mercy by sending others to bring the gospel to the English. The moral of Edwards's story was that "we are no better than you in no respect only as God has made us to differ and has been pleased to give us more Light and now we are willing to give it to you."[52]

The requirements for salvation would be the same for Indian and English: a mixture of repentance and divine grace. If repentance is earnest, Edwards preached to the Stockbridge Indians, "there is forgiveness offered to all nations," for Christ "did not die only for one nation," but he made clear "his design of making other nations his People," even those that "had been Heathens."[53] Christ offered himself "readily and freely" to suffer for sinners, "let 'em be who they will of what nation soever they are."[54] In a baptismal sermon, Edwards preached, "'tis the will of Christ that all nations shall be taught." Christ recognized "no difference" among the nations; Christ had "died for some of all / all need / all alike."[55] The offer of salvation is open to all, "for God is a merciful God and would have all men saved and come to the knowledge of the truth."[56]

To the Stockbridge Indians, whose suffering he regularly witnessed, Edwards proffered Christ as refuge, comforter, and friend. In his sermon on Revelation 3:20, Edwards evoked a bleeding Christ standing at the door and knocking: "He invites you all men and women, young and old. You that have been the greatest sinners, drunkards, quarrellers, Lyars. If any of you have been guilty of fornication adultery murder or whatever wickedness." However great the sin, "the great Saviour the King of Heaven and Earth" is now "come to your door." All that was needed was "to let Him in."[57] The message was clear: the offer of salvation was not restricted to particular nations.

Edwards used his pulpit to counsel the Stockbridge Indians and offer comfort during difficult times. In a sermon preached in August 1753 at the height of the controversy over the management of the mission, Edwards warned his listeners that sometimes it is necessary "to wait till we get to another world before we have our reward."[58] One particularly poignant sermon preached in August 1756, in the midst of the French and Indian War, captures Edwards's encouragement offered to sinners and his empathy for the plight of his Indian congregants. "You that are poor you that have but few Friends," urged Edwards, "if any of you are weary of sin, if you are weary of seeing so much wickedness in the world," or "weary of seeing others drunk, weary of contention," then do not "walk in the ways of drunkness [sic] and do the works of darkness" but instead "chose [sic] heaven as your house. . . . Trust in Christ." Edwards promised that in heaven, the saints would find "bounty without deformity . . . friends and no enemies . . . and nothing but peace and love and no contention," something both Edwards and the Stockbridge Indians found elusive in this world.[59]

If Edwards often offered comfort to his Indian congregation, he did not spare them the hard doctrines of Calvinism. He warned them, too, that access to the gospel brought greater obligations: "you had better know your duty more than others and God has done more for you than others and therefore if you don't do your duty you will have a better place in Hell than the Heathen that never heard of Jesus Christ."[60] But Edwards often balanced these harsh bits of Calvinist doctrine with assurances that sinfulness was the natural state of *all* humanity, and therefore Indians had as good a chance of being saved as any others who had heard the gospel. In his sermons to the Indians, the hard doctrines of Calvinism were couched in a gentler way so that original sin became the guarantor of spiritual equality.

This theme reappears in Edwards's treatise on *Original Sin*, written during his years at Stockbridge. *Original Sin* was to be part of Edwards's grand campaign against the spirit of Arminianism, which he believed had made dangerous inroads in New England society. [61] His experiences with his English congregations at Northampton and Stockbridge had convinced him that even those with the best education in gospel principles were liable to backsliding and very un-Christian behavior. Had it not been for his mission experience, Edwards might not have emphasized in *Original Sin* the equality in human depravity to the extent that he did. In this treatise, while the American Indians, together with other examples of "pagan" peoples, serve as examples of the absolute necessity of divine revelation in acquiring knowledge of "true religion," the conclusion to be drawn was that all humanity would be in a similar state were it not for the grace of God.[62] Europeans had not shown a lesser tendency toward sin. Rather, God's grace had been more readily available to them.

At the end of the treatise, Edwards underscored what he saw to be the ethical implications of the doctrine of original sin. Far from resulting in "an ill opinion of our fellow-creatures" thereby promoting "ill-nature and mutual hatred," as his opponents – John Taylor in particular – argued, the affirmation of the doctrine of original sin would, in fact, induce a welcome humility. By contrast, to disown "that sin and guilt, which truly belongs to us," in Edwards's view, leads only to a "foolish *self-exaltation* and *pride*." Acceptance of the doctrine would have the salutary effect of teaching "us to think no worse of others, than of ourselves," and convincing people that "we are *all*, as we are by nature, *companions* in a miserable helpless condition." This, in turn, "tends to promote a mutual *compassion*." If the doctrine of original sin is abandoned in favor of faith in human reason, then sin becomes a matter of choice, and so one is free to believe "that the generality of mankind are very wicked, having made themselves so by their own free choice, without any necessity: which is a way of becoming wicked, that renders men truly *worthy of resentment*."[63] In a strange way then, *Original Sin* emerges as a call to human fellowship rooted in a conviction of the universality of depravity.

In the Calvinist doctrine of human depravity, Edwards found grounds to affirm the equality of Indian and English. It was the related doctrine of the necessity of divine grace through Christ's salvific work that fostered the missionary impulse in Edwards and other Christians. Thus it was the universalizing core of Christianity that in Edwards's hands both promised equality and sponsored colonialism. On this latter point, Edwards was very much a man of his times, fully sharing in the conviction of English cultural superiority and the necessity of extinguishing Indian "savagery" in order to make room for English "civility" and Christianity.

Linking Edwards's theological and philosophical writings with his immediate social context is a tricky business: Edwards himself certainly did not consciously reflect on the implications of his encounter with the Stockbridge

Indians for his theology. In part, this failure reflects the realities of colonial power; Edwards could hold to his Christian convictions without any conscious challenge from his mission experience, while Mahicans could not pretend to be unaffected by the European presence.

Edwards's most enduring contribution to the mission field was not his own labors at Stockbridge, but his publication of the *Life of Brainerd*, his most frequently reprinted work. Even in his lifetime, missionaries carried copies of Edwards's *Life of Brainerd* into the field with them.[64] It was in the nineteenth century, however, that the work made its greatest impact, as it inspired generations of missionaries to emulate Brainerd's self-sacrificing ethic as they fanned out across the globe in displays of disinterested benevolence. The *Life of Brainerd* was particularly important in that it helped to immunize missionaries against becoming too disheartened when their efforts were rewarded with many hardships and few conversions; the greater the deprivations and hardships of mission work, the more secure they were in the knowledge that their motives were purely disinterested.[65] Edwards's New Divinity disciples turned their attention as well to a number of other reform movements in the late eighteenth and early nineteenth century.[66]

Far more difficult to measure is Edwards's legacy as missionary rather than as promoter of missions. In basic outline, the story of Stockbridge differs little from that of other Anglo-Protestant missions: purportedly benevolent missionary projects sought to "civilize" and Christianize native peoples. Invariably, Christian Indians found the bar for entrance into "civilized" society raised ever higher until they were excluded on the basis of seemingly immutable racial difference. The Stockbridge Indians became Christian farmers and fought side by side with their white neighbors in war after war.[67] And yet, by the conclusion of the Revolution, the Stockbridge Mahicans found it impossible to remain in Stockbridge, their lands reduced to a tiny fraction of their original holdings.[68] By 1787 most of the tribe had resettled in New York, settling on Oneida land. This would be just the first of many removes that would eventually bring the Stockbridge Mohicans to the reservation they now occupy in Wisconsin.

Edwards arguably played an important role in cementing the loyalty of the Stockbridge Indian community both to Christianity and to the British and later American governments.[69] During his short tenure as missionary, Edwards proved himself to be a loyal friend and defender of the Stockbridge Indians; and there are at least some clues that they developed considerable respect and affection for Edwards. His satisfaction alone suggests that Edwards enjoyed a good working relationship with his Indian congregants, and other sources suggest that his presentation of Christian doctrine left its mark. Hendrick Aupaumut, future sachem of the Stockbridge Indians, was

born at Stockbridge in the months after Edwards's death in 1758. Aupaumut grew up as a committed Christian and advocate for his people. Even
after the Stockbridge Indians were driven from their Massachusetts home,
Aupaumut maintained a friendship with Edwards's son Timothy. In one letter, Aupaumut requested of Timothy that he might borrow a copy of his
father's *Religious Affections* or *Freedom of the Will.* Later in his life, Aupaumut frequently opposed all forms of nativism – whether the racism of white
Americans or the nativism of Indian leaders such as the Shawnee Prophet –
affirming instead a vision of human equality and imagining a future in which
there would be "no distinction between the different Tribes, wheather white,
red or black."[70]

Whether or not Aupaumut was directly influenced by Jonathan
Edwards's teachings is impossible to document, but like Edwards, he too
found in Christianity confirmation of a universal brotherhood, and this idea
often provided the basis for his advocacy of Indian rights. More broadly,
despite betrayal after betrayal by government officials, the tribe – now known
as the Stockbridge-Munsee Band of Mohican Indians, with a reservation
located in Wisconsin – has maintained a steady commitment both to the
Christian religion and to the importance of education in Euro-American
ways, even while sustaining and reviving interest in traditional culture.[71]

In sum, Jonathan Edwards's work as a missionary reveals him to be a
man of his times, with some notable differences. He shared in the common
assumptions of his day, namely, of Indian cultural inferiority and the centrality of education in the "arts of civilization" to any missionary program.
Clearly, Edwards had long been committed to evangelism as his role in the
revivals of the 1740s testifies, and in some respects Edwards's work as missionary can be understood as simply an extension of that role. In Northampton and Stockbridge, Edwards understood his work to be an expression of
his love for and duty to God. But the particular circumstances of Edwards's
tenure at Stockbridge – his dismissal from Northampton and the continued struggle with the Williams family – inclined him to greater affection
for his Indian congregation than he might otherwise have felt. This affection translated into a defense of Indian rights at Stockbridge and a message
preached from the pulpit that emphasized the equality of Indian and English
before God. Edwards's treatise on *Original Sin*, written during his tenure as
missionary, was one more prong in his attack on Arminianism. Edwards
argued that holding fast to the doctrine of original sin served as a check
against thinking too highly of oneself and thus served as a basis for compassion toward one's fellow humans. Like Edwards, Stockbridge Indian leaders
over the years have consistently emphasized the importance of education
and the imperatives of justice.[72]

Notes

1. The work of Perry Miller helped to revive scholarly interest in the Puritans and Edwards. Perry Miller, *Jonathan Edwards* (New York: William Sloane Associates, 1949). Norman Fiering challenged much of Miller's interpretation of the intellectual context in which Edwards worked. Norman Fiering, *Jonathan Edwards's Moral Thought and Its British Context* (Chapel Hill: University of North Carolina Press, 1981).

2. Patricia J. Tracy's biography of Edwards is the only full-fledged social history account of Edwards's life and thought (*Jonathan Edwards, Pastor: Religion and Society in Eighteenth-Century Northampton* [New York: Hill and Wang, 1979]). Kenneth P. Minkema's unpublished dissertation provides an invaluable social history of the extended Edwards family over several generations. "The Edwardses: A Ministerial Family in Eighteenth-Century New England" (Ph.D. dissertation: University of Connecticut, 1988). George M. Marsden's massive new biography weaves together the insights of recent decades of scholarship. *Jonathan Edwards: A Life* (New Haven: Yale University Press, 2003). See also Minkema, "Old Age and Religion in the Writings and Life of Jonathan Edwards," *Church History* 70 (Dec. 2001): 674–704; Ava Chamberlain, "The Immaculate Ovum: Jonathan Edwards and the Construction of the Female Body," *William and Mary Quarterly*, 3rd ser., 57 (2000): 280–322; idem, "Bad Books and Bad Boys: The Transformation of Gender in Eighteenth-Century Northampton, Massachusetts," *New England Quarterly* 75 (2002): 179–203.

3. During the raid, French-allied Indians devastated the town, killing about 50 of the 275 inhabitants and taking captive an additional 112. Eight members of the Williams household were taken captive and three were killed. Edwards was related to this Williams family through his maternal grandmother, Esther Warham Mather Stoddard. Evan Haefeli and Kevin Sweeney, *Captors and Captives: The 1704 French and Indian Raid on Deerfield* (Amherst: University of Massachusetts Press, 2003), 1, 114. Kevin Sweeney's unpublished dissertation is the definitive source on the Williams family and on the seventeenth- and eighteenth-century Connecticut Valley context. Kevin Sweeney, "River Gods and Related Minor Deities: The Williams Family and the Connecticut River Valley 1637–1790" (Ph.D. dissertation: Yale University, 1986), 753.

4. There had been one earlier effort in 1733, sponsored by the Society in Scotland for Propagating Christian Knowledge, which sent three missionaries to work at English forts. The attempt to copy French methods failed miserably, as Stoddard himself recognized. Samuel Hopkins, *Historical Memoirs Relating to the Housatonic Indians* (Boston, 1753), 2–3.

5. Stoddard, *Whether God Is Not Angry* (Boston, 1723). This commitment was also suggested by the colony's seal, which featured an Indian with outstretched hands pleading, "come over and help us."

6. For an overview of Brainerd's career and Edwards's editing and publication of his journal, see Norman Pettit, "Introduction," WJE, 7:1–85.

7. Brainerd reported that when God enabled him to "set before them the Lord Jesus Christ as a kind and compassionate Saviour," it was surprising to "see how their Hearts seem'd to be pierc'd with the tender and melting Invitations of the Gospel,

when there was not a Word of Terror spoken to them." *Mirabilia Dei Inter Indicos* (Philadelphia, n.d. [1746]), 17–19, 202, 208.

8. Edwards's farewell sermon to his Northampton congregation makes precisely this point, emphasizing his willingness to labor in a thankless job with no concern for his own happiness, but only for the eternal welfare of his flock. *A Farewel-Sermon Preached at the First Precinct in Northampton after the People's Publick Rejection of Their Minister, and Renouncing Their Relation to Him as Pastor of the Church There on June 22, 1750* (Boston, 1751).

9. Brainerd observed the same strict standards of admission, thus supporting Edwards's position by "transporting the ideology of the Northampton pulpit into the wilderness" (WJE, 7:15).

10. Marsden's biography provides a synthesis of recent scholarly discussions of the "communion controversy." *Jonathan Edwards*, 346–74. More detailed accounts can be found in Tracy, *Jonathan Edwards, Pastor*, 171–94; Kevin Sweeney, "River Gods," 429–57; WJE, 12:44–86.

11. For Edwards's own account of the relationship of Stockbridge affairs with the Williams family's involvement in the communion controversy, see especially his letter to William Hogg (WJE, 16:549–52).

12. WJE, 16:355–6; Ola Elizabeth Winslow, *Jonathan Edwards, 1703–1758* (New York: Collier, 1961 [1st ed. 1940]), 243.

13. "Minutes," Dec. 11, 1749, New England Company Records, 1685–1784, New England Historic Genealogical Society, Boston, Massachusetts (hereafter NEC Records); Marsden, *Jonathan Edwards*, 379–80. For a more extended discussion, see Edmund S. Morgan, *The Gentle Puritan: A Life of Ezra Stiles, 1727–1795* (New Haven: Yale University Press, 1962), 82–9.

14. The most famous line from this letter laments the shame that a "head so full of divinity should be so empty of politics." Ephraim Williams, Jr., to Jonathan Ashley, May 2, 1751, in Wyllis Wright, ed., *Colonel Ephraim Williams: A Documentary Life* (Pittsfield: Berkshire County Historical Society, 1970), 61.

15. WJE, 16:386–7. Edwards is here quoting Thomas Gillespie's previous letter to him. Gillespie was one of his Scottish correspondents.

16. "Minutes," May 9, 1750, NEC Records; WJE, 16:505.

17. Winslow suggests that Edwards was present at the 1734 meeting at Stoddard's house in which the mission was first proposed (*Jonathan Edwards*, 249). On Stoddard's reasons for the proposal, see Samuel Hopkins, *Historical Memoirs Relating to the Housatonic Indians* (Boston, 1753), 3.

18. The classic account of New England Indian relations is James Axtell, *The Invasion Within: The Contest of Cultures in Colonial North America* (New York: Oxford University Press, 1985). More recently, see Laura M. Stevens, *The Poor Indians: British Missionaries, Native Americans, and Colonial Sensibility* (Philadelphia: University of Pennsylvania Press, 2004). On Eliot, see Richard W. Cogley, *John Eliot's Mission to the Indians before King Philip's War* (Cambridge: Harvard University Press, 1999).

19. On the Stockbridge mission, see Patrick Frazier, *The Mohicans of Stockbridge* (Lincoln: University of Nebraska Press, 1992); Rachel Wheeler, "Living upon Hope: Mahicans and Missionaries, 1730–1760" (Ph.D. dissertation: Yale University, 1998); "In a Letter from a Friend in the Country," *Boston Post Boy*, Sept. 2, 1739.

20. Kevin Sweeney, "River Gods," 357–60; Lion Miles, "The Red Man Dispossessed: The Williams Family and the Alienation of Indian Land in Stockbridge, 1736–1818," *New England Quarterly* 67 (March 1994): 46–76.

21. "In a Letter from a Friend in the Country," *Boston Post Boy*, Sept. 3, 1739; Kenneth P. Minkema, "Hannah and Her Sisters: Sisterhood, Marriage and Courtship in the Edwards Family in the Early Eighteenth Century," *New England Historical and Genealogical Society* 146 (1992): 35–56.

22. WJE, 16:424.

23. For example, see the petition from several Stockbridge Indian residents to the General Court in September 1750 protesting that Williams had encroached on their land. Williams requested that the petition be dispensed as "vexatious and groundless." The Court found that "it would be inconvenient for sd Williams not to have it," and so rejected the petition (*Massachusetts Archives*, vol. 32, pp. 61–4, 72–3, 76, Boston).

24. Gideon Hawley, "A Letter from Rev. Gideon Hawley of Marshpee, Containing an Account of His Services among the Indians of Massachusetts and New York, and a Narrative of His Journey to Onohoghgwage," *Massachusetts Historical Society Collections*, ser. 1, vol. 4 (1794): 55.

25. On Puritan tribalism, see Edmund Morgan, *Visible Saints: The History of a Puritan Idea* (New York: New York University Press, 1963), 114–25.

26. Hopkins, *Historical Memoirs*, 165.

27. William Kellaway, *The New England Company, 1649–1776: Missionary Society to the American Indians* (London: Longmans, 1961), 272–5; WJE, 16:422–30, 497, 550–1, 630–1.

28. Marsden, *Jonathan Edwards*, 395–6.

29. WJE, 16:423–5, 428, 550–1. The Indians' contempt for Williams predated Edwards's arrival. Sergeant recorded in his journal that Stockbridge chief Umpachenee complained to him that, "Capt Williams and I were the occasions of his Apostacy." John Sergeant, diary entries dated Oct. 21 and Nov. 29, 1739, Stiles Papers, Beinecke Rare Book and Manuscript Library, Yale University, New Haven, Connecticut.

30. WJE, 16:590; Marsden, *Jonathan Edwards*, 400.

31. The Mohawks, in fact, left in the spring of 1754 (Marsden, *Jonathan Edwards*, 405). Edwards took notes on the back of a sermon manuscript of a meeting between himself and the principal Mohawk leaders about their decision to leave. They gave as the reason for their departure: "those People that lately had the management of affairs at the Boarding School that had discouraged them." Luke 1:77–9, Dec. 1753, 13/1051 Jonathan Edwards Collection, 1696–1972, Gen MSS 151 (hereafter JEC), Beinecke Rare Book and Manuscript Library.

32. Marsden, *Jonathan Edwards*, 404–5. As in King Philip's War in the previous century, even friendly Indians became suspect (Frazier, *Mohicans*, 105–23).

33. WJE, 16:420.

34. Marsden, *Jonathan Edwards*, 5–6, 36–7.

35. WJE, 16:434–47.

36. See especially Edwards's letter to Speaker of the Massachusetts House of Representatives, Thomas Hubbard (WJE, 16:528–33); Acts 11:12–13, Jan. 1751, 14/1091 JEC.

37. WJE, 3:151.

38. "Private Meeting on Occasion of Mssrs W—ge's Hawley Going into the Country of the Six Nations," Acts 14:26–7, May 1753, 14/1092 JEC.
39. Ibid.
40. Axtell, *Invasion Within*, 131–78.
41. WJE, 16:431.
42. Ibid., 407–14.
43. "Profession of Faith," n.d., 21/1245 JEC.
44. Of roughly 1,200 surviving manuscript sermons, approximately 190 of these were composed for the Stockbridge Indians. Counting these and repreached Northampton sermons, Edwards preached approximately 233 sermons to the Stockbridge Indians. All numbers are drawn from an analysis of the finding aid to the Jonathan Edwards Collection Gen MSS 151, by Elizabeth A. Bolton, Beinecke Rare Book and Manuscript Library, 1995. Numbers should be taken as approximate, as some sermon manuscripts Edwards marked with "St. Ind" are not identified in the index as Indian sermons.
45. WJE, 16:604. Gideon Hawley, schoolmaster to the Stockbridge Indians and friend of Edwards, commented in his journal that he "was pleased with both his [Edwards's] discourses. The first to the Indians was from John 10:27." Hawley, July 14, 1754, The Papers of Gideon Hawley, American Congregational Library, Boston. Sermons preached to the two congregations can be distinguished not only by stylistic markers, but also by Edwards's headings. He labeled the sermons to the Indians "St. Ind" followed by the date and the preaching text. Those without the "St. Ind." were clearly preached to the English congregation, as is apparent by the different style and vocabulary.
46. WJE, 3:160. In *Freedom of the Will*, Edwards distinguished between the meaning of words as understood by the "common" people and as used in philosophical discourse without any sense that a lack of an appreciation or capacity for metaphysical disputation in any way lessened a person's likelihood of experiencing saving grace. See, for example, Part IV, Section 4, "It Is Agreeable to Common Sense, and the Natural Notions of Mankind, to Suppose Moral Necessity to Be Consistent with Praise and Blame, Reward and Punishment," WJE, 1:357–71.
47. Hawley, "A Letter," 51.
48. Of the 165 sermons marked as preached to the English congregation at Stockbridge, only 29 were original compositions. See also WJE, 16:504–9.
49. Indeed, New Testament texts outnumber Old Testament texts by a ratio of five to three, as compared to a nearly equal balance in those preached to his English congregations.
50. Wilson H. Kimnach, "Introduction," WJE, 10:213–27.
51. I have made this argument at greater length in Rachel Wheeler, "'Friends to Your Souls': Jonathan Edwards's Indian Pastorate and the Doctrine of Original Sin," *Church History* 72 (2003): 736–65.
52. "To the Mohawks at the Treaty," Aug. 16, 1751, in *The Sermons of Jonathan Edwards, A Reader*, Wilson H. Kimnach, Kenneth P. Minkema, and Douglas A. Sweeney, eds. (New Haven: Yale University Press, 1999), 105–10.
53. Luke 24:47, Oct. 1751, 14/1078 JEC.
54. Revelation 3:20, Feb. 1751, 14/1141 JEC.
55. Undated fragment from baptismal sermon on back of letter dated Dec. 28, 1756, JEC.

56. "To the Mohawks," 105–10.

57. Revelation 3:20, Feb. 1751, 14/1141 JEC. See also, John 1:12, Feb. 1751, 14/1079 JEC.

58. Luke 9:23, Aug. 1753, 13/1061 JEC.

59. Revelation 22:5, Aug. 1756, 14/1149 JEC. For Edwards's view of the state of the world at this time, see his letter to Gideon Hawley (WJE, 16:690).

60. The manuscript provides no further hints as to the occasion or date of the lecture. Edwards, "Lecture on the Problem of Drink," 14/1155 JEC.

61. Marsden, *Jonathan Edwards*, 447–58.

62. Wheeler, "'Friends to Your Souls.'"

63. Emphasis in the original. WJE, 3:424.

64. Gideon Hawley wrote from his mission post among the Oneida, "I read my Bible & Mr. Brainerds life the only Books I bro't with me, and from them have a little support." June 3, 1753, The Papers of Gideon Hawley, American Congregational Library, Boston Massachusetts.

65. On Brainerd and disinterested benevolence, see Joseph Conforti, *Jonathan Edwards, Religious Tradition and American Culture* (Chapel Hill: University of North Carolina Press, 1995), 62–86. In his introduction to the Yale Edition, Pettit notes that Brainerd observed the same strict standards of admission, and thus supported Edwards's position by "transporting the ideology of the Northampton pulpit into the wilderness" ("Introduction," WJE, 7:15).

66. See especially Joseph Conforti, *Samuel Hopkins and the New Divinity Movement: Calvinism, the Congregational Ministry, and Reform in New England between the Great Awakenings* (Grand Rapids: Eerdmans, 1981).

67. For the Stockbridge Indians' military service in the eighteenth century, see Frazier, *Mohicans*; Colin G. Calloway, *The American Revolution in Indian Country: Crisis and Diversity in Native American Communities* (Cambridge: Cambridge University Press, 1995), 85–107.

68. Miles, "Red Man Dispossessed," passim.

69. It should be noted, however, that the Stockbridge Indians' commitment was never unquestioning.

70. I have written on Aupaumut more extensively in Rachel Wheeler, "Hendrick Aupaumut: Christian Mahican Prophet," *Journal of the Early Republic* 25 (July 2005): 187–220.

71. The tribal website contains autobiographical sketches of the tribal elders, many of which demonstrate these commitments. "Esteemed Elders," http://www.mohican-nsn.gov/Elders/EsteemedElders.htm (18 January 2006).

72. On the history of the Stockbridge Indians in the nineteenth and twentieth centuries, see James W. Oberly, *A Nation of Statesmen: The Political Culture of the Stockbridge-Munsee Mohicans, 1813–1972* (Norman: University of Oklahoma Press, 2005).

Part III

Edwards's legacy and reputation

11 Evangelical tradition in America

DOUGLAS A. SWEENEY

Ever since the eighteenth century, Jonathan Edwards's legacy and the fate of evangelicals in America have been symbiotically linked.[1] As Edwards's reputation has fared, so has the evangelical movement. There are many reasons for this, not all of them anchored in his eminence. Yet more than any other thinker, Edwards has aided evangelicals in gaining credibility and in furthering their agenda in American public life. Not surprisingly, then, evangelicals have usually championed Edwards more wholeheartedly – less hesitantly, and often much less critically – than has any other group. Not all of them have favored Edwards's Calvinistic commitments. Since the time of the Civil War, most have dissented from Calvinism. But all have shared in Edwards's passionate pursuit of "true religion," the kind of vital Christian piety that stems from regeneration (spiritual rebirth) and sets its subjects apart from nominal Christianity.

As Edwards preached in 1740, "[t]here is such a thing as conversion," and "'tis the most important thing in the world; and they are happy that have been the subjects of it and they most miserable that have not."[2] This doctrine has since become a hallmark of the evangelical movement, distinguishing it from other forms of traditional Protestantism. Indeed, for the purposes of this chapter, evangelicalism will be defined as orthodox[3] Protestantism transformed and reconfigured by the transatlantic awakenings of the early eighteenth century. "Evangelical" is a term that has been put to many uses. But so-called modern evangelicals, as members of the movement typically labeled "evangelical," are those who joined together in the heat of the revivals for the sake of spreading the gospel ecumenically. They transgressed the ethnic, geographical, and confessional zoning system that had long divided the citizens of Western Christendom – for the sake of promoting revival and conversion cooperatively. Along the way, they exported Edwards's "true religion" globally, turning him into their country's best-known theologian.[4]

In the remainder of this chapter, I take a roughly chronological approach to Edwards's legacy in America's evangelical tradition. After treating Edwards's role in the eighteenth-century revival and charting subsequent evangelical uses of his work, I conclude with a discussion of recent evangelical efforts to transmit his spiritual legacy into the future.

THE EVANGELICAL REVIVAL

By all accounts, Edwards proved to be the theological genius of his era's "Great Awakening." George Whitefield (1715–70) preached more, usually to much larger crowds. John Wesley (1703–91) did far more to organize revival forces. But Edwards made the best sense of spiritual "signs and wonders," interpreting them in relation to traditional Protestant thought. For those struggling to understand their era's Protestant revolution, he drafted several major treatises on revival and rebirth: his now-classic *Faithful Narrative of the Surprising Work of God* (1737);[5] *Distinguishing Marks of a Work of the Spirit of God* (1741), delivered at Yale's commencement; *Some Thoughts Concerning Revival* (1742), a controversial tract for the times; and most beloved of all, a book on *Religious Affections* (1746). These writings continue to shape evangelical spirituality.

It was Edwards's work on the doctrine of the freedom of the will that exerted the greatest force on evangelical theology.[6] Outside of Wesleyan circles, which were comparatively slow to form in Britain's American colonies, Calvinistic evangelicals usually led revival efforts. Some of them held forbiddingly strict views of the scope of Christ's atonement for the sins of fallen humanity – views that, early in the revival, placed a drag on spiritual outreach. To like-minded Calvinists harboring qualms about the awakening and its use of what was then called "indiscriminate" evangelism – that is, the revivalists' practice of extending the gospel promises to everyone, without stressing that God redeems only those elected for salvation – Edwards provided an analysis of the *Freedom of the Will* (1754) that distinguished between a non-elect sinner's "natural ability" (or constitutional capacity) to repent and turn from sin, and his or her "moral inability" (or ineradicable unwillingness) to do the same. Everyone gets what he or she wants, Edwards's treatise told its readers. The problem is that hardened sinners never *want* to submit to God. They *will not* kneel at the foot of the cross unless God draws them by his grace. They have themselves to blame, therefore, for their refusal to convert.

It may seem strange today that Christian conservatives hindered the revivals, that there were Calvinists at the time whose views of election and predestination kept them from preaching to people outside their own communities. But by the time of the awakening, there was a long and hallowed tradition in Great Britain especially, whose adherents thought it presumptuous to suggest to perfect strangers that it was possible for any of them to repent and be reborn.[7] Edwards's doctrine cleared the way for many such people to preach revival and to evangelize outside of their own churches and ethnic groups. It helped them share the gospel freely without suggesting in the process that non-Christians had the power to save themselves.

In New England, Edwards's colleagues, known as New Divinity preachers, did the most to spread this doctrine of natural ability. By the time the awakening ended, they were but one of several groups who sought control of New England's churches. But by the early nineteenth century, these Edwardseans would win the hearts and minds of most of their peers, enculturating the region with their leader's New Divinity.[8] Led at first by Edwards's colleagues Joseph Bellamy (1719–90) and Samuel Hopkins (1721–1803), they soon attracted the brightest college students at Yale. They promoted church renewal and evangelical conversion, all on the basis of Edwards's notion of natural ability.

New Divinity theologians developed other distinctive doctrines, too, but they secured their region's churches with their institutional work. They came to dominate New England's ministerial associations, playing a major role in examining and licensing future pastors. Ministering as they did before the rise of modern seminaries, they founded "schools of the prophets" (*schola prophetarum*) in which to train New England's clergy. Seasoned pastors led the schools, welcoming recent college graduates headed for ministry into their homes, supervising their doctrinal study, and letting them practice preaching and counseling in their churches under their watch. They spread Edwardsean doctrinal views by publishing scores of tracts and treatises – both Edwards's and their own. They organized concerts of prayer, common fasts, and conference meetings, all in support of further revival in the region and abroad. Finally, they worked at tightening up their churches' sacramental practice, reversing a century-old tradition pioneered by Edwards's grandfather, Solomon Stoddard (1643–1729), which allowed upstanding churchgoers, unable (or unwilling) to give account of their conversions, to participate in the Lord's Supper anyway.[9]

Edwards's reputation grew up with the modern evangelical movement, exerting a formative effect on its fledgling doctrines and institutions. By the dawn of the nineteenth century, both were poised to flourish as never before in the new United States. Edwards's evangelical heirs would take advantage of the liberties of independent America to market "true religion" with fewer restraints from state churches and their doctrinal confessions.

THE SECOND GREAT AWAKENING

America's Second Great Awakening proved much larger than the first. It also featured more theological and practical diversity. Though it is often represented in terms of doctrinal decline – both of Calvinism generally and of Edwards's New Divinity – such depictions are usually rendered by disgruntled, present-day Calvinists, or scholars who fail to grasp the complexities of doctrinal history, and rarely account for the full range of the revivals. The fact is that Calvinism did survive the Second Awakening. Indeed, Edwardseanism thrived as never before. Other groups now played a part in the nation's spiritual revivals. The old state churches were disestablished and upstart evangelical groups such as Wesley's Methodists, the Baptists, and an assortment of Restorationists now contributed significantly to the evangelical cause. But even some of these would soon fall under Edwards's spell. And in New England, a recontextualized Edwardsean tradition – soon to be called the New England Theology – expanded its tent to cover the bulk of the spiritual landscape. By the early 1830s, Edwards's legacy grew so large that he might well have been dubbed "America's evangelical."[10]

The Second Great Awakening blanketed several different regions – most famously New England, western New York, and the Cumberland Valley – each of which had its own unique style and doctrinal accents. The first major theater of revival was New England, where the New Divinity preachers held sway. Indeed, the Second Great Awakening played a greater role than the first in the Edwardsean enculturation of New England. In the late 1790s Edwardsean leaders such as Timothy Dwight (1752–1817), the grandson of Jonathan Edwards and president of Yale, began to promote renewal among the young and in key churches. By the 1810s and 1820s a major revival was underway. By the early 1830s nearly every Calvinist church in Massachusetts and Connecticut, and many in northern New England, had been attracted to the New Divinity platform.

Dwight's students led the way in spreading revival through the region. Pastor and activist Lyman Beecher (1775–1863) preached up a storm in his parish churches (first in Litchfield, Connecticut, then in Boston), promoting the cause of home missions wherever he went. Yale professor Nathaniel Taylor (1786–1858) taught evangelistic theology and preached revival in churches near New Haven. Most importantly, itinerants such as the strenuous Asahel Nettleton (1783–1844) tied New England's Christians together with a common, Calvinist message. Each of these ministers modified his New Divinity inheritance in ways that led to division among their churches. As their movement and its resources expanded exponentially, they began to disagree over what it should mean to carry Edwards's mantle through the nineteenth century. But they did so, to a person, in the service of revival, heralding Edwards's New Divinity, in one form or another, all the way.

The other major theaters of the Second Great Awakening featured less Edwardseanism, but even they showed vestiges of Edwards's legacy. In western New York especially, Edwards was read among the clergy and played a role in shaping spiritual expectations for the revival. Presbyterians and Congregationalists predominated in the region, though a sprinkling of Baptists and Methodists worked there too. A large number of these leaders had family roots back east in New England, but proved less interested than their cousins in conserving New England ways. More progressive in their outlook as well as in their methods of revival, they were also less conservative in their Calvinism. Consequently, they raised the eyebrows of the Edwardseans in New England, creating controversy within the Reformed community.

The most important leader by far of the revivals in New York was Presbyterian-turned-Congregationalist Charles Grandison Finney (1792–1875). Though he was born in western Connecticut, Finney was raised in western New York. He began his career as a lawyer, but then underwent a dramatic conversion experience in 1821. He quit the law and entered the ministry, studying theology with his pastor, George Gale (1789–1861) of Adams, New York. He was ordained by Presbyterians in 1824 and spent several years as an itinerant evangelist in New York as well as in cities such as Boston and Philadelphia. In 1832 he settled down in New York City, first at the Chatham Street Chapel (Presbyterian) and then at the Broadway Tabernacle (Congregational). In 1835 he accepted a call to move to Ohio and serve as professor of theology at the fledgling Oberlin College, which had been founded by a group of antislavery evangelicals. He spent the following four decades teaching theology at Oberlin, preaching regularly in the First Congregational Church of Oberlin (from 1837 to 1872), touring the nation as a revivalist, leading Oberlin as president (from 1851 to 1866), and publishing his lectures and collections of his sermons. He was the single most influential evangelical of his day.[11]

Finney taught (controversially) that "religion is the work of man," and that revival "is not a miracle" but "the result of the right use of the appropriate means."[12] As a Christian supernaturalist, he acknowledged with the Calvinists that revival and conversion do not occur without the help of the Holy Spirit. But as an experienced revivalist, he claimed that such things rarely occur without some human effort either. In the providence of God, means are used to promote revival. Grace is necessary, of course, but God does not coerce the lost or save the spiritually complacent. Rather, grace is that which persuades of the truth of Christianity. It enables anxious sinners to pick themselves up by their own bootstraps, and it is promised to all who seek it earnestly.

Finney also taught that "the state of the world is still such, and probably will be till the millennium is fully come, that religion must be mainly promoted by means of [revivals]." Human sin and its deadening effects "can only be counteracted by religious excitements."[13] And so evangelicals ought to be doing all that they can to bring them about. In keeping with this conviction, Finney developed several revivalistic methods that he believed were most conducive to the arousal of spiritual fervor. Known ever since as the "new measures," though they were really not new at all, they included mass advertising, "protracted" revival meetings, lay leadership, public prayers offered by men and women alike, and – most controversial of all – the "anxious bench."[14] The anxious bench was a pew placed at the front of the congregation where anxious sinners sat for prayer and special attention during the meetings. Finney's critics thought it symbolic of all that was wrong with his "new measures" and with the manipulative approach to Christian conversion he represented.

Finney's controversial tactics led by 1827 to a showdown with the Edwardseans of New England. Beecher, Nettleton, and their colleagues expressed concern about the "new measures." A conference was called in New Lebanon, New York, in July of 1827, at which the New Englanders hoped to curtail the excesses of Finney and his followers. In the end, however, the Edwardseans failed to suppress the Finneyites. In fact, the longer Finney defended himself, the more he impressed his opponents with his passion and sincerity. Ironically, he was preaching in Beecher's backyard just five years later – with the support of most of Boston's Edwardsean pastors, Beecher included. When pressed, Finney defended his measures by claiming Edwardsean patrimony. He said his emphasis on the capacity of sinners for moral effort and on the need for revival planning among the spiritually complacent derived from Edwards's own emphasis on human natural ability and insistence on the pursuit of true religion.[15]

Clearly, Finney represented the wave of the evangelical future. Revivalism had become the movement's premier institution. Successful revivalists were now the movement's leading authorities. Edwards's legacy was being spent in unintended ways, but ways that multiplied his influence among an increasingly broad range of the nation's evangelicals.

EVANGELICAL MISSIONS

As Stuart Piggin has claimed, "Jonathan Edwards was massively constitutive of modern Protestant missions."[16] Not only did his writings inspire numerous Calvinist ministers to promote "indiscriminate" or cross-cultural evangelism, but his example as a missionary and missionary biographer also inspired a surge of intercultural ministries. In 1747 Edwards promoted a transatlantic, evangelical Concert of Prayer "for the revival of religion and the advancement of Christ's kingdom."[17] In 1736 his congregation in

Northampton had helped to found a frontier Indian mission in Stockbridge, Massachusetts. Then in 1751 Edwards moved to Stockbridge himself, becoming a leading missionary in the colonies.[18]

Most significant of all for the rapid spread of Protestant missions was Edwards's *Life of David Brainerd* (1749), the best-selling book to come from his pen. Brainerd ministered as a missionary to Indians in New Jersey as well as New York and Pennsylvania. He was a protégé of Edwards. And he represented to Edwards, as to millions ever since, "a remarkable instance of true and eminent Christian piety" – the ideal, outward-reaching, gospel-driven evangelical.[19] Brainerd died of tuberculosis at the age of twenty-nine, drawing his final breath from a bed in the Edwards parsonage, but he had kept a strikingly intimate spiritual diary for years. Edwards organized his *Life of David Brainerd* around selections from the diary. Although Brainerd served for less than five years on the mission field, Edwards's *Life* transformed him into a Christian hero. His rather ordinary tombstone in Northampton's cemetery became a virtual Protestant shrine, attracting pilgrims far and wide. His name was hallowed through the halls of the early missions institutions. His legendary example of personal sacrifice for Christ – some have called it martyrdom – inspired multitudes to missionary service.[20]

Eighteenth-century Americans were not the first Protestants to enter the mission field. Europeans had dabbled in missions from the time of the Reformation. The British Puritans founded the first formal missions to Native Americans. Moravian Pietists proved the first global force in Protestant missions. And the English founded the early international sending agencies. But American evangelicals have commissioned the most missionaries. It took them a while to begin, but by the antebellum period their ministries were burgeoning, thanks in large part to the legacy of Edwards.

Not until nearly 1800 did the New Divinity "men"[21] commence America's first indigenous societies for missions. And even then their organizations devoted themselves to what would later be called the work of "home missions." Both the Connecticut Missionary Society (1797–8) and the Massachusetts Missionary Society (1799) – whose efforts culminated in the larger American Home Missionary Society (1826) – promoted preaching, church planting, and the distribution of Christian books and pamphlets among the pioneers and Indians of the West. They exerted a moral force on the formation of the new nation, but none of these groups made much of a difference overseas.[22]

It took a group of college boys to expand their elders' horizons and to stimulate investment by Americans abroad. In the summer of 1806, Samuel J. Mills (1783–1818) invited several fellow Williams College students to join him for prayer in Sloan's meadow, not far from their campus in rural

Williamstown, Massachusetts. A recent revival at the college, which had become an Edwardsean school, aroused concern throughout the community for world evangelization. Mills and his friends agreed to unburden their hearts in prayer for Asian ministry. But caught in a thunderstorm, they ran for refuge under a haystack, where they continued in prayer and committed themselves to service in foreign lands. This event has long been known as the "Haystack Prayer Meeting."[23]

These men continued to meet for prayer regarding the progress of the gospel. Two years later they founded an organization for international missions. Known as the Society of the Brethren (1808), it was the first foreign missions institution in the United States. "We can do it if we will," read the group's Edwardsean motto. All of its members planned to travel overseas as missionaries. And at least three of them – Samuel Mills, Gordon Hall (1784–1826), and James Richards (1784–1822) – continued their training at the recently established Andover Seminary (1808), the nation's first post-baccalaureate, Protestant theological school. They aroused support there for their cause, attracting other seminarians such as Samuel Newell (1784–1821), Samuel Nott, Jr. (1788–1869), and the later-renowned Adoniram Judson (1788–1850). These men earned their school its moniker, "the missionary seminary."[24]

In 1810 Judson, Newell, Nott and Hall presented themselves for foreign service before the General Association of Massachusetts (a Congregationalist organization). The following day they helped to found their country's first sending agency for international missions, called the American Board of Commissioners for Foreign Missions (ABCFM). In 1812 the American Board sent Judson, Nott, Newell, Hall and Luther Rice (1783–1836), along with their wives, to found a mission near Calcutta. By the end of the second decade of the nineteenth century, the Board had also made deep inroads into Ceylon (Sri Lanka), the Sandwich Islands (Hawaii), and Palestine, and among Native Americans.

Scores of missionary wives, as well as single female missionaries, received their education at Mt. Holyoke Female Seminary. Founded in 1837 by the Edwardsean theologian and educator Mary Lyon (1797–1849), Mt. Holyoke trained its students in liberal arts, domestic work, and ministry. Lyon sought to shape the whole woman, as she told her benefactors. She also aimed to "teach nothing that cannot be made to help in the great work of converting the world to Christ."[25] Her school was nestled amid the rolling hills of western Massachusetts, roughly eighty miles from Andover, well situated for partnership with the latter school in missions. Countless couples left from these schools to engage in missions overseas. And as the nineteenth century wore on, women enjoyed a greater freedom to serve in missions on their own. Schools such as Lyon's proved indispensable to their labors.[26]

Edwards's followers continue to spur the work of modern evangelical missions. Scholars often slight this aspect of Edwards's legacy. His missionary heirs have played a greater role than any other group in spreading his reputation abroad.[27]

THE NEW ENGLAND THEOLOGY

As distinguished from the rest of the theology of New England, "the New England Theology" was uniquely Edwardsean. A tradition of variations on certain key Edwardsean themes, it represented the nation's first indigenous theological movement.[28] In the words of Edwards A. Park (1808–1900), the last leader of this movement,

> It signifies the formal creed which a majority of the most eminent theologians in New England have explicitly or implicitly sanctioned, during and since the time of Edwards. It denotes the spirit and genius of the system openly avowed or logically involved, in their writings. It includes not the peculiarities in which Edwards differed, as he is known to have differed, from the larger part of his most eminent followers; nor the peculiarities in which any one of his followers differed, as some of them did, from the larger part of the others; but it comprehends the principles, with their logical sequences, which the greater number of our most celebrated divines have approved expressly or by implication.[29]

By the early 1850s, these "principles" were summarized under three main heads: "that sin consists in choice, that our natural power equals, and that it also limits, our duty."[30] All three were controversial, and all derived, ultimately, from the doctrine of natural ability.

The New England Theology might be said to have gone through three major phases: a phase succeeding the Great Awakening, when Edwards's New Divinity followers systematized his doctrinal views; a phase at the height of the Second Awakening, when Edwardseans such as Taylor recontextualized these views, making them serviceable for evangelism in early national America; and a phase in the antebellum period, when myriad evangelicals claimed a New England doctrinal pedigree, but the movement grew so large that it began to pull apart – and Edwards A. Park tried desperately to stitch it together.

In phase one, several leading New Divinity doctrines characterized the New England Theology. Edwardsean preachers called their hearers to "immediate repentance," to "disinterested benevolence," and to a "willingness to be damned," if necessary, for God's glory. They were not perfectionists, but they had grown dissatisfied with the ineffectual piety of establishmentarian Protestantism. Few favored disestablishing New England Congregationalism, but all of them championed an evangelical view of religion, calling parishioners to personal faith, genuine conversion, and self-sacrifice in service of the needy. New Divinity leaders, such as Hopkins and even Jonathan Edwards, Jr., are best known for their antislavery work. They developed a new atonement theory – universal in scope – stressing that all that kept sinners from appropriating the atonement's benefits was their ongoing rebellion, or refusal to convert. And they opposed Solomon Stoddard's liberal sacramental policy, denying the Eucharist to those who would not testify to some measure of genuine religion, and restricting the rite of baptism to families of the converted, thus abandoning New England's older Half-Way Covenant too.[31]

In phase two, the New England Theology was characterized by Taylor's controversial modifications, changes that split the Congregationalists of Connecticut and beyond and led to disruption in the Presbyterian Church. Taylor redefined the New Divinity doctrine of the will and the related view of original sin so as to exclude the teaching that all of us (that is, all human beings) labor under the guilt of Adam unless and until our souls are supernaturally renovated. Taylor granted that all are born with dreadfully sinful human natures, natures that lead to sin "in all the appropriate circumstances of our being." He denied, however, that we are born with natures that are burdened with a positive sinful charge, a physical quality that would render sin inevitable. "Sin is in the sinning," Taylor taught his students at Yale. "It is man's own act," not the fault of our first parents, for every sinner has genuine "power to the contrary." Indeed, though Edwards had distinguished between the unregenerate sinner's "natural ability" and "moral inability" to repent, Taylor scuttled inability altogether. He admitted that sin is "certain" prior to spiritual rebirth. But he denied that it is in any way "necessary." Thus Taylor altered Edwardsean doctrine, at least rhetorically and semantically. But he did so for a classic Edwardsean reason: he sought to keep the unrepentant from blaming God for their moral problems.[32]

In phase three, the New England Theology expanded to the breaking point. Finney and other westward-oriented evangelical pragmatists now adapted it for their purposes, using Edwards's cachet to fortify their new agenda. In the end, they rid the movement of nearly all but its three "principles." However, they used these three principles to animate what some have called their antebellum evangelical "righteous empire," sharing a truncated version of Edwards's theological legacy with an unprecedented number of Americans.[33]

By the time of the Civil War, the New England Theology was dying. Intramural competition over Edwards's spiritual mantle, as well as extramural losses to new, progressive Christian leaders, led to a period when the most important Edwardsean achievements came in the form of testy defenses of their tribe from criticism and historical reconstructions of the unity of their movement.[34] Edwards's spirit did live on to wander the cultural hinterlands, but the New England Theology, as a vital intellectual movement, soon expired.

OTHER EVANGELICALS

The New England theologians were not the only evangelicals to make good on Edwards's legacy. Throughout the United States, many thousands of evangelicals honored Edwards as a founder of their movement for revival as well as a theological genius, appealing to him selectively in pursuit of true religion. None of them did so with more vigor than the Baptists and Presbyterians.

Baptist use of Edwards's legacy dates to the time of the Great Awakening, when Isaac Backus (1724–1806) mimicked much of Edwards's evangelical Calvinism. But Edwardseanism infiltrated the ranks of Baptist thinkers much more thoroughly during the time of the Second Awakening. New England Baptists such as Jonathan Maxcy (1768–1820), who held the presidencies of Rhode Island College, Union College, and, late in his life, the University of South Carolina, contributed significantly to the New Divinity platform. Maxcy published a well-known "Discourse Designed to Explain the Doctrine of Atonement" in 1796, which became a standard source of Edwardsean views.[35] Early Southern Baptist leaders also shared in Edwards's legacy. William Bullein Johnson (1782–1862), a faithful protégé of Maxcy, along with William T. Brantly (1787–1845), Luther Rice (1783–1836), and Jesse Mercer (1769–1841), are only the best-known examples of Edwardsean activists who played important roles in shaping Southern Baptist faith and practice, most importantly through the formation of the Triennial Convention in 1814, predecessor to the Southern Baptist Convention formed in 1845.[36]

Presbyterians, north and south, also drew upon Edwards's legacy, disagreeing among themselves about the merits of New Divinity. During the First Great Awakening, Presbyterians divided into Old and New Side camps (1741–58). Old Side leaders opposed the revivals and their leaders' disorderly methods. They were nervous about New England and its impact on their church. New Side Presbyterian leaders supported the revivals and New England, viewing Edwards and the Edwardseans as allies in their cause. They founded the College of New Jersey in 1746, later Princeton University, whose first three presidents hailed from Edwards's New England. The second of these was Edwards's son-in-law, Aaron Burr (1716–57). The third was Edwards himself, whose body is buried in Princeton's cemetery. Soon after Edwards died, Gilbert Tennent (1703–64), the leading New Side Presbyterian organizer, offered the following testimony to his party's sympathies: "On Wednesday the 22nd [of March], departed this life, the reverend and worthy Mr. Jonathan Edwards . . . ; a person of great eminence, both in respect of capacity, learning, piety, and usefulness; a good scholar, and a great divine."[37]

During the Second Great Awakening, Edwardsean Presbyterianism grew as never before (or since). Southern Presbyterian leaders such as Hezekiah Balch (1741–1810) and Gideon Blackburn (1772–1838) spread Edwardsean views through North Carolina, Tennessee, and central Kentucky, finding them institutional homes in the early Synod of Tennessee, the Brainerd Mission to the Cherokees of southern Tennessee, Greeneville College (later Tusculum), Southern and Western Seminary (later Maryville College), East Tennessee College (later the University of Tennessee), and Danville College (later Centre College).[38]

More significant to the institutional history of Presbyterians, northern Presbyterian leaders signed an agreement with their Congregational colleagues in Connecticut that would expedite church planting in the West. This Plan of Union (1801) guaranteed collaboration on the frontier, as well as a wide Edwardsean inroad into the Presbyterian Church. The "Presbygational" churches it yielded could enter either denomination. However, they usually chose to join the Presbyterians. As a result, hundreds of Presbyterian churches dotted the West, led by clergy who were enamored of the spirit of New England. They founded colleges and seminaries throughout the old northwest, in the Mississippi Valley and beyond, schools such as Beloit, Carleton, Grinnell, and Illinois College. Along the way, they altered the ethos of American Presbyterianism, causing concern back East, raising hackles in the deep South, and sparking controversy regarding the use of the church's confessional standards that would persist into the late twentieth century.[39]

In fact, the Presbyterian schism between the Old and New Schools (1837 ff.) erupted largely over the issue of Edwardseanism. Many Old School leaders admired Edwards's Calvinism, but detested what had become of New England Theology. They leveled heresy charges against their fellow Presbyterian ministers who had adopted Taylor's evangelistic theology, most notably against Lyman Beecher in 1835 and against Albert Barnes, in 1830–1 and 1835. Then, at the Presbyterian General Assembly of 1837, they annulled the Plan of Union, expurgating the four synods it had produced. The nation's sectional controversy only exacerbated the schism. New School Presbyterians split over slavery in 1857. Old Schoolers split in 1861 as the Civil War began.

Old and New School in the South would reunite during the war (1864), but in the North reunion would not occur until 1869.[40]

The Princetonians, especially, champions of Old School theology, sought to sever Finney, Park, Taylor, and others from Edwards's legacy. Most of them questioned Edwards's doctrine of the sinner's natural ability. They regretted Edwards's tendency to indulge in metaphysics, but they praised his opposition to modern infidelity and they delighted in his rout of Arminianism. Charles Hodge (1797–1878), Lyman Atwater (1813–83), and Benjamin Breckenridge Warfield (1851–1921) all delivered fierce attacks against the New England Theology. But none of them phrased the Old School message quite as clearly as Warfield would nearly half a century after the end of the New School controversy. He wrote, "It was Edwards' misfortune that he gave his name to a party; and to a party which, never in perfect agreement with him in its doctrinal ideas, finished by becoming the earnest advocate of (as it has been sharply expressed) 'a set of opinions which he gained his chief celebrity in demolishing.'"[41]

Edwards's legacy outside New England was always hotly contested; as a result, it remained at the forefront of modern evangelical consciousness. It declined at century's end, along with the evangelical movement. But by the 1940s and 1950s, an Edwards renaissance had emerged, one that enhanced his reputation, inspired a host of Edwards scholars, and renewed evangelical interest in Edwards's mantle.

THE EDWARDS RENAISSANCE

The so-called Edwards renaissance has received a great deal of attention.[42] Much less studied is its bearing on America's evangelicals. A few scholars have begun to comment seriously on the relation. Kenneth P. Minkema has noted that, since the 1990s especially, "Evangelical scholars, seminarians, pastors, and religious leaders have taken up Edwards as a theologian, preacher, and revivalist in a way not seen since before the Civil War."[43] Sean Michael Lucas has published a bibliographic essay on their efforts.[44] In the main, however, the scores of evangelical groups who claim, study, revere, or propagate Edwards remain *terra incognita* to the academic community. Mark Noll explains that "twentieth-century evangelical Protestants came late to the recovery of Edwards." Nevertheless, continues Noll, "[a]t the start of the twenty-first century, evangelical Protestants, who in many ways are the modern constituency closest to Edwards' own religious concerns, have at last begun to learn from him themselves."[45]

As Minkema has demonstrated, evangelicals now produce the bulk of scholarship on Edwards's theological activity.[46] But perhaps more important for the extension of his legacy, evangelical leaders now convene the largest conferences, dispense the most literature and audio-visual matter, build the most popular websites, and raise the most interest related to Edwards's life and theological ministry. An exhaustive survey of their efforts is simply not possible here. But a summary will help to show that evangelicals continue to appropriate Edwards more than any other group, past or present.

The leading pioneer of the evangelical Edwards renaissance was John H. Gerstner (1914–96), faculty member at the Presbyterian Pittsburgh Seminary as well as Trinity Evangelical Divinity School. Gerstner promoted Edwards with hundreds of pastors, seminarians, and evangelical laity, devoted his summers to poring over Edwards's manuscripts at Yale, and published several books on Edwards's theology.[47] He also made disciples, most importantly R. C. Sproul (b. 1939), who founded Ligonier Ministries in the early 1970s near Gerstner's home in western Pennsylvania. A deeply Edwardsean institution,[48] Ligonier Ministries moved to Orlando, Florida, in 1984. Today it sponsors *Renewing Your Mind*, a radio program heard by millions; *Tabletalk*, a monthly magazine for Reformed evangelicals; a multimedia group; as well as numerous seminars. It also owns a similar ministry named Soli Deo Gloria, which was founded in 1984 by Don Kistler (b. 1949), another Edwards partisan, at a California megachurch, Grace Community Church, pastored by the well-known dispensational media figure John MacArthur. In 1986 Kistler moved to Pennsylvania and connected himself to Gerstner. A long-time colleague of Sproul as well, Kistler speaks at conferences and publishes the writings of the Puritans, sharing Edwards's legacy in typical evangelical fashion – not by zooming closely onto a few of his doctrinal protrusions, but by offering a panoramic view of his evangelical eminence, promoting a broadly Reformed, Christian spirituality.

Iain Murray (b. 1931) and his Banner of Truth Trust, though not American, have also played a role in the recent Edwards renaissance, prompting thousands of America's more thoughtful evangelicals to study Edwards's life and ministry. Murray is peripatetic. He has worked as a Protestant minister both in England and Australia and as a publishing executive in Scotland. He cofounded the Banner of Truth Trust in 1957 to propagate Reformed and evangelical literature. Through its magazine (*The Banner of Truth*), its scores of Calvinistic reprints, and, most importantly, Murray's devout biography of Edwards,[49] he has done almost as much as Gerstner, Sproul, and their associates to spread Edwardsean faith throughout America. The Banner of Truth even operates an office in Pennsylvania, not too distant from the Gerstners' Ligonier.[50]

John Piper (b. 1946) is now America's most famous Edwardsean minister. He pastors Bethlehem Baptist Church in Minneapolis, Minnesota, publishes widely popular books on Edwards's thought and spirituality,[51] and heads a national center, named Desiring God Ministries, devoted in part to sharing Edwardsean views with other evangelicals. Through his books, tapes, the Internet, and major pastoral conferences, he shares his passion for Edwards's spirituality, especially for what he refers to as Edwards's Christian "hedonism," known more technically as Christian eudaemonism. He has also inspired others with similar evangelical ministries. John H. Armstrong (b. 1949), a former pastor in Wheaton, Illinois (Reformation and Revival Ministries), Samuel Storms (b. 1951), a former professor based in Kansas City, Missouri (Enjoying God Ministries), and C. J. Mahaney (b. 1953), a megachurch minister in Washington, D.C. (Sovereign Grace Ministries), are only the best-known examples of the scores of evangelicals who are attempting to combine assorted Edwardsean commitments with contemporary evangelical practices.

The Southern Baptist Convention is now the single largest Protestant denomination in America. Not surprisingly, then, its doctrine has diversified significantly, allowing for Calvinist, Arminian, and Anabaptist views. However, since 1982, a group of pastors and theologians has worked to revive and strengthen Calvinism in Southern Baptist churches. They have done so, moreover, with frequent claims to Edwards's legacy. Led by Tom Ascol (b. 1957), their Southern Baptist "Founders Movement" has grown rapidly during the past two decades. Today it organizes several conferences per year, sponsors outreach on the Web, and prints a journal (*Founders Journal*) and other items through its publishing division (Founders Press). The Founders Movement has also created a sizable market for Edwards's writings, especially among pastors. Thus in recent years a growing number of Southern Baptist scholars have published editions of Edwards's sermon manuscripts.[52]

A large array of other leaders has also promoted Edwards recently to evangelical Christians in America. Professional scholars such as Richard Lovelace (b. 1930) of Gordon-Conwell Seminary,[53] George Marsden (b. 1939) of Notre Dame,[54] Gerald McDermott (b. 1952) of Roanoke College,[55] Stephen Nichols (b. 1970) of Lancaster Bible College,[56] and Mark Noll (b. 1946) of Wheaton College,[57] not to mention leaders such as William C. Nichols (b. 1950) of International Outreach (Ames, Iowa)[58] and Brandon G. Withrow (b. 1971) of Passion for Truth (now in suburban Philadelphia),[59] continue to carry Edwardseanism – in dozens of different shapes and sizes – into the future.

To be sure, Edwards's legacy has now survived his tercentennial birthday, October 5, 2003. We no longer live in a day when Edwardseans can dominate the mainstream of American academe. But if they cooperate with others and work with a view to the commonweal, perhaps they can play a role in promoting their eponym well into the future, both among their own constituents and throughout what Edwards referred to, in the hope of millennial glory, as "all nations... the whole habitable world."[60]

Notes

1. My thanks to Robert Caldwell, Jason Dahlman, David Kling, Scott Manetsch, Cindy Sleasman, and Brandon Withrow for expert advice on drafts of this chapter. The bibliography on Edwards's legacy among American evangelicals is immense. In the notes that follow, I have listed only those sources most important to the development of the themes of this chapter. For a more complete listing, consult the "Select Bibliography" in Douglas A. Sweeney and Allen C. Guelzo, eds., *The New England Theology, 1734–1852: America's First Indigenous Theological Tradition, From Jonathan Edwards and the New Divinity to Edwards Amasa Park* (Grand Rapids: Baker, 2006).

2. Jonathan Edwards, "The Reality of Conversion," in Wilson H. Kimnach, Kenneth P. Minkema, and Douglas A. Sweeney, eds., *The Sermons of Jonathan Edwards: A Reader* (New Haven: Yale University Press, 1999), 83, 92.

3. That is, doctrinally orthodox Protestantism. The terms "orthodox" and "orthodoxy" are hotly contested today, but they prove more accurate as descriptors of the evangelical movement than the term "conservative." Evangelicals have always been doctrinally conservative, but they have not always proven culturally or politically conservative.

4. I have developed this approach to evangelical history in Douglas A. Sweeney, *The American Evangelical Story: A History of the Movement* (Grand Rapids: Baker, 2005), a volume from which I have drawn in parts of this chapter. Though it offers an insider's history of the evangelical movement, it may also help others to negotiate the meanings of the word "evangelical" and the varied interpretations of modern evangelical history.

5. As noted in D. W. Bebbington's contribution to this volume, the *Faithful Narrative* quickly became an international best-seller. First published in London (1737) and Edinburgh (1737), it was soon revised and published in Boston (1738) before appearing in translation both in Germany (1738) and Holland (1740). It attracted international attention to the revival, encouraging Wesley to preach out of doors and drawing Whitefield to America. See also David W. Bebbington, "Remembered Around the World: The International Scope of Edwards's Legacy," and M. X. Lesser, "An Honor Too Great: Jonathan Edwards in Print Abroad," in David W. Kling and Douglas A. Sweeney, eds., *Jonathan Edwards at Home and Abroad: Historical Memories, Cultural Movements, Global Horizons* (Columbia: University of South Carolina Press, 2003), 177–200, 297–319.

6. The best treatment of this doctrine and its roles in American history is Allen C. Guelzo, *Edwards on the Will: A Century of American Theological Debate* (Middletown, CT.: Wesleyan University Press, 1989).

7. In Edwards's day there were English Dissenters, such as the Calvinistic Baptists John Gill (1697–1771) and John Brine (1703–65), who taught this could only be said with confidence in the confines of a rightly ordered, covenanted community. For a helpful recent discussion of Edwards's impact on such ministers, see D. Bruce Hindmarsh, "The Reception of Jonathan Edwards by Early Evangelicals

in England," in Kling and Sweeney, eds., *Jonathan Edwards at Home and Abroad*, esp. 207–12.

8. On the notion of an Edwardsean enculturation of Calvinist New England, see Douglas A. Sweeney, *Nathaniel Taylor, New Haven Theology, and the Legacy of Jonathan Edwards* (New York: Oxford University Press, 2003), 13–65.

9. On these institutional efforts, see Joseph Conforti, *Samuel Hopkins and the New Divinity Movement: Calvinism, the Congregational Ministry, and Reform in New England between the Great Awakenings* (Grand Rapids: Christian University Press, 1981); David W. Kling, *A Field of Divine Wonders: The New Divinity and Village Revivals in Northwestern Connecticut, 1792–1822* (University Park: Pennsylvania State University Press, 1993); Sweeney, *Nathaniel Taylor, New Haven Theology, and the Legacy of Jonathan Edwards*.

10. Philip F. Gura, *Jonathan Edwards: America's Evangelical* (New York: Hill and Wang, 2005), esp. 222–38.

11. On Finney's life and work, see Charles Hambrick-Stowe, *Charles G. Finney and the Spirit of American Evangelicalism*, Library of Religious Biography (Grand Rapids: Eerdmans, 1996); Keith Hardman, *Charles Grandison Finney, 1792–1875: Revivalist and Reformer* (Syracuse: Syracuse University Press, 1987).

12. Charles Grandison Finney, *Lectures on Revivals of Religion*, ed. William G. McLoughlin (Cambridge, MA: Belknap Press of Harvard University Press, 1960), 9–13.

13. Ibid., 10–11.

14. Finney's own interpretation of the "new measures" is found in ibid., 250–76.

15. On Finney's Edwardsean pedigree, consult Allen C. Guelzo, "Oberlin Perfectionism and Its Edwardsian Origins, 1835–1870," in Stephen J. Stein, ed., *Jonathan Edwards's Writings: Text, Context, Interpretation* (Bloomington: Indiana University Press, 1996), 159–74; idem., "An Heir or a Rebel? Charles Grandison Finney and the New England Theology," *Journal of the Early Republic* 17 (Spring 1997): 61–94. See Hambrick-Stowe, *Charles G. Finney and the Spirit of American Evangelicalism*.

16. Stuart Piggin, "The Expanding Knowledge of God: Jonathan Edwards's Influence on Missionary Thinking and Promotion," in Kling and Sweeney, eds., *Jonathan Edwards at Home and Abroad*, 266.

17. *An Humble Attempt to Promote Explicit Agreement and Visible Union of God's People in Extraordinary Prayer for the Revival of Religion and the Advancement of Christ's Kingdom on Earth, Pursuant to Scripture-Promises and Prophecies concerning the Last Time* (WJE, 5:307–436).

18. On Edwards's work at the Stockbridge mission, see Chapter 10 of this book.

19. WJE, 7:96.

20. Joseph Conforti, "David Brainerd and the Nineteenth-Century Missionary Movement," *Journal of the Early Republic* 5 (Fall 1985): 309–29.

21. Though scholars often refer to these ministers as New Divinity "men," there were several notable women in their ranks. Sarah Osborn and Susanna Anthony (of Newport, Rhode Island) are by far the best known. Osborn has received the most attention. See Samuel Hopkins, ed., *Memoirs of the Life of Mrs. Sarah Osborn* (Worcester, MA: Leonard Worcester, 1799); Mary Beth Norton, ed., "'My Resting Reaping Times': Sarah Osborne's Defense of Her 'Unfeminine' Activities, 1767," *Signs: Journal of Women in Culture and Society* 2 (Winter 1976): 515–29;

Charles E. Hambrick-Stowe, "The Spiritual Pilgrimage of Sarah Osborn (1714–1796)," *Church History* 61 (December 1992): 408–21; Catherine Brekus, *Sarah Osborn's World: Popular Christianity in Early America* (New York: Knopf, forthcoming).

22. On Edwardsean home missions, see James R. Rohrer, *Keepers of the Covenant: Frontier Missions and the Decline of Congregationalism, 1774–1818*, Religion in America Series (New York: Oxford University Press, 1995); Genevieve McCoy, "The Women of the ABCFM Oregon Mission and the Conflicted Language of Calvinism," *Church History* 64 (March 1995): 62–82; Victor B. Howard, *Conscience and Slavery: The Evangelistic Calvinist Domestic Missions, 1837–1861* (Kent, OH: Kent State University Press, 1990).

23. See David W. Kling, "The New Divinity and the Origins of the American Board of Commissioners for Foreign Missions," *Church History* 72 (Dec. 2003): 791–819; idem., "The New Divinity and Williams College, 1793–1836," *Religion and American Culture* 6 (Summer 1996): 195–223.

24. On Andover Seminary and missions, see *Memoirs of American Missionaries, Formerly Connected with the Society of Inquiry Respecting Mission, in the Andover Theological Seminary* (Boston: Peirce and Parker, 1833); Leonard Woods, *History of the Andover Theological Seminary* (Boston: James R. Osgood, 1885); Henry K. Rowe, *History of Andover Theological Seminary* (Newton, MA: Thomas Todd, 1933).

25. Quoted in Dana L. Robert, *American Women in Mission: A Social History of Their Thought and Practice* (Macon, GA: Mercer University Press, 1996), 98.

26. Amanda Porterfield, *Mary Lyon and the Mount Holyoke Missionaries* (New York: Oxford University Press, 1997); Elizabeth Alden Green, *Mary Lyon and Mount Holyoke: Opening the Gates* (Hanover, NH: University Press of New England, 1979).

27. For more on Edwards's legacy in evangelical missions, consult Andrew F. Walls, "Missions and Historical Memory: Jonathan Edwards and David Brainerd," in Kling and Sweeney, eds., *Jonathan Edwards at Home and Abroad*, 248–65; Ronald E. Davies, *Jonathan Edwards and His Influence on the Development of the Missionary Movement from Britain* (Cambridge: Currents in World Christianity Project, 1996).

28. Scholarly literature on the New England Theology is vast and contentious. For an historiographical summary, see Douglas A. Sweeney, "Edwards and His Mantle: The Historiography of the New England Theology," *New England Quarterly* 71 (March 1998): 97–119. Cf. The "Select Bibliography" in Sweeney and Guelzo, eds., *The New England Theology*.

29. Edwards A. Park, "The New England Theology; with Comments on a Third Article in the Biblical Repertory and Princeton Review, Relating to a Convention Sermon," *Bibliotheca Sacra* 9 (January 1852): 174.

30. Ibid., 175.

31. Consult, Sweeney and Guelzo, eds., *The New England Theology* for a description of these doctrines and a selection of the relevant primary sources. On New England's Half-Way Covenant (a term that dates from the 1740s rather than from the seventeenth century), see Robert G. Pope, *The Half-Way Covenant: Church Membership in Puritan New England* (Princeton: Princeton University Press, 1969).

32. The locus classicus of these modifications is Taylor's *Concio ad Clerum: A Sermon Delivered in the Chapel of Yale College, September 10, 1828* (New Haven: H. Howe, 1828). For more on his theology, see Sweeney, *Nathaniel Taylor, New Haven Theology, and the Legacy of Jonathan Edwards.*

33. See Martin E. Marty, *Righteous Empire: The Protestant Experience in America* (1970; reprint, New York: Harper Torchbooks, 1977).

34. Edwards A. Park, the "last of the consistent Calvinists," is well-known for such efforts at historical reclamation. See Frank Hugh Foster, *The Life of Edwards Amasa Park, Abbot Professor, Andover Theological Seminary* (New York: Fleming H. Revell Company, 1936); Anthony C. Cecil, Jr., *The Theological Development of Edwards Amasa Park: Last of the "Consistent Calvinists"* (Missoula, MT: Scholars' Press, 1974); Joseph Conforti, "Edwards A. Park and the Creation of the New England Theology, 1840–1870," in Stein, ed., *Jonathan Edwards's Writings,* 193–207.

35. Maxcy's "Discourse" was later anthologized by Edwards A. Park in what has become the standard New Divinity volume on the subject, Edwards A. Park, ed., *The Atonement: Discourses and Treatises by Edwards, Smalley, Maxcy, Emmons, Griffin, Burge, and Weeks* (Boston: Congregational Board of Publication, 1859). On the Edwardsean view of atonement, see also Dorus Paul Rudisill, *The Doctrine of The Atonement in Jonathan Edwards and His Successors* (New York: Poseidon, 1971); David Wells, "The Debate over the Atonement in 19th-Century America," *Bibliotheca Sacra* 144 (April–June 1987): 123–43 (July–Sept. 1987): 243–53 (Oct.–Dec. 1987): 363–76; Bruce M. Stephens, "An Appeal to the Universe: The Doctrine of the Atonement in American Protestant Thought from Jonathan Edwards to Edwards Amasa Park," *Encounter* 60 (Winter 1999): 55–72.

36. Much work remains to be done on the history of Baptist Edwardseanism. Good places to begin include E. Brooks Holifield, *Theology in America: Christian Thought from the Age of the Puritans to the Civil War* (New Haven: Yale University Press, 2003), 282–4; Anthony L. Chute, *A Piety above the Common Standard: Jesse Mercer and Evangelistic Calvinism* (Macon, GA: Mercer University Press, 2004); Robert Snyder, "William T. Brantly (1787–1845): A Southern Unionist and the Breakup of the Triennial Convention" (Ph.D. dissertation, Southern Baptist Theological Seminary, 2005); Tom J. Nettles, "Edwards and His Impact on Baptists," *Founders Journal* 53 (Summer 2003): 1–18.

37. Quoted in Iain H. Murray, *Jonathan Edwards: A New Biography* (Edinburgh: Banner of Truth Trust, 1987), 442.

38. The tiny Independent Presbyterian Church (1813–63), most influential in South Carolina, was only marginally Edwardsean but did practice some of the New Divinity. See Harold M. Parker, Jr., "The Independent Presbyterian Church and Reunion in the South, 1813–1863," *Journal of Presbyterian History* 50 (Summer 1972): 89–110. On later Edwardseans among the southern "New School" Presbyterians (on the New School, see below), cf. idem., *The United Synod of the South: The Southern New School Presbyterian Church* (Westport, CT: Greenwood Press, 1988); E. T. Thompson, *Presbyterianism in the South* (3 vols. Richmond, VA: John Knox, 1963–73). Much work remains to be done on southern Presbyterian Edwardseans. The best place to begin is Sean Michael Lucas, "'He Cuts up Edwardsism by the Roots': Robert Lewis Dabney and the Edwardsian Legacy in

the Nineteenth-Century South," in D. G. Hart, Sean Michael Lucas, and Stephen J. Nichols, eds., *The Legacy of Jonathan Edwards: American Religion and the Evangelical Tradition* (Grand Rapids: Baker Academic, 2003), 200–214 (though Lucas focuses on an opponent of the Edwardseans). Further bibliographical leads may be found in Sweeney, *Nathaniel Taylor, New Haven Theology, and the Legacy of Jonathan Edwards*, 180–1, n. 71, 244–5, nn. 20, 22.

39. Largely due to their proximity to Yale and its alumni, New York State and northern New Jersey were major centers of northern Presbyterian Edwardseanism. On the Plan of Union, see Zebulon Crocker, *The Catastrophe of the Presbyterian Church, in 1837, Including a Full View of the Recent Theological Controversies in New England* (New Haven: B. and W. Noyes, 1838); William S. Kennedy, *The Plan of Union* (Hudson, OH: Pentagon Steam Press, 1856); Williston Walker, *The Creeds and Platforms of Congregationalism* (1893; reprint, New York: Pilgrim Press, 1991), 524–41.

40. For the Old School abrogation of the Plan of Union at the 1837 General Assembly, see *Minutes of the General Assembly of the Presbyterian Church in the United States of America, from A.D. 1821 to A.D. 1837 Inclusive* (Philadelphia: Presbyterian Board of Publication and Sabbath-School Work, n.d.), esp. 604–14. On the schism of 1837–8 and its role in shaping subsequent Presbyterian Edwardseanism, see Crocker, *The Catastrophe of the Presbyterian Church*; Earl Pope, *New England Calvinism and the Disruption of the Presbyterian Church* (1962; reprint, New York: Garland, 1987); George M. Marsden, *The Evangelical Mind and the New School Presbyterian Experience: A Case Study of Thought and Theology in Nineteenth-Century America* (New Haven: Yale University Press, 1970).

41. Benjamin Breckenridge Warfield, "Jonathan Edwards and the New England Theology," in Mark Noll, ed., *The Princeton Theology, 1812–1921: Scripture, Science, and Theological Method from Archibald Alexander to Benjamin Warfield* (1983; reprint, Grand Rapids: Baker Academic, 2001), 314. For more on nineteenth-century Presbyterian responses to Edwards, see Mark A. Noll, *America's God, from Jonathan Edwards to Abraham Lincoln* (New York: Oxford University Press, 2002); idem., "Edwards' Theology after Edwards," in Sang Hyun Lee, ed., *The Princeton Companion to Jonathan Edwards* (Princeton: Princeton University Press, 2005), 292–308.

42. See especially Joseph Conforti, *Jonathan Edwards, Religious Tradition, and American Culture* (Chapel Hill: University of North Carolina Press, 1995); Donald Weber, "Perry Miller and the Recovery of Jonathan Edwards," in Perry Miller, *Jonathan Edwards* (Amherst: University of Massachusetts Press, 1981), v–xxv; idem, "The Figure of Jonathan Edwards," *American Quarterly* 35 (Winter 1983): 556–64; idem, "The Recovery of Jonathan Edwards," in Nathan O. Hatch and Harry S. Stout, eds., *Jonathan Edwards and the American Experience* (New York: Oxford University Press, 1988), 50–70. For a track record of Edwards scholarship since World War II, see the bibliographies of M. X. Lesser: *Jonathan Edwards: A Reference Guide* (Boston: G. K. Hall, 1981); *Jonathan Edwards: An Annotated Bibliography, 1979–1993*, Bibliographies and Indexes in Religious Studies, no. 30 (Westport, CT: Greenwood Press, 1994).

43. Kenneth P. Minkema, "Jonathan Edwards in the Twentieth Century," *Journal of the Evangelical Theological Society* 47 (Dec. 2004): 677.

44. Sean Michael Lucas, "Jonathan Edwards between Church and Academy: A Biblio-graphic Essay," in Hart, Lucas, and Nichols, eds., *The Legacy of Jonathan Edwards*, 228–47.

45. Noll, "Edwards' Theology after Edwards," 305.

46. "A survey of journal articles on Edwards published during the 1990s shows, of 105 articles tallied, the following breakdown among types of journals: Evangelical: 64 (61.0 percent); mainline: 7 (6.7 percent); nonreligious: 34 (32.3 percent). An indication that this trend will continue is that, of thirty-two dissertations on Edwards from 2001–3, fourteen were completed at state or secular private universities, while eighteen were completed at seminaries, schools of theology, or religiously affiliated institutions. Within this latter group, it is interesting to note that the two institutions supporting the most graduate work on Edwards (three dissertations each) within these three years were Westminster Theological Seminary (Presbyterian) and Marquette University (Jesuit). Minkema, "Jonathan Edwards in the Twentieth Century," 677, n. 55.

47. The following are Gerstner's best-known publications: *Steps to Salvation: The Evangelistic Message of Jonathan Edwards* (Philadelphia: Westminster Press, 1959); *Jonathan Edwards on Heaven and Hell* (Grand Rapids: Baker, 1980); *Jonathan Edwards: A Mini-Theology* (Wheaton, IL: Tyndale House, 1987); *The Rational Biblical Theology of Jonathan Edwards* (3 vols. Orlando: Ligonier, 1991–3). Gerstner's wife Edna has also fostered interest in Edwards, most significantly through her novel entitled *Jonathan and Sarah – An Uncommon Union: A Novel Based on the Family of Jonathan and Sarah Edwards (the Stockbridge Years, 1750–1758)* (Morgan, PA: Soli Deo Gloria, 1995).

48. Sproul's Edwardsean publications include *Chosen By God* (Wheaton, IL: Tyndale House, 1986); *Willing to Believe: The Controversy over Free Will* (Grand Rapids: Baker, 1997); with Archie Parrish, *The Spirit of Revival: Discovering the Wisdom of Jonathan Edwards* (Wheaton, IL: Crossway, 2000).

49. Murray, *Jonathan Edwards: A New Biography*.

50. Early in his career (1956–9), Murray worked as an assistant to David Martyn Lloyd-Jones (1899–1981), a Welsh physician who became a Calvinist preacher and leader of British evangelicals and also a great promoter of Jonathan Edwards. See Murray's two-volume biography of Lloyd-Jones, *D. Martyn Lloyd-Jones: The First Forty Years, 1899–1939* (Edinburgh: Banner of Truth Trust, 1982); *D. Martyn Lloyd-Jones: The Fight of Faith, 1939–1981* (Edinburgh: Banner of Truth Trust, 1990).

51. Piper's best-known publications include *Desiring God: Meditations of a Christian Hedonist* (Sisters, OR: Multnomah, 1986); *The Supremacy of God in Preach-ing* (Grand Rapids: Baker, 1990); *The Pleasures of God* (Sisters, OR: Mult-nomah, 1991); *God's Passion for His Glory: Living the Vision of Jonathan Edwards* (Wheaton, IL: Crossway, 1998); Piper and Justin Taylor, eds., *A God Entranced Vision of All Things: The Legacy of Jonathan Edwards* (Wheaton IL: Crossway, 2004).

52. See especially Richard A. Bailey and Gregory A. Wills, eds., *The Salvation of Souls: Nine Previously Unpublished Sermons on the Call of Ministry and the Gospel by Jonathan Edwards* (Wheaton, IL: Crossway, 2002); Michael D. McMullen, ed., *The Blessing of God: Previously Unpublished Sermons of Jonathan Edwards* (Nashville: Broadman and Holman, 2003).

53. See especially his best-known book, Richard Lovelace, *Dynamics of Spiritual Life: An Evangelical Theology of Renewal* (Downers Grove, IL: InterVarsity Press, 1979).

54. See especially George Marsden, *Jonathan Edwards: A Life* (New Haven: Yale University Press, 2003).

55. Edwards looms large in many of Noll's scholarly writings. See especially, Mark Noll, *The Scandal of the Evangelical Mind* (Grand Rapids, Eerdmans, 1994), 77–81, passim.

56. See especially Gerald McDermott, *Seeing God: Twelve Reliable Signs of True Spirituality* (Downers Grove, IL: InterVarsity Press, 1995); idem, *Can Evangelicals Learn from World Religions? Jesus, Revelation, and Religious Traditions* (Downers Grove, IL: InterVarsity Press, 2000).

57. See especially Stephen Nichols, *Jonathan Edwards: A Guided Tour of His Life and Thought* (Phillipsburg, NJ: P & R, 2001); idem, *An Absolute Sort of Certainty: The Holy Spirit and the Apologetics of Jonathan Edwards* (Phillipsburg, NJ: P & R, 2003).

58. See especially William C. Nichols, ed., *Seeking God: Jonathan Edwards' Evangelism Contrasted with Modern Methodologies* (Ames, IA: International Outreach, 2001); idem, ed., *Knowing the Heart: Jonathan Edwards on True and False Conversion* (Ames, IA: International Outreach, 2003); idem, ed., *The Torments of Hell: Jonathan Edwards on Eternal Damnation* (Ames, IA: International Outreach, forthcoming).

59. See especially Brandon Withrow, "Introduction," in Peter Van Mastricht, *A Treatise on Regeneration*, ed. Brandon Withrow (Morgan, PA: Soli Deo Gloria, 2002), vii–xxxii; idem, "An Empty Threat: Jonathan Edwards on Y2K and the Power of Preaching," *Reformation and Revival Journal* 9 (Winter 2000): 69–92; idem, "Jonathan Edwards: Revival, Millennial Expectations, and the Vials of Revelation," *Trinity Journal* 22 (Spring 2001): 75–98; idem, "Jonathan Edwards and Justification: Help for Current Evangelical Discussion? Part One," *Reformation and Revival Journal* 11 (Spring 2002): 93–109; idem, "Jonathan Edwards and Justification: Help for Current Evangelical Discussion? Part Two," *Reformation and Revival Journal* 11 (Winter 2002): 98–111.

60. *Humble Attempt*, WJE, 5:329.

12   The reputation of Edwards abroad

D. W. BEBBINGTON

Jonathan Edwards was not just an American. Though living in "the American plantations," the theologian was conscious of being an inhabitant of "the British dominions."[1] He was a Briton who delighted in the discomfiture of the French and longed for news of "the notions that prevail in our nation."[2] Yet he was also a Christian whose sympathies extended beyond British territories "into Holland, Zeeland, and other Protestant countries, and all the visible church of Christ.[3] Edwards had a cosmopolitan dimension, fostered by his grand apocalyptic vision of the future spread of the gospel. So it is not surprising that others saw in him more than an American. For Isaac Taylor, a commentator on his works writing in 1831, there was no doubt that Edwards shared his own English identity. "We claim Edwards as an Englishman," asserted Taylor: "he was such in every respect but the accident of birth in a distant province of the empire."[4] But Samuel Hopkins, Edwards's first biographer, recognized the complementary truth that Edwards won fame not only in America and Britain but also in the Netherlands and Germany.[5] Although Edwards appealed particularly to his compatriots in England, Scotland, and Wales, he enjoyed a European reputation even during his lifetime and eventually gained a measure of celebrity in specific circles elsewhere. Jonathan Edwards was a figure who contributed to intellectual life far beyond New England.

Apart from a sermon that appeared in 1731, Edwards's first work to come before the public, his *Faithful Narrative*, was published not in America but in England. Although a sample was put into print in Boston in December 1736, the whole text was initially issued in London in the following year.[6] The English capital was the natural place to publish a book aiming for a substantial Anglophone audience, and there it could be commended by Isaac Watts, the intellectual leader of the Congregational denomination to which Edwards belonged, and his fellow minister John Guyse. The work established Edwards's fame in England, with seven British editions of the title following by 1750. Other books by Edwards, though normally published first in New England, subsequently appeared in English editions.

The *Distinguishing Marks*, complete with its introduction by the Boston Congregationalist William Cooper, was republished in London in 1741. Likewise the *Religious Affections* came out in a London version in 1762, abridged by William Gordon, another Congregational minister. Edwards particularly appealed to the Congregationalists at a time when, like their American cousins, they were emerging into a period of awakening, but Anglicans of evangelical persuasion were also drawn to him. John Newton, the clergyman who was near the center of the cluster of revival supporters in the Church of England, initially thought highly of Edwards. Although greatly admiring George Whitefield, the transatlantic revival preacher, Newton is reputed to have believed that there was as much divinity in Edwards's little finger as in Whitefield altogether.[7] Among those identified with the evangelical revival in England, Edwards was revered as a publicist and example of the same movement in America.

In Scotland there was, if anything, even stronger endorsement of Edwards's principles and practice. The Calvinist inheritance of the land provided a firm bond with the American theologian. The *Faithful Narrative* came out in Edinburgh hard on the heels of the London edition. In 1742 the venerable John Willison, minister of Dundee South Parish Church and perhaps the leading devotional writer of the age, recommended a Glasgow edition of the *Distinguishing Marks* to Scottish readers as "a most excellent, solid, judicious, and scriptural Performance."[8] In the following year, some of the ministers associated with revival in the town of Cambuslang established contact with Edwards in order to compare notes about the awakenings on the two sides of the Atlantic. William McCulloch, minister at Cambuslang, was initially wary of *Some Thoughts Concerning the Present Revival of Religion*, Edwards's sequel to the *Distinguishing Marks*. Edwards seemed too favorably inclined to "Impressions & Impulses & Immediate Revelation &c" for the cautious Scot.[9] Yet McCulloch, together with his friends, soon decided that Edwards was sound in his views and maintained a steady transatlantic correspondence with the American over the rest of his life. It was from this circle that there arose the suggestion of a concert of prayer for the worldwide spread of the gospel that bore fruit in Edwards's *Humble Attempt*. These men frequently reissued extracts from the *Faithful Narrative* in their publications, thus disseminating Edwards's celebrity as a spokesperson of revival. When a Scottish edition of Hopkins' memoir of Edwards eventually appeared in 1785, it is not surprising that the subscribers to the volume included a coal-hewer, a gardener, a hammer man, a laborer, and a nailer.[10] Edwards had become a name to conjure with among the common people of Scotland.

The most frequent Scottish correspondent of Edwards was John Erskine, joint minister of Old Greyfriars, Edinburgh, and the leader of the evangelicals

in the Church of Scotland. Erskine kept Edwards supplied with the latest theological literature, sending over nearly one-third of the American's library.[11]
Although Erskine had reservations about Edwards's views on justification,[12]
he entirely agreed with the leading features of his thought. Immediately after
Edwards's death, Erskine ensured that his reputation was not exploited in
Scotland for mistaken ends. Lord Kames, a leading lawyer and friend of the
freethinking David Hume, had published in favor of a fatalist philosophical
position, and attempts were made to use Edwards's *Freedom of the Will* to vin-
dicate his scheme. Erskine published a letter he had received from Edwards
protesting this misrepresentation of his opinions as *Remarks on the Essays*.
The letter was included in the 1768 edition of *Freedom of the Will* and long
retained its place in the preliminaries to the volume. Erskine never lost his
esteem for Edwards. In 1774 he published for the first time Edwards's *History
of the Work of Redemption*, consisting of a set of the author's sermons, and
he followed that with a volume of Edwards's actual sermons in 1788, his *Miscellaneous Observations on Important Theological Subjects* in 1793 and his
Remarks on Important Theological Controversies in 1796. All were published
in Edinburgh rather than America because Erskine was convinced that the
whole Christian church needed Edwards's writings. "I do not think," Erskine
wrote to McCulloch on hearing the news of Edwards's untimely death, "our
age has produced a divine of equal genius or judgment."[13] Edwards stood
high in the esteem of the evangelicals of Scotland.

It was not only the Reformed communities of Great Britain that
responded enthusiastically to Edwards's writings. John Wesley, the Anglican clergyman whose followers emerged as the Methodist movement, was
a lifelong Arminian opponent of Calvinism, and yet he rejoiced in Edwards
the champion of revival. He abridged the *Faithful Narrative* (1744), the *Distinguishing Marks* (1744), and the *Life of Brainerd* (1768) for publication.
Some Thoughts Concerning the Present Revival of Religion appeared in 1745,
although, with characteristic disregard for the wishes of an author, Wesley
struck out the first word of Edwards's title so that the book appeared as
Thoughts.... When Wesley came to edit *Religious Affections* in 1773 for his
Christian Library, a set of classics designed for the Methodist people, he was
even more cavalier. Edwards's twelve signs of authentic faith were reduced
to eight, and the length of the whole work shrank to a mere one-sixth of
the original. This drastic pruning was designed not only to make the book
more accessible, but also to eliminate what Wesley judged to be error. "Out
of this dangerous heap," he explained, "wherein much wholesome food is
mixed with much deadly poison, I have selected many remarks and admonitions which may be of great use to the children of God."[14] The problem, as
he explained in his *Thoughts upon Necessity* (1774), was with Edwards the

metaphysician. The New Englander argued that human actions were determined; Wesley, in contradiction of Edwards, inferred that on that scheme
there was no human liberty, and without choice, he concluded, there was
no such thing as morality. Like many others after him, Wesley was singling
out an aspect of Edwards for praise and another for blame. When purged
of the necessitarian doctrine that went along with his Calvinism, however,
Edwards seemed a potent force for good. By circulating his revival writings
widely in condensed form, Wesley did much to propagate Edwards's fame
in England.

On the continent of Europe, as in the British Isles, the first impact of
Edwards was through the *Faithful Narrative*. The general superintendent
of Magdeburg in Prussia, Johann Adam Steinmetz, received a copy of the
publication soon after its appearance in London. Steinmetz was the editor
of the works of Philip Spener, the pioneer of the Pietist movement, and
part of the network of German church leaders who were on the lookout
for signs of spiritual vitality in international Protestantism.[15] He set about
translating Edwards into German and published the book in his home town
in 1738. His hope of reviving devotion in the region is plain from the addition of an account of soul-saving in Germany as well as New England, but
his apprehensions are equally evident. Perhaps, he mused, "the Lord might
finally remove his candlestick from ungrateful Europe and give the glory of
Lebanon to the American wilderness."[16] After such an early beginning to
German knowledge of Edwards, however, there was a total collapse. Subsequent theologians showed little or no awareness of the American, and even
those with Pietist sympathies lost sight of him. In a predominantly Lutheran
setting, a Calvinist exercised little appeal. The German interest in Edwards
turned out to be a false start.

It was Steinmetz's translation of the *Faithful Narrative*, however, that
opened the way into the much more responsive environment of the Netherlands. Once more, as in Scotland, a Reformed land felt an affinity for Edwards.
The crucial figure in the earliest reception of Edwards in the Netherlands was
Isaac Le Long, a member of a prosperous Huguenot family that had found
refuge in Frankfurt and then Amsterdam. He was a cosmopolitan polymath,
but possessed no discernible connection with the English-speaking world.
Le Long was most at home in Pietist circles, and in collaboration with the
Moravian August Gottlieb Spangenburg he translated a number of German
works into Dutch.[17] Edwards's account of revival in the New World naturally appealed to Le Long, and in 1740, two years after its appearance in
German, he translated Steinmetz's version so that it would be available to the
Dutch people. The work enjoyed some success, for it reached a second edition
ten years later. The awareness of Edwards created by Le Long's translation

probably explains why the *Life of Brainerd* was published in Dutch translation at Utrecht in 1756. Bound with Brainerd's own account of his mission
to the Indians, the book gave evidence of remarkable developments in North
America. The initial attraction of Edwards in the Netherlands, as in the British
Isles, was as a reporter of dramatic new signs of gospel triumphs on the other
side of the globe.

The Dutch, unlike the Germans, made the transition to seeing Edwards
as a great theologian. In 1774 there was published at Utrecht a translation
of the *Freedom of the Will*, prefaced by a short original life and appraisal of
Edwards. Although these were written by another hand, the man responsible for the publication was probably Gijsbert Bonnet, Professor of Divinity
at Utrecht. Bonnet had engaged in a controversy with Henry Goodricke, an
English member of the Reformed Church at Groningen, over the value of
confessions of faith. Goodricke wanted to appeal to the Bible and reason
alone, but in 1770 Bonnet had contended that articles of faith had their
place.[18] The dispute had attracted the attention of John Erskine, the former
correspondent of Edwards in Edinburgh, who approved the stance adopted
by Bonnet. Although already in his fifties, Erskine learned Dutch in order
to correspond with the Dutch professor.[19] It must have been Erskine who
drew Bonnet's attention to Edwards as a defender of Reformed orthodoxy. In
1776 the *History of Redemption*, still unpublished in America, was translated
into Dutch from the Edinburgh edition, again supplied by Erskine. Appearing in Utrecht, the book received the official approval of the local classis,
which would probably have been secured by Bonnet. The same translator
produced a Dutch version of the life of Edwards, issued by the university
publisher at Utrecht in 1791. Interest in Edwards, however, was spreading
to others in the Netherlands. Marinus van Werkhoven, a regular translator
of English theologians, produced Dutch editions of *Religious Affections* in
1779, *Two Dissertations* in 1788, and *Original Sin* in 1790, the last with the
imprimatur of the classis of Schieland, near Rotterdam. It was also commended by Johannes Conradus Appelius, a respected parish minister who
had championed Reformed teaching in print.[20] Edwards had come to be
widely appreciated in the Netherlands as a powerful writer who blended an
unaffected piety with a firm orthodoxy.

The reputation of Edwards among his contemporaries abroad therefore
showed a distinct pattern. Initially he was valued for his revival reports. That
was true in England, Scotland, Germany, and the Netherlands alike. Among
those who shared Edwards's passion for spiritual awakening but not his
doctrinal position, the interest stopped there. Both Wesley and the Germans
failed to look beyond the accounts of revival to the theological works. Those
who formed part of the international Calvinist network, however, recognized

in Edwards an astute advocate of their viewpoint. The Congregationalists of England, the Presbyterians of Scotland, and the Reformed of the Netherlands developed a taste for the polemical writings of the American. The case of John Newton in the Church of England is particularly instructive. At first attracted by Edwards, he then drew back.[21] Although himself a Calvinist, Newton believed in keeping his partisan doctrinal views to himself and appealing to the Bible alone for his teaching. It was only when people were as willing as Edwards to align themselves in public with the Reformed tradition that they found an enduring resource in his writings. In these overtly Calvinist circles, Edwards became an apologist of whom they were proud.

In the next generation, among those who had not known Edwards as an early advocate of the Great Awakening, friends as well as foes saw him as a thinker of standing. Over the decades beginning in the 1770s but lasting well into the nineteenth century, he was treated as a major reference point in British intellectual debate. There were, it is true, dismissive comments from some of those who saw his thought as dated. A reviewer in the London *Monthly Review*, for example, condemned the *History of Redemption* on its publication as "a long, laboured, dull, confused rhapsody." The book, continued the reviewer, was "merely an attempt to revive the old mystical divinity that distracted the last age with pious conundrums: and which, having, long ago, emigrated to America, we have no reason to wish should ever be imported back again."[22] Others, however, even when disagreeing with Edwards, treated his opinions with respect. In 1777 Joseph Priestley, the most advanced thinker among the English Presbyterians who were turning toward religious liberalism, felt that he had to meet Edwards's defense of the Almighty from the charge of being the author of sin.[23] Sir James Mackintosh, a leading exponent of the philosophy of the Scottish school at the turn of the nineteenth century, disagreed with Edwards's ethical views, holding that they implied unmeaning assumptions about degrees of existence, but he nevertheless treated him as a "remarkable man, the metaphysician of America," showing a "power of subtle argument, perhaps unmatched, certainly unsurpassed among men."[24] And Dugald Stewart, the most influential propagator of common-sense philosophy in the same period, regarded Edwards as the ablest champion of necessitarianism of the eighteenth century. Although, Stewart observed, the New World was normally less concerned with abstract science than with business affairs, there was one American who, "in logical acuteness and subtility, does not yield to any disputant bred in the universities of Europe."[25] The author of *Freedom of the Will* had earned himself a lasting place in British philosophical discussion.

At one point the legacy of Edwards became the focus of an intensely felt exchange. In the wake of the French Revolution, its principles were defended in England at a popular level by Thomas Paine, but its weightiest apologist was William Godwin. Although he is now best known for being the husband of the feminist Mary Wollstonecraft, Godwin was notorious in his day for trying, in his *Enquiry Concerning Political Justice* (1793), to commend liberty, equality, and fraternity at a time when Britain was going to war against revolutionary France. Godwin had been trained for the Dissenting ministry under Joseph Fawcett, who was a follower of Jonathan Edwards, and had absorbed Edwards's writings even before that.[26] Hence Godwin's thought, though transposed into a secular key, carried strong echoes of the teaching of Edwards. "The mind," Godwin wrote, "cannot first choose to be influenced by a motive, and afterwards submit to its operation: for in that case the preference would belong wholly to this previous volition." The argument is attributed to Edwards, who is said to show the impossibility of free will "with great force of reasoning." Likewise, Godwin rejected gratitude as a motive, contending that "to prefer one man to another, from some other consideration than that of his superior usefulness or worth" would make "something true to me...which cannot be true to another man," and so could not be true in itself. Again the contention about the need to subordinate private affections for the sake of benevolent neutrality is explicitly drawn from the writings of Edwards, in this case the *Nature of True Virtue*.[27] Godwin was claiming the authority of the American for his revolutionary apologetic.

The inferences Godwin drew from Edwards's premises were particularly alarming to more conservative thinkers who were committed to the existing order in Britain. From the rejection of free will, Godwin reached the conviction that human beings were not strictly responsible for their behavior. Vice was no more than "an infectious distemper," deserving reformatory cure rather than retributive punishment. "[U]nder the system of necessity the ideas of guilt, crime, desert and accountableness have no place."[28] Consequently the whole system of criminal justice was called into question. From the downgrading of gratitude, Godwin came to the conclusion that social inferiors owed no debt of appreciation for the protection they received from their superiors. The ranking of society was called into question, allowing the preference to be given to French egalitarianism. To refute the subversive notions of Godwin, conservatives believed, was a priority of the times. One of his leading opponents, Samuel Parr, an advanced Whig clergyman but a champion of the existing state of affairs in Britain, preached a sermon in 1800 to lay bare Godwin's error in dismissing gratitude as a foundation of the social structure. Parr took occasion to notice Edwards's *Freedom of the Will*. The preacher explained that he had been charmed with "the metaphysical acuteness and the fervent piety of the writer," remarking that Edwards improves his readers even where he does not convince. Edwards's inability to carry conviction, however, was crucial. There was no reason, Parr's hearers would conclude, to abandon the normal Anglican view of the period that human beings possessed free will and therefore must be responsible agents. The main thrust of the sermon, however, was to show that, though Edwards did demonstrate that gratitude was not part of true virtue in his limited sense of the term, he would not have denied that it was connected with justice. Hence Godwin was misrepresenting the American, whose authority could not be claimed for the rejection of gratitude as a motive for deference.[29] The interpretation of Edwards had become an issue of political debate. The episode reveals how significant a place Edwards had earned in British intellectual life as a whole.

It was in the theological sphere, however, that Edwards's star shone most brightly. In England, his impact as a doctrinal writer was greatest on the Particular Baptists, the Calvinistic denomination that practiced believer's baptism. Their Reformed beliefs had not hampered their initial growth in the seventeenth century, but in the eighteenth many of their ministers adopted a higher form of Calvinism that inhibited them from making free offers of the gospel. Since God had chosen the elect before the foundation of the world and since he would infallibly bring about his purposes, there seemed no point in preaching to the unconverted. It might verge on blasphemy to try to achieve on his behalf what the Almighty could do for himself. Yet ministers wanted their hearers to come to salvation. How could they make a summons to repentance and faith consistent with their fundamental convictions? Jonathan Edwards showed them the answer. The distinction between natural and moral inability embodied in the *Freedom of the Will* was the solution to their difficulties. On the Edwardsean view, sinners possessed a natural ability to believe the gospel, so that nothing in the capacities with which they had been endowed by their Creator prevented them from becoming Christians. What they might display, however, was a moral inability to embrace the gospel, an expression of refusal to repent of their sins, which was their own fault. Consequently all human beings had an obligation to accept salvation, and every minister could proclaim the gospel without reservation. Edwards's central theological teaching provided hitherto inhibited Calvinists with a new and pressing sense of mission.

The higher type of Calvinism, though not universal among the Particular Baptists, had prevailed in London and was widespread elsewhere in England. In about 1775, however, John Ryland, son of the minister of College Street Baptist Church, Northampton, discovered Edwards's *Freedom of the Will* and, under its influence, moved to a lower version of Calvinism that was congruent with vigorous evangelistic endeavor.

His circle of friends in the midlands became committed to the same standpoint. In 1784, having been sent a copy of the *Humble Attempt* by John Erskine from Scotland, they published a new edition, began a monthly prayer meeting on the lines it recommended, and, partly as a result, launched in 1792 the Baptist Missionary Society, the first of the modern British missionary societies. Ryland, who became co-minister with his father and in 1786 sole minister, turned into a devoted disciple of the American, even giving one of his sons the forenames "Jonathan Edwards." That "blessed man," he explained to a fellow minister in 1790, "has been more useful to me than any other." Ryland's enthusiasm encompassed other works alongside the *Freedom of the Will*. If he were forced to part with all human compositions, he told the friend in the same letter, the last to go would be the *Life of Brainerd*, the *Religious Affections*, and Joseph Bellamy's *True Religion Delineated*, bearing, as it did, Edwards's seal of approval. But *Freedom of the Will*, which Ryland assumed his correspondent knew, was foundational.[30] From 1793 to 1825, Ryland taught its principles to the two hundred or so candidates for Baptist ministry who passed through Bristol Baptist Academy while he was president. He was contributing to a revolution in the teaching prevalent among English Baptists.

Even more influential than Ryland was Andrew Fuller, the Particular Baptist minister at Soham in Cambridgeshire and later at Kettering in Northamptonshire. Fuller accepted Edwards's distinction between natural and moral inability, making it the groundwork of his work *The Gospel Worthy of All Acceptation* (1781). "He found much satisfaction in this distinction," the author explained in the preface to his work, "as it appeared to carry with it its own evidence – to be clearly and fully contained in the Scriptures – and calculated to disburden the Calvinistic system of a number of calumnies with which its opponents have loaded it."[31] As a result Fuller called on preachers to urge their hearers to embrace the gospel and on sinners to accept that they had a responsibility to believe. Fuller became associated with the principle of "duty faith," which Baptists committed to a higher Calvinism repudiated but those following Fuller's moderate version embraced. As founding secretary of the Baptist Missionary Society, Fuller put into practice his principles of spreading the gospel as widely as possible. In his last letter to Ryland before his own death in 1815, Fuller remarked that if detractors "preached Christ half as much as Jonathan Edwards did, and were half as useful as he was, their usefulness would be double what it is."[32] As the ablest theologian produced by the Baptists in his generation, Fuller more than anyone else ensured that the substance of Edwards's teaching exerted an enduring influence over his denomination for most of the nineteenth century. In the

1890s David Gracey, principal of the Pastors' College founded in London by the great Baptist preacher Charles Haddon Spurgeon, was still commending Edwards's methods as approved by Fuller.[33] Edwards became the touchstone of Baptist orthodoxy.

In Scotland the standing of Edwards was high as a result of Erskine's advocacy during and after the American's lifetime, but it became even more entrenched through its endorsement by Thomas Chalmers, the evangelical leader in the Church of Scotland in the early nineteenth century. Chalmers, who had been powerfully influenced by Andrew Fuller, revered Edwards for his union of genuine devotion with metaphysical ability. "The American divine," Chalmers wrote in 1821, "affords, perhaps, the most wondrous example, in modern times, of one who stood richly gifted both in natural and spiritual discernment: and we know not what most to admire in him, whether the deep philosophy that issued from his pen, or the humble and child-like piety that issued from his pulpit."[34] Edwards, according to Chalmers, supplied the best vindication of God from being the author of sin, and he incontrovertibly demonstrated that the doctrine of necessity did not undermine moral responsibility, in both cases surpassing Leibniz in the cogency of his argument.[35] Although Edwards might be faulted for "an occasional lapse into merely verbal reasoning," his great achievement was to "remove from evangelical religion the discredit of exerting a slavish or depressing influence upon superior minds."[36] Chalmers transmitted his enthusiasm for Edwards to the students he trained, first as professor of divinity at Edinburgh from 1828 to 1843, then as the holder of the equivalent post in the Free Church of Scotland that he led out of the established church. The incomparable prestige of Chalmers among Presbyterians of all parties did much to ensure the continuing fame of Edwards in Victorian Scotland.

There were many symptoms of Edwards's enduring place in Scottish affections. Even when William Cunningham, Chalmers' successor as principal of the Free Church College in Edinburgh, tried to free Calvinism from association with necessitarianism, which he felt was under pressure from the philosophers of the day, he admitted his own leaning toward necessity because of the power of Edwards's argument against the self-determining power of the will. Despite reservations about the imputation of Adam's offense, Cunningham still thought the American's *Original Sin* "one of the most valuable, permanent, possessions of the Christian Church."[37] Two additional volumes of Edwards's collected works appeared in Edinburgh in 1847. His practical books circulated even more widely than his doctrinal writings. *Faithful Narrative* and *Some Thoughts* were both republished in the second quarter of the century, and *Life of Brainerd* appeared in five new Scottish editions between 1824 and 1851. Most popular of all, according to the theologian

James Orr, was *Religious Affections*. At the start of the twentieth century, Orr noted that although acquaintance with this "pearl of Edwards's religious writings" was fading in the rising generation, it had been well known to their parents and grandparents.[38] Nineteenth-century Scottish Presbyterians, still bonded to the New Englander by their common Calvinism, owed him a great debt.

In Wales, the language barrier had initially limited the reputation of Edwards. He had been known to the revivalist Howell Harris as early as 1743,[39] but Edwards exerted little or no influence over the Welsh speakers of his own denomination, the Congregationalists (known as Independents in Wales) until Edward Williams, principal of the Independent academies successively at Oswestry and Rotherham, publicized his works at the opening of the nineteenth century. Williams's *Essay on the Equity of the Divine Government* (1809), based on the distinction between natural and moral inability, set out an Edwardsean framework for theology. John Roberts, Independent minister at Llanbrynmair, Montgomeryshire, one of Williams's former students, had already started to argue for Edwards's position in Welsh in 1807. Two years later he published some extracts from *Religious Affections* and in 1814 a refutation of the views of higher Calvinists in a booklet called *An Humble Attempt*.[40] Roberts was propagating what was called in Wales the "New System," a mediating position between high Calvinism and the Arminianism of the Wesleyan Methodists, which became the mainspring for the spread of Independency in north Wales. Translations of Edwards's works into Welsh followed: *History of Redemption* (1829), *Religious Affections* (1833), *Freedom of the Will* (1865), *Two Dissertations* (c. 1865), and *Original Sin* (1870). All of them were produced by Independent ministers. Although the response of the denomination in Wales to Edwards was delayed, his reception was thorough, molding several generations of the ministry.

English Congregationalists, seeing Edwards as one of their own, owed him hardly less. The first collected edition of Edwards's works to appear anywhere in the world was assembled in eight volumes between 1806 and 1811 by the Welshman Edward Williams and Edward Parsons, Congregational minister at Leeds, Yorkshire, where the edition was published. Declaring their plans to edit next the works of John Owen, the great English Congregational divine of the seventeenth century, they avowed that, "were we disposed to hold up the writings of any fallible men, as forming our standard of faith, we should not hesitate to give our most decided preference to EDWARDS and OWEN."[41] Other prominent Congregationalists also promoted Edwards. The poet James Montgomery introduced an edition of the *Life of Brainerd* (1829), the Birmingham minister John Angell James wrote a preface for *Faithful Narrative* (1839), and the theologian John Pye Smith did the same (1827). Pye Smith, who served as tutor at Homerton College from 1800 to 1850, frequently quoted Edwards or referred to his works while lecturing to his students for the ministry. Like Chalmers, he specially valued Edwards's defense of the Almighty against the charge of being the author of sin, chiding Edward Williams, though Pye Smith had been his pupil, for failing to do the American justice on the subject. Nor was he impressed by the doctrinal side of Edwards alone, for he urged his students to read the New Englander's resolutions for life "*frequently*, and with *self-application.*"[42] Edwards naturally had a particular appeal for his coreligionists.

The greatest monument to Edwards among English Congregationalists was the two-volume set of his works produced by Henry Rogers, who spent most of his career teaching in Congregational colleges but who moved to the chair of English language and literature at University College, London, two years after publishing the collection in 1834. This version was long to remain standard, reaching a twelfth edition in 1879. In the extensive introductory evaluation, Rogers, a man of unusual ability, was unstinting in his praise for Edwards. "By the concurrent voice of all who have perused his writings," Rogers claimed, "he is assigned one of the first, if not the very first place, amongst all the masters of human reason." It was Edwards's greatness to possess "a mind peculiarly adapted for *deductive* reasoning; a mind, whose delight it is to draw inferences from known or supposed premises." Yet this characteristic carried its own defect. Edwards was unsuited for induction from a range of phenomena, taking facts about comets for granted and dog-matizing on them. The resulting blend of "acuteness and absurdity, such vig-orous logic and such inconclusive premises," was reminiscent of Descartes.[43] The image of Edwards that this text conveyed to the majority of midcentury readers was therefore ambiguous. He was undoubtedly an intellectual figure of great eminence, but he was also weak on the investigative side of intelli-gence that Victorians valued so highly. This one-sided understanding of the American by a firm Congregational devotee prepared the way, as we shall see, for others to criticize him more trenchantly.

The identification of Edwards with the missionary cause ensured that his fame spread beyond Britain. The Baptist Missionary Society, whose pio-neer, William Carey, had called *Life of Brainerd* "almost a second Bible,"[44] continued to draw inspiration from Edwards. Likewise Henry Martyn, the evangelical Anglican missionary to Iran, was attracted to overseas gospel work by the *Life of Brainerd*, which the Church Missionary Society later abridged in its periodical before reissuing it as a free-standing publication.[45] Robert Murray McCheyne, an exemplar for several Scottish generations of missionaries, was himself confirmed in his allegiance to the cause of mis-sions by reading the *Life of Brainerd*.[46] The Congregationalists' own agency for foreign missions, called in its early days simply the Missionary Society, was responsible for another version of *An Humble Attempt* in 1814.[47] Missionaries carried awareness of Edwards across the world. In Calcutta, the capital of the Bengal region that Carey served, was published in 1859 a new edition of *An Humble Attempt*.[48] It was probably through agents of the Continental Society that the same book was translated into French in 1823. It was published in Switzerland in French in 1838 and in German thirteen years afterward. *History of Redemption*, which appeared in French in 1854, was actually translated into Arabic in Beirut fourteen years later, with an attribution to "the Learned Chief Jonathan Edwards." There was a global interest in Edwards that owed its existence largely to the missionary impetus that he had helped to stir up.

Nevertheless, the legacy of Edwards outside America in the period of his greatest influence was largely a British phenomenon. His writings appeared not only in the usual publishing centers of London, Edinburgh, and Glasgow, but also in Bristol, Bungay (Suffolk), Carlisle, Halifax (Yorkshire), Leeds, Liverpool, Newport (Isle of Wight), and Penryn (Cornwall). The English provinces were stirred. Although the American's celebrity as a philosopher made his teachings a subject of public debate, it was his many-sided theological oeuvre that chiefly fostered his influence. He was widely admired for his devotional life, but his greatest single contribution was the creation of a doctrinal paradigm for mission. The English Baptists, the Scottish Presbyterians, and the Congregationalists of England and Wales all embraced a framework of moderate Calvinism that bore the stamp of Edwards. Even the evangelicals in the Church of England, who were usually wary of avowing their debt to non-Anglican sources, sometimes adhered to Edwards's synthesis. Thomas Scott, one of their leading doctrinal writers, avoided referring to Edwards and yet, in an overview of his theological system, expounded the distinction between natural and moral inability in the Edwardsean manner.[49] Theologians naturally took issue with the American on particular points, and they normally went beyond him in embracing the governmental theory of the atonement that had been propounded by Edwards's disciple Joseph Bellamy. They could better be described, in fact, as exponents of the "New England Theology" inaugurated by Edwards than as simple Edwardseans. Yet their view of the world was essentially that of Edwards – a warm-hearted interpretation of the Reformed tradition that actively encouraged evangelism at home and abroad. The evangelical Calvinism that flourished in Britain during the nineteenth century owed more to Edwards than to any other writer.

From an early point in the nineteenth century, however, and overlapping with the period of Edwards's doctrinal ascendancy in many quarters, there was a reaction against his views. The alteration in Edwards's standing was associated with the rise of the Romantic spirit. The rational temper of Edwards, acceptable to an earlier age, seemed increasingly out of place in an era that exalted will and emotion in human affairs. His style seemed desiccated, his thinking artificial. In Germany, where Romanticism flourished most, Edwards was little known during the whole nineteenth century. The philosopher J. H. Fichte held "this solitary thinker of North America" in esteem for rising to "the deepest and loftiest ground which can underlie the principle of morals."[50] Toward the end of the century, a survey of the history of doctrine by K. R. Hagenbach registered Edwards's existence, but did not evaluate his thought.[51] These writers, however, were exceptional in Germany in alluding to the New Englander at all. More remarkably, Edwards ceased to exercise any significant sway over the Dutch intellect. After 1791 Edwards's titles ceased to appear in the Netherlands. Willem Bilderdijk, the central figure in the Dutch Reveil movement that was the national equivalent of the Evangelical Revival, possessed a copy of *Freedom of the Will,*[52] but he was a poet whose taste was formed by the Romantic spirit of the times. For him and his contemporaries, the native traditions of theology more deeply rooted in the Reformation had much greater appeal. They loved what they called the "old writers," who did not include Edwards. The American may still have been valued for his piety, but there was no equivalent on the continent to the British evangelical Calvinist synthesis based on Edwards's thinking.

In England the beginnings of a turn against Edwards can be detected in the thinking of the enormously influential Romantic poet Samuel Taylor Coleridge. He assured John Ryland in 1807 that he admired Edwards's works, but was convinced that "Kant in his Critique of Pure Reason has completely overthrown the edifice of Fatalism."[53] Coleridge was misinterpreting Edwards as a fatalist and so, with a typical appeal to an idealist philosopher, he dismissed "the New England system."[54] Others who shared Coleridge's Romantic attachment to free will began to doubt Edwards's value. The future prime minister, William Ewart Gladstone, when twenty-nine years old, devoted a month in 1839 to working out his estimate of Edwards's position. Gladstone appreciated the theologian's devotional spirit, but found the argument of *Freedom of the Will* unconvincing. He recognized the cruciality of the distinction between natural and moral inability, but refused to follow Edwards as he contended for the compatibility of the decrees of God with human liberty. A large cross, Gladstone's sign of dissent, appears in the margin of his copy of the book at this point, and many others appear elsewhere.[55] Even Edwards's admirers, such as the Congregationalist Henry Rogers, found something missing in the American's manner. Reason so controlled Edwards, according to Rogers, that it was rare to discover in his pages any "glowing sensibility... lofty enthusiasm... [or] touches of pathos."[56] The man was a dry stick, devoid of appropriate emotion. What a new age demanded of its favorite authors was absent in Edwards.

Theologians swayed by the novel cultural influences began to repudiate Edwards's doctrinal convictions. They chose a much milder presentation of the faith than the one they found in the American. Thomas Erskine, a Scottish Episcopalian who was the nephew of Edwards's admirer John Erskine, acknowledged in 1837 that Edwards was "a good and holy man," but asserted that *Freedom of the Will* was "directly opposed to the gospel of Jesus Christ." God was "the common Father of men," not confining his love to the elect.[57] Erskine's fellow Scot, John McLeod Campbell, wrestled with Edwards's version of Calvinism, preferring it to more recent varieties but ultimately condemning it for replacing the New Testament God of love with a God of justice.[58] And the mentor of the Broad Churchmanship movement in the Church of England, F. D. Maurice, though praising Edwards's manliness, criticized him in 1862 for capitulating to the spirit of the eighteenth century, seeing the Almighty as a "happy Being" remote from the miseries of his creatures.[59] Believing that Calvinism was untenable, these theologians proposed to replace it with a new theological understanding based on divine love, human sympathy, and the doctrine of the incarnation. The fresh pattern necessarily swept away the doctrinal structure erected by Edwards.

Conservative theological opinion refused to follow the new trend. In the Highlands of Scotland, where evangelical Calvinism remained hegemonic long after it had decayed elsewhere, Edwards's reputation was green. In 1844 the secretary of the Society for the Support of Gaelic Schools in the Highlands referred to an episode in the life of the American on the assumption that it would be familiar to his readers.[60] Edwards's *Sinners in the Hands of an Angry God* was translated into Gaelic for distribution in the Highlands in 1848 and reprinted in 1851; another edition was published in 1863 and reprinted in 1870, 1876, and 1889. A further sermon, *Great Question*, was similarly translated by a Free Church of Scotland minister in the Highlands at an uncertain date.[61] But it was not only in remote corners of the British Isles that Edwards was still honored. Joseph Angus, the principal of the Baptists' Regent's Park College, London, spoke of Edwards's treatment of the hatred of sin as "solemn and impressive."[62] J. C. Ryle, the Evangelical bishop of Liverpool from 1880 to 1900, wrote appreciatively of *Religious Affections*.[63] And the Welsh Independent Robert Thomas, who had translated *Freedom of the Will* into his native tongue in 1865, continued to teach within an Edwardsean doctrinal framework at Bala College, the leading denominational institution, until 1880.[64] Many of the men whom he trained for the ministry must have still been serving in the chapels when the Welsh Revival broke out in 1904, and they may well have applied Edwards's tests to its authenticity.

A living legacy of Edwards survived in the churches until the beginning of the twentieth century.

Thinkers of broader views in the later Victorian years sometimes showed a certain respect for Edwards even though they stood far apart from his theological stance. The Unitarian philosopher James Martineau, in the process of vindicating the case for free will, conceded that Edwards had made a strong case for the opposite on the basis of Scripture.[65] Likewise John Stuart Mill, the freethinking Liberal utilitarian, recognized that Edwards had argued the determinist case "as keenly as any modern."[66] W. E. H. Lecky, the historian of rationalism in Europe, was appalled by Calvinist tenets, but acknowledged Edwards as having expounded them with "undoubted genius."[67] The most thorough and perceptive appreciation of Edwards from this school was written by Leslie Stephen, the agnostic intellectual who launched the *Dictionary of National Biography*. Descended from an evangelical family, Stephen felt some affinity for Edwards even while deploring his Calvinism, his style, and much of his content. He found the precocious four-year-old Phebe Bartlett, converted in the Northampton revival, a "detestable infant" and the hellfire in which she believed "the most repulsive of all theological dogmas," yet he warned the reader not to dismiss in consequence what Edwards had to say. The American displayed "genuine feeling," "shrewd mother-wit," and a capacity for "elevated conceptions of truth." He had developed something akin to Spinozan pantheism and – here Stephen anticipates Perry Miller – the theologian was interesting because he connected the old Calvinism of the Puritans with the transcendentalism of Ralph Waldo Emerson. Edwards was, Stephen concluded, "formed by nature to be a German professor, and accidentally dropped into the American forests."[68] Edwards compelled grudging admiration even from many of those who most disliked his convictions.

In Britain, however, there was little disposition among those not sharing his religious views to turn Edwards into a great hero from the past. Whereas in America the theologian began to be treated as a national icon, in Britain he now seemed an alien. The nearest approximation to the reinvention of Edwards that took place in the United States was the attempt to revive his fame by Alexander Grosart, a minister of the United Presbyterian Church of Scotland who specialized in reissuing Puritan divines. Grosart crossed the Atlantic in 1853 to examine the Edwards papers with a view to writing a biography and coediting his works with his descendant Tryon Edwards. The Civil War intervened, the project languished, and all that came of it in 1865 was a privately printed selection from the manuscripts.[69] The role of early Georgian seer, assigned to Edwards in America, was occupied in Britain by Joseph Butler, the bishop of Durham, who wrote the *Analogy of Religion* (1736). Chalmers, Maurice, and the *Encyclopaedia Britannica* all drew parallels between Edwards and Butler, seeing them as equivalent figures in their respective lands.[70] Edwards was therefore largely superfluous in Britain, except, perhaps, to a handful of Congregationalists mindful of their tradition. It was such people who were responsible for selecting Edwards as one of the sixty doctors of the church to be depicted in the stained glass windows of the chapel of Mansfield College, Oxford, when it opened in 1889 as the Congregational seat of learning in the university.[71] Outside those circles, the reputation of Edwards beyond the United States was in decay.

It was left to the twentieth century to revive the fame of the New Englander abroad. One early attempt to rehabilitate him was in the Netherlands, where the confessional movement led by Abraham Kuyper applauded Edwards's defense of the Reformed faith. The theologian Herman Bavinck refers appreciatively to Edwards in each of the four volumes of his *Reformed Dogmatics* (1895–1901).[72] The attitude of these firm Calvinists, however, was by no means uniformly favorable. Jan Ridderbos, later professor at Kampen Theological University, obtained a doctorate in 1907 for a thesis on Edwards. Ridderbos professed a high regard for Edwards's assault on Arminianism, but the American was insufficiently single-minded in his attachment to a Calvinist line. His position, according to Ridderbos, was "not entirely thought out, sometimes swinging towards the mechanistic worldview and over time swinging towards pantheism."[73] Although Ridderbos was to publish a sympathetic article on Edwards in 1957 shortly before his own death, his considerable influence over conservative Dutch Protestants made them cautious about the American. Edwards was not reinstated to the prestige that he had once enjoyed in the Netherlands.

Edwards was neglected in Britain down to the mid-twentieth century. Where he was mentioned, it was usually as a theologian of merit in spite of his Calvinism. Thus Albert Peel, a leading Congregational historian, praised the "lyrical quality" of his writings while registering "the pitiless logic of his system."[74] In 1929, however, Martyn Lloyd-Jones, an able Welsh Presbyterian, discovered Edwards and became a devotee.[75] Lloyd-Jones, who ten years later was minister of Westminster Chapel at the heart of London, commended Edwards's Reformed faith to a wide audience, especially through his annual Puritan Conference during the 1950s and 1960s. Gathering young supporters such as J. I. Packer and Iain Murray, Lloyd-Jones initiated an Edwardsean movement for the propagation of a practical Calvinism tinged with revivalism. The greatest impact was in Wales, where Lloyd-Jones's Evangelical Movement of Wales spread the message, but the influence was felt throughout the English-speaking world. Murray's publishing agency, the Banner of Truth

Trust, issued the *Select Works of Jonathan Edwards* in 1958 and his biography of Edwards in 1987, carrying the fame of the American to new readers in many lands. Once more a version of evangelical Calvinism inspired by Edwards was current in the churches.

The esteem for Edwards as something other than a Reformed theologian had never entirely died away. Missionaries sometimes remembered him, with an article appearing in 1948 to mark the bicentennial of the appearance of *An Humble Attempt.*[76] Edwards was also recalled as an advocate and diagnostician of revival. This evaluative role came to the fore when, from the 1960s, the charismatic renewal movement claiming special manifestations of the power of the Holy Spirit gathered force. Because the legitimacy of the new movement was called into question, commentators appealed to Edwards for a verdict. In 1989, for example, J. I. Packer added an afterword, drawing on Edwards's criteria for true revival, to an English study of charismatic renewal called *Delusion or Dynamic?*[77] When, in 1994, the Toronto Blessing carried prostrations and animal noises including "holy laughter" round the world, the controversy reached a fresh intensity. Guy Chevreau, a leader of the Toronto Airport Vineyard Fellowship where the evangelical charismatic phenomenon began, defended it at length from the pages of Edwards. His *Catch the Fire* (1995), soon translated into German, was but one of the popular books published at this time either for or against the blessing. Edwards, it was said, was "being studied with increasing urgency by Christians throughout the world."[78] The episode meant that Edwards the advocate of revival became known beyond Reformed circles because of his contemporary value.

The other dimension of the twentieth-century revival of interest in Edwards was the mushrooming of international academic attention. There had been an isolated instance of scholarly scrutiny of Edwards's immaterialism in 1888 in France, a result of the national penchant for philosophy.[79] But in general the process of academic rehabilitation began in the late 1950s, in large part a byproduct of the publication of the Yale Edition of his works. Interest in Edwards outside America, whether primarily philosophical, literary, or theological, was initially almost entirely restricted to western Europe. The chief exception was J. L. Borges, the national librarian of Argentina, who in 1967 published an account of Edwards in a handbook on the literature of North America. Evidently Edwards appealed to Borges' taste for the bizarre, since two years later he wrote a Spanish sonnet about Edwards, describing his world as a "vessel of wrath."[80] A literary study of Edwards appeared in Russia in 1981, and the first Asian publication on him was an article in Japanese that came out in 1992.[81] In 1997 there followed the first discussion of Edwards in Czech.[82] By the end of the twentieth century, the scholarly engagement with Edwards had become global.

The celebrity of Edwards was therefore by no means confined to America. "Though far removed from the ancient seats of learning," wrote Henry Rogers in 1834, "Edwards has spoken in a voice which has echoed through the halls of European science and philosophy."[83] That eulogistic estimate was accurate but insufficiently discriminating. Because Edwards was essentially a Reformed theologian, he exerted his strongest influence over the like-minded international Calvinist network. Even in that world, his thought did not reach everywhere, being delayed in permeating Wales and never becoming known in the large Calvinist community of Hungary.[84] Among the Congregationalists and Baptists of England, the Presbyterians of Scotland, and the Reformed of the Netherlands, however, his fame became widespread well before the end of the eighteenth century. In Britain, evangelical Calvinism was founded on the template of his theology. Protestants who were wary of robust Reformed teaching – Germans, Methodists, and many evangelical Anglicans – nevertheless admired Edwards as a publicist of revivals and often as a spiritual mentor and advocate of missions. Even philosophers of little or no religious conviction respected the American's case for necessity. But there was a reaction in the Romantic age, with Edwards's reputation on the continent being extinguished and his appeal becoming limited to conservative theological circles in Britain. When his standing was revived in the twentieth century, it was chiefly as a Calvinistic champion, as a scrutineer of revival, or as a subject of academic inquiry. In each of these respects Edwards had become, by the opening of the twenty-first century, a figure of worldwide reputation.

Notes

1. Letter to William McCulloch, January 21, 1746–7, WJE, 16:220; and letter to John MacLaurin, May 12, 1746, WJE, 16:204.
2. Letter to John Erskine, Dec. 11, 1755, WJE, 16:679.
3. Letter to a correspondent in Scotland, Nov. 1745, WJE, 16:183.
4. Jonathan Edwards, *An Inquiry into the Modern Prevailing Notions Respecting the Freedom of the Will . . . with an Introductory Essay by the Author of "Natural History of Enthusiasm"* (London: James Duncan, 1831), xxi n.
5. Samuel Hopkins, *The Life and Character of the Late Rev. Mr. Jonathan Edwards* (Boston: S. Kneeland, 1765), 84.
6. Thomas H. Johnson, *The Printed Writings of Jonathan Edwards, 1703–1758: A Bibliography* (Princeton: Princeton University Press, 1940), 5. This book is the basis for much of the otherwise unattributed bibliographical information in this chapter. I am grateful to Mark Noll of Wheaton College for help with its interpretation and for much other guidance.
7. Edward Morgan, *John Elias: Life, Letters and Essays* [1844–7] (Edinburgh: Banner of Truth Trust, 1973), 122.
8. John Willison, "Preface to the Scots Reader," in Edwards, *The Distinguishing Marks of a Work of the Spirit of God* (Glasgow: T. Lumisden and J. Robertson, 1742), v.

9. William McCulloch to Howell Harris, Nov. 4, 1743, in G. M. Roberts, *Selected Trevecka Letters (1742–1747)* (Caernarvon: Calvinistic Methodist Bookroom, 1956), 120.

10. Samuel Hopkins, *The Life and Character of the Late Reverend, Learned, and Pious Mr. Jonathan Edwards* (Glasgow: David Niven for James Duncan, 1785), 397–408.

11. C. W. Mitchell, "Jonathan Edwards's Scottish Connection and the Eighteenth-Century Scottish Evangelical Revival, 1735–1750" (Ph.D. dissertation, University of St. Andrews, 1998), 233.

12. J. R. McIntosh, *Church and Theology in Enlightenment Scotland: The Popular Party, 1740–1800* (East Linton, East Lothian: Tuckwell Press, 1998), 167.

13. Sir Henry Moncreiff Wellwood, *Account of the Life and Writings of John Erskine* (Edinburgh: George Ramsay for Archibald Constable, 1818), 224.

14. A. C. Outler, ed., *John Wesley* (New York: Oxford University Press, 1964), 473.

15. Nicholas Hope, *German and Scandinavian Protestantism, 1700–1918* (Oxford: Clarendon Press, 1995), 189–90.

16. W. R. Ward, *The Protestant Evangelical Awakening* (Cambridge, UK: Cambridge University Press, 1992), 91.

17. D. Nauta, ed., *Biografisch Lexicon voor de Geschiedenis van het Nederlands Protestantisme* (3 vols. Kampen, Netherlands: J. H. Kok, 1978–90), 1:255–7. I am grateful to Jan Oosthoek, formerly of the University of Stirling, and to Roel Kuiper of the Erasmus University for help with Dutch sources.

18. Ibid., 2:78–80. See also John Erskine, *Sketches and Hints of Church History and Theological Controversy* (2 vols. Edinburgh: for M. Gray and Archibald Constable, 1790–7), 1:1–4.

19. Wellwood, *Erskine*, 315–16.

20. Nauta, *Biografisch Lexicon*, 1:32–4.

21. D. Bruce Hindmarsh, *John Newton and the English Evangelical Tradition between the Conversions of Wesley and Wilberforce* (Oxford: Clarendon Press, 1996), 167.

22. WJE, 9:86.

23. Joseph Priestley, *The Doctrine of Philosophical Necessity Illustrated* (London: J. Johnson, 1777), 122–4.

24. Sir James Mackintosh, *Dissertation on the Progress of Ethical Philosophy* (Edinburgh: Adam and Charles Black, 1836), 182.

25. Dugald Stewart, *Dissertation: Exhibiting the Progress of Metaphysical, Ethical and Political Philosophy, since the Revival of Letters in Europe* (Edinburgh: Thomas Constable, 1854), 424.

26. William Godwin, *Enquiry Concerning Political Justice and Its Influence on Morals and Happiness*, ed. F. E. Priestley (3 vols. Toronto: University of Toronto Press, 1946), 3:18 n, 49 n.

27. Idem, *An Enquiry Concerning Political Justice* (2 vols. London: for G. G. J. and J. Robinson, 1793), 1:302, 84.

28. Ibid., 1:314.

29. Samuel Parr, "A Spital Sermon, Preached at Christ Church," in John Johnstone, ed., *The Works of Samuel Parr, Ll. D.* (8 vols. London: Longman, Rees, Orme, Brown and Green, 1828), 2:381–93, quoted at 491.

30. John Ryland to Joseph Kinghorn [1790], in M. H. Wilkins, *Joseph Kinghorn of Norwich* (Norwich: Fletcher and Alexander, 1855), 183.

31. Andrew Fuller, *The Gospel Worthy of All Acceptation*, in H. L. McBeth, *A Source-book for Baptist Heritage* (Nashville, TN: Broadman Press, 1990), 133.

32. Andrew Fuller to John Ryland, April 28, 1815, in John Ryland, *Life and Death of the Rev. Andrew Fuller* (Charlestown, MA: Samuel Etheridge, 1818), 332–3, cited by M. X. Lesser, *Jonathan Edwards: A Reference Guide* (Boston: G. K. Hall, 1981), 26. I am strongly indebted to this guide for this chapter.

33. David Gracey, *Sin and Unfolding Salvation* (London: Passmore and Alabaster, 1894), 28–9.

34. Thomas Chalmers, *The Christian and Civic Economy of Large Town* (3 vols. in 1. Glasgow: for William Collins, n.d.), 1:318.

35. Idem, *Institutes of Theology* (2 vols. Edinburgh: Sutherland and Knox, 1849), 2: 386; idem, *Prelections on Butler's Analogy, Paley's Evidences of Christianity and Hill's Lectures in Divinity* (Edinburgh: Sutherland and Knox, 1849), 131.

36. [Thomas Chalmers], "Edwards' Inquiry, with Introductory Essay," *Presbyterian Review*, II (1831): 244, 238. The authorship of the article is identified by Henry Rogers (see n. 41), xxxi n.

37. William Cunningham, *The Reformers; and the Theology of the Reformation* (Edinburgh: T. and T. Clark, 1862), 471–83, 512, 520.

38. *Congregationalist and Christian World*, October 3, 1903, 467.

39. G. M. Roberts, *Selected Trevecka Letters (1742–1747)* (Caernarron: Calvinistic Methodist Bookroom, 1956), 199.

40. William Evans, *An Outline of the History of Welsh Theology* (London: James Nisbet, 1900), 126, 131; John Roberts, *Cyfarwyddiadau ac Anogaethau i Ggredinwyr* (Bala: R. Sanderson, 1809). I am grateful to Professor D. Densil Morgan of the University of Wales, Bangor, for this reference.

41. [Edward Williams and Edward Parsons, eds.], *The Works of President Edwards* (8 vols. London: for James Black and Sons, 1817), 1:v.

42. John Pye Smith, *First Lines of Christian Theology*, ed. William Farrer (London: Jackson and Walford, 1854), 5, 155.

43. Henry Rogers, "An Essay on the Genius and Writings of Jonathan Edwards," in *The Works of Jonathan Edwards, A. M.* (12th ed. London: William Tegg, 1879), i, iii, v.

44. Joseph A. Conforti, *Jonathan Edwards, Religious Tradition and American Culture* (Chapel Hill: University of North Carolina Press, 1995), 69 n.

45. Ibid; Josiah Pratt, *The Life of the Rev. David Brainerd* (London: R. B. Seeley and W. Burnside, 1834), vii–xvi.

46. A. A. Bonar, *Memoir and Remains of the Rev. Robert Murray M'Cheyne* (Dundee: William Middleton, 1844), 19.

47. J. A. de Jong, *As the Waters Cover the Sea: Millennial Expectations in the Rise of Anglo-American Missions* (Kampen: J. H. Kok, 1970), 182.

48. *Extracts from the Call to Extraordinary Prayer Published in 1748 by President Edwards* (Calcutta: for Calcutta Christian Tract and Book Society, 1859).

49. Thomas Scott, *Remarks on the Doctrines of Original Sin, Grace, Free-Will, Justification by Faith, Election and Reprobation, and the Final Perseverance of the Saints* (2nd ed. London: A. Macintosh, 1817), 94.

50. J. H. Fichte, *System der Ethik*, Bd I, s. 544–5, par. 225, quoted by M. C. Curtis, "Kantean Elements in Jonathan Edwards," in *Philosophische Abhandlungen: Max Heinze zum 70* (Berlin: Ernst Siegfried Mittler, 1906). I am grateful to Dan

Holder of Muhen, Switzerland, for this reference and for other help with German sources.

51. K. R. Hagenbach, *History of Christian Doctrines* (3 vols. Edinburgh: T. and T. Clark, 1880–1), 3:283.

52. J. van Eijnatten, *Hogere Sferen: De ideeenwald van Willem Bilderdijk (1756–1831)* (Hildershum, 1998), 670. I am grateful to Roel Kuiper for this reference.

53. Earl Leslie Griggs, ed., *Collected Letters of Samuel Taylor Coleridge* (6 vols. Oxford: Clarendon Press, 1955–71), 3:35.

54. S. T. Coleridge, *Aids to Reflection*, ed. John Beer (Princeton, NJ: Princeton University Press, 1993), 157.

55. [Williams and Parsons, eds.], *Works of President Edwards*, 1:151–2, 239. Gladstone's copy of the book is at St. Deiniol's Library, Hawarden, Flintshire.

56. Rogers, "Essay," xix.

57. Thomas Erskine, *The Doctrine of Election* (2nd ed. Edinburgh: David Douglas, 1878), 347–8.

58. John McLeod Campbell, *The Nature of the Atonement* (London: James Clarke, 1959), 63.

59. F. D. Maurice, *Modern Philosophy* (London: Griffin, Bohn, 1862), 470.

60. *Thirty-Third Annual Report of the Society for the Support of Gaelic Schools* (Edinburgh: for the Society, 1844), 15. I am grateful to Professor Donald Meek of the University of Edinburgh for this and the next references.

61. Donald Maclean, ed., *Typographica Scoto-Gadelica* (Edinburgh: J. Grant, 1915), 114–15.

62. Joseph Angus, *Six Lectures on Regeneration* (London: Alexander Shepheard, 1897), 68.

63. J. C. Ryle, *Holiness* (3rd ed. London: William Hunt, 1887), vi.

64. *The Dictionary of Welsh Biography down to 1940* (London: Honourable Society of Cymmrodorion, 1959), 963.

65. James Martineau, *A Study of Religion* (2 vols. Oxford: Clarendon Press, 1888), 2:277.

66. As reported by John Morley: Asa Briggs, ed., *Gladstone's Boswell: Late Victorian Conversations* (Brighton: Harvester Press, 1984), 203.

67. W. E. H. Lecky, *History of the Rise and Influence of the Spirit of Rationalism in Europe* (2 vols. London: Longman, Green, Longman, Roberts and Green, 1865), 1:477.

68. Leslie Stephen, "Jonathan Edwards," *Hours in a Library (Second Series)* (London: Smith, Elder, 1876), 44, 54, 59, 101, 105.

69. A. B. Grosart, *Selections from the Unpublished Writings of Jonathan Edwards of America* (n.p.: printed for private circulation, 1865), 11, 16.

70. Chalmers, *Prelections*, 131; Grosart, *Selections*, 15; Maurice, *Modern Philosophy*, 459–68 (immediately before Edwards).

71. D. A. Johnson, *The Changing Shape of English Nonconformity, 1825–1925* (New York: Oxford University Press, 1999), 176.

72. Herman Bavinck, *Gereformeerde Dogmatiek* (4 vols. Kampen: J. H. Bos, 1908), 1:202; 2:381; 3:89, 101, 116; 4:161, 163–4.

73. Jan Ridderbos, *De Theologie van Jonathan Edwards* ('s-Gravenhage: Johan A. Nederbragt, 1907), 312.

74. Albert Peel, *The Congregational Two Hundred, 1530–1948* (London: Independent Press, 1948), 96.
75. Iain H. Murray, *D. Martyn Lloyd-Jones* (2 vols. Edinburgh: Banner of Truth Trust, 1982–90), 1:253–4.
76. John Foster, "The Bicentenary of Jonathan Edwards' 'Humble Attempt,'" *International Review of Missions* 37 (1948): 375–81.
77. Gervais Angel, *Delusion or Dynamic? Reflections on a Quarter-Century of Charismatic Renewal* (Eastbourne, Sussex: MARC, 1989).
78. Robert Backhouse, comp., *Experiencing God: Jonathan Edwards: Select Readings from His Spiritual Classics* (London: Marshall Pickering, 1995), vi.
79. Georges Lyon, "L'Immaterialisme en Amerique – Jonathan Edwards," *L'Idealisme en Angleterre au XVIIIe Siecle* (Paris: Ancienne Librairie Germer Bailliere et Cie, 1888), 406–39.
80. Lesser, *Reference Guide*, 282.
81. Idem, *Jonathan Edwards: An Annotated Bibliography, 1979–1993* (Westport, CT: Greenwood Press, 1994), 32, 147.
82. Josef Smolik, *Kristus a jeho Lid* (Prague: Oikumene, 1997), 143–7. I owe this reference to the author.
83. Rogers, "Essay," xi.
84. I am grateful to Janos Pasztor of the Reformed Academy at Debrecen for this point.

13 Edwards and American literature

PHILIP F. GURA

Jonathan Edwards published his many sermons and books a century before anyone devoted a substantial work to the topic of "American literature" and even longer before the subject existed as an academic discipline. Indeed, in his day no one even conceived the category "American literature." Like Cotton Mather, Benjamin Franklin, and other representatives of what subsequently was termed, first, "colonial American literature" and then "early American literature," Edwards was an Englishman in British North America, a provincial who labored on the periphery of empire. When such a colonist wrote, it was as an Englishman, to be read across the Atlantic as well as by fellow colonists. Edwards explicitly acknowledged this dual audience, reminding himself in one of his early notebooks, "*Before I venture to publish in London, to make some experiment in my own country,*" and thus "*to play at small games first, that I may gain some experience in writing.*"[1] Beginning in the 1730s he began to realize this plan, publishing his first sermon in Boston and a few years later having the first edition of his *Faithful Narrative of the Surprising Work of God in the Conversion of Many Hundred Souls in Northampton* issued in London under the sponsorship of the prominent Nonconformist clergymen Isaac Watts and John Guyse. By the time of his death in 1758 Edwards had, indeed, become a participant in Europe's larger intellectual conversation, an English thinker of the first rank.

In the aftermath of the American Revolution, as the newly formed United States sought to parade cultural and intellectual achievement equal to that of European nations, the first assessments of American literature per se began to appear. Concurrently, Edwards's reputation as a religious thinker underwent something of a resurrection and transformation, having languished in the immediate decades after his death when few printers seemed interested in publishing excerpts from his voluminous manuscripts and none in issuing his complete works.[2] In particular, new champions of revivalism, laboring in what became known as the Second Great Awakening, claimed Edwards as their spiritual godfather and his evangelical writings as their models for piety. By the late 1820s some of his works, edited by the American Tract Society, were widely reprinted, so that Edwards's influence was more pervasive than it had been a century earlier when he led the New England revivals.

This was the context for Edwards's inclusion in Samuel Lorenzo Knapp's *Lectures on American Literature* (1829), the first book-length publication devoted to the topic. Knapp viewed the English language's migration across the Atlantic as part and parcel of the triumph of Anglo-Saxon civilization. As he put it, "As Empire travels westward with us," the English tongue, "whose origin and history, copiousness, strength, beauty, sweetness, and importance, have occupied our past hour, will carry with it the blessings of sound political and civil institutions, the blessings of letters and science, of virtue and religion."[3] As this suggests, Knapp was broadly inclusive in his understanding of literature, considering it whatever of written expression added to the stock of human knowledge. For Knapp and his cohort, "literature" might be a sermon, an exploration tract, a theological treatise, or a political disquisition, as well as a novel, poem, or drama – in short, what our own generation terms "discourse," not, that is, just belles-lettres, what literature connoted after the institutionalization of the English profession in the late nineteenth and early twentieth centuries.

Even though much of the early written expression from British America was in fact church-related, Edwards merited only brief mention in one of Knapp's lectures on eighteenth-century writing, and certainly not in the way, for example, that his nineteenth-century contemporaries spoke of Richardson's *Pamela,* Shakespeare's plays, or Coleridge's poetry. Knapp believed that Edwards's most significant work, his chief contribution to "American literature," was his *Freedom of the Will* (1754), a book, he wrote approvingly, that "requires the grasp of a vigorous and mature mind," for its "subject of inquiry . . . commenced with the first man and will end only with the last; and will never be thoroughly explained by any one." Acknowledging the book's still considerable influence in theological and philosophical circles (even as Edwards's more accessible pietistic works proliferated in abbreviated editions among the rank and file), Knapp concluded, "It is no common mind that can produce any thing worthy of notice on such a mysterious subject." To him, Edwards had distinguished himself as a profound thinker whose contribution to philosophical and theological argument merited his inclusion (if not at great length) in a work on American expression. Importantly, Knapp also noted Edwards's increasingly pervasive influence on nineteenth-century religious thought, observing, for example, that his *Religious Affections* was "a work much read by all classes of Christians of the present day."[4]

Given Knapp's desire to prove the United States to be Europe's intellectual equal, he also noted Edwards's extensive reputation abroad. Two decades later, at the height of the period in literature subsequently dubbed the

"American Renaissance," Rufus Griswold, the period's most inveterate anthol-ogizer and irrepressible booster of American writing, struck this same emphasis. In his *Prose Writers of America* (1846), he praised Edwards's transatlantic reputation as a logician and theologian, "the first man of the world during the second quarter of the eighteenth century," as he termed him. But given Griswold's immersion in the New York literary scene, where the constant refrain was for the development of "Young America in litera-ture," and when even sermons were beginning to be praised more for their beauty than their doctrine, he struggled to find any transcendent "literary" value in Edwards's works.[5]

Griswold finally settled on what he termed Edwards's "uncommonly good" style, so "suitable to his subjects," adding that "he seldom has been sur-passed in perspicuity and precision" when addressing theological issues. And if Edwards occasionally was "deficient in harmony" and lapsed into faults "of a mechanical sort," at least the Northampton minister's wit redeemed him: it was, Griswold reported, "of the Damascus sort, shining and keen."[6] Six years later, Evart and George Duyckinck, Griswold's rivals in their attempts to sur-vey and command New York's burgeoning literary marketplace, agreed. If Edwards had devoted himself to belles-lettres, they wrote, he would have been "an acute critic and poet." Unfortunately, they observed, he was a New Englander and thus an inheritor of "the ghostly line of Puritanism." The unfortunate but, to the chauvinistic Duyckincks, altogether expected result was that "all his powers were confined to Christian morals and metaphysics."[7]

Antebellum literary historians thus were reticent to claim for Edwards a more prominent place in the literary pantheon because his approach to his primary subject matter – theology – seemed increasingly desiccated and outdated at a time when both readers and critics preferred that their religious and moral concerns be addressed in more belletristic terms. Undeniably, in the 1850s Christianity was as much a part of the lives of Americans as it ever had been, but in ways that an Emerson, a Melville, or a Stowe now enunciated more powerfully than a theologian like Edwards. It is telling, for example, that such nineteenth-century theologians as Lyman Beecher, Charles Grandison Finney, and Edwards Amasa Park did not find places in the emergent histories of American literature, even though their cultural work was comparable to Edwards's a century earlier. Although he had a place in American history, Edwards's prominence in the emergent canon of American literature was assured only by his priority – as an example from an earlier period of a well-published and respected intellectual whose writings seemed more and more anachronistic.

Such implicit criticism of Edwards on the grounds of his donnée per-sisted through the remainder of the century, accompanied by the same grudging nods to his stature as theologian and philosopher. Moses Coit Tyler, for example, author of the first genuinely scholarly study of early American literature, is typical. Edwards, he noted in 1878, was "the most acute and original thinker" the nation had yet produced (overlooking the fact that there was no United States when Edwards wrote). But like the Duyckincks, Tyler struggled to praise Edwards as much for his expression as for his thought. He filled a large place in "ecclesiastical and philosophical history," Tyler opined, and "had the fundamental virtues of a writer," that is, "abundant thought, and the utmost precision, clearness, and simplicity in the utterance of it." Tyler could even cite "many examples of bold, original, and poetic imagery" in Edwards's works. But like his predecessors, he fell back on Edwards the philosopher. "As a theologian, as a metaphysician, as the author of The Inquiry into the Freedom of the Will [sic], as the mighty defender of Calvinism, as the inspirer and the logical drill-master of innumerable minds in his own country, and in Great Britain," Tyler concluded, Edwards "fills a large place in ecclesiastical and philosophical history" – but not, in other words, in the history of literature as Tyler's contemporaries William Dean Howells, Henry James, and Mark Twain now conceived it.[8]

Tyler's near-contemporary, the literary historian Charles F. Richardson, put it more explicitly. Rejecting his competitors' inclusive historical approach to the subject, in his *American Literature, 1607–1885,* Richardson argued for literary criticism on more objective, aesthetic grounds. American literature in the colonial period, he opined, was "promising indeed, but without great achievement." No doubt with Tyler's two-volume work in mind, he complained, "We have had enough description"; now "we want analysis." Why, he asked, "should writings which have passed into obscurity in England be magnified beyond their deserts, merely because they were written on the American coast?" To Richardson, literature was not intellectual history but "the written record of valuable thought, having other than merely practical purpose."[9] To his credit, he understood Edwards's undeniable influence on subsequent theologians, particularly Samuel Hopkins, Joseph Bellamy, and Nathaniel Emmons, even if, like virtually all his predecessors, he was unable to move Edwards to the front row of writers as *writer* rather than as mere *thinker.*

Richardson's sense that there was little from the colonial period that justified intensive study accords with his contemporary Mark Twain 's reaction to Edwards. In the spring of 1867 the humorist wrote his friend and fellow author Harriet Beecher Stowe (who much more successfully than her father Lyman Beecher had married her prose to her culture's interest in religion) about his recent encounter with Edwards's *Freedom of the Will.* This author, whose character Huck Finn admitted that he had read now and then in John Bunyan's *Pilgrim's Progress* and found it "interesting but tough," had an even worse experience with Edwards. "Continuously until near midnight," Twain wrote, "I wallowed and reeked with Jonathan in his insane debauch; rose immediately refreshed and fine at 10 this morning, but with a strange and haunting sense of having been on a three days' tear with a drunken lunatic. . . . All through the book," Twain noted, he saw the "glare of a resplendent intellect gone mad – a marvelous spectacle. No, not *all* through the book," Twain corrected himself. "The drunk does not come on till the last third, where what I take to be Calvinism and its God begins to show up and shine red and hideous in the glow from the fires of hell. . . . I was ashamed," Twain admitted to his friend, "to be in such company."[10]

And so were a lot of others, including members of Boston's elite Radical Club, who at one of their meetings in the 1880s heard Oliver Wendell Holmes (who earlier had pilloried New England Calvinism in his famous poem, "The Deacon's Masterpiece; or the Wonderful 'One-Hoss Shay'") speak respectfully of Edwards. After hearing Holmes favorably review what most of the audience, imbued as they were with "liberal" religion, considered Edwards's repugnant beliefs, Unitarian minister David Wasson forthrightly declared that "he did not believe any good ever came out of Edwards's philosophy."[11] James Freeman Clarke, another Unitarian clergyman, agreed. "I cannot see," he commented, "that Jonathan Edwards is likely to exercise a permanent influence, either as a metaphysician, theologian, or mystic." Edwards will be chiefly remembered, he concluded, "as a powerful thinker, whose thoughts produced no lasting results."[12] By the late nineteenth century, in other words, in venues where literature was written and discussed, Edwards was fast fading from consideration, his autocratic principles and exclusive religion out of step with the times, his prose a relic of what many took as a discredited part of the nation's past.

At the same time, American literature finally was emerging as its own field of academic study as English departments offered more courses focused on the development of national literatures rather than on pedantic philology. The monument to this effort to give American writing a presence equal to that of the centuries-long parade of English literature was the multivolume *Cambridge History of American Literature,* edited by William P. Trent and others, which appeared in 1917. Eschewing Richardson's attempt to make the turn into aesthetics, the editors announced in their preface that the book comprised "a survey of the life of the American people as expressed in their writings rather than a history of *belles-lettres* alone."[13] One would thus expect Edwards to have had very much a place in their pageant, but Paul Elmer More's chapter on him, primarily biographical in orientation, comes across as virtually apologetic, as if even Edwards's significance as a revivalist and philosopher somehow no longer could be of major interest except as an historical curiosity. Unable to make a convincing case for Edwards as writer, More could only conclude, deferentially, "He remains one of the giants of the intellect and one of the enduring masters of religious emotion," someone whom few could study "without recognizing the force and honesty of his genius." How precisely he expressed something of the American experience in his writings remained unexplored.[14]

Such efforts to understand Edwards as formative of the American mind continued for decades, even as attempts to claim a place for him in literary histories remained unconvincing. Further, as scholars worked toward the development of this emergent national narrative, they treated significant writing produced prior to 1776 primarily as a prelude to the mid-nineteenth-century flowering subsequently dubbed the American Renaissance, what I elsewhere have termed the "continuities" thesis.[15] To succeed in this mode of assessing early American literature in the early twentieth century, however, they had to combat an increasingly virulent reaction to Puritanism among critics in the vanguard of the Modernist movement. If, as one later exponent of this "continuities" school has written, "Puritanism contained the seeds of political and social ideals, structures of thought and language, and literary themes which inspired both the content and the forms of much American writing from 1700 to the present," it first had to be rehabilitated as a field of inquiry.[16] Only then could one plot Edwards's position in the master narrative.

In a period in which Freud's theories quickly gained influence, praising New England's Calvinist heritage was no easy task; thus Edwards was absent from two seminal works of the 1920s by critics who were central to the rise of literary Modernism. D. H. Lawrence, for example, who in his irreverent but highly influential *Studies in Classic American Literature* (1923) exemplified the new generation's disdain for any writing that contributed to what they saw as America's deep repression of pleasure, could not find a word for Puritanism or Edwards. Instead, he began his book with Benjamin Franklin, the secular incarnation of the ever-driven and never happy Puritan, always suspicious of the flesh. In his comparably influential *In the American Grain* (1925), Lawrence's contemporary, William Carlos Williams, exemplar of the new spirit in American literature, acknowledged the significance of New England's Puritan past to American literature but chose for its exemplar Cotton Mather, whose books comprised "the flower of that religion, that unreasonable thing, on which they prided themselves for their purity." In Mather's work, Williams identified Puritanism's fascinating allure, promising as it did a "steel-like thrust from the heart of each isolate man straight into the tabernacle of Jehovah without embellishment or softening," a description that certainly applies as well to Edwards's descriptions of true religious experience.[17] But like most other cultural critics, Williams chose not to conjure America's past with the name "Edwards."

One exception was Lewis Mumford, who a year after Williams published his study began a scholarly career that spanned half a century. In his influential *The Golden Day* (1926), Mumford found room for Edwards but decried him as "the last great expositor of Calvinism," an outdated faith. He knew that Edwards was important; but, like so many other Modernists, he viewed Edwards's thinking and influence of little significance to contemporary problems. Edwards, he observed dismissingly, "wrote like a man in a trance, who at bottom is aware that he is talking nonsense." Admittedly in love with the beauty of the soul, Mumford continued, Edwards unfortunately remained so ensnared "in the premises of determinism that, with a heavy conscience, he followed his dire train of thought to its destination" and thus was prevented from seeing man in his true dignity and power.[18] To realize the "Golden Day," Mumford believed, Edwards's successors, both religious and secular, had to reject so dark and closed a vision. Mumford went on to celebrate the ebullience of Emerson and Whitman, writers who had broken from Calvin's snare to become midwives to a truly American literature.

Echoing this view was Mumford's contemporary, Vernon Louis Parrington, whose *Main Currents of American Thought* (1927) still comprises one of the most inclusive assessments of American writing. Parrington's bogey was not the psychological repression singled out by Lawrence and Williams, nor the determinism that so appalled Mumford. Rather, he focused on the authoritarian and undemocratic aspects of Puritanism, which he saw everywhere in Edwards's writings. In his study, Parrington celebrated what he viewed as the inexorable rise of liberal democracy over three hundred years of American history and thus he championed, in early American thought, such mavericks as Roger Williams and Thomas Jefferson. As for Edwards, he was "a theologian equipped with the keenest dialectics, a metaphysician endowed with a brilliantly speculative mind, [and] a psychologist competent to deal with the subtlest phenomena of the sick soul." But, Parrington continued, like Cotton Mather before him (and whom Parrington had given a good trouncing), Edwards never contributed significantly to the true American spirit because he was "the unconscious victim of a decadent ideal [that is, divine sovereignty] and a petty environment," by which Parrington presumably meant insular and religion-obsessed New England.[19]

By the 1930s, however, the tide rose in Edwards's favor, particularly after the revivification of New England Puritanism as a field of serious academic study. Concurrent with Arthur O. Lovejoy's championing of the history of ideas, several American scholars, most notably the Harvard professors, Perry

Miller, Samuel Eliot Morison, and Kenneth Murdock, turned a new and powerful spotlight on America's colonial period, studying Puritanism seriously as a complex belief system whose cultural work had never been adequately assessed. These individuals, some in history departments but the most influential in departments of English, were not content merely to describe and then (as had their predecessors in the academy) condemn Calvinism's tenets, but asked what these added up to as imaginative and social constructions. The results were as exhilarating as they were liberating.

In these years the signal moment for Edwards as a writer was the appearance of Clarence H. Faust and Thomas H. Johnson's *Jonathan Edwards: Representative Selections* (1935) in the prestigious "American Writers Series," edited by literary historian Harry Hayden Clark.[20] Indeed, Edwards was one of only two writers representative of the colonial period chosen for the series; predictably, Benjamin Franklin was the other. But why was Edwards now on the shelf in the company of Bryant, Cooper, Emerson, Irving, Melville, and other undeniably belletristic authors? The answer lies in who else had a hand in this particular volume. Johnson, for example, had written his doctoral dissertation on "Edwards as a Man of Letters" at Harvard under the direction of F. O. Matthiessen, Miller's, Murdock's, and Morison's colleague who subsequently achieved fame for his magisterial *American Renaissance: Art and Expression in the Age of Emerson and Whitman* (1941). For his part, Faust had worked on "Edwards as a Thinker" with R. S. Crane at the University of Chicago where Miller had done his graduate work. And both editors thanked two others at Harvard – Miller and Murdock – for help on the book's introduction.

Thus, the making of Edwards's modern reputation in American literature was linked to Miller and his cohort's larger revisionist project, one that forever changed our understanding of American Puritanism. The Edwards whom Faust and Johnson presented through lengthy extracts from his works fit precisely into the master narrative about the development of American culture that Miller had begun to promulgate, of how European ideas were indelibly transformed once they were transplanted across the Atlantic.[21] To him, Edwards, with his grand philosophical and theological vision, was a central transitional figure into the age of the American Revolution and beyond.

But in what terms? Certainly not in the ways that writers such as Donne, Herbert, or Milton were being praised by the most influential high Modernist critics. Faust and Johnson still praised Edwards more as a "thinker" than for his contribution to American literature as T. S. Eliot and his cohort understood it. Typically, for example, in his section on "Edwards as a Man of Letters," coeditor Johnson celebrated him in a tradition of English religious and philosophical polemicists. Further, Johnson argued Edwards's inclusion in the series primarily on the grounds of his "eminence or popularity" (attested to, he claimed, by the frequency with which his works were published in Europe and America between 1721 and 1800), not on any continuing literary significance. Indeed, Johnson played this section in an oddly minor key. Edwards had a "sparse and conventional" style, and his rhetoric was "seldom heightened" except when he sought "to arouse an emotion of powerful yearning or revulsion," certainly not attributes that would catch Eliot's eye.[22] Despite the name of the series in which the book appeared, Faust and Johnson still presented Edwards as a philosopher and theologian, not as a writer per se.

So too did Robert E. Spiller and his coeditors when in the wake of World War II they published their *Literary History of the United States* (LHUS) (1948). The LHUS was an ambitious project with many contributors, who agreed with Parrington that American literature's uniqueness was defined by "the ideals ... and practices developed in democratic living." Further, they believed that the nation now had existed long enough for literary historians to agree on genuine masterworks "in which aesthetic, emotional, or intellectual values [were] made articulate by excellent expression." The contributors thus were presenting nothing less than "the record of man made enduring by the right words in the right order."[23] In this work, on the strength of his earlier anthology, Johnson drew the assignment of Edwards and thus gained another opportunity to assess his significance. But given this agenda, when Johnson treated Edwards, he succumbed fully to the "continuities" thesis, reviewing the Northampton minister's meditations on fate and free will, good and evil, and the nature of true virtue, only to conclude that his interests anticipated the concerns of the greatest authors of the American Renaissance. "The voice, through these many American years, is the voice of Hawthorne, and Melville, and Emerson, and Whitman, and Adams," Johnson concluded. "But the hand is the hand of Jonathan Edwards."[24] It did not matter that none of these individuals himself testified to any influence from (nor even interest in) Edwards. Simply put, the fascination Edwards held for the two subsequent generations of scholars in American literature lay in his championing by a group of scholars and their acolytes, who viewed the emergence of a truly distinctive American literature as in good measure indebted to nineteenth-century's writers' ongoing conversation with America's Calvinist past.

In these years, Edwards's reputation as a distinctive thinker attained its greatest height through Miller's influential biography, *Jonathan Edwards,* published in the "American Men of Letters" series in 1949. Miller based his own assessment on Edwards's imaginative engagement with what he regarded as the still central questions about the relation of man to things eternal. In this light, Miller declared that Edwards was "one of America's five or six greatest artists who happened to work with ideas instead of poetry or fiction."[25] Thus, Miller's *Jonathan Edwards* is not "about" literature in the same way that his contemporaries, the "New Critics" Cleanth Brooks and Robert Penn Warren, conceived it. Instead, Miller followed such nineteenth-century admirers of Edwards as Stowe, who viewed Edwards as both metaphysician and poet, someone whose conception of things was as different from those of "common men" as that of Dante or Milton. As Stowe put it in her popular *Oldtown Folks* (1867), Edwards had "sawed the great dam and let out the whole waters of discussion all over New England, and that free discussion led to all shades of opinion in modern days." "Little as he thought of it," she continued, "yet Waldo Emerson and Theodore Parker were the last results of the current set in motion by Jonathan Edwards."[26] Similarly, Alexander Allen, one of Edwards's late nineteenth-century biographers, agreed. He noted that Edwards's *A Divine and Supernatural Light* resembled "so closely the later Transcendentalist thought of New England as almost to bridge the distance between Edwards and Emerson," making Edwards "the forerunner of the later New England Transcendentalism quite as truly as the author of a modified Calvinism."[27] Ever the assiduous researcher, Miller quite probably had gleaned what his contemporaries considered two of his most brilliant insights – of Edwards as supreme artist and as a connector to the Transcendentalists – from his omnivorous reading in nineteenth-century sources.

Further, despite the title of the series in which the book appeared, it is important to recall that Miller was not constitutionally disposed to treat Edwards as a man of letters, for he was singularly uninterested in the stylistic achievement of the Puritans whom he studied. For example, he never devoted any significant time to the boldly original poet Edward Taylor, whose manuscripts had first been transcribed by Johnson himself, with whom Miller had coedited the landmark anthology *The Puritans* (1938). We cannot underestimate the importance of the recovery of Taylor's corpus for early American literary study, for between 1950 and 1975 the fact that he stood shoulder to shoulder with such heavyweights as Herbert and Milton gave new direction to the field, even as it marginalized others such as Edwards who were primarily theologians. Scholars who knew only Anne Bradstreet's and Michael Wigglesworth's poetry marveled at Taylor's intricate meter and startling language; and the pages of the *New England Quarterly* and *American Literature*, two beacons for those interested in early American literature, frequently carried explication of Taylor's work, only occasionally of Edwards's. Thus, when essays on Edwards appeared in literary journals, they tended to explore patterns of imagery in his sermons or other works, the sort of investigation that "New Critics" of literature, following in the steps of Robert Penn

Warren and René Wellek, could sanction. On the contrary, Miller's Edwards, when he could be found in the secondary literature, surfaced more often in journals devoted to history or American studies. Still, in this tug of war, the Millerites carried the day. On the strength of their belief in Edwards's centrality to the development of the American mind, for twenty-five years all serious students of American civilization wrestled with his theology.

By the mid-1970s, with the rise of the new social history, particularly its disdain for narratives built on the work of great and exceptional minds, interest in Edwards declined, not to recover until Sacvan Bercovitch, the chief scholar of early American literature in the three decades after Miller's death, turned his attention to him. Bercovitch brought to the field wide and deep learning in scriptural exegesis, and he found in the seventeenth and eighteenth centuries what Miller usually had missed (or when he did see it, as he had in Roger Williams's work, he simply misread): the elaborate use of scriptural analogy that literary critics call *typology.* Bercovitch's first major contribution to early American literary study, his landmark anthology, *Typology and Early American Literature* (1972), awakened scholars to how extensively and intricately Puritan writers built their texts on typological principles.[28] Later in his most influential work, *The American Jeremiad* (1978), Bercovitch ascribed to Edwards a central role in the extension in the eighteenth century of the "ritual of consensus" that explained the persistence of American ideology through four centuries.[29] The important thing to recognize is that, while Miller had privileged Edwards for his protomodernism, by focusing on his rhetoric Bercovitch directly engaged his language and thus made him available in a new way as an historical figure for students of literature. To be sure, Bercovitch decoded Edwards's typology primarily to note its service to the promulgation of a rhetoric of middle-class values that by the nineteenth century were hegemonic in American culture. To him, Edwards confirmed and continued the rhetoric of American exceptionalism that derived from the first generation of Puritan divines; but he had done so, Bercovitch argued, through the undeniably significant typological grounding of his prose, a matter of living rhetoric.

For almost two decades the explanatory power of Bercovitch's scholarship on Edwards and other central figures of early American literature (particularly Cotton Mather) precluded other, complementary work. This is the more unusual because, during these same years, the Yale Edition of Edwards's writings made available more and more primary material that shed light on his development as thinker and writer. Simply put, by the mid-1990s the action in early American literature had shifted. There were, for example, efforts to enlarge greatly the geographical boundaries of the discipline, to all the lands that comprised Europe's colonial empire from the sixteenth through the eighteenth centuries. In this regard, early American literary study began to resemble more a subfield of comparative literature as scholars read texts in Spanish, French, and Portuguese alongside hitherto canonized work in English. With the entire "Atlantic Rim" now in their purview, many viewed the very notion of American literature as that written *only in English* as a matter of postcolonial arrogance.[30]

With studies in race, gender, and class ascendant, scholars' interests shifted to figures whose works speak directly to such topics. Thus, at the millennium there was much interest in the late eighteenth- and early nineteenth-century writers of the "Black Atlantic," as well as in women whose poetry or novels explored the implications of political liberty to a culture still in thrall to sharp gender distinctions. Even with more and more volumes of the Yale Edition available, Edwards could not find a central place in such scholarship. If anything, on matters of race, gender, and class, he seemed a man inextricably tied to his time, someone inclined to spiritual transcendence but who had no overt concern for the political or philosophical questions that subsequently made figures like Franklin, Jefferson, Olaudah Equiano, or Judith Sargent Murray of interest.[31]

We can readily gauge the nature and degree of the discipline's interest in Edwards in the late twentieth century in two recently published large-scale histories of American literature. In *The Columbia Literary History of the United States* (CLHUS) (1988), edited by Emory Elliott, a work comprised of many-score hands, Alan Heimert (Miller's chief disciple and inheritor of his mantle at Harvard) drew the assignment of Edwards in a contribution that stresses his centrality to eighteenth-century British American intellectual life. In particular, Heimert views Edwards's unique "creativity" as arising from the crucible of the colonial revivals. If as Heimert put it, Edwards has "come to be recognized as perhaps the finest mind ever to emerge in America" and as well "by some, as among our supreme architects of prose," his stature derived primarily from "his participation in, commentaries on, and obsessions with the issues raised" in the Great Awakening.[32]

Unlike Bercovitch, however, who was fixated on the typological underpinning of Edwards's thought and on the ideology that the theologian's corpus valorized, Heimert locates Edwards's stylistic achievement in his revivification of the "oratorical" mode that Matthiessen had identified as the hallmark of the supreme American vernacular. "Assonance, alliteration, repetition, progressive and rhythmic expansion of clauses" – these, Heimert declares, were Edwards's attempts "to address the ear as well as the eye," and the marks of a brilliant literary stylist. But, following Miller's lead, he argued that such rhetoric finally was subordinate to the sublime *ideas* that Edwards described in his theological summa. Edwards's greatest achievement, Heimert concludes, was as a central architect of the American mind, one the few great "intelligences" of his era who had "set the agenda, in the years between the Awakening and the Revolution, for our endless debate over the nature of the American character and society."[33] To know Edwards, in other words, is to know America.

Bercovitch's own project – he is general editor of the multivolume *Cambridge History of American Literature* (CHAL) – treated Edwards differently. Therein he appears under the rubric of "New England Puritan Literature," in an essay contributed by Elliott, editor of the CLHUS and with a long history as a proponent of the "continuities" thesis in American literature. Indeed, for scholars of early American literature who have struggled to enlarge their notion of the discipline, Elliott has been a bogey. William Spengemann, for example, who pioneered the notion of treating American literature more largely – in his case, as a subset of the literature of British America, that is, including the Caribbean and other regions that were dominated by the British, and thus, by the English language – dismisses Elliott, Bercovitch, and others because they have been led to their conclusions about the continuities in American literature by "a kind of verbal shell game, in which the prestidigitator places his thematic pea under one shell labeled 'Puritan,' makes a lot of rapid movements with his typewriter, and then produces the pea from under another shell marked 'American literature.'"[34]

Spengemann's witty riposte is as applicable to Elliott's chapter on "Reason and Revivalism" in the CHAL as it was to Elliott's earlier work, for in his emphasis on Edwards's attempts to capture the ineffable experience of grace, Elliott tells the reader, the minister "moves to employ a poetic language that many readers have seen as anticipating the style of the Transcendentalists.... Using highly figurative and lyrical language," Elliott argues, the minister "struggles to find words capable of conveying the complexity of his emotions." In Elliott's respectful recital, Edwards is the dying ember of New England Calvinism, for, "at his desk in the frontier village of Stockbridge thinking of the awesome power of the Creator," he "in some way captures the peculiar ambiguity of Puritan literary history" and its connections to subsequent American thought. Recalling Miller's insistence on Edwards's significance to the twentieth century, for example, Elliott proposes as Edwards's most "arresting" feature "the mixture of Ramist logic with poetic visions that are at once medieval and modernist" that permeates his best work.[35]

If we take Heimert and Elliott as our guides, in the early twenty-first century Edwards's contemporary reputation among scholars of American literature thus continues to swing, as it always has, between two poles. On the one hand, there remains a sense that his writings have been (and continue to be) essential to a larger understanding of the American mind, primarily through how they revivified our country's values and goals through his memorialization of the eighteenth-century revivals. On the other, Edwards represents the artist as mystic, struggling with words to express how he had come to be at home in the universe. No longer is he denigrated, as he was so commonly in the nineteenth and early twentieth centuries, for allegiance to an outdated and repressive creed, for both Heimert and Elliott convince us that he transcended Calvinism's restrictions and liberated himself and his readers into new understanding of the end for which God created the world. And both these critics, importantly, believe that he did this through his powerfully evocative language, as a great writer must do.

We know, then, that Edwards will continue to be read both for what he offers in helping us to understand the relationship of revivalism to American nationhood and for what he teaches and exemplifies of the spiritual life. But there remains the matter of his final influence in American literature, that is, of how his works themselves have figured in literary history as inspiration or templates for subsequent writers. Fully to understand Edwards as an American writer in this way involves consideration of what literary historian Lawrence Buell has characterized as this nation's "Calvinist literary culture," of which Harriet Beecher Stowe is the prime example, and of what Douglas Sweeney, in his recent book on Nathaniel William Taylor, has described as "Edwardsian enculturation of Calvinist New England during the first third of the nineteenth century." As Sweeney explains, nineteenth-century Edwardseanism included "not only those approved by self-appointed Edwardsian gatekeepers, but all who participated in and took their primary religious identification from the expanding social and institutional network that supported and promoted Edwardsian thought."[36]

With Buell's and Sweeney's injunctions in mind, Edwards's true legacy in American literature may most reside in his contribution to what literary and cultural historians term the discourse of "sentimentalism," particularly as it was conceived, utilized, and modified in its literary exfoliation by such newly recovered and appreciated writers as Stowe, Maria Cummins, and Susan Warner as well as by more canonical authors like Nathaniel Hawthorne, Herman Melville, and Walt Whitman. In particular, Edwards's emphases on emotion as a central component to the religious life and on disinterested benevolence as one of the signs of true spirituality indelibly marked antebellum literature.

The center of Edwards's influence as a writer, then, is not located in his lengthy theological treatises, which had their greatest currency among other theologians and philosophers, and which accounted for his initial canonization by our earliest literary historians, from Knapp on. Rather, it resides in those writings that had a much wider circulation in antebellum America, such works of practical divinity as his *Religious Affections* and *Life of David Brainerd,* as well as the "Conversion of President Edwards" (taken from his *Personal Narrative*) and the "Account of Abigail Hutchinson" (excerpted from his *Faithful Narrative*), which the American Tract Society reprinted in thousands upon thousands of copies. In these works we return over and over to Edwards's insight, offered in his *Religious Affections,* that "if the great things of religion are rightly understood, they will affect the heart."[37] The vibration of one heart to the stirrings of another, the sympathy which unites souls of all class, race, or gender, a benevolence to being in general, is what more than anything else defined sentimentalism, and this emotion derived in good measure from Edwardsean principles and language.

By the nineteenth century, in other words, Edwards's ideas about goodness and virtue had become so internalized that they were finally inescapable, precisely the "enculturation" that Sweeney describes. Edwards's influence is clear and highly visible in Stowe's *Minister's Wooing* or in Cummins's *The Lamplighter,* for example; but it also is found in those authors whom Matthiessen enshrined as the torchbearers of the American Renaissance. We cannot come to terms, for example, with Emerson's moving passage upon the loss of his son in his great essay "Experience" without understanding the sentimental conventions that accrued around the death of a child. Nor can we fully interrogate Hawthorne's understanding of interpersonal relationships in his *Blithedale Romance* without considering sentimental attitudes toward self and other. Further, even in so radical a poet as Whitman we find the message that these same bonds of sympathy are sacred between all beings, male and female, black and white, rich and poor. Hitherto we have leapt when we have come upon those rare moments when we have seen Edwards named explicitly in some work of nineteenth-century literature – as when, in Melville's "Bartleby the Scrivener, for example," the narrator invokes "Edwards on the Will and Priestley on Necessity."[38] But more important, nineteenth-century sentimentalism (*pace* Ann Douglas, who viewed it as the hallmark of an eviscerated or emasculated culture), in fact, received much vigor and currency from Edwardsean language and metaphor.[39]

In American literature, Edwards always has been the odd man in, someone whose discourse is not self-consciously belletristic, even as it is incantatory in its evocative power. To a large extent, Perry Miller got it right when he asked readers to consider Edwards as finally an artist who worked primarily with ideas, principal among them, grace, community, love, and sensibility. But he underestimated how much Edwards's staying power as an author depended on his incessant struggle to embody those ideas in a language that carried their full weight and meaning. Edwards's most astute readers, from the early nineteenth century on, have recognized this achievement, even if they had to do so by eschewing those of his works most commonly encountered in literary anthologies and sampling his whole corpus. The essential Edwards, that is, will not be found in *Sinners in the Hands of an Angry God* or the apostrophe to Sarah Pierpont, his future wife, but rather in those texts such as *Religious Affections* and *Life of Brainerd* that embody his profound spirituality, as well as in the searching treatises in which he pushes language to its limits to describe what he has come to know of the universe and its Creator.

Edwards's self-consciousness about his medium of expression thus remains the hallmark of his stature as an important writer. Consider, for example, what he has to say on this topic in his *Treatise Concerning Religious Affections* as he seeks to draw the distinction between the "affections" and mere passions. "It must be confessed," Edwards observes, "that language is here somewhat imperfect, and the meaning of words in a considerable measure loose and unfixed, and not precisely limited by custom, which governs the use of language"[40] Similarly, in his notes on "The Mind" he complains, "We are used to apply the same words a hundred different ways," so that "ideas being so much tied and associated with the words, they lead us into a thousand real mistakes."[41] Or, as he put it in his *Freedom of the Will*, too often "due care has not been taken to conform language to the nature of things, or to any distinct clear ideas."[42] Born in part of his early appreciation of John Locke's writings and buttressed with his own language experiments, from the pulpit as well as on the page, Edwards crafted a prose style hypnotic in its cadence and seductive in its persuasive power because of his sensitivity to the inherent imprecision of words, a writer's main set of tools. In text after text throughout his career, he struggled with the relation of words to the ideas they represent, and he sought a verbal precision that effectively tied his opponents in knots as they tried to parry the thrusts of his verbal logic. Wrestling with this angel, he emerged blessed in his gifts, and able to bestow his wisdom upon subsequent generations through his finely honed prose. It is no small achievement, in American literature as in American thought more largely conceived.

Notes

This chapter is the result of the author's recent reconsideration of Edwards's place in American letters, the results of which were offered at the "Jonathan Edwards at 300" conference in 2003 as well as in the pages of *Early American Literature*. See Philip F. Gura, "Jonathan Edwards in American Literature," *Early American Literature* 39 (2004): 147–67.

1. *Natural Philosophy*, WJE, 6:194.
2. See Philip F. Gura, "Jonathan Edwards in American Literature," *Early American Literature* 39, no. 1 (2004): 147–66.

3. Samuel L. Knapp, *Lectures on American Literature, with Remarks on Some Passages in American History* (New York: Elam Bliss, 1829), 22.

4. Ibid., 82.

5. Rufus Wilmot Griswold, *The Prose Writers of America* (1846; reprint, Philadelphia: A. Hart, 1852), 53.

6. Ibid., 56.

7. Evert A. and George L. Duyckinck, *Cyclopedia of American Literature* (2 vols. New York: Charles Scribner, 1855), 1:92.

8. Moses Coit Tyler, *A History of American Literature* (2 vols. New York: G. P. Putnam's Sons, 1879), 2:177, 191.

9. Charles F. Richardson, *American Literature, 1607–1885* (1886, reprint New York: Putnam, 1891), xvi, xviii, xx.

10. Cited in Henry F. May, "Jonathan Edwards and America," in Nathan O. Hatch and Harry S. Stout, eds., *Jonathan Edwards and the American Experience* (New York: Oxford University Press, 1988), 23–4.

11. Mrs. John T. Sargent, ed., *Sketches and Reminiscences of the Radical Club* (Boston: James R. Osgood, 1880), 370.

12. Ibid., 375.

13. William Peterfield Trent et al., eds., *The Cambridge History of American Literature* (4 vols. New York: G. P. Putnam's Sons, 1917–21), 1:iii.

14. Ibid., 71.

15. Philip F. Gura, "The Study of Colonial American Literature, 1966–1987: A *Vade Mecum*," *William and Mary Quarterly* 45, no. 2 (April 1988): 305–41.

16. Emory Elliott, ed., *Puritan Influences in American Literature* (Urbana: University of Illinois Press, 1979), xi–xii.

17. D. H. Lawrence, *Studies in Classic American Literature* (1923; reprint, New York: Viking Press, 1964); William Carlos Williams, *In the American Grain* (Norfolk, CT: New Directions, 1925), 111.

18. Lewis Mumford, *The Golden Day: A Study in American Experience and Culture* (New York: Boni and Liveright, 1926), 32–3.

19. Vernon Louis Parrington, *Main Currents in American Thought* (3 vols. New York: Harcourt, Brace, 1930), 1:148, 162–3.

20. Clarence Faust and Thomas H. Johnson, eds., *Jonathan Edwards: Representative Selections* (New York: American Book Company, 1935).

21. See especially Perry Miller, *Errand into the Wilderness* (Cambridge, MA: Harvard University Press, 1956).

22. Ibid., cxi.

23. Robert E. Spiller et al., eds., *Literary History of the United States* (3 vols. New York: Macmillan, 1948), 1:xvi.

24. Ibid., 81.

25. Perry Miller, *Jonathan Edwards* (New York: William Sloane Associates, 1949), xii.

26. Harriet Beecher Stowe, *Oldtown Folks* (1867; reprint, Cambridge, MA: Harvard University Press, 1966), 260, 387.

27. Alexander V. G. Allen, *Jonathan Edwards* (Boston: Houghton, Mifflin, 1894), 388.

28. Sacvan Bercovitch, *Typology and Early American Literature* (Amherst: University of Massachusetts Press, 1972).

29. Idem, *The American Jeremiad* (Madison: University of Wisconsin Press, 1978).

30. See, for example, Susan Castillo and Ivy Schweitzer, eds., *The Literatures of Colonial America* (Oxford: Blackwell, 2001).

31. See, for example, Vincent Carretta, ed., *Unchained Voices: An Anthology of Black Authors in the English-Speaking World of the Eighteenth Century* (Lexington: University of Kentucky Press, 1996); Adam Potkay and Sandra Burr, eds., *Black Atlantic Writers of the Eighteenth Century* (New York: St. Martin's Press, 1995); Frances Foster Smith, *Written by Herself: Literary Production of African American Women, 1746–1892* (Bloomington: Indiana University Press, 1993); Amanda Porterfield, *Female Piety in Puritan New England: The Emergence of Religious Humanism* (New York: Oxford University Press, 1992).

32. Alan Heimert, "Jonathan Edwards, Charles Chauncy, and the Great Awakening," in Emory Elliott, ed., *Columbia Literary History of the United States* (New York: Columbia University Press, 1988), 113–14.

33. Ibid., 126.

34. William Spengemann, "Review Essay," *Early American Literature* 16 (1981): 184.

35. Emory Elliott, "Reason and Revivalism," in Sacvan Bercovitch, ed., *The Cambridge History of American Literature, Volume One: 1580–1820* (Cambridge: Cambridge University Press, 1994), 302, 306.

36. Lawrence Buell, *New England Literary Culture: From Revelation through Renaissance* (New York: Cambridge University Press, 1986), 268–75; Douglas A. Sweeney, *Nathaniel William Taylor, New Haven Theology, and the Legacy of Jonathan Edwards* (New York: Penguin, 1986).

37. WJE, 2:120.

38. Herman Melville, "Bartleby, the Scrivener" (1855), in idem, *Billy Budd, Sailor and Other Stories* (New York: Penguin, 1986), 55.

39. Ann Douglas, *The Feminization of American Culture* (New York: Knopf, 1977).

40. WJE, 2:97.

41. Ibid., 6:345.

42. Ibid., 1:349.

14 Edwards in "American culture"

M. X. LESSER

In 1858, a hundred years after Jonathan Edwards died, "The Deacon's Masterpiece: or The Wonderful 'One-Hoss-Shay.' A Logical Story" appeared in *The Atlantic Monthly*.

> Have you heard of the wonderful one-hoss-shay,
> That was built in such a logical way
> It ran a hundred years to the day,
> And then, of a sudden, it – ah, but stay,
> I'll tell you what happened without delay,
> Scaring the parson into fits,
> Frightening people out of their wits,
> Have you ever heard of that, I say?

Other than that perfect bit of timing, both the date of construction of the chaise –"Seventeen hundred and fifty-five" – and the measure of its history hint at Edwards and *Freedom of the Will*, first published in 1754.[1] More directly, if less rhythmically, Oliver Wendell Holmes later castigates Edwards in more than two dozen pages of the *International Review*, declaring his theology a "barbaric, mechanical, materialistic, pessimistic" system. And, returning to a fictive account at about the same time, Holmes identifies the "real aim" of his novel *Elsie Venner, A Romance of Destiny*, as a "test" of original sin and "human responsibility for the disordered volition."[2]

That the poem found its way onto the pages of *The Atlantic* during its first year may be little more than public notice for one of its founders, much like the lines of Emerson, Longfellow, and Lowell, its first editor. Yet its publication proved significant for Edwards, not so much in its form as its forum, "a magazine," as the cover leaf of *The Atlantic* had it, "of literature, art, and politics." But for a piece on Edwards's observations of flying spiders in the *American Journal of Science and Arts* in 1832, critical estimates of him in American periodicals were confined to theological ones, the first of them the *Connecticut Evangelical Magazine* in 1808.[3] The year that "The Deacon's Masterpiece" appeared in *The Atlantic*, "Jonathan Edwards and the

Successive Forms of the New Divinity" appeared in *Biblical Repertory*, part of an ongoing paper war about Edwards's legacy, here a skirmish over its appropriation by those who had "broad and irreconcilable differences" with him.[4] Other journals in the nineteenth century, and other poems and novels as well, offer another Edwards, an iconic figure still, but one less the concern of seminarians and their professors. After decades of relative neglect at the turn of the century, Edwards springs fully armed in an academic recovery halfway through it and in an evangelical reclamation at its close. Possessed of him, American culture seems not quite certain of his place.

Early estimates of Edwards start, modestly enough, in the front matter to his printed work. *God Glorified,* published in 1731 "at the Desire of several, Ministers and Others, in *Boston,* who heard it," convinced two of them, Thomas Prince and William Cooper, that it was surety that the *"Evangelical Principles"* of Solomon Stoddard would *"shine"* in his grandson. *A Divine and Supernatural Light* followed three years later with a short note by Edwards and a hymn by Isaac Watts. When *Faithful Narrative* appeared in London in 1737, it had a long preface by Watts and fellow dissenting minister John Guyse that, while recommending the "astonishing" work of God, faulted its "pious" recorder for his "Style," "Inferences," and "Defects," and for the conversion narratives of Abigail Hutchinson, a dying young woman, and Phebe Bartlett, a precocious toddler – "Childrens Language," they harrumphed, "always loses its striking Beauties at second-hand." The first American edition, published the following year, struck Watts and Guyse from one of its three issues, restored it to the other two, and added to each a commendatory preface by four Massachusetts ministers and an attestation by another six.[5] In 1737, Edwards explained his selection of sermons in his preface to *Five Discourses* and complained about divines "in endless controversy and dispute," but he withheld comment from *Sinners in the Hands of an Angry God* and a funeral sermon on the death of his uncle William Williams, both published in 1741. *Distinguishing Marks,* delivered later that year, carried a defense by Cooper and occasioned a broadside reply, a fifty-page rebuke, and no further invitations to speak at Yale. With the publication two years later of *Some Thoughts Concerning the Revival,* the battle was decidedly joined, as the Reverend Charles Chauncy of Old Brick Church, Boston, took the text apart, section by section, often page by page, in a rebuttal nearly a hundred pages longer than the original.[6] Although there was another caustic critique following the publication of his amended qualifications for communion,[7] it was after Edwards's death that questions about his words gathered direction, and then about the Stockbridge texts, not the Northampton. The first full-scale assault on *Freedom of the Will* occurred in 1770, some sixteen years after its initial publication, and another on *The Nature of True Virtue,* a year later. His other major works – *Religious Affections, Life of Brainerd, Original Sin,* and *History of Redemption*– went unremarked in the eighteenth century.[8]

In 1803, the Edwards centennial, a few lines addressed *Distinguishing Marks,* fewer still *Freedom of the Will*.[9] Within three years, the first of the eight volumes of the Leeds edition of his works was published, with the *Life* by Samuel Hopkins and *Freedom of the Will* and *End of Creation,* texts of his exile; two years later, the first of the eight volumes of the first American, or Worcester, edition appeared, with Hopkins once again, but now with *Farewell Sermon, Result of a Council at Northampton, An Humble Inquiry,* and *Misrepresentations Corrected,* documents of his dismissal.[10] Individual titles continued to be published, but there was a change in kind and number. *Faithful Narrative,* which set Edwards's reputation here and abroad through countless editions and translations in the eighteenth century, was reprinted only four times in America in the nineteenth century, all before 1833. *Sinners* was reprinted six times in the nineteenth, the last in 1845 in Choctaw for the Cherokee Nation. Although *Original Sin* was reprinted only twice, *Freedom of the Will* drew press time – and fire – more than a dozen times before 1882, an effort led by the publishers of the revised Worcester. A similar service by the American Tract Society produced 70,000 copies of *Life of Brainerd* from 1833 to 1892; 60,100 of *History of Redemption* from 1838 to 1875, both undated, both abridged; and nearly 150,000 copies of *Personal Narrative* between 1823 and 1875.[11] But these texts and others in the canon brought little comment, except on matters of style. For readers, Edwards's language was, variously, uncouth, vulgar, inelegant, or repellent. So pervasive was the view that his was one of "the most remarkable specimens of bad writing" of the time that an editor of *Religious Affections* abridged the text to rid it of ambiguities and tautologies, and another prepared *Sinners* in "other language" for the modern, that is, 1826, reader.[12]

By the time of "The Deacon's Masterpiece," Edwards had become, in the minds and prose of some academic theologians, a type of Christianity gone wrong, and some of the rancor spilled onto the pages of Harriet Beecher Stowe. "Views of Divine Government," Chapter 23 of *The Minister's Wooing,* traces New England theocracy from its founding to an exchange of letters between Samuel Hopkins and Jonathan Edwards, the younger, on the scheme of the universe, free agency, original sin, and regeneration. Stowe notes the "almost unearthly disinterestedness" of their lives and the "unflinching consistency" of their sermons, adding that the elder Edwards preached sermons "so terrific in their refined poetry of torture, that very few persons of quick sensibility could read them through without agony." Taken by the energy and clarity of his belief – she cites the *Personal Narrative* for its stark beauty – she is put off by the morbidity of its application, and thus betrays the characteristic ambivalence toward Edwards of a later time. Systems such as his "differ from the New Testament as the living embrace of a friend does from his lifeless body, mapped out under the knife of the anatomical demonstrator; every nerve and muscle is there, but to a sensitive spirit there is the very chill of death in the analysis." A decade later, her *Oldtown Folks* repeats some familiar observations about Edwards, but ventures some new ones. Edwards united in himself the soul of the poet and the mind of the metaphysician, she remarks, a widely held notion then and one shared, for example, by her brother Henry Ward Beecher in *Norwood*.[13] But Harriet Beecher Stowe also suggests that Edwards rationalized scriptural matters "far more boldly and widely" than many of his editors let on. In time, such matters as he explored led quite unexpectedly to transcendentalism: "Little as he thought it, yet Waldo Emerson and Theodore Parker were the last results of the current set in motion by Jonathan Edwards." Finally, she turns to Edwards's wife, as Holmes and others would as the century wore on, offering her in gentle reproof to his grim doctrines. She quotes approvingly his paean to Sarah in New Haven and refers to his account in *Some Thoughts* of her religious crisis in January 1742, concluding that her "saintly patience" tempered his difficulties in Northampton and his loneliness in Stockbridge.[14]

In much the same way, John Greenleaf Whittier singles out Sarah's religious experience and its effect in "The Preacher" (1860), a poem largely about George Whitefield and the Great Awakening. Edwards forges "The iron links of his argument" in the solitary reaches of the "dark Northampton woods," brightened by the light of the Lord he discovers there and by the vision of Sarah at home, her "sweet, still countenance . . . rapt in trance."[15] In fact, Sarah was so attractive a counter to Edwards that she became for some the locus of imaginative recreations as lover, helpmeet, and mother, the stable and affectionate center of the household. So the Reverend Amos Delos Gridley scours the Edwards memoirs, a recently published history of Stockbridge, and other "Historical Discourses" to gain "an inside view" of Sarah's life, arranging the material as diary entries and letters from January 9, 1726, her sixteenth birthday, to September 22, 1758, exactly six months after her husband's death and ten days before her own. In between, Gridley dotes upon young love and married bliss, and he reports Whitefield's visit, Brainerd's death, Edwards's dismissal, the Stockbridge troubles, his unpolished style, and the call to Princeton, all pieced together like so much gossip, devoting whole patches to a short history of New England life and customs for Mrs. John Erskine, the wife of Edwards's Scottish admirer and editor.[16] At a further remove, *Esther Burr's Journal*, the creative devising of the Reverend

Jeremiah Eames Rankin, records the chatty details of Edwards's family life, from the first entry of February 13, 1741, the ninth birthday of his third daughter, to the last entry in April 1758, a reprint of a letter "from my dear widowed mother to poor widowed me."[17] But the darker Edwards persists. In Paul Leicester Ford's *Janice Meredith: A Story of the Revolution,* the heroine's father recalls the time in Princeton years ago when he and his wife heard Edwards, "that strange combination of fire and logic," deliver two sermons on infant damnation. So convinced that her four children who recently died would suffer everlasting torment, she became then and forever remained a "stern, unyielding woman."[18] And in one of James Lane Allen's Kentucky romances, *The Mettle of the Pasture,* a character discovers Edwards "most prominent" among the doctrinal tracts of "black-browed" seminarians on the family bookshelves, "hoarsest of the whole flock of New World theological ravens."[19]

From such phantom letters and current fiction, interest widens in the popular accounts to include genealogy, particularly after the family reunion at Stockbridge in early September 1870, coming to a climax of sorts in the fabricated eugenics at the turn of the century. Essays appear in general periodicals – about Edwards's birthplace in *Putnam's,* his life among the Housatonics in *Harper's,* his "delusional insanity" in *New England Magazine* – and in specialized ones like the *American Journal of Education.*[20] Readings of his theology still occupy the usual journals, but it is his philosophy, more often his idealism and its sources, that merits attention now, as it does in the first doctoral dissertation on him in 1899. The only full-length appraisal of Edwards in the century comes late in it and characterizes his style as "thinking aloud," his speculative thought an exercise "in confusion, if not failure," and indicts him for the "great wrong" of his doctrine of divine sovereignty, his dogged belief in original sin, and the "false premises" of his theology.[21] As is often the case at the century's end, the mystical Edwards is the valuable Edwards, the "imperishable element" in him in this account and the saving remnant of his faith. A decade earlier, the first professor of American literature, Moses Coit Tyler, regrets even more Edwards's calling and suggests that he could have been "one of the great masters" of physical science or imaginative literature, a writer of clear expression, bold imagery, and keen wit.[22]

Unlike the Stockbridge reunion and its puffery thirty years before, the gathering at the First Church of Christ, Northampton, on June 22, 1900, to mark the sesquicentennial of Edwards's dismissal, was "a serious attempt" to take his measure, in papers on his place in history, his influence on spiritual life in New England, and his imaginative appeal. Somewhat less profound, the gatherings in October 1903 at Andover and Yale, South Windsor and

Stockbridge, Berkeley and Brooklyn, to celebrate the bicentennial of his birth ranged from a 166-line poem comparing him to Dante to a sermon proclaiming, "Think what it would be ... if every one of us were a Jonathan Edwards!"[23] Between the Northampton retrospective and the dedication of a memorial gate to him at South Windsor in 1929, publication of his work all but ceased, and commentary became sparse. The Moody Bible Institute, Chicago, published extracts of *Life of Brainerd* in 1900, and the Baptist Book Concern, Louisville, distributed *Sinners* for five cents a copy in 1901. *Ten New England Leaders* numbered him among them; *The Edwardean,* a quarterly journal begun in October 1903, folded after four issues; and the "real" Edwards arrived five years later. Mark Twain claimed Edwards a " drunken lunatic," a "resplendent intellect gone mad"; and Teddy Roosevelt assured an anxious public nearing war that Edwards had a strong sense of duty, that "there wasn't a touch of the mollycoddle about him." In the 1920s, Modern Students Library published selections from Franklin and Edwards – a coupling probably first suggested by Mrs. Stowe fifty years earlier – and his great-great-grandson reprinted *Sinners,* a sermon "second only" to the Sermon on the Mount.[24] The Hall of Fame for Great Americans unveiled a bust of Edwards, and the *Hampshire Gazette* reported a proposal to name a hotel after him.[25] *Main Currents in American Thought* dismissed him as an "anachronism," and *Evangelized America* labeled him a "spiritual hypochondriac."[26] At South Windsor, the Connecticut Society of Colonial Dames heard about his family, his theological significance, and his mind, and at Ann Arbor, a doctoral candidate, Henry Bamford Parkes, put the finishing touches to "New England and the Great Awakening." Within a year it had morphed into *Jonathan Edwards: The Fiery Puritan.*[27] It was 1930, and it signaled more than a change in title.

With Edwards now proclaimed a "classic" American, early studies probe his radicalism and godliness, and the next ten years produce eleven dissertations, three more than the previous thirty years.[28] In 1932 Columbia grants its first doctorate on the decline of New England theology after Edwards, the University of Chicago its first on Edwards and penology, and Harvard its first on Edwards's philosophy. *Harper's* publishes a full-length study of "one of the most stimulating and forceful minds" in America; the "Inheritance of Our Fathers" series issues *Wicked Men Useful in Their Destruction Only,* the first of a dozen of his sermons that it reprints over the next fifty years; and Yale dedicates Jonathan Edwards College.[29] In 1935 two newly minted Ph.D.s – Clarence H. Faust, author of "Jonathan Edwards's View of Human Nature" (University of Chicago, 1935), and Thomas H. Johnson, author of "Jonathan Edwards as a Man of Letters" (Harvard, 1934) – gather representative selections for the American Writers Series, with over a hundred pages of introductory remarks, the juvenilia, about a dozen letters, as many sermons, and parts of the major treatises. In 1940, Johnson compiles a descriptive bibliography of Edwards's printed writings; Perry Miller of Harvard explores the continuities of the Puritan tradition from Edwards to Emerson; and Ola Elizabeth Winslow of Goucher College traces Edwards along the "inner curve of spiritual experience."[30] In the first of three essays in 1948, Miller discovers "a revolution in sensibility" in Edwards's typological use of nature; in the second, he suggests that for Edwards grace operates within a social, as well as an individually psychological context; and in the third, he relates Edwards's sense of the heart to his "radical" empiricism. The year following, Miller charts the "drama of his ideas" in the "American Men of Letters" series, with Edwards emerging as "intellectually the most modern man of his age," a philosopher "infinitely more" than a theologian, a "major" artist.[31] In the 1950s, Miller writes of Edwards and Locke, the *History of Redemption*, and the Great Awakening; he brings together some of his earlier pieces on the "movement of European culture into the vacant wilderness of America," including four on Edwards; and he becomes general editor of the nascent Yale Edition of Edwards's works, the first volume, *Freedom of the Will*, edited by Paul Ramsey of Princeton, "a kind of intellectual ecumenicity in the Ivy League." Within a year a sort of battle of the books was at hand, as two texts derived from eighteenth-century collected editions appear: the first volume of *Select Works*, over a Banner of Truth imprint, with *Faithful Narrative* and three sermons; and *Jonathan Edwards on Evangelism*, over a Grand Rapids imprint, with parts of *Faithful Narrative, Some Thoughts, Religious Affections, Treatise on Grace*, and three other sermons. The following year, 1959, Yale published *Religious Affections*, and the Banner of Truth ten more sermons.[32] For all that, the "fiery Puritan" still haunts the popular imagination.

"Ode to Jonathan Edwards" in *Woman's Home Companion* dwells on infant damnation for nine stanzas, offering not orthodoxy but the mischief of his children as the doctrinal key.

> O Children dear, what have you done
> To papa Edwards, Jonathan, John?
> Come, with your constant cry for food,
> Between him and his wrathful God?
> Had a fight at his time of prayer?
> Left your toys on the attic stair
> And laughed like fiends when he took a fall?
> Conceived in sin, O vipers all!

Another poem, "The Theology of Jonathan Edwards," begins,

> Whenever Mr. Edwards spake
> In church about Damnation
> The very benches used to quake
> For awful agitation.

Men would "roll their eyes," women "swoon," and children "shudder," for Edwards's God was

> Not God the Father or the Son
> But God the Holy Terror.

And "Mr. Edwards and the Spider," Robert Lowell's poem based upon *Sinners*, "The Future Punishment of the Wicked," and "Of Insects," all of them closely read as he prepared and later abandoned a biography of Edwards, fuses the language of both sermons with the occasion of the young naturalist's observations,

> As a small boy
> On Windsor Marsh.

Beyond the flying spiders of Edwards's youthful records, Lowell develops the figure of the "hourglassblazoned" spider, "the Black Widow, death," and deepens the terror through an allusion to Josiah [Joseph] Hawley. The suicide of Edwards's uncle becomes the particular focus of the forty-six line companion poem, "After the Surprising Conversions," which expands upon the relevant passage in *Faithful Narrative*. He borrows far more from Edwards here, taking whole lines and phrases, but he alters the tone of the narrative and shifts the date:

> September twentysecond, Sir, the bough
> Cracks with the unpicked apples, and at dawn
> The small-mouth bass breaks water, gorged with spawn.

Edwards, according to Lowell, fails to understand the fatal, human consequence of his preaching divine terror and stands in stark contrast to the autumnal ripeness about him.[33]

Apart from a "ghostly interview" with Edwards about liberal theology, the only fiction of the time, unlike the verse, clearly reflects the developing critical attitude toward Edwards, if not its precision. *Consider My Servant* by Jack Duncan Coombe gets at the "human" Edwards during the time between his ordination and farewell sermon by going beneath his "scholarliness and Puritan composure." All the characters of a life are here – Solomon Stoddard,

Joseph Bellamy, George Whitefield, Gilbert Tennent, David Brainerd, Robert Breck – and all the events, but they are unrecognizable somehow. Major Joseph Hawley, instrumental in Edwards's dismissal, sought his forgiveness five years after the affair; yet here Hawley apologizes the very evening of the ministerial council's rejection. And Samuel Sewall attends Edwards's first public lecture on July 8, 1731, although the bewitched judge died a year and a half earlier.[34]

From 1960 to 1989, publications on Edwards – books, articles, dissertations, reviews, fugitive references, newspaper notices, reprints – tripled over the previous thirty years, from nearly four hundred items to nearly twelve hundred. Obviously, such an increase arose from more than Miller's serial efforts, as other studies conceived yet another Edwards. But just as Edwards had become a "center of consciousness" for Miller, so Miller became a center of consciousness for a generation of scholars.[35] Though the majority of dissertations are given over to exploring pastoral and theological matters, a growing number point elsewhere, to Edwards's social and psychological theories, stylistics, the public square, his ministerial family, and, as one explained, his "common consciousness" with Nathaniel Hawthorne.[36] That kind of reading becomes fairly standard over time, Edwards linked now to Dickinson, Emerson, Faulkner, Poe, Thoreau, and Whitman; *Sinners* providing a gloss to "The Minister's Black Veil" and "The Pit and the Pendulum," and *Freedom of the Will* to "Bartleby, the Scrivener"; his sensationalism recalling Mrs. Rowlandson's in *A Narrative of the Captivity,* the account of his conversion, Adam's in *Paradise Lost,* Book X.[37] A veritable Homeric catalogue of other relationships crowds other pages. One reader detects remarkable similarities between Edwards and Hassidic masters in their psychology of the religious experience; another finds his theology more comprehensible as an adaptation of Gregory of Nyssa's Christian Neoplatonism. Still others join Edwards to Aristotle and Augustine, John Brown and Charles Brockden Brown, John Dewey and William James, Mary Baker Eddy and Charles Grandison Finney, Sigmund Freud and B. F. Skinner, H. Richard Niebuhr and Josiah Royce, and, least among a host of others, Huck Finn and Heinrich Himmler. And the number of volumes of the Yale Edition increased by seven.[38]

The popular novels of the time are slow to change, recounting Sarah's trials as had the late nineteenth century. *The Prospering,* a novel set in Stockbridge, includes the sometimes bitter days that an "aristocratic" Sarah and a "cold stern" Jonathan spend there among the Mahicans and the Williamses. But impressions soften after the narrator reads Edwards's *Life of Brainerd* and discovers his God of "indescribable wonder" behind the "awful wrath" of his preaching.[39] In a "parable for the befuddled woman," *Marriage to a*

Difficult Man offers another Edwards, the "socially bumbling" pastor and theologian as loving husband and father. Sarah darts into his study during the day, "confident that no matter how intent he was on his writing, he would put down his pen and turn to her with lighted face," their "uncommon union" surviving dismissal in a "harvest of middle-age love."[40] The Stockbridge years draw a more sympathetic, more accommodating Robert Lowell to Edwards as well. In "Jonathan Edwards in Western Massachusetts," he again draws upon Edwards's words, from such disparate sources as his apostrophe to Sarah and his letter to the Princeton trustees, at 102 lines the longest of his poems:

> I love you faded,
> old, exiled and afraid
> to leave your last flock, a dozen
> Housatonic Indian children;
> afraid to leave
> all your writing, writing, writing,
> denying the Freedom of the Will.

In "The Worst Sinner, Jonathan Edwards's God," Lowell's last, he again turns to Edwards the man, "a good man," he calls him, but one, like the poet, steeped in sin. Both are part of a heritage of depravity and, therefore, they can no more "drink away the venom in the chalice" than can God.[41]

That kind of sympathy, common to a good many readers of Edwards over these years, distinguishes the poetry in the popular press. In *The New Yorker*, "Awaiting Winter Visitors: Jonathan Edwards, 1749" discovers Edwards days after a failed sign, months before his dismissal, watching his congregation slip from him, reckoning "the fervor would not hold its bloom." Sarah still clings to "the hard faith" amid want and death and a spring of "merciless speedwell." So, Edwards ends,

> I shall retire and read St. Paul,
> who called the human corpse a seed.[42]

And in *Yankee*, "Sermon for Jonathan Edwards" glimpses Edwards returning home against the cold, "his greatcoat swirling," Sarah kneeling to unpin him – "Oh, he was forever disassembling God's book" – holding his words to the light,

> her knees ached,
> from hard prayer,
> from shadow,
> from stone.

All this comes to an end in the unlikely pages of a dissertation and a festschrift, thirty-nine lines of a "triptych journey" in one, a Shakespearean sonnet in the other.[43]

A shift in the academic study of Edwards occurs as well, as scholars all but abandon Miller's paradigm. In the hunt for literary analogues, both Dickinson and Emerson survive the 1990s, as does Melville, in a piece tying Captain Ahab to Edwards, not the whale; but the effort flags, and although surveys of his indebtedness and influence in broader categories persist, their numbers dwindle. What remains, and continues, is the parsing of his theology and the conviction of his ministry, distilled as *America's Theologian* and *America's Evangelical*.[44] Dissertations, once again, light the territory ahead. Between 1990 and 2004, the number increased by almost twenty or a fifth over the previous fifteen years, those by seminarians by almost thirty or three-fifths. A few report on Dickinson and Melville and on other relationships, some previously vetted (John Dewey and Alfred North Whitehead), others freshly proposed (Cotton Mather and Nathaniel Taylor).[45] The overwhelming number argue theological issues, revisiting some (revelation, salvation, trinitarianism), uncovering others (assurance, hermeneutics, historiography); on pastoral matters, all take an evangelical turn.[46]

Over the same period, the definitive Edwards grew to twenty-three volumes – five of published and unpublished sermons, four of unpublished "Miscellanies," one of extant letters, as well as writings on typology, ecclesiology, Scripture, the Trinity, faith, and grace – and Yale published two readers.[47] Other houses, chiefly evangelical, issued smaller collections or single titles, often in paperback or pamphlet, many of well-worn texts. *Sinners*, "Made Easier to Read" in 1996, in Phillipsburg, New Jersey, was rendered difficult again later that year in Paradise Valley, Arizona; *Distinguishing Marks*, by the "Pastor of the Church of Christ at Northampton, in Connecticut," published in Salem, Ohio, in 1998, was "modernized" two years later in Wheaton, Illinois. Edwards's writings appeared as *The Wrath of Almighty God* and *Altogether Lovely* in Morgan, Pennsylvania; as *His Redeeming Love* in Ann Arbor, Michigan; and addressed *To the Rising Generation* in Orlando, Florida, only the last drawn from the manuscripts. The 1834 two-volume collected works, the source for many more selections, was reprinted in facsimile in Peabody, Massachusetts. The only fictional accounts were about the "rare and beautiful relationship" between Jonathan and Sarah in Stockbridge and a book for young readers that has more to do with its twelve-year-old heroine than "the infamous revivalist."[48]

Hardly the local celebrations of a century ago, the Edwards's tercentenary brought together scholars of a wide range of interests and dispositions, from the country over and abroad, to read over a hundred papers at nine gatherings, eight in the last fifteen years, and held at venues as diverse as

Wheaton College and Yale University, Indiana University and the University of Miami, Arch Street Friends Meetinghouse and Westminster Presbyterian Church, Princeton Theological Seminary and Desiring God Ministries, and the Library of Congress.[49] At the last of them, and typical of most, papers review the familiar, only to revise it: Edwards was fixed now, not to a particular writer, but to the tradition of the eighteenth-century sentimental novel; others set him in an historical context but couched in a present concern – for example, Edwards and the politics of sex in New England. That mix of the old, or the old rejuvenated, and the new fairly describes the contents of books of the period, as well as the houses that published them. Semiotics comes to Edwards; studies in Catholicism and Deism vie with those on aesthetics and revivalism, with a shelf of enhanced readings of theology, another of reprints.[50] *Christian History* and the *Journal of Religious Ethics* devote an issue to him, and half a dozen bibliographies not only review the work but often recast it. One traces the publishing history of Edwards abroad, two in the same journal take on the latest volumes of the Yale Edition and the books of the 1980s, a fourth creates an "Edwards for Preachers," a fifth tries to "bridge the wide chasm between church and academy" in the 1990s by separating the two, and the sixth sorts the whole by categories, if only to summon readers in two of them, history and theology, to a common enterprise, a more fully realized, because shared, Edwards.[51]

George Marsden's biography of Edwards attempts much the same thing – to "take seriously his religious outlook on his own terms," his "Calvinistic heritage" and his personal, "eternal relationship to God," and to depict him as a "real person in his own time," at once a philosopher and a theologian, pastor and college president, missionary and family man, a "revered figure" in the "international Reformed movement" and in "broader evangelicalism" – concluding in his opening words, "Edwards was extraordinary."[52] Others have thought him "always and everywhere interesting," "enigmatic and slippery," "inexhaustible and impossible to pin down."[53] And the good doctor, jotting down the date – "First of November – the Earthquake-day" – recorded that

> The parson was working his Sunday's text,
> Had got to *fifthly*, and stopped perplexed
> At what the – Moses – was coming next.
> All at once the horse stood still,
> Close by the meet'n'- house on the hill.
> First a shiver, and then a thrill,
> Then something decidedly like a spill,
> And the parson was sitting upon a rock,
> At half past nine by the meet'n'- house clock.

Not a bad figure that – for Jonathan Edwards in American culture.

Notes

1. The first issue of *The Atlantic Monthly* was published in Boston in November 1857; the poem appeared the following September as part of "The Autocrat at the Breakfast-Table" (pp. 496–7). For the most sustained treatment of Edwards in American culture, see Joseph A. Conforti, *Jonathan Edwards, Religious Tradition, and American Culture* (Chapel Hill: University of North Carolina Press, 1995). For earlier approaches, see Donald L. Weber, "The Image of Jonathan Edwards in American Culture" (Ph.D. dissertation, Columbia University, 1978); Nathan O. Hatch and Harry S. Stout, eds., *Jonathan Edwards and the American Experience* (New York: Oxford University Press, 1988). For a later approach, see "Edwards and American Culture," in David W. Kling and Douglas A. Sweeney, eds., *Jonathan Edwards at Home and Abroad: Historical Memories, Cultural Movements, Global Horizons* (Columbia: University of South Carolina Press, 2003), 85–174. The present reading draws upon my published bibliographies, *Jonathan Edwards: A Reference Guide* (Boston: G. K. Hall, 1981) [hereafter RG]; *Jonathan Edwards: An Annotated Bibliography, 1979–1993* (Westport, CT: Greenwood Press, 1994) [hereafter AB]; and my revision of Thomas H. Johnson, *The Printed Writings of Jonathan Edwards* (Princeton: Princeton Theological Seminary, 2003) [hereafter PW]. Many of the citations that follow in the endnotes are to numbered entries in these three bibliographies. The two annotated bibliographies are arranged chronologically and, within a given year, alphabetically, each entry numbered in order. The descriptive bibliography is arranged by title and numbered consecutively throughout the text. Within a title, editions appear in order of date of publication; small caps identify sequential editions of the same title by the same publisher.

2. RG, 1880.6, p. 24. Holmes read a shorter version at the April meeting of the Radical Club (RG, 1880.9); a complete text was reprinted in his *Pages from an Old Volume of Life* (RG, 1883.3). Although *Elsie Venner* was first published in 1861 (Boston: Ticknor and Fields), it was not until the preface to the second edition (New York: Grosset and Dunlop, 1883), ix, that Holmes asserted this. In the preface to the third edition (Boston: Houghton Mifflin, 1891), xii, he restated "the motive idea" for the novel and questioned "the most hardened theologian" on imputation. See also references to Edwards in the text itself (pp. 62, 317 ff). In another, longer poem read at the 250th anniversary of Harvard, Holmes declared, "O'er Princeton's sands the far reflections steal, / Where mighty Edwards stamped his iron heel" (RG, 1887.4). A scattering of verse was published before Holmes: an anonymous elegy and a couple of lines from two Connecticut Wits, Joel Barlow and Edwards's grandson Timothy Dwight (RG, 1758.1, 1778.1, 1788.3).

3. In the first issue appeared, for example, Emerson's "Days" and "Brahma," pp. 47–8; Longfellow's "Santa Filomena," pp. 22–3; and Lowell's "Sonnet" ("The Maple Puts Her Corals on in May"), p. 120 – all unsigned. For the articles, see RG, 1808.2 and 1832.6. In the eighteenth century, the London *Monthly Review* published four anonymous and highly critical reviews of *Freedom of the Will, Original Sin, Justice of God*, and *History of Redemption* (RG, 1762.1, 1767.1, 1774.1, and 1775.1).

4. [Lyman H. Atwater], *Biblical Repertory and Princeton Review* 30 (Oct. 1858): 614. The question of Edwards's theological "improvements" and his successors, proposed by his son in the latter's collected works and argued in its reviews,

became the point of dispute over the years in the sometimes angry pages of *Bibliotheca Sacra* (Andover), *Biblical Repertory* (Princeton), and *The New Englander* (Yale). For the younger Edwards, see RG, 1842.3; for the reviews by Atwater and Enoch Pond, see RG, 1843.2 and 1844.5. For another view of the dispute, see Edwards Amasa Park (RG, 1852.9); for a nineteenth-century summary of the conflict after it had abated, see George Nye Boardman (RG, 1899.2).

5. Thomas Prince and William Cooper, "To the Reader," in idem, *God Glorified in the Work of Redemption* (Boston: S. Kneeland and T. Green, 1731), i–ii; *A Divine and Supernatural Light, Immediately Imparted to the Soul by the Spirit of God* (Boston: S. Kneeland and T. Green, 1734), the hymn, "The Sovereignty of Grace" (p. 32). For the London, Edinburgh, and American editions, see PW, 9–12B. On the flyleaf of his presentation copy (Beinecke Rare Book and Manuscript Library, Yale University), Edwards wrote, "It must be noted that the Rev. publishers of the ensuing narrative, by much abridging of it, and altering the phrase and manner of expression, and not strictly observing the words of the original, have through mistake, published some things diverse from fact, which is the reason some words are crossed out: and besides there are some mistakes in the preface, which are noted in the margins." From 1816 to 1875, the New England Tract Society (later the American Tract Society [hereafter ATS]) published over 150,000 copies of *An Account of Abigail Hutchinson, a Young Woman Hopefully Converted at Northampton*; Phebe is still unaccounted for. John Wesley abridged *Faithful Narrative* and four other works (*Distinguishing Marks*, *Some Thoughts*, *Life of Brainerd*, and *Religious Affections*), but wrote a preface only to the last (PW, 158); all were frequently reprinted.

6. *Discourses on Various Important Subjects* (Boston: S. Kneeland and T. Green, 1737), ii; *Sinners in the Hands of an Angry God* (Boston: S. Kneeland and T. Green, 1741); *Resort and Remedy of Those that Are Bereaved by the Death of an Eminent Minister* (Boston: G. Rogers, 1741); William Cooper, "To the Reader," *The Distinguishing Marks of a Work of the Spirit of God* (Boston: S. Kneeland and T. Green, 1741), i–xviii. For comments on the last, see Stephen Sims and William Rand (RG, 1741.2 and 1743.3). *Some Thoughts Concerning the Present Revival of Religion in New England* (Boston: S. Kneeland and T. Green, 1742), 378 pp.; Charles Chauncy, *Seasonable Thoughts on the State of Religion in New-England* (Boston: Rogers and Fowle, 1743), 472 pp.

7. *An Humble Inquiry into the Rules of God Concerning the Qualifications Requisite to a Complete Standing and Full Communion in the Visible Christian Church* (Boston: S. Kneeland, 1749): Solomon Williams, *The True State of the Question Concerning the Qualifications Necessary to Lawful Communion in the Christian Sacraments* (Boston: S. Kneeland, 1751). For Edwards's reply, see *Misrepresentations Corrected, and Truth Vindicated* (Boston: S. Kneeland, 1752).

8. For the publication histories of *Religious Affections* in the eighteenth century, see PW, 143–57; of *Life of Brainerd*, PW, 198–204; of *Freedom of the Will*, PW, 260–7; of *Original Sin*, PW, 282–9; of *The Nature of True Virtue*, PW, 311–13; of *History of Redemption*, PW, 321–31. *Charity and Its Fruits* was first published in 1852: PW, 443. For the attack on *Freedom of the Will*, see RG, 1770.2, and on *The Nature of True Virtue*, see RG, 1771.2. There was also a minor exchange abroad over the reissue of *The Justice of God in the Damnation of Sinners* (PW, 316); see RG, 1789.2 and 1789.4. For the critical engagement of Edwards abroad,

see "Edwards around the World," Kling and Sweeney, eds., *Jonathan Edwards*, 177–319; for a bibliography of his works published abroad, see pp. 304–13, and for a list of translations, PW, 241–2.

9. J. Hughs, Preface, *The Marks of a Work of the True Spirit* (Pittsburgh: John Israel, 1803), iii–viii; Samuel Miller, *A Brief Retrospect of the Eighteenth Century* (New York: T. and J. Swords, 1803), 2:30–1.

10. For the Leeds, see PW, 505; and for the first American, or Worcester, see PW, 509. The Leeds was reprinted once, in 1817 (PW, 506); but seventeen years later, Edward Hickman, pastor of the Congregational Church, Denton, Norfolk, published a two-volume, double-columned edition, which was reprinted probably a dozen times over the next sixty years (PW, 512–512H).

11. For the publication history of *Faithful Narrative*, see PW, 28, 34–6; for *Sinners*, PW, 99–101, 103–4; *Original Sin*, PW, 290, 294; *Freedom of the Will*, PW, 268, 271, 275, 277–277K; *Life of Brainerd*, PW, 209–10, 214–15 (ATS imprints, PW, 221–3, 231 [in German]); *History of Redemption*, PW, 333, 337, 349–50 (ATS imprints, PW, 343–6, 351 [in Welsh]); and *Personal Narrative*, PW, 360 (ATS imprints, PW, 359–59D, 363 [in German]). The Worcester, enlarged in 1843, was reprinted nineteen times by 1881 and became the American standard before the Yale Edition: PW, 513–13S.

12. For commentary on *Freedom of the Will*, for example, see the thousand pages of Henry Philip Tappan: RG, 1839.8, 1840.6, and 1841.4; on matters of style, RG, 1808.5, 1811.2, 1822.4, and 1824.1; on the altered texts, RG, 1817.1 and 1826.1.

13. *The Minister's Wooing* (New York: Derby and Jackson, 1859), 335–7, 339; *Oldtown Folks* (Boston: Fields, Osgood, 1869), 363; *Norwood* (New York: Charles Scribner, 1868), 326. For a different and largely positive effect Edwards had on Susan Warner and her popular *The Wide, Wide World* (New York: G. P. Putnam's Sons, 1850), see Sharon Y. Kim, "Beyond Men in Black: Jonathan Edwards and Nineteenth-Century Women's Fiction," in Kling and Sweeney, eds., *Jonathan Edwards*, 137–53.

14. For the transcendental connection, see *Oldtown Folks*, 229; for Sarah, *The Minister's Wooing*, 265–6; and for Harriet Beecher Stowe, *Poganuc People* (New York: Fords, Howard, and Hulbert, 1878), 225; for Oliver Wendell Holmes, *Over the Teacups* (Boston: Houghton Mifflin, 1891), 249–50, where he invokes Sarah to counter Edwards's doctrine of imputation, calling him "the great master of logic and spiritual inhumanity."

15. John Greenleaf Whittier, *Home Ballads and Poems* (Boston: Ticknor and Fields, 1860), 165–6. The shift in focus from Edwards to his wife confirms in an obvious way the more subtle workings of sentimentalized religion outlined by Ann Douglas (RG, 1977.11). See also Amanda Porterfield (AB, 1980.37) and Julie Ellison (AB, 1984.7). On the question of gender in Edwards, see Sandra Gustafson, "Jonathan Edwards and the Reconstruction of 'Feminine' Speech," *American Literary History* 6 (Summer 1994): 185–212; Ava Chamberlain, "Bad Books and Bad Boys: The Transformation of Gender in Eighteenth-Century Northampton, Massachusetts," *New England Quarterly* 75 (June 2002): 179–203.

16. A. D. Gridley, "Diary and Letters of Sara Pierpont," *Hours at Home* (Aug. 1867): 295–303 (Sept. 1867): 417–25.

17. Jeremiah Eames Rankin, *Esther Burr's Journal* (Washington, DC: Harvard University, 1901); RG, 1901.9.

18. Paul Leicester Ford, *Janice Meredith: A Story of the American Revolution* (New York: Grosset and Dunlap, 1899); RG, 1899.5.

19. James Lane Allen, *The Mettle of the Pasture* (New York: Macmillan, 1903); RG, 1903.1.

20. For genealogy, see RG, 1871.5; for eugenics, RG, 1900.20; and for the journals, RG, 1869.2, 1871.1, 1890.3, and 1877.1.

21. John Henry MacCracken, "Jonathan Edwards Idealismus" (Ph.D. dissertation, University of Halle, 1899, in German, was published in part in English (*RG*, 1902.7). For commentary on Edwards's idealism, see RG, 1897.7 and 1902.12. Alexander V. G. Allen, *Jonathan Edwards* (Boston: Houghton Mifflin 1889), 337–8, 386, 388.

22. Moses Coit Tyler, *A History of American Literature* (New York: G. P. Putnam's Sons, 1878), 2:178.

23. For the sesquicentennial of his dismissal, see RG, 1901.6; for the bicentennial celebrations, RG, 1903.17 and 1904.14; for the sermon, RG, 1903.28; and for newspaper and journal coverage, RG, 1903.3–16.

24. For the *Brainerd* text, see PW, 237A; for *Sinners*, PW, 109B and 111; and for Franklin-Edwards, PW, 475. For *Ten New England Leaders*, see RG, 1901.14; for *The Edwardean*, RG, 1903.44 and 1904.15; for "The Real Jonathan Edwards," RG, 1908.2; for Twain's February 1902 letter, RG, 1917.6; and for Roosevelt's February 1916 letter, RG, 1916.6. Stowe remarked in *Oldtown Folks* (p. 458) that the "average New England character" combines the materiality of Franklin with the spirituality of Edwards. For a brief history of the idea, see RG, 1896.10, 1915.1, 1923.2, and 1962.7. Yale University held a conference on the two in February 1990; *The New York Times Book Review* joined them in pastel caricature on its cover leaf, July 6, 2003.

25. For the Hall of Fame, see RG, 1900.17, 1901.7, and 1926.1–4. One of twenty-nine elected in 1900, Edwards received eighty-one votes to Washington's ninety-seven and Hawthorne's seventy-three. Edwards's bust by Charles Grafly, installed May 12, 1926, reads, "Dynamic figure in the 'Great Awakening' religious revival of the mid-18th century." Apparently, the proposal for a hotel in Northampton failed, but a motel of the same name thrives on Cape Cod; a sundial marks the Edwards parsonage on Main Street in Stockbridge.

26. For Vernon Louis Parrington's charge of anachronism, see RG, 1927.2. See also H. Richard Niebuhr, "The Anachronism of Jonathan Edwards," in William S. Johnson, ed., *Theology, History, and Culture: Major Unpublished Writings* (New Haven: Yale University Press, 1996), 123–33, an address delivered at First Church of Christ, Northampton, March 9, 1958. For *Evangelized America*, see RG, 1928.5.

27. For the Colonial Dames, RG, 1929.7; for Henry Bamford Parkes's dissertation, see RG, 1929.10, and for its publication, see RG, 1930.10.

28. For the classic Edwards, see RG, 1931.4; for his radicalism, RG, 1931.5; and for his godliness, RG, 1931.10. For a chronology of dissertations, see RG, p. 379.

29. For the dissertations, see RG, 1932.4, 11, and 13; for the study, RG, 1932.10; and for the sermon, PW, 457.

30. For dissertations by Faust and Johnson, see RG, 1935.2 and 1934.4; for their anthology, RG, 1935.3; for Johnson's bibliography, RG, 1940.7; for Miller's essay, RG, 1940.9; and for Winslow's biography, RG, 1940.10.

31. For Miller's essays, see RG, 1948.7–9; for his *Jonathan Edwards*, RG, 1949.9; for a spirited reaction, RG, 1952.12.

32. For Miller's essays, see RG, 1950.13, 1951.12, 1952.4, 1956.8. On ecumenicity, see RG, 1958.4; on Banner of Truth, PW, 481–2; on Eerdmans, PW, 480; and on Yale, PW, 515–16. In 1961, Banner of Truth published *Religious Affections*, PW, 484; except for reconfigurations and reprints, it was the last volume of *Select Works*. Another paper by Miller, "Sinners in the Hands of a Benevolent God," was published posthumously in his *Nature's Nation* (Cambridge: Harvard University Press, 1967), 279–89.

33. For the poems, see RG, 1954.4, 1960.11, 1946.3. In an interview with Frederick Seidel, Lowell recalls "heaping up books and taking notes" on Edwards, "getting more and more numb on the subject . . . and feeling less and less a calling." "The Art of Poetry III: Robert Lowell," *Paris Review* 7, no. 25 (1961): 64.

34. For the "ghostly interview," see RG, 1959.2; for the novel, see RG, 1957.5.

35. See, for example, five studies from the 1960s: John H. Gerstner, *Steps to Salvation: The Evangelistic Message of Jonathan Edwards* (Philadelphia: Westminster Press, 1960); Alfred Owen Aldridge, *Jonathan Edwards* (New York: Washington Square Press, 1964); Conrad Cherry, *The Theology of Jonathan Edwards: A Reappraisal* (Garden City, NY: Doubleday, 1966); James Carse, *Jonathan Edwards and the Visibility of God* (New York: Charles Scribner's Sons, 1967); Roland A. Delattre, *Beauty and Sensibility in the Thought of Jonathan Edwards* (New Haven: Yale University Press, 1968). The phrase is Alan Heimert's in "Perry Miller: An Appreciation," *Harvard Review* 2 (Winter 1964): 35.

36. For dissertations on theology, see RG, 1962.14 and 1971.20; AB, 1981.38, 1986.10, 1986.15; on psychology, RG, 1974.5; on social theory, RG, 1968.21; on stylistics, RG, 1973.11; on the public square, AB, 1989.33; on the Edwards family, AB, 1988.30; on Edwards and Hawthorne, RG, 1978.22.

37. For Dickinson, see RG, 1961.15; for Emerson, RG, 1968.32; for Faulkner, AB, 1983.17; for Poe, RG, 1972.35; for Thoreau, AB, 1982.1; for Whitman, RG, 1976.2. For Hawthorne's short story, see RG, 1973.22; for Poe's, AB, 1980.51; and for Melville's, RG, 1969.28, 1976.19. For Rowlandson's narrative, see RG, 1973.31, and for Milton's epic, RG, 1969.34.

38. For the Hassidic masters and Gregory of Nyssa, see RG, 1973.29, 1978.24; for Aristotle and Augustine, AB, 1982.13 and 1981.15; for Brown and Brown, RG, 1970.28, and AB, 1983.44; for Dewey and James, RG, 1975.12, and AB, 1983.21; for Eddy and Finney, AB, 1983.18, and RG, 1969.19; for Freud and Skinner, AB, 1981.40, and RG, 1974.41; for Niebuhr and Royce, RG, 1976.41, and AB, 1983.37; for Huck Finn and Himmler, RG, 1974.3, and AB, 1980.32. For the Yale Edition, see PW, 517–23.

39. Elizabeth G. Speare, *The Prospering* (Boston: Houghton, Mifflin, 1967), 284, 306, 329.

40. Elizabeth D. Dodds, *Marriage to a Difficult Man* (Philadelphia: Westminster Press, 1971), 8–9, 11, 96, 162.

41. Robert Lowell, "Jonathan Edwards in Western Massachusetts," *For the Union Dead* (New York: Farrar, Straus and Giroux, 1964), 40–4; idem, "The Worst Sinner, Jonathan Edwards's God," *History* (New York: Farrar, Straus and Giroux, 1973), 73. Additionally, there is a discursive life of Edwards cast as verse: RG, 1967.11.

42. Andrew Hudgins, "Awaiting Winter Visitors: Jonathan Edwards, 1749," *New Yorker*, 24 (March 1980), 46.

43. Mary Ann Waters, "Sermon for Jonathan Edwards," *Yankee*, October 1985, 218. For the triptych journey, see AB, 1988.5; and for the sonnet, see David Levin, "To Jonathan Edwards," in R. W. Crump, ed., *Order in Variety: Essays and Poems in Honor of Donald E. Stanford* (Newark: University of Delaware Press, 1991), 74.

44. For Dickinson, see AB, 1990.30; for Emerson, AB, 1991.15; for Melville, AB, 1991.20. Robert W. Jenson, *America's Theologian: A Recommendation of Jonathan Edwards* (New York: Oxford University Press, 1988); Philip F. Gura, *Jonathan Edwards: America's Evangelical* (New York: Hill and Wang, 2005).

45. William M. Vaughn, "The Sublime and the Dutiful: Ethics and Excess from Edwards to Melville" (Ph.D. dissertation, University of Illinois at Urbana-Champaign, 1998); Mary L. S. Huffer, "Emily Dickinson's Experiential Poetics" (Ph.D. dissertation, University of Florida, 2002); James Good, "John Dewey, Jonathan Edwards, and New England Theology" (Ph.D. dissertation, Rice University, 2001); Kendra G. Hotz, "The Metaphysics of Otherness: A Comparative Examination of the Thought of Alfred North Whitehead and Jonathan Edwards" (Ph.D. dissertation, Emory University, 2000); Julie Whitman, "Cotton Mather and Jonathan Edwards: Philosophy, Science, and Puritan Theology" (Ph.D. dissertation, Indiana University, 1993); Douglas A. Sweeney, "Nathaniel William Taylor and the Edwardsean Tradition" (Ph.D. dissertation, Vanderbilt University, 1995).

46. Allyn L. Ricketts, "The Primacy of Revelation in the Philosophical Theology of Jonathan Edwards" (Ph.D. dissertation, Westminister Theological Seminary, 1995); Richard M. Weber, "'One-Step' Salvation: The Knowledge of God and Faith in the Theology of Jonathan Edwards" (Ph.D. dissertation, Marquette University, 2002); Stephen J. Nichols, "'An Absolute Sense of Certainty': The Holy Spirit and the Apologetics of Jonathan Edwards" (Ph.D. dissertation, Westminster Theological Seminary, 2000); Thomas F. Atchison, "Towards Developing a Theology of Christian Assurance from 1 John with Reference to Jonathan Edwards" (Ph.D. dissertation, Trinity Evangelical School, 2004); Robert E. Brown, "Connecting the Sacred with the Profane: Jonathan Edwards and the Scripture History" (Ph.D. dissertation, University of Iowa, 1999); David E. Clark, "Leveling Mountains, Drying up Rivers: Jonathan Edwards' Historiography Applied" (Ph.D. dissertation, Westminster Theological Seminary, 2001); F. Allan Story, Jr., "Promoting Revival: Jonathan Edwards and Preparation for Revival" (Ph.D. dissertation, Westminster Theological Seminary, 1994; Christopher W. Morgan, "The Application of Jonathan Edwards's Theological Method to Annihilationism in Contemporary Evangelicalism" (Ph.D. dissertation, Mid-American Baptist Theological Seminary, 1999).

47. For the Yale edition to 2003, see PW, 524–36. *The "Miscellanies," 1153–1360*, was added in 2004. For the "Readers," see PW, 495, 499.

48. For *Sinners*, see PW, 122, 124; for *Distinguishing Marks*, PW, 83, 85; for the first three selections, PW, 496–7, 501; for the facsimile, PW, 512J. For the fiction, see Edna Gerstner, *Jonathan and Sarah: An Uncommon Union* (Morgan, PA: Soli Deo Gloria, 1995); Norma Jean Lutz, *Maggie's Choice: Jonathan Edwards and the Great Awakening* (Uhrichsville, OH: Barbour, 1997), p. 134. A 1999 reprint adds the subtitle.

49. Wheaton College, Wheaton, IL, Fall 1984: Hatch and Stout, eds., *Jonathan Edwards and the American Experience*; Yale University, New Haven, CT, February 22–4, 1990: Barbara B. Oberg and Harry S. Stout, eds. *Benjamin Franklin, Jonathan Edwards, and the Representation of American Culture* (New York: Oxford University Press, 1993); Indiana University, Bloomington, IN, June 2–4, 1994: Stephen J. Stein, ed., *Jonathan Edwards's Writings: Text, Context, Interpretation* (Bloomington: Indiana University Press, 1996); University of Miami, Coral Gables, Fl, March 9–11, 2000: Kling and Sweeney, eds. *Jonathan Edwards*; Arch Street Friends Meetinghouse, Philadelphia, PA, October 3–5, 1996: Sang Hyun Lee and Allen C. Guelzo, eds., *Edwards in Our Time: Jonathan Edwards and the Shaping of American Religion* (Grand Rapids, MI: William B. Eerdmans, 1999); Westminister Presbyterian Church, Lancaster, PA, October 26–8, 2001: D. G. Hart, Sean Michael Lucas, and Stephen J. Nichols, eds., *The Legacy of Jonathan Edwards: American Religion and the Evangelical Tradition* (Grand Rapids, MI: Baker Academic, 2003); Princeton, NJ, April 10–12, 2003, "Jonathan Edwards the Theologian"; Minneapolis, MN, October 2003: John Piper and Justin Taylor, eds., *A God Entranced Vision of All Things: The Legacy of Jonathan Edwards* (Wheaton, IL: Crossway, 2004); Library of Congress, Washington, DC, October 3–4, 2003: Harry S. Stout, Kenneth P. Minkema, and Caleb J. D. Maskell, eds., *Jonathan Edwards at 300: Essays on the Tercentenary of His Birth* (Lanham, MD, University Press of America, 2005).

50. Stephen H. Daniel, *The Philosophy of Jonathan Edwards: A Study in Divine Semiotics* (Bloomington: Indiana University Press, 1994); Anri Morimoto, *Jonathan Edwards and the Catholic Vision of Salvation* (University Park: Pennsylvania State University, 1995); Gerald R. McDermott, *Jonathan Edwards Confronts the Gods: Christian Theology, Enlightenment Religion, and Non-Christian Faiths* (New York: Oxford University Press, 2000); Louis J. Mitchell, *Jonathan Edwards on the Experience of Beauty* (Princeton: Princeton Theological Seminary, 2003); Helen K. Hosier, *Jonathan Edwards, the Great Awakener* (Uhrichsville, OH: Barbour, 1999); Stephen R. Holmes, *God of Grace and God of Glory* (Edinburgh: Clark, 2000); Mark A. Noll, *America's God: from Jonathan Edwards to Abraham Lincoln* (New York: Oxford University Press, 2002). Among the reprints, see Elisabeth D. Dodds, *Marriage to a Difficult Man* (Laurel, MS: Audubon Press, 2004); Perry Miller, *Jonathan Edwards* (Lincoln: University of Nebraska Press, 2005).

51. See "Jonathan Edwards: The Warm-Hearted Genius behind the Great Awakening," *Christian History* 22 (1:2002): 1–47; "Focus: Jonathan Edwards," *Journal of Religious Ethics* 31 (Summer 2003): 181–321; M. X. Lesser, "'An Honor Too Great': Jonathan Edwards in Print Abroad," in Kling and Sweeney, eds., *Jonathan Edwards*, 297–319; Michael J. McClymond, "The Protean Puritan: The Works of Jonathan Edwards, Volumes 8 to 16," *Religious Studies Review* 24 (Oct. 1998): 361–7; Roland A. Delattre, "Recent Scholarship on Jonathan Edwards," *Religious Studies Review* 24 (October 1998): 369–75; David O. Filson, "Jonathan Edwards for Pastors: A Bibliographic Essay," *Presbyterian* 24 (1998): 110–18; Sean M. Lucas, "Jonathan Edwards between Church and Academy," in Hart, Lucas, and Nichols, eds. *The Legacy of Jonathan Edwards*, 228–47; Kenneth P. Minkema, "Jonathan Edwards in the Twentieth Century," *Journal of the Evangelical Society* 47 (December 2004): 659–87.

52. George M. Marsden, *Jonathan Edwards, A Life* (New Haven: Yale University Press, 2003), 1–2, 4, 9–10.

53. Allen, *Jonathan Edwards*, v; Donald Weber, "The Figure of Jonathan Edwards," *American Quarterly* 35 (Winter 1983): 564; Henry F. May, "Jonathan Edwards and America," in Hatch and Stout, eds., *Jonathan Edwards*, 30.

15 Edwards's intellectual legacy

STEPHEN D. CROCCO

Students of Jonathan Edwards now look back to the tercentenary celebrations of his birth in 2003 as the culmination of nearly fifty years of effort to prepare a critical edition of his works. The publication of several volumes in the Yale Edition and conferences in Washington, D.C., Princeton, and elsewhere that year heralded Edwards's many contributions and his ongoing significance. For some, the publication of George M. Marsden's *Jonathan Edwards: A Life* was the high point. Finally, there was a usable, modern biography of a colonial figure who shaped his own era and continues to shape America and the world nearly 250 years after his death. Marsden's book made the cover of the *New York Times Book Review*.[1] Edwards had arrived!

Those who know the history of Edwards's reception know he did not always occupy such a prominent place in the national psyche. Generations of scholars have learned a *common* account of Edwards's legacy that goes something like this. Edwards's theological legacy died out by the end of the nineteenth century. He began the twentieth century with few friends and plenty of critics. His greatness was admired from a distance, if at all. In the 1920s, he was called an anachronism for his failure to imbibe the budding democratic spirit of his own age. Edwards was pitied for being a theologian when he could have turned his prodigious mental abilities to philosophy, science, or belles lettres. He was scorned for degrading God and human beings by his insistence on the essential truths of Calvinism. Yet for the most part, he was ignored.[2]

In the 1930s, the common account continues, when world events were challenging scientific and progressive conceptions of history, religion got a fresh hearing. Edwards finally and suddenly received attention from unexpected sources, namely Neo-Orthodox theologians. The agnostic Harvard professor, Perry Miller, gave Edwards a boost with his 1949 biography and almost single-handedly rescued Edwards and colonial New England from years of neglect. Miller devoted the rest of his life to the Yale Edition of Edwards's *Works*, initiating a midcentury revival of interest in him. The edition was fast out of the gate in the 1950s, stumbled in the 1960s, only to regain its balance in the 1980s, creating the momentum that led to celebrations of the tercentenary of his birth in 2003 and the near completion of the Yale Edition.

While this common account has been serviceable, it tends to minimize the kinds and number of conversations about Edwards's legacy among scholars interested in religion. The argument of this chapter is that Edwards did not go through a period of visibility, followed by a period in the shadows, only to be made visible again. Rather, it is that Edwards had been the subject of a steady stream of attention from a variety of sources, including intellectuals interested in religion who were not necessarily interested in theology or ecclesiology. In the first half of the twentieth century, literary scholars, philosophers, and historians made numerous efforts to come to terms with Edwards's legacy for their own descriptive and constructive work. Although Edwards was certainly ignored by some and lifted up by others as a negative example, there were scholars from a variety of disciplines who debated his legacy and how to reshape it to fit current needs.

In arguing this point, this chapter selects a few episodes from the Edwards historiography to illustrate distinctive debates or positions promoted by intellectuals from the turn of the twentieth century to the present. The second section of the chapter sets the nineteenth-century background for these discussions, which included dismissals of Edwards for his imprecatory sermons and attempts to strip him of his pessimism about human nature. The third section samples debates about Edwards's legacy from the first three decades of the last century when he was often dismissed as a tragic figure, but sometimes embraced as a timeless thinker. Section four considers the so-called "Neo-Orthodox" recovery, where Edwards was positioned to interrogate a modern but chastened culture. The fifth section considers Perry Miller and his claim that Edwards was a man ahead of his time, and possibly our time, in spite of being a colonial pastor. The sixth and final section discusses efforts after Miller to produce a critical edition of Edwards's works. Since the 1980s, the Yale Edition office became a clearinghouse for Edwards studies and sponsor of national Edwards conferences.

This chapter is best read alongside M. X. Lesser's *Jonathan Edwards: A Reference Guide* and *Jonathan Edwards: An Annotated Bibliography, 1979–1993*.[3] These reading guides, with bibliographic essays and extensive lists of secondary literature, reveal virtually every nook and cranny where Edwards's influence has been felt. But rather than summarize Lesser and the scholarship that appeared since his second book – an impossible task and a continual temptation – this chapter will spell out some of the cultural, intellectual, institutional, and even personal factors that prompted twists and turns in discussions of Edwards's legacy among religious intellectuals.

This chapter mostly bypasses discussions of Edwards's reputation in ecclesiastical settings or in purely theological scholarship, though hard lines between theological and wider intellectual interests are difficult to draw, especially in the nineteenth century.

NINETEENTH-CENTURY BACKGROUND

In 1757, following the death of Aaron Burr, trustees of the College of New Jersey in Princeton tried to persuade Edwards to assume the presidency. One appeal to Edwards must have been the opportunity to institutionalize experiential Reformed thought as an organizing principle for life and as the basis for engaging Enlightenment faith in a setting at the heart of the colonies. His brief tenure (as well as that of his immediate and sympathetic successors) meant that his intellectual program had little chance to grow. When John Witherspoon became president at Princeton in 1768, he enthusiastically rooted out vestiges of Edwards's Lockean epistemology in favor of Scottish Realism – a tradition Edwards knew and treated with suspicion.[4] Francis Hutcheson, for example, did not exclude God; but God was mentioned "so slightly" that it gave Edwards reason to be skeptical.[5] With Edwards unseated in Princeton, the center of his influence shifted north, where he reigned as the titular head of various New England theological and philosophical traditions.[6] Denominational colleges and seminaries, including Yale, were homes of a vital intellectual culture directly inspired by Edwards. *Freedom of the Will, Original Sin, The Nature of True Virtue,* and *The End for Which God Created the World* were high-level contributions in discussions of "mental philosophy," epistemology, metaphysics, and ethics. He was the original genius and inspiration of the New England schools, but not the rule by which all truth was measured. Some of Edwards's followers embraced his innovations, but not his orthodoxy. Others embraced his orthodoxy, but not his innovations. Over the years, debates raged over the meaning of what Edwards wrote, whether his disciples departed from him in significant ways, what he would have written had he lived longer, and whether or not his disciples hid a manuscript which revealed his heterodoxy.[7] Edwards's ideas were also spread far and wide by missionaries and by educators eager to take their teacher's ideas into the new territories. With the help of zealous students, impressive progeny, and a remarkable written legacy, Edwards put a powerful stamp on nineteenth-century New England churches, colleges, social service organizations, and politics.[8] This activity, buttressed by judgments about what was valuable or not, or true to Edwards or not, reached its apex, at least symbolically, with the celebrations of the bicentennial of his birth in 1903.

It is undeniable that by the turn of the twentieth century the native New England theological traditions were changing and many would say declining. Theology itself was not in decline. However, the long line of New England theologies with Edwards at the head – the New Divinity, the Old Calvinists, the New Haven Theology – was rapidly giving way at places like Yale and Andover to new theologies and philosophies influenced by Enlightenment religion. Nothing in Edwards's writings and reputation aided the decline, distanced him more from enlightened readers, and prevented him from having a wider hearing than his imprecatory sermons, particularly his widely published *Sinners in the Hands of an Angry God,* delivered in Enfield, Massachusetts, in 1741. In 1901, at the 150th anniversary of Edwards's dismissal from the Northampton Church, Yale Divinity professor George Park Fisher noted that the appreciative gathering was "reparation for somewhat hard treatment of him in bygone days" – a barrage of harsh words for the author of the Enfield sermon. Fisher went on to say "that in this country so many of 'the merely literary' – as [Cardinal John Henry] Newman would style them – appear to know nothing of his writings save passages in the Enfield sermon. They would find, if they looked for them, in [Anglican theologian] Jeremy Taylor, 'the Shakespeare of preachers,' delineations of future torment which rival the pictures of terror in that sermon."[9]

In spite of Fisher's defense of Edwards's imprecatory language – and he was not the only one defending him who employed an "everyone did it then" argument – *Sinners* was the one piece by Edwards known by everyone. It was a rallying call in just about every discussion. This sermon was often pointed to as *the* example of the offensive character of his theology, or as something to be apologized for or "gotten over" before he could be appreciated. Cheap shots at Edwards abound in the secondary literature, much of it citing what more than one called the worst sermon of all time. One of the harshest critics was Oliver Wendell Holmes, of whom one defender of Edwards wrote, "He has left argument . . . [to adopt] a severity toward Jonathan Edwards which is nothing short of a gag."[10]

Some religious intellectuals seemed to deal with the author of *Sinners* by accepting him for what he was – an eighteenth-century Augustinian theologian with remarkable talents – and left it at that. To them, the "offense" question was largely misplaced. If they had a motto, it would have been, "Let Edwards be a figure of his time!" Edwards was not an anachronism as much as those who insisted on taking him to task for being an honest son of the eighteenth century – albeit a son of the early eighteenth century. Yet, it was not uncommon for these scholars to add a hypothetical lamentation, often without rancor: "Ah, if Edwards had only turned his prodigious abilities away from theology to philosophy, science, or literature!" Perhaps Fisher had one of his colleagues in mind, Yale professor of English Henry A. Beers, who published an *Outline Sketch of American Literature* in 1887. Although Edwards's writings belonged to theology, Beers argued they had merit for the student of American literature. "[T]here is an intensity and a spiritual elevation about them, apart from the profundity and acuteness of the thought, which lift them here and there into the finer ether of purely emotional or imaginative art."[11] Of course, Beers's point was that Edwards excelled in the art of using words to describe terrors instead of comforts.[12]

In 1931, Henry Seidel Canby, lecturer in English at Yale, published a sympathetic and sensitive account of Edwards in his introduction to *Classic Americans: A Study of Eminent American Writers from Irving to Whitman*. Canby even took a dig at those who dismissed Edwards as a hellfire preacher. These critics, wrote Canby, "have clearly read no further in his writing, whereas the weight of the New England will upon later literature is better explained by his towering metaphysics." According to Canby, Edwards was a first-rate Calvinist mind at the end of the period of Calvinist dominance in New England. His hellfire sermons and passionate devotion to study were marks of the age and were not incompatible with Edwards being an affectionate human being. In spite of his enthusiasm for Edwards and his desire to see him portrayed fairly, Canby regrets that his theological agenda kept his literary instincts "powerfully suppressed" and thus "bent a first-rate talent to other ends."[13] Canby's was the kind of regret that did not make a normative claim on Edwards. He was interested in Edwards's ideas for their own sake. He approached Edwards in a detached fashion with a kind of objectivity that accompanied good academic work. Scholars like him may have had their own religious commitments, but they bracketed them for the sake of description, saving normative engagement with Edwards for more appropriate venues.

At the turn of the last century, George A. Gordon, pastor of the Old South Church, Boston, was not willing to hand Edwards over completely to detached scholars. Gordon embraced liberal Christianity; however, he argued that a viable New England theology needed to be tempered by the best insights of the great Edwards. In his 1901 essay, "The Significance of Edwards Today," Gordon set out the contours of an enlightened Edwardsean theology.[14] Before Edwards could be restored to preeminence as a leader of a truly modern theology, he had to escape the control of the repristinators who let his answers set the questions of the day. Why? Because, Gordon said, as "a whole, Edwards is incredible, impossible. He is nearly as much in the wrong as he is in the right. He carries his vast treasure in the earthen vessel of radical inconsistency and fundamental error." Gordon wrote that the truth in Edwards "is massive and precious, but it lies as gold lies in the rock. It must be delivered from encompassing error, set free, purified and brought to its full value through the fires of a happier experience." Further, writes Gordon, "The one supreme thing in him that insures his permanence as a teacher is his thought of God. What Being was to Parmenides and Plato, what the one Substance was to Spinoza, what the Absolute was to Hegel, God was to Edwards." Regrettably, according to Gordon, Edwards's great flaw was that his passion for God came at the expense of humanity. "Nothing could be sublimer [sic] than his conception of God at its best; nothing could be more incredible than the treatment to which he subjects the race under God." For this reason, "Edwards thus becomes the theologian of chief interest for our time. All the contradictions that work in the church today are in him forced into fierce antithesis. And in him, too, is the source and promise of deliverance." Edwards, Gordon continues, "is not a temple, he is a quarry. No free man of our time can live in the system of Edwards; but the material in him for building purposes is abundant and much of it is of the highest quality."[15] An Edwards set free from his pessimistic view of human nature could breathe new life into the New England theology. Perhaps it could, but in reality it did not.

EDWARDS IN THE EARLY TWENTIETH CENTURY

The period from the Civil War to the 1930s was the heyday of liberal Protestantism in America. In *The University Gets Religion,* D. G. Hart argues, "As sentimental and moralistic as it could sound, Protestant educators [in this period] were committed to propagating at their institutions an Enlightened Christianity that would yield all of the positive aspects of Christian teaching without the theological baggage."[16] Perhaps it is more accurate to say these educators were committed to a liberal Protestantism that would create new forms of Christian teaching compatible with enlightened interests. As discussions about the broader American tradition emerged in Protestant-oriented colleges and universities across the country in the late-nineteenth century – founding myths, the meaning of the American experience, and notions of American destiny – scholars in a variety of relatively new academic disciplines found they had a stake in the shape of Edwards's legacy. University divinity schools and, later, religion departments fostered this interest; but they were hardly the only places in the university where religious questions, including questions about Edwards's legacy and reputation, were valued. Arguments about the importance of colonial New England for understanding American culture – which were made by a host of scholars, including Perry Miller – now seem curiously quaint and even downright chauvinistic given current sensitivities to the contributions of other peoples and places. But in the first five decades of the last century, such arguments were routinely made by the enlightened Protestant establishment seeking to export the best of American civilization to the world. In that context, scholars flocked to discussions about what was interesting, important, and salvageable in Edwards for America's mission to the world.

These discussions are often missing from the common account of Edwards's legacy which by the early twentieth century was supposedly lying on its deathbed. If Edwards was "recovered" by Neo-Orthodox theologians in the 1930s, as the common account suggests, the question is, "From what did he need to be recovered?" It was certainly not from neglect. Take, for example, a sample of publications in a five-year period from 1927 to 1932, that is, the period before the beginning of a so-called recovery of Edwards. In 1927, Vernon Louis Parrington published "The Anachronism of Jonathan Edwards," perhaps the most famous example of the detractor literature.[17] A year later, Winfield Burggraaff and W. A. Visser't Hooft both published historical studies claiming Edwards played a positive, though unwitting, role in the development of American liberal thought. Visser't Hooft wrote, "The place of Edwards in the history of American thought, both theological and philosophical, is one of the most hotly debated and interesting problems in the history of American thinking."[18] The place of Edwards *is* – not *was* – one of the most interesting problems. This was a remarkable statement for a figure supposedly in eclipse. Henry Bamford Parkes published in 1930 his diatribe *Jonathan Edwards: The Fiery Puritan*, in which he argued that Edwards had no positive influence on America.[19] That same year philosopher Herbert W. Schneider dismissed Parkes' book and published a largely positive account of Edwards's enduring idealism in *The Puritan Mind*.[20] William Warren Sweet's *The Story of Religion in America* also appeared in 1930, giving Edwards a major role in the narrative.[21]

In 1931 Charles Angoff entered the debate over Edwards's legacy with his conclusion that Edwards made no contribution to enlightened American thought.[22] Edward H. Dewey remarked on what Edwards could have done in literature had he not, sadly, given his abilities over to Calvinism.[23] In "The Radicalism of Jonathan Edwards," Frederic Carpenter saw expressions of Edwards's profound mysticism in Transcendentalism, Walt Whitman, William James, and others.[24] Harvey G. Townsend described Edwards's unique and positive contributions to American philosophy in the same year.[25] In publications in 1931 and 1932, Joseph Haroutunian praised Edwards's radically theocentric Calvinism.[26] Also in 1932, Arthur Cushman McGiffert, Jr., published *Jonathan Edwards* – a "balanced" biography in contrast to Parkes – showing Edwards's enduring influence in America.[27] These works, representing expressions of general contempt, endorsements of his distant contributions, efforts to refashion him, attempts to give him his own voice, and so forth, are a sample of Edwards traditions and the claims and counter-claims made about his legacy from roughly the bicentennial of his birth in 1903 to the Edwards "revival" in the 1950s centered on the Yale Edition of his *Works*.

For many scholars interested in religion, the issue was not about accusing Edwards or forgetting him, as his detractors suggested. Rather it was about how he should be remembered. Was Edwards a false start, a road block, a bridge figure, or a destination? Upon whom did he have an influence? Who carried his work forward? Who are his true followers today?[28] Of what use was Edwards in a modern intellectual program? The question, "Was Edwards a stepping stone or a hindrance to enlightened thought?" became a matter of widespread interest. There was no denying Edwards was a towering figure on the American landscape. Yet did he serve any positive purpose other than simply as an illustration of a first-rate Calvinist mind at the end of the Puritan period?

There was plenty of interest in Edwards as an early illustration of American genius. His capacity for observing the natural world won him the admiration of historians of science. Since sermons were a major genre of colonial writing, and since Edwards bridged the beginning and end of the colonial period, scholars of American literature had to deal with him. Historians tried to connect the dots between Puritanism, Edwards, Deism, the American Revolution, Transcendentalism, and beyond. Psychologists saw in Edwards's writings some rudimentary forms of psychoanalysis.[29] Comparisons and contrasts between Edwards and the Mathers, Benjamin Franklin, and Ralph Waldo Emerson were common. Some emphasized patterns of continuity, whereas others emphasized sharp differences. Edwards and Franklin were the subjects of numerous comparative studies asking what each contributed to or represented about America. Most claimed both men represented something essential, if not permanent, about the nation.[30]

Edwards's ability as a metaphysician gave him pride of place in discussions of the origin and development of American philosophy. Some thought the question whether Edwards was in debt to George Berkeley's idealism was *the* question in the history of American speculative thought. Edwards's various roles in narratives supporting American philosophical traditions gave credence to Visser't Hooft's remark about his prominence. Edwards's reputation as the first American philosopher was secure. In much of the nineteenth century, the arguments in *Freedom of the Will* and *The Nature of True Virtue* were frequently considered in discussions and courses on moral philosophy. Such courses, often taught by college and university presidents, eventually gave way to the creation of departments of philosophy. Many American

philosophers who were part of the enlightened Protestant establishment –
including William James and Josiah Royce – remained open to religious
concerns well into the twentieth century.[31] And Edwards remained a subject
of interest in this context. However, less attention was paid to his "philosophical" writings as such and more to the enduring questions associated with his
life. James was familiar with Edwards's writings on revival and conversion
and referred to him with a respectful impartiality.[32]

In 1911, Royce declared that before James, there were only two representative American philosophers: Jonathan Edwards and Ralph Waldo Emerson.
According to Royce,

> Edwards was an originator. For he actually rediscovered some of the
> world's profoundest ideas regarding God and humanity simply by
> reading for himself the meaning of his own religious experience....
> If the sectarian theological creed that he defended was to our minds
> narrow, what he himself saw was very far-reaching and profound....
> Edwards and Emerson had given tongue to the meaning of two
> different stages of our American culture. And these were thus far our
> only philosophical voices.[33]

James completed Royce's triumvirate and secured Edwards's place in the
process.

Enlightened readers struggled to get past what Royce judiciously called
"narrow" in Edwards. Since Edwards as a "whole" was unpalatable, many
proposed to put Edwards in a refiner's fire (separating precious metal from
dross) or in a threshing machine (separating wheat from chaff). Liberal
Protestantism and Enlightenment religion stoked the fires and drove the
thresher. Invariably, it was aspects of Edwards's Calvinist orthodoxy that
were to be burned up and discarded.[34] Another approach, using a slightly
different image, was to peel back the various layers around Edwards to identify his essential or fundamental insight. When the extraneous layers and
various accretions, mainly owing to his historical context as a Puritan pastor,
were stripped away and peeled back, Edwards's deep God-consciousness and
natural mysticism were exposed and with them the raw power of his mind.
In his 1926 survey, *The American Spirit in Letters,* Yale professor of English
Stanley Thomas Williams wrote, "As a thinker and writer he stands like a
peak between two ages. In one pure, strong mind met all the ideals, all the
aspiration of Puritan New England. Edwards is, in the broadest sense of the
term, the supreme Puritan.... He also looks forward.... For, strip from him
his system of Calvinism, and he is a transcendentalist."[35]

Visser't Hooft thought Edwards was interesting and important because
there was something in him besides the Calvinist. "It is the Edwards of

mystic experience who writes in terms of sublime personal piety of the wonderful immediacy between God and the human soul . . . who gives a new formulation to the doctrine of divine immanence."[36] This distinction was close to the heart of the "enlightened" Edwards tradition – a rival to earlier New England traditions as well as efforts by repristinators and conservatives to promote his legacy. Theories of an enlightened Edwards later diverged over the question of whether Edwards's doctrine of sin was a liability or an asset in understanding the human condition. Efforts to separate Edwards from his Calvinism by burning, threshing, peeling, stripping, and chiseling produced some sort of *Ur-Edwards* – pre-Christian in nature – a figure in the company of Plato, Dante, Spinoza, Hegel, and other timeless thinkers.

In the early twentieth century, the jury was out on whether Emerson would have made the pantheon of the world's timeless thinkers, but an Edwards stripped of his Calvinism was a shoo-in. These ideas were echoed by I. Woodbridge Riley, Herbert W. Schneider, and other professional philosophers who took religion seriously. Riley, a professor of philosophy at Vassar College, was no friend to Edwards's brand of philosophical theology. However, in publications in the early decades of the twentieth century, he professed an admiration for Edwards's idealism, pantheism, monism, and mysticism.[37] Columbia philosopher Herbert W. Schneider looked to the New England Puritan tradition to understand "the specious present" that is "unintelligible unless it be illuminated by the past."[38] Schneider was reacting to the sudden demise of the New England theological tradition, or, as he calls it, "the mental world of New England." By 1930, the problems and ideas of Puritan New England – and the Edwardsean traditions associated with that world – have "all but disappeared. . . . Even Emerson, who helped dig the grave, already stands cold and classic, an immortal monument over a buried past. New teachers, new ideas, and other languages, have shaped our minds. Our grand-parents are aliens in our country and we in theirs."[39] Schneider had no use for Puritan theology. However, by studying the Puritans he sought to revive an imaginative adventure of eternal ideas. More than anything, it was Edwards's idealism that captured Schneider's attention. "Esthetic categories are the last which one might expect to find in a rigid Calvinist philosophy, written in New England, by a Puritan of Puritans. Yet it is precisely on the theory of beauty, of harmony, of proportion, and of love, that Edwards now erected his imposing idealism."[40] Schneider also valued Edwards's ideas because they offered a profound description of the cosmic tragedy of human experience and a realistic response to optimistic views of the human condition. In this light, Edwards's ideas were brilliant and stimulating again. Schneider had far fewer positive things to say about Edwards's followers or Edwards himself.[41]

NEO-ORTHODOX RECOVERY

The common account of Edwards historiography bypassed many of the active discussions of his contributions in favor of focusing on his dilapidated reputation as a reflection of a general lack of interest in American religious history in the 1920s. In that account, Vernon Louis Parrington in 1927 ("Edwards as an anachronism"[42]) and Henry Bamford Parkes in 1930 ("Edwards as a blight upon posterity"[43]) delivered knockout blows to Edwards's already reeling legacy. Then, seemingly out of nowhere, American "Neo-Orthodox" thinkers Joseph Haroutunian and H. Richard Niebuhr gave him a fresh hearing that struck a chord with Perry Miller a decade later.[44] Since Haroutunian and Niebuhr were first- and second-generation immigrants, respectively, they came to the study of American religious history with different eyes and agendas than Edwards's usual interlocutors. They had no natural entree to the cultural enclaves where Edwards's influence was felt. Arguably, they had more in common with the Polish or Italian immigrants in Northampton than the descendants of the Mayflower who, on the two-hundredth anniversary of his birth, celebrated Edwards as a cultural icon. In that sense only, their studies did come out of "nowhere."

Haroutunian came to Edwards through debates about American religion that were still in vogue at Columbia University's Department of Philosophy and Union Theological Seminary. Although naturalism was in ascendance at Columbia, Haroutunian's mentors, including Herbert Schneider, published on Edwards as part of longstanding discussions about the New England religious tradition. John Dewey was a fixture at Columbia when Haroutunian was still a graduate student. Dewey's pilgrimage from liberal Congregationalist to religious humanist may have been well known.[45] Haroutunian's *Piety versus Moralism: The Passing of the New England Theology* was best seen as one in a series of rival narratives of the New England tradition, taking into full account the claims and counterclaims made by many others about the legacy of Edwards. It is probably best viewed as a counternarrative to Frank Hugh Foster's *A Genetic History of New England Theology* and a supplement to his teacher's *The Puritan Mind*.[46] In *Piety versus Moralism*, Haroutunian argued that the vital intellectual piety of Edwards – his Calvinism or theocentrism – was gradually transformed by his followers. "It was the faith of the fathers ruined by the faith of their children," a faith that was not Calvinism. In the nineteenth century, "[g]ood and intelligent Christians discarded such Calvinism with little remorse. They were busy men, proclaiming the fatherhood of God, the brotherhood of men, and the moral ideal set up by the 'gentle Jesus'.... They were great optimists."[47] Foster and others were right about the death of the New England theology. However, they were wrong about the cause. According to Haroutunian, it was liberalism, not Calvinism, that killed it. There never seems to have been a time when the young Haroutunian struggled to give up liberalism and become orthodox in a new way. If anything, he went from being an agnostic to being a "happy Calvinist," but one with deep feelings for the tragic sense of life.[48]

H. Richard Niebuhr first came to Edwards in the context of efforts to "Americanize" his midwestern, German, immigrant denomination. As a student at Eden Theological Seminary, he learned that to understand America one needed to understand Edwards.[49] Niebuhr made Edwards the central figure of his 1937 volume, *The Kingdom of God in America*. And thus Edwards became the keystone of Niebuhr's repudiation of the strictly economic, philosophical, religious, and sociological explanations of American Christianity in his much heralded 1929 book, *The Social Sources of Denominationalism*. Like Haroutunian, Niebuhr offered a rival interpretation of the American religious tradition that infused theology – indeed infused "God" – back into history with Edwards pointing the way. In the preface to *The Kingdom of God in America*, Niebuhr wrote, "A final conviction [underlying the book] is that American Christianity and American culture cannot be understood at all save on the basis of faith in a sovereign, living, loving God. Apart from God the whole thing is meaningless and might as well not have been." Niebuhr hoped his book would serve as a "stepping stone" to the work of a "Jonathan Edwards *redivivus* who will bring down to our time the *History of the Work of Redemption*."[50] Whether Niebuhr was ever a chastened liberal who then embraced Neo-Orthodoxy is a debated question. What is clear is that as Niebuhr distanced himself from the theology of his mentors and colleagues at Yale, he found Edwards to be a profoundly realistic theocentric thinker. With few exceptions, Edwards's God was Niebuhr's God.

Haroutunian and Niebuhr were not interested in minimizing Edwards's nineteenth-century followers as much as they were interested in maximizing Edwards's God. As they considered various accounts of the origins and destiny of America, they looked back and found Edwards. Looking for the roots of a spiritual crisis in America, Haroutunian and Niebuhr were impressed by how Edwards resisted anthropocentric and humanistic onslaughts in his day. They believed readers attuned to the events of the day and the great traditions of the church had much to learn from Edwards. By portraying him as the lonely Calvinist or the great religious thinker in a sea of mediocre ones, Haroutunian and Niebuhr were not doing poor historical work. Instead, they formed a theory about why the earlier Edwardsean traditions had gone to seed. In effect, Haroutunian and Niebuhr turned the tables on many of Edwards's interpreters. In a stunning move – the great contribution of

Neo-Orthodoxy – they submitted the traditions of the repristinators, the New England theologians, the detractors, the enlightened Edwardseans, and, by extension, their own theologies, to Jonathan Edwards, who was the refiner's fire and the threshing machine. Their theory that just about all of Edwards made more sense than modern enlightened theologies, particularly those of the optimistic variety, struck a chord with a generation of thinkers. Under the inspiration of Reinhold Niebuhr and with the guidance of Joseph Haroutunian and H. Richard Niebuhr, numerous enlightened readers, chastened and otherwise, came to think about Edwards and American religious history in fresh ways. Many were impressed. In the years immediately following their publications, neither Haroutunian's nor Niebuhr's books figured a great deal in publications on Edwards. This gives credence to the idea that their place in the story to "recover" Edwards has been read back from the vantage point of Miller's years.

Neither Haroutunian nor Niebuhr ever wrote much specifically about Edwards. *Piety versus Moralism* was about Edwards's followers, and *The Kingdom of God in America* covered a lot of ground. Haroutunian embraced certain aspects of Edwards's theology in his second book, *Wisdom and Folly in Religion,* a confrontational Protestant critique of twentieth-century theology and culture. As part of his assessment, he blasted liberal, orthodox, and Neo-Orthodox theologies as being helplessly anthropocentric. He called Edwards an advocate of "tough-minded religion ... perhaps the first and greatest of those who sought to incorporate the spirit of modern science and empiricism into Christian theology."[51] Niebuhr wrote the preface to *Wisdom and Folly in Religion.* There he asserted, "Luther, Calvin and Edwards – read with a humble desire to understand their meaning rather than with a sense of superiority – have illuminated for the author the state of every man in need of God. In them he has found that resolute facing of the hard and unpalatable facts about man and God which the twentieth-century mind demands."[52] Haroutunian abandoned efforts to write a book on Edwards years later when he found himself embroiled in contemporary theological discussions.

Niebuhr wrote little specifically about Edwards. Yet he relied heavily upon him as a conversation partner, especially in his writings on faith. His most important piece on Edwards was a sermon preached in 1958 on the bicentennial of his death. In "The Anachronism of Jonathan Edwards," Niebuhr asked why people were gathering to honor his memory if they were not willing to honor the cause for which he stood, and that cause was "nothing less than the glory of God." Niebuhr admitted modern people "[w]ill concede perhaps that man is as wicked as Edwards said. What we do not know – or do not yet know – is that God is as holy as Edwards knew him to be."[53]

Incidentally, both men were invited to edit volumes of Edwards for the Yale Edition. Haroutunian declined the offer, and Niebuhr died before he could get started on his assignment to edit Edwards's ethical writings.

PERRY MILLER AND EDWARDS'S LEGACY

Any account of Edwards's legacy to religious scholarship needs to recognize Perry Miller and his enormous efforts to gain new readers to the author of *Sinners in the Hands of an Angry God.* The common account rightfully gives Miller a major role. However, it treats him as it does the Neo-Orthodox interpreters, as a figure largely without a context. In Miller's case, his great contributions to Edwards scholarship came in the midst of a steady stream of publications on Edwards by others dealing with the same issues as those in the late 1920s and early 1930s. In other words, the debates of the 1920s on Edwards's legacy were still working themselves out in the 1940s.[54]

Miller's career in the Office of Strategic Services during World War II interrupted his general excavations of the New England mind. After the war, Miller resumed his work at Harvard with a new focus on Jonathan Edwards. Miller considered Edwards's theology to be "the supreme achievement of the New England mind...considered philosophically and artistically."[55] In 1947 Miller was preparing Edwards's *Miscellany* 782 ("Sense of the Heart") and *Images and Shadows of Divine Things* for publication.[56] His enthusiasm for Edwards was not based on the well-known treatises and sermons, as important and interesting as they were. Rather, Miller was fascinated by the forward-thinking ideas he believed were buried in unpublished notebooks and manuscripts in the vaults of the Sterling Library at Yale. These manuscripts, when revealed, would open new ways of seeing Edwards and America. His problem was getting Yale University excited about its own greatest son and the treasure-trove of manuscripts in its care.

Miller's *Jonathan Edwards* prompted considerable interest in Edwards when it was published in 1949.[57] Miller judged Ola Winslow's 1940 biography successful in describing Edwards's life.[58] With Winslow's work done, Miller could turn his attention to the mind of Edwards.

> The truth is, Edwards was infinitely more than a theologian. He was one of America's five or six major artists.... If I read him correctly – though Edwards remains, as he was even to himself, an enigma – he repays study because, while he speaks from a primitive religious conception...yet at the same time he speaks from an insight into science and psychology so much ahead of his time that our own can hardly be said to have caught up with him.[59]

Reinhold Niebuhr wrote a very favorable review of the volume; the review highlighted his admiration of Miller as much as Miller's handling of Edwards.[60] Reviews of Miller were generally mixed along the lines that the book was both brilliant and brilliantly wrongheaded. Miller admitted there were problems with his interpretation, arguably his view that Edwards was a closet naturalist.[61] Incidentally, Miller's contention was a variation of the "essence of Edwards" approach favored by enlightened interpreters who looked behind Edwards the theologian for the *real* Edwards. Perhaps the greatest contribution of Miller's biography was that it generated an interest in Edwards that his book could not satisfy.

With his naturalistic interpretation admired but largely discredited, Miller became more interested in giving Edwards his own voice. That was a natural move for Miller, who believed Edwards did not need defenders as much as he needed readers. Nineteenth-century editions of Edwards were still the mainstay of research. However, they left out large amounts of manuscript material. The texts they included often contained editorial errors. Many were "improved" by well-meaning editors. Apart from sending interested readers to the manuscripts at Yale University and Andover Newton Theological School, which was not a very practical solution, the only reliable source Miller could recommend was a reader edited by Clarence H. Faust and Thomas H. Johnson, published in 1935. Incidentally, the editors of that volume thanked Miller for reading a draft of the introduction.[62]

In 1951 there was serious talk of an Edwards edition at Yale with Miller as the general editor. While waiting for funding, Miller planned the edition – determining the size and scope of the project, negotiating with Yale University Press, and lining up potential editors and Editorial Committee members. Norman Holmes Pearson, a professor of American literature, was the "point man" for the edition at Yale. While Pearson's initial estimates of scope were for an edition of fifty to sixty volumes, at that time Miller thought it could be done in twelve to fifteen volumes. Miller was not convinced that everything Edwards wrote needed to be published. Many of the "*Miscellanies*," for example, were simply notes from books that Edwards was reading or extended biblical exegesis. Although there was a ceremonial interest in Edwards at Yale, Miller's task was to translate that interest into a substantial critical edition supported by the university. In 1953, there was no editorial committee, no formal assignments, no office, no support staff, no census of the manuscripts, and still no funding. During this time, Miller did recruit two young church historians to the project. These would-be editors, Thomas A. Schafer and John H. Gerstner, worked on the manuscripts while Miller waited for funding. A grant from the Bollingen Foundation was formally announced in June 1954. A week later, Miller, Pearson, and

Yale Divinity School Dean Liston Pope met to get the newly funded project off the ground.

Much has been made of Miller's agnosticism, though evidence for it is rare. If he was an agnostic, he was a *Protestant* agnostic who gathered around him a committee of more or less Protestant scholars of enlightened and Neo-Orthodox stripes. In fact, there is probably no better illustration of the prominence of the Protestant establishment in academia generally, and Edwards studies in particular, at the midpoint of the twentieth century than the proposals for the original editorial committee of the Yale Edition. When it came time to assemble an Editorial Committee, Miller suggested Yale's Sydney E. Ahlstrom (Lutheran), Chicago's Sidney E. Mead (Unitarian), and Harvard's Amos Wilder (Congregationalist) and George H. Williams (Congregationalist-Unitarian). Pearson (Congregationalist) suggested Yale's John E. Smith (Episcopalian). Pope named Vincent Daniels (minister at Old Greenwich Congregational Church), Princeton's Paul Ramsey (Methodist), Duke's H. Shelton Smith (American Free Church Protestant), and Yale's H. Richard Niebuhr (Congregationalist) and Roland Bainton (Quaker).[63] Most of these scholars had little experience with Edwards. It is fair to say some were more interested in working with Miller than working on Edwards. Yet in the end they came to believe in the edition.

A few years into the project, in a letter on maintaining high editorial standards, Miller wrote that "while we are a band of Christians, for the purposes of this publication we are basically a band of scholars."[64] This remark, arguably a throwaway line for Miller, reflects the early Committee's desire to present Edwards's words in a detached fashion. Editors' introductions were to tell modern readers what they had in their hands – the background of the work, textual matters, and so forth. But editors were not discouraged from engaging Edwards and his interpreters. They could be polemical. For example, in his introduction to *Religious Affections*, John E. Smith talked about the contemporary relevance of Edwards for enduring religious questions by saying things like, "To the revivalist in our time Edwards has a sobering word," without being an advocate for Edwards, his friends, or his opponents.[65]

Jonathan Edwards College at Yale commemorated the publication of Paul Ramsey's edition of *Freedom of the Will* in 1957. A few weeks later, Thomas H. Johnson, of "Faust and Johnson," wrote a laudatory review in the *New York Times Sunday Book Review*. In "He Speaks to Our Time," Johnson asked why an edition of Edwards made sense in 1957, when it would have been unthinkable forty years earlier?[66] Johnson's answer echoed earlier sentiments by Christian intellectuals who came to appreciate Edwards's theological vision in an age of chastened liberalism. Like a host of others before him, Johnson contended that Edwards refused to assert humanity at the expense of God, refused to substitute humanitarianism for ethics, and refused to deny the unpleasant facts of life. "Edwards was the most revolutionary thinker of his day. He wished to face naked truth, not defend traditions.... If the volumes to follow adhere to the standard set by Paul Ramsey in the first, Edwards will have achieved the monument he deserves."[67] The second volume, *Religious Affections*, edited by philosopher John E. Smith, was published in 1959. The edition was off to a fast start.

Yet by 1960 the whole project was in the doldrums. The Editorial Committee waited for either Gerstner or Schafer to produce a volume of manuscript material. In the meantime, there was very little in the pipeline, though a number of volumes had been assigned. Since precious Bollingen money was tied up with manuscript projects, there was no funding for other volumes and no likelihood for going back for more. The Editorial Committee hoped a volume under H. Richard Niebuhr's name could restart the stalled edition. Niebuhr balked at such a big project, especially when the Committee wanted to include two brief manuscripts on ethics in the volume to fulfill the terms of the Bollingen grant requiring previously unpublished manuscript material to be produced.[68] Niebuhr died on July 5, 1962.[69] Miller died the next year before either Schafer or Gerstner came through with a third volume of Edwards.

Funding problems and delays in the manuscript projects led to an eleven-year gap between *Religious Affections* and the next volume, Clyde A. Holbrook's *Original Sin*, in 1971. In spite of all of the early activity, conditions in 1963 had not changed much from a decade earlier. There was still no editorial office, no support staff, no funding to speak of, and no budget. Yale University's failure to support its own project made it difficult to raise external support. It was also unfortunate that Miller's goal to lure modern readers to Edwards with lengthy and creative introductions by well-known scholars put the edition at odds with then emerging standards of edition science that minimized the editor's role. Since grants were often tied to the new standards, the Edwards edition missed opportunities to be underwritten, while editions of Thomas Jefferson, Benjamin Franklin, and others did not.

While the Yale Edwards edition appeared to be on hold in the 1960s, new General Editor John E. Smith pushed the edition ahead on several fronts. During this time a pattern emerged that had lasting effect on Edwards scholarship. Since the publication of Miller's biography and the first two volumes of the Yale Edition, anyone working on Edwards had reason to believe there might be buried treasure in the unpublished manuscripts, particularly the "*Miscellanies.*" When the imminent publication of the "*Miscellanies*" became less and less likely due to the enormity of the task, scholars sought permission to consult Thomas Schafer's transcriptions. Gradually, from the 1960s through the 1980s, Schafer became the de facto gatekeeper of Edwards research and publication. Although this delayed his own editorial work, it had the effect of slowly inviting a community of graduate students and scholars from various disciplines and perspectives into the grand project to publish Edwards's works in a modern, critical edition. Over the years, a number of these scholars were invited to edit volumes in the edition. Along the way, volume editors and many others were introduced to the stories and struggles of the modern effort to give Edwards his own voice, as well as the claims and counterclaims put on the legacy of Edwards. It took the actual publication of additional volumes to open Edwards scholarship beyond those with the time and resources to travel to Yale to consult transcriptions and manuscripts.

COMPLETION OF THE YALE EDITION

The Yale Edition is a scarlet thread through the escalating number of publications on Edwards from the 1950s to the present. At the center of those publications are, of course, the Yale volumes themselves: two appeared in the 1950s, none in the 1960s, three in the 1970s, and four in the 1980s. Since 1990, over a dozen volumes have been published. Progress came swiftly when the edition was infused with funds in the 1980s. Those funds created an actual office at Yale Divinity School that supported editors and the publication of volumes of sermons, "*Miscellanies*," treatises, letters, and notebooks. Harry S. Stout, now Jonathan Edwards Professor of American Christianity at Yale, replaced Smith as General Editor in 1991. A reinvigorated office of The Works of Jonathan Edwards also sponsored or cosponsored a number of conferences beginning in the 1980s. These conferences became, in effect, hotbeds of rival Edwards traditions where explications of his texts and arguments about his legacy received sustained attention in supportive environments.[70] Papers delivered at these conferences became chapters in books, and many chapters became books.

The first national Edwards conference was held in 1984 at Wheaton College, in part to recognize the role evangelical scholars played in promoting Edwards. In his opening address, Henry F. May asked the audience why they were there. "Why is it that Edwards has attracted not just a passing glance, but the devotion of years of hard work on the part of so many fine scholars? Is it because you believe him, love him, admire him? Is it because you find him complex and baffling, a perfectly engaging puzzle, a figure eternally subject to profound reinterpretation? Is it because he seems to some of you, as he did to [Perry] Miller and others, to offer a key to the understanding of American culture?" May ended his address by wondering, "Is it possible to have a fruitful discussion of a great religious thinker with the frank participation of believers, rejecters, and agnostics?"[71] The answer was clearly "Yes" – as the success of the Yale-sponsored conferences has shown – but not always, and not always easily.

Although each of the Edwards conferences had specific themes reflected in the titles of the conference, the papers themselves were on a wide variety of topics.[72] Some papers raised perennial questions about Edwards's relationship to Puritanism, Franklin, and nineteenth-century theology, for example. Another group of papers brought Edwards into normative discussions of contemporary theology, ethics, and ministry. A third set of papers delved into new areas of research, looking at previously unknown or little-known texts by Edwards, particularly in newly published volumes of "*Miscellanies*," letters, notebooks, and sermons.[73] Here scholars brought to light new angles on Edwards and thus new angles on Edwards traditions. For example, Edwards's deep interest in public theology and non-Christian religious traditions came as surprises to many readers.[74] A fourth group of papers reflects the present age's interest in Edwards on gender, race, class, and postmodern concerns. Edwards's newly published letters and notebooks give up secrets about his daily life as well as his interest in daily life. Papers covering Edwards on politics, economics, slavery, women, and children have gone a long way to humanize him and show him as a man of his time. It is tempting to see this stream of publications as pointing to new kinds and levels of Edwards scholarship. Certainly, the number of publications has grown and the availability of previously unpublished materials has opened up fresh areas of research. However, recent publications on Edwards generally continue the same kinds of discussions and debates about Edwards's legacy that have evoked and provoked scholars for many decades.

In conclusion, it seems that at every national Edwards conference, usually after a particularly dense paper, someone stands up and says, "I'm no scholar and I haven't been able to follow that last paper at all, though I'm sure that what it says is important. What I want to say is that I'm a minister of the gospel, and I love Jonathan Edwards because he helps me to understand God better. Next to the Bible, Edwards is the most inspiring reading I know." These comments are usually followed by an embarrassing period of silence. Some lower their heads. Others gaze out the window. A few shoot glances around the room, joining in a collective hope that the speaker will sit down. Some raise eyebrows indicating disapproval, annoyed that Edwardsean fundamentalism continues to be present in scholarly settings. Others are sympathetic with the comment made, though they wince at the way it was made. Still others are amazed that Jonathan Edwards continues to make disciples and provoke controversy more than any other American religious thinker. These "interruptions" and reactions to them, whether voiced or not, are not wasted moments. They are occasions, once again, to debate the legacy of Edwards, giving scholars interested in American religion fresh material for historical studies and cultural analysis.

Notes

1. Gary Wills, "Soul on Fire," Review of George M. Marsden, *Jonathan Edwards: A Life* (New Haven: Yale University Press, 2003), *New York Times Book Review*, Sunday (July 6, 2003): 10.

2. Henry F. May's seminal essay, "The Recovery of American Religious History," has been the backbone of a common account of Edwards historiography (*American Historical Review* 70 [1964]): 79–92. See also Donald Weber, "The Recovery of Jonathan Edwards," in Nathan O. Hatch and Harry S. Stout, eds., *Jonathan Edwards and the American Experience* (New York: Oxford University Press, 1988), 50–70.

3. M. X. Lesser, *Jonathan Edwards: A Reference Guide* (Boston: G. K. Hall, 1981); *Jonathan Edwards: An Annotated Bibliography, 1979–1993* (Westport, CT: Greenwood Press, 1994). Lesser is currently preparing a complete and updated reference guide to be published by Eerdmans.

4. See Edwards's remarks on Francis Hutcheson in *The Nature of True Virtue*, WJE, 8:537–627; Michael J. McClymond, *Encounters with God: An Approach to the Theology of Jonathan Edwards* (New York: Oxford University Press, 1998).

5. "If true virtue consists partly in a respect to God, then doubtless it consists *chiefly* in it" (*The Nature of True Virtue*, WJE, 8:553).

6. I am grateful to Nicole Kirk for her observation that "Edwards Lane" in present-day Princeton is a dead-end street.

7. On the last point, in 1903 George Park Fisher published *An Unpublished Essay of Edwards on the Trinity* (New York: Scribner's, 1903). After half a century of speculation about Edwards's heterodoxy, Fisher put suspicions to rest.

8. All of this Edwards activity produced a lively intellectual culture that is documented in Joseph Conforti's *Jonathan Edwards, Religious Tradition, and American Culture* (Chapel Hill: University of North Carolina Press, 1995).

9. George Park Fisher, "Greetings from Yale University," in *Jonathan Edwards: A Retrospect*, H. Norman Gardiner, ed. (Boston: Houghton, Mifflin, 1901), 78 ff.

10. David Gregg, "Jonathan Edwards: His Theological Creed and Its Influence" (Brooklyn, NY: Eagle Press, 1903), 8. To return to Fisher's remark, it is worth noting Edwards's "hard treatment" for *Sinners* continued throughout the twentieth century and is arguably the single most important factor to account for a prejudice against him that led to delays in the timely completion of the Yale Edition.

11. Henry A. Beers, *An Outline Sketch of American Literature* (New York: Scribner's, 1887), 42.

12. It is worth noting that one of the passages Beers quotes from *Sinners* to illustrate Edwards's penchant for terror is really his paraphrase of Isaiah 63:3b: "[F]or I will tread them in mine anger and trample them in my fury; and their blood shall be sprinkled upon my garments, and I will stain all my raiment."

13. Henry Seidel Canby, *Classic Americans* (New York: Harcourt, Brace, 1931), 12, 22.

14. George A. Gordon, "The Significance of Jonathan Edwards To-Day," in H. Norman Gardiner, ed., *Jonathan Edwards: A Retrospect* (Boston: Houghton Mifflin), 51–74.

15. Ibid., 52, 59, 65–6, 69.

16. D. G. Hart, *The University Gets Religion* (Baltimore: Johns Hopkins University Press, 1999), 37. Theological baggage was not the issue as much as the kind of theology. See also Edward Shils, "Order of Learning in the United States," in Alexandra Oleson and John Voss, eds., *The Organization of Knowledge in Modern America, 1960–1920* (Baltimore: Johns Hopkins University Press, 1979), 35–6.

17. Vernon Louis Parrington, *Main Currents in American Thought* (2 vols. New York: Harcourt, Brace), I:148–63.

18. W. A. Visser't Hooft, *The Background of the Social Gospel in America* (Haarlem: H. D. Tjeenk Willink and Zoon, 1928), 89 ff.

19. Henry Bamford Parkes, *Jonathan Edwards: The Fiery Puritan* (New York: Minton, Balch, 1930).

20. Herbert W. Schneider, "Review of *Jonathan Edwards: The Fiery Puritan* by Henry Bamford Parkes," *Nation* 131 (Nov. 26, 1930): 584–5. See also idem, *The Puritan Mind.* Studies in Religion and Culture: American Religion Series, no. 1 (New York: Henry Holt, 1930).

21. William Warren Sweet, *The Story of Religion in America* (New York and London: Harper and Brothers, 1930).

22. Charles Angoff, *A Literary History of the American People*, vol. 1 (2 vols. New York: Knopf, 1931).

23. Edward Hooker Dewey, "Jonathan Edwards," in John Macy, ed., *American Writers on American Literature* (New York: Horace Liveright, 1931).

24. Frederic I. Carpenter, "The Radicalism of Jonathan Edwards," *New England Quarterly* 4 (Oct. 1931): 629–44.

25. Harvey G. Townsend, "An Alogical Element in the Philosophy of Edwards and Its Function in His Metaphysics," in Gilbert Ryle, ed., *Proceedings of the Seventh International Congress of Philosophy* (Oxford: Oxford University Press, 1932).

26. Joseph Haroutunian, "Jonathan Edwards: A Study in Godliness," *Journal of Religion* 11 (July 1931): 400–19; idem, *Piety versus Moralism: The Passing of the New England Theology*, Studies in Religion and Culture: American Religion Series, no. 4 (New York: Henry Holt, 1932).

27. Arthur Cushman McGiffert, Jr., *Jonathan Edwards,* Creative Lives Series (New York: Harper and Brothers, 1932).

28. See, for example, Alexander V. G. Allen, who asserted that those "in whom the God-consciousness is supreme, are the true continuers of the work of Jonathan Edwards." *Jonathan Edwards* (Boston: Houghton, Mifflin, 1890), 389.

29. Edwin E. Slosson, "Jonathan Edwards as a Freudian," *Science* 52 (Dec. 24, 1920): 609.

30. See, for example, Carl Van Doren, *Benjamin Franklin and Jonathan Edwards: Selections from Their Writings* (New York: Charles Scribner's Sons, 1920).

31. Bruce Kuklick, *A History of Philosophy in America* (New York: Oxford University Press, 2001), xiii. See also Shils, "Order of Learning in the United States," 78–80.

32. John E. Smith, "Introduction" to William James, *The Varieties of Religious Experience* (Cambridge, MA: Harvard University Press, 1985), passim.

33. Josiah Royce, "William James and the Philosophy of Life," in John J. McDermott, ed., *The Basic Writings of Josiah Royce* (2 vols. Chicago: University of Chicago Press, 1969), 1:206.

34. Revivalists and conservatives had their own version of the refiner's fire for Edwards. While the essential revivalist Edwards was quite different from the enlightened Protestant version, the dross was the same in both cases, namely Calvinism. Conservative readers wanted to salvage Edwards from defects inherent in his writings as well as the various "liberal" accretions to his thought over the years made by his followers. See B. B. Warfield, "Edwards and the New England Theology," *Encyclopaedia of Religion and Ethics*, vol. 5, edited by James Hastings (New York: Scribner's, 1912), 5:221–7.

35. Stanley Thomas Williams, *The American Spirit in Letters* (New Haven, CT: Yale University Press, 1926), 43–4.

36. Visser't Hooft, *Background of the Social Gospel*, 90.

37. See, for example, I. Woodbridge Riley, "Jonathan Edwards," in idem, *American Philosophy: The Early Schools* (New York: Dodd, Mead, 1907), 126–87; idem, "The Real Jonathan Edwards," *Open Court* 22 (Dec. 1908): 705–15.

38. Herbert W. Schneider, *The Puritan Mind* (Ann Arbor, MI: University of Michigan Press, 1958), 3. In his review of *The Puritan Mind*, Arthur Cushman McGiffert, Jr., wrote:

> Curiously little attention has recently been paid to the development of religious thought in America.... [T]he church historian and the historical theologian have concerned themselves primarily in the modern period with European life and thought. Now, almost simultaneously, the publication of two books gives hope that American historical scholarship will again become domesticated and endeavor to interpret our religious tradition in terms of indigenous and familiar minds and events. The two centers of this interest are Chicago and Columbia, under the leadership of Professor [William Warren] Sweet [author of *The Story of Religions in America* (1930)] and Professor Schneider.

 "The New England Philosophy of Life" [Review of *The Puritan Mind* by Herbert W. Schneider], *Journal of Religion* 11:2 (April 1931): 306–7. Note that Harvard is not included.

39. Schneider, *The Puritan Mind*, 3–4.

40. Ibid., 142.

41. Ibid., 155. Schneider wrote, "I shall leave it to others to dissect the theological bones of a once living religion" (ibid., 7). That job fell to Schneider's graduate student Joseph Haroutunian.

42. Parrington, "The Anachronism of Jonathan Edwards," I:148–63.

43. Parkes, *Jonathan Edwards: The Fiery Puritan*, 249.

44. Neo-Orthodoxy is one of those terms that seems to have an enduring usefulness even though many people given that label (or tarred with that brush) seem to go out of their way to show why it does not work for them. Both Haroutunian and Niebuhr wrote pages on the problems of Neo-Orthodoxy and by implication, why they were not Neo-Orthodox.

45. Bruce Kuklick, an historian at the University of Pennsylvania, argues for a line of continuity between Edwards and Dewey via the religious liberalism that emerged during the nineteenth-century debates over Edwards's legacy. According to

Kuklick, both Edwards and Dewey "were engaged in a dialogue that in the eighteenth and nineteenth centuries was widely recognized as religious. Both saw that salvation was contingent on relegating the self to its appropriate place in the scheme of things. But in another sense, Dewey and Edwards were at odds. For Edwards, only supernatural grace could overcome the natural and achieve the proper integration of the individual and the cosmos.... Dewey succeeded in infusing the ostensibly natural instrument of science with this supernatural power.... He had thought literate Americans out of the categories of Jonathan Edwards." Bruce Kuklick, *Churchmen and Philosophers: From Jonathan Edwards to John Dewey* (New Haven: Yale University Press, 1985), 252 ff. *Churchmen and Philosophers* is its own retelling of the common account of Edwards's legacy, arguing for the demise of the New England Edwards tradition as well as the liberal version of a palatable Edwards (pp. 252 ff.). Haroutunian might have suggested that Kuklick change the title of his book to "Christian Moralism and Moral Philosophy: From Charles Chauncy to John Dewey."

46. Frank Hugh Foster, *A Genetic History of New England Theology* (Chicago: University of Chicago Press, 1907).

47. Joseph Haroutunian, *Piety versus Moralism: The Passing of the New England Theology* (New York: Henry Holt, 1932), 281–2.

48. James W. Hoffman, "Happy Calvinist," *Presbyterian Life* 6:1 (Jan. 10, 1953): 12–15.

49. William G. Chrystal, "Samuel D. Press: Teacher of the Niebuhrs," *Church History* 4 (1984): 511.

50. H. Richard Niebuhr, *The Kingdom of God in America* (Chicago: Willett, Clark, 1937), xiv.

51. Joseph Haroutunian, *Wisdom and Folly in Religion* (New York: Scribner's, 1940), 89.

52. H. Richard Niebuhr, "Introduction," in Joseph Haroutunian, *Wisdom and Folly in Religion*, viii–ix.

53. H. Richard Niebuhr, "The Anachronism of Jonathan Edwards," in William Stacy Johnson, ed., *H. Richard Niebuhr: Theology, History, and Culture* (New Haven: Yale University Press, 1996), 126, 132.

54. Thomas H. Johnson, *The Printed Writings of Jonathan Edwards 1703–1758: A Bibliography* (Princeton: Princeton University Press, 1940).

55. Perry Miller, *The New England Mind*, vol. 1 (2 vols. New York: Macmillan, 1939), 176.

56. Perry Miller, ed., "Introduction," to *Images and Shadows of Divine Things by Jonathan Edwards* (New Haven: Yale University Press, 1948), 1–41; idem, "Jonathan Edwards on the Sense of the Heart," *Harvard Theological Review* 41 (April 1948): 123–45.

57. Perry Miller, *Jonathan Edwards*. The American Men of Letters Series (New York: William Sloane Associates, 1949).

58. Ola Elizabeth Winslow, *Jonathan Edwards, 1703–1758: A Biography* (New York: Macmillan, 1940). Miller described Winslow's biography as the "most readable as well as the most reliable biography." Miller, "Speculative Genius," Review of *Jonathan Edwards, 1703–1758* by Ola Elizabeth Winslow, *Saturday Review*, 21:25 (1940): 6–7.

59. Perry Miller, *Jonathan Edwards*, xii–xiii.

60. Reinhold Niebuhr, "Backwoods Genius," Review of *Jonathan Edwards* by Perry Miller, *The Nation*, 169:27 (Dec. 31, 1949): 648.

61. Reinhold Niebuhr wrote, "One might raise . . . questions about Edwards's alleged 'naturalism' when he is expounding a fairly traditional doctrine of the realm of 'grace' above the level of the natural good" ("Backwoods Genius," 648). In his review, Joseph Haroutunian made a similar point when he wrote, "Edwards' empiricism does not make him a naturalist" (*Theology Today* 7 [1950–1]: 555).

62. Clarence H. Faust and Thomas H. Johnson, eds., *Jonathan Edwards: Representative Selections, with Introduction, Bibliography, and Notes* (New York: American Book Company, 1935), v. It is worth noting that there was a trickle of publications on Edwards's manuscripts and letters. Miller was aware of this activity, but it was negligible compared to the effort needed to edit and publish thousands of pages of manuscript materials at Yale and Andover Newton. On the occasion of the 250th anniversary of Edwards's birth in 1953, Vergilius Ferm published a thick volume of Edwards's writings, including some manuscript material, *Puritan Sage: Collected Writings of Jonathan Edwards* (New York: Library Publishers, 1953).

63. George H. Williams and H. Shelton Smith were not part of the original editorial committee, though their names were considered along with others during the period.

64. Miller to John H. Gerstner, Oct. 18, 1957, Gerstner file, Office of the Works of Jonathan Edwards, Yale Divinity School. Used with permission.

65. John E. Smith, "Introduction," WJE, 2:52.

66. Yet Johnson himself prepared a successful Edwards reader nearly twenty years earlier. Faust and Johnson, eds., *Jonathan Edwards: Representative Selections*.

67. *New York Times Sunday Book Review*, June 23, 1957, p. 7.

68. The manuscripts were "Signs of Godliness" (WJE, 21:469–510) and "Christ's Example" (WJE, 21:511–19).

69. For a detailed discussion of Niebuhr's volume and how it was taken over by Ramsey, see Stephen D. Crocco, "Paul Ramsey and The Works of Jonathan Edwards," *Annual of the Society of Christian Ethics* (1992): 157–72.

70. Major Edwards conferences were held in Wheaton (1984), New Haven (1990), Bloomington (1994), Philadelphia (1996), Miami (2000), and Washington, D.C. (2003). The Wheaton papers were published as Nathan O. Hatch and Harry S. Stout, eds., *Jonathan Edwards and the American Experience* (New York: Oxford University Press, 1988); the New Haven papers as Barbara B. Oberg and Harry S. Stout, eds., *Benjamin Franklin, Jonathan Edwards, and the Representation of American Culture* (New York: Oxford University Press, 1993); the Bloomington papers as Stephen J. Stein, ed., *Jonathan Edwards's Writings: Text, Context, Interpretation* (Bloomington, IN: Indiana University Press, 1996); the Philadelphia papers as Sang Hyun Lee and Allen C. Guelzo, eds., *Edwards in Our Time: Jonathan Edwards and the Shaping of American Religion* (Grand Rapids, MI: Eerdmans, 1999); the Miami papers as David W. Kling and Douglas A. Sweeney, eds., *Jonathan Edwards at Home and Abroad: Historical Memories, Cultural Movements, Global Horizons* (Columbia, SC: University of South Carolina Press, 2003); and the Washington papers as Harry S. Stout, Kenneth P. Minkema, and Caleb J. D. Maskell, eds., *Jonathan Edwards at 300: Essays on the Tercentenary of His Birth* (Lanham, MD, University Press of America, 2005). There were other conferences,

some cosponsored by the Yale Edition, such as the one in Princeton in 2003. Most of the papers from that conference were published in Sang Hyun Lee, ed., *The Princeton Companion to Jonathan Edwards* (Princeton, NJ: Princeton University Press, 2005).

71. Harry F. May, *The Divided Heart: Essays on Protestantism and the Enlightenment in America* (New York: Oxford University Press, 1991), 127, 144.

72. The main exception to this is the second Edwards conference, "The National Conference on Edwards and Franklin," in New Haven in February 1990. Most of these papers dealt with Edwards *and* Franklin.

73. When Edwards's biblical writings are all published and studied, he may be best known as a scholar of Scripture.

74. See Gerald R. McDermott, *One Happy and Holy Society: The Public Theology of Jonathan Edwards* (State College: Pennsylvania State University Press, 1992); idem, *Jonathan Edwards Confronts the Gods: Christian Theology, Enlightenment Religion, and Non-Christian Faiths.* (New York: Oxford University Press, 2000).

16 Edwards and social issues

AVA CHAMBERLAIN

In March 1753 Jonathan Edwards wrote a letter to his twenty-one-year-old daughter Esther, who had been living away from home since her marriage the previous year to Aaron Burr, the president of the College of New Jersey and the pastor of a congregation in Newark. This letter was a reply to one Esther had written her mother, informing her that she was still suffering from "extreme weakness and distressing pains" and asking for her comfort and advice. "Mothers," Laurel Thatcher Ulrich observes, "represented the affectionate mode in [the] essentially authoritarian mode of childrearing" practiced in colonial New England.[1] Although Esther had received the "unwearied kindness and tender care of" her husband during her illness, she was also homesick and in need of a little mother-love. But her precarious physical and spiritual state demanded the stronger hand of a father. Edwards begins his letter in an affectionate fatherly tone, assuring his daughter that he and Sarah "are glad to hear that you are in any respect better," and expressing their concern "at your remaining great weakness." He quickly shifts, however, from his paternal to his pastoral voice, to address his daughter's spiritual condition, a topic more urgent than her physical health.[2]

This new voice sounds distant, even cold and aloof. Taking Esther's illness as an occasion for her spiritual growth, Edwards severs the intimate parental bond that should tie a father to his sick child and positions his daughter at the same remove any seriously ill member of his congregation would occupy. He does not comfort her with the reassuring message that suffering and sickness are rare interruptions in a normally happy life. "I would not have you think," he cautions, "that any strange thing has happened to you in this affliction." His newly married daughter should not develop a sentimental hope for a future of domestic bliss, for it is "the course of things in this world," he observes, "that after the world smiles, some great affliction soon comes." She should not "depend on worldly prosperity," such as that obtained by marrying one of the most prominent men in colonial New England, but should anticipate a life of affliction and trial. Her "travel" through the "wilderness" of the world will be full of "weariness, pain and

325

trouble," whether sick or well, whether in Newark with her husband or in Stockbridge with her family. Earthly existence offers no real comfort. "If you lived near us," he writes, "yet our breath and yours would soon go forth, and we should return to our dust, whither we are all hastening." And so, instead of reassuring his daughter with the hope that she will soon recover her health, Edwards twice observes that she may not. Like all pious Christians, she should improve what brief moments she may have before death seeking her "heavenly Father," her only true source of comfort.[3]

Edwards's counsel to his daughter seems to support the common image of the dour Puritan divine, so rigidly attached to the cruel doctrines and strict morality of Calvinism that his life was without warmth, sympathy, and affection. The remainder of the letter, however, places this image in question. This letter is written on two sides of one quarto leaf. Edwards's exhortation on the religious life occupies the whole front of the leaf, so the first line on the verso comes as some surprise. "As to means for your health," Edwards writes, "we have procured one rattlesnake, which is all we could get." This abrupt shift from the universal to the particular is rather comic, especially since it is clear from the context that Edwards has enclosed the snake with the letter, and would have sent several more if he could have found them. In addition to this one rattlesnake, Edwards also included in the package some ginseng, whose man-shaped root was widely acknowledged to have great curative properties. He also recommended to his daughter his own favorite restorative, horseback riding, and recorded in the letter's postscript his wife's recipe for "a conserve of raisins" and "a tea made of the leaves of Robin's plantain," which she had found "very strengthening and comfortable to her in her weakness."[4]

These paragraphs reveal a new image of Edwards, as comfortable handling snakes and ginseng as he is contemplating the doctrine of innate depravity, an Edwards not divorced from ordinary reality but deeply embedded in the popular culture of eighteenth-century New England. According to David D. Hall, Puritan ministers "imagined sin as something almost physical" and believed "the health of their bodies depended on their overcoming sin."[5] Although Edwards surely embraced this supernatural perspective, nowhere in the letter does he suggest his daughter's illness is a consequence of sin, nor does he call her to repentance. He focuses on the natural and reveals an impressive knowledge of the medical arts. It was not uncommon in New England for ministers to practice medicine, but no evidence exists to suggest Edwards treated persons outside his family in a professional capacity. What Edwards displays in this letter is not elite medical knowledge but healing lore shared widely in colonial New England culture. His belief in the efficacy of rattlesnake and ginseng root locates him as a participant in that culture.[6] His theological erudition at times placed him in conflict with popular beliefs. Like other eighteenth-century elites, for example, he worked to suppress occult healing practices, which, according to Jon Butler, flourished among the common folk.[7] But despite his education and social status, his patterns of belief reflected those of the wider culture. In fact, in dispensing medical advice to his daughter, he does not elevate himself as the sole authority. Throughout this part of the letter, he speaks for both himself and Sarah, frequently employing the first person plural, and he encourages Esther to act as her own authority in matters of personal health. Voicing a common prejudice against professionalized medicine, he says, "I should think it best pretty much to throw by doctors, and be your own physician, harkening to them that are used to your own constitution."[8] Healing should be a family matter, he suggests, guided not by the knowledge contained in medical texts but by personal experience.

In prescribing folk remedies for his daughter's illness, Edwards acts as a concerned parent, whose authority derived from his position within the family and was available to all similarly situated persons. Likewise, the attitude toward sickness and death he expresses in the first half of the letter reflects his participation in the popular culture of his time. According to Charles Hambrick-Stowe, Puritanism was primarily a devotional movement, defined as much by a rigorous daily regimen of Bible reading and prayer as the profession of strict doctrine. This "popular piety infused the experience of nearly everyone in New England," Hambrick-Stowe writes, "though obviously in varying degrees."[9] It called both clergy and laity alike to experience life as a pilgrimage in preparation for death, to strive daily for the implantation and glorification with Christ that came only after death. Because illness was a reminder of the reality of death, it presented a special opportunity for intense devotion. Edwards, as the spiritual head of his family, exhorts his daughter Esther to contemplate in her illness her impending death and the weary journey she must travel in her "progress towards an heavenly home."[10] In this counsel he speaks neither as a theologian nor as a pastor but, once again, as a father. Even the most gifted thinker of his time occupied in the context of his family the ordinary role of father, and throughout the letter he comfortably maintains this position. The abrupt shift from the spiritual to the physical is more apparent than real. Edwards's beliefs not only about rattlesnake and ginseng but also about suffering and death reveal him as a man of his time.

This letter is a small example of what social history has to offer the study of Jonathan Edwards. The image of the rattlesnake forcefully situates Edwards in the eighteenth century and challenges us to integrate this social location into seemingly unrelated areas of his life and thought. With some prominent exceptions, however, Edwards scholars have ignored the snake and the world it represents. There are a number of obvious reasons for this omission. Social history was first advanced as a response and corrective to the dominance of figures like Edwards in the favored narrative of American religious history. This narrative identified men of ideas as the primary agents of history and focused on New England as the region most fertile in ideas and texts. The new social history shifted attention away from individual men of genius to outsiders and ordinary folk whose historical significance lay less in their individuality than in their membership in communities, classes, and groups. Because members of these groups only rarely left behind published texts, their voices had to be recovered from new sources. To reconstruct the intimate details of the lives of women, African Americans, and poor and working-class Americans, social historians turned to diaries, court and probate records, personal correspondence, and other manuscript sources generally ignored by all but antiquarians. As new stories emerged using these new methods, the grand narrative collapsed, as did the central place of New England, the Puritans, and Jonathan Edwards.

Perry Miller, who was in large part responsible for positioning Edwards as a central figure in the grand narrative of American religious history, had undisguised contempt for those charmed by the snake.[11] Because, in Miller's view, the "real life of Jonathan Edwards at Northampton and Stockbridge was the continuous inner monologue" that he recorded in his manuscript writings, intellectual history was the proper approach. Further driving a wedge between Edwards and social historians, Miller emphasized the modernity of Edwards's ideas. According to Miller, Edwards's study of John Locke and other Enlightenment figures placed him so ahead of his time "that our age is better prepared to comprehend Edwards than was his own."[12] The only creature that makes its way into Miller's writings is, therefore, the spider – not only the flying spider, whose "amazing works" a young Edwards described for the Royal Society of London, but also the "loathsome insect" that hangs over the fire "by a slender thread."[13] Unlike the snake, these spiders represent Edwards's modernism. "Edwards found the route from Locke's sensationalism to the burning spider inescapable," Miller observes. Were this route blocked, Edwards would, in Miller's estimation, be "only a shouting evangelist who drummed up hysteria with hell-fire and brimstone" and "would pertain to social history . . . but not to literature and not to philosophy."[14]

Social historians have, therefore, tended to neglect Jonathan Edwards because of their methodological predilection to study history from below, and Edwards scholars have favored a more intellectual approach, at least in part because of Perry Miller's inescapable influence. But since the advent of modern Edwards scholarship, a minority report has also irregularly been issued by historians applying the tools of social and cultural analysis to the study of Edwards. As a result, a substantial body of literature now exists focusing on such categories as class, age, gender, sex, and race. This literature does employ textual analysis, but because Edwards rarely addressed the social divisions and cultural practices of eighteenth-century New England in his published treatises, it also draws upon such unpublished manuscript sources as sermons and letters. To move beyond the identification of Edwards's own views to a consideration of how gender and other social constructions shaped his pastoral role as minister and evangelist, Northampton town and church records, as well as Hampshire County court records, have also been fruitfully employed. The remainder of this chapter will survey some results of this analysis, considering how Edwards during his Northampton ministry approached, first, age and class division; second, gender and sexual conflict; and, finally, race and African slavery.

Edwards's life and ministry spanned the first half of the eighteenth century, a crucial transitional period in colonial New England history. During this period the frontier villages established by the first generation of Puritan emigrants became urban commercial centers. The population increased, as did poverty and class division. Individualism and self-interest began to fragment communities once unified by traditional hierarchical bonds of deference and respect. Land, which had supported in abundance several generations of yeoman farmers, grew scarce, creating financial insecurity, increased mobility, and new career choices. Local markets supplied by subsistence economies developed into regional and international free markets that imported new European luxury goods into the colonies. The free trade of ideas also flourished. Enlightenment philosophy advocated the rational scrutiny of traditional religious beliefs and political arrangements, while evangelical pietism promoted a religion of the heart, which privileged the emotions and created new forms of religious authority. And the rapid pace of social change increased contention, litigiousness, and intergenerational conflict.

This social ferment formed the context of Edwards's ministry in Northampton, and his successes and failures as a pastor were directly related to his ability to negotiate this dynamic situation. His youth ministry represented, at least for a time, a notable success. The Northampton youth, those young men and women between the ages of fifteen and twenty-six who were preparing to make choices about career, marriage, and family formation, were the group most affected by changing social and economic conditions. As with youth throughout New England, the burden of growing land scarcity fell disproportionately on their shoulders, increasing the conflicts and anxieties of adolescence. Although according to Patricia Tracy "the land problem was not really desperate" during Edwards's tenure in Northampton, the effects of scarcity were clearly present. The town had ended granting home lots to young men in the process of household formation in 1703; after this time, they could acquire land only through inheritance, purchase, or emigration to the frontier. No large-scale emigration occurred until the 1760s, but during Edwards's pastorate there was a spike in men choosing to move to another town, with twenty-five leaving in the 1730s and twenty-nine in the following decade. Purchase of land presented difficulties of its own. If a father's resources were insufficient to buy land for his son, a youth was unlikely to save enough money to purchase land on his own, for the possibilities of lucrative employment were few, and the land available for purchase was generally in small lots of poor quality. Likewise, it was difficult to get enough capital to set up a shop, if a young man chose to forego farming and enter a craft or trade.[15]

Most men acquired land, therefore, through inheritance, but inheritance was not a solution but another symptom of the land problem. New Englanders did not practice primogeniture, so large families distributed property in small lots among several sons. And with increasing life expectancy, if fathers did not give land to their offspring prior to death, sons often had to wait until middle age to inherit. In 1730 Northampton did open a "safety valve" to alleviate some of the pressures of land scarcity. The town voted to divide the remaining 14,000 acres in the southwestern corner of the original Northampton land grant among the descendants of the town's first families, thereby creating the village of Southampton. Despite its rocky, mountainous terrain, this new settlement grew rapidly; in five years it contained about twenty families, and within thirteen years it had gathered a church and called a minister. But the establishment of a satellite village whose land grants were available only to the town's elite simply delayed the inevitable crisis. "After 1730," Tracy notes, "there was no hope that Northampton as a corporate enterprise could provide adequate land for those coming of age."[16]

Lacking land, young people who should be entering adulthood through the crucial rites of passage of marriage and household formation were left in a state of protracted adolescence and dependence upon their parents. Intergenerational tensions inevitably increased, as did the average age at marriage, which rose to 28.6 years. A distinctive youth culture began to develop, marked by rebellious and socially unacceptable behavior. Edwards reported that at the beginning of his pastorate the Northampton youth were "very much addicted to night-walking, and frequenting the tavern, and lewd practices." They would meet together for "frolics," that is, "conventions of both sexes, for mirth and jollity," and "would often spend the greater part of the night in them." Only twenty-five years old when he became pastor of the Northampton church, Edwards was sympathetic to the youth in his congregation, and he paid close attention to them in his preaching and pastoral activities. They proved – perhaps because of their anxious and uncertain futures – particularly responsive to his calls for reform. Under his ministry "the young people shewed," Edwards noted, "more of a disposition to hearken to counsel, and by degrees left off their frolicking." Instead of meeting in the evenings for "mirth and jollity," they gathered for prayer and Bible reading, and became models of piety for their elders.[17] The youth, therefore, became the vanguard of the revival that inflamed Northampton and much of the surrounding Connecticut Valley area in 1734 and 1735. And when George Whitefield brought revival to Northampton in 1740, the young people were again among the first affected.[18]

Congregational ministers throughout New England had a longstanding concern for the reform and conversion of young people. In addition to his success with this age group, Edwards also extended his ministry to children, even those younger than seven, generally considered the age of reason. In *A Faithful Narrative*, an account of the Connecticut Valley awakening, Edwards describes two model conversions. The first, the deathbed conversion of a young unmarried woman named Abigail Hutchinson, exemplified the central role of youth in the awakening. The second, however, was of a four-year-old girl named Phebe Bartlett. Edwards observed how "five or six times a day" she would retire to her closet for "secret prayer." There she begged God to forgive her sins and cried out in fear of going to hell. After her conversion, she exhorted members of her family to seek salvation and "took her opportunities to talk to the other children about the great concern of their souls." Although Phebe's own parents at first "supposed her not capable of understanding" the gospel, Edwards not only judged her subject to genuine spiritual convictions but also presented her as a model convert to be emulated by Christians of all ages.[19]

Edwards's Calvinism led him to reject a sentimental view of children as sinless innocents. "As innocent as children seem to be to us," he famously observed, "yet if they are out of Christ, they are not so in God's sight, but are young vipers, and infinitely more hateful than vipers."[20] Unlike the rattlesnake enclosed in the letter to his sick daughter Esther, this viper appears to confirm modern belief in the cruelty of Puritanism. But Edwards's Calvinism was tempered by his evangelicalism. As Catherine Brekus notes, "besides defending the traditional view of children's depravity, he also subtly undermined it." He ignored the apparent irrationality of even small children like Phebe Bartlett and judged them capable of conversion and the religious life. During the Connecticut Valley awakening, he admitted twenty children under the age of fourteen to full membership in the Northampton church and invited them to participate in the Lord's Supper. "By passing the bread and cup to them," Brekus notes, "he treated them as full spiritual equals." Edwards's evangelical vision created "a topsy-turvy world where children could be superior to adults" and where adults were less likely to embrace the gospel than children.[21]

According to the hierarchical society of colonial New England, age took precedence over youth, and elderly men and women were considered models of wisdom and virtue, worthy of younger persons' deference and respect. Edwards supported this traditional ordering of society, frequently praising the virtues of his elders. For example, in his funeral sermon for Colonel John Stoddard, an aged Northampton patriarch, Edwards stated that "a man in authority" must be "one advanced in years, one that has long been in authority, so that it has become as it were natural for the people to pay him deference, to reverence him, to be influenced and governed by him."[22] But he reserved particularly harsh judgment for persons over fifty, the beginning of old age, who had not embraced the gospel. As role models for the young, elderly persons should display their lifelong commitment to the Christian faith. If they have lived a sinful life, the deeply entrenched habit will be difficult to overcome. Again privileging youth over age, he judged that "[e]arly religion is most acceptable to God." Elders should earn their veneration by growing old in piety, for "[t]hose that are converted late are under disadvantages."[23] Edwards frequently used a botanical metaphor to express this spiritual inversion. "Man, when he first comes into the world, is like a young twig, easily bent," he noted in an early sermon on Psalms 95:7–8, "but the longer you suffer yourself to grow at random, the more you will be like an inflexible tree: your heart hardens so fast, that you will find the work of religion much more difficult the longer delayed."[24] Of course, elderly persons were not outside the reach of God's grace; in *A Faithful Narrative,* Edwards reports that during the awakening, twenty persons over age fifty were converted in his congregation.[25] But perhaps because of the intergenerational bias of Edwards's evangelism, they tended to oppose revival religion.[26]

Edwards may also have undermined his support among Northampton's older established householders by criticizing their political contentiousness and self-interested business practices. He notes that a principal source of conflict in the town has "been a sort of settled division of the people into two parties, somewhat like the Court and Country party in England." Edwards in many ways supported the hierarchical elitism of the Court party, whose leaders were "some of the chief men in the town, of chief authority and wealth, that have been great proprietors of their lands."[27] God has so ordered the world, he writes, "that mankind should be under heads, princes, or governors, to whom honor and subjection, and obedience should be paid." These rulers are "wiser and stronger" than those "in subjection" to them," who are "less knowing and weaker."[28] But Edwards was also, as Gerald McDermott has argued, sympathetic to the Country party's fear of a ruler's tendency to abuse power.[29] His suspicion of political power was not, however, founded simply on a desire to protect civil rights and liberties. Edwards feared only the power of the unredeemed. He condemned as "vicious persons" and "public enemies" those "men of influence" who do not have "the fear of God before their eyes and don't govern themselves by the rules of his Word."[30] Such ungodly men were unfit to lead; instead of promoting the public good, they used their offices to pursue self-interested aims and to stir up contention and party spirit.

Edwards also criticized the business practices that were rapidly trans-forming Northampton into western Massachusetts's largest economic center and many of the town's yeoman farmers into wealthy businessmen and merchants. In the eighteenth century, population growth and the devel-opment of a free market restructured the economy of New England. Port towns and other major urban areas became part of an international trade network that employed new monetary practices and formalized debt instru-ments. Market fluctuations created not only new accumulations of wealth but also inflationary prices and widespread indebtedness. In Northampton and many other New England towns, people enticed by new economic oppor-tunities and discouraged by the land shortage, increasingly turned to trade. "With trade came," as Mark Valeri notes, "a new class of rich, aggressive entrepreneurs, artisans, and merchants."[31] A sign of the prominence of this rising entrepreneurial class came in 1737 with Northampton's completion of its new meetinghouse. Abandoning the traditional order for the assignment of pews, the church for the first time gave wealth precedence over age and usefulness.[32]

Himself a wealthy man with the largest salary of any minister in west-ern Massachusetts, Edwards objected not to wealth per se but to the way it was acquired and employed. Merchants and traders should use their wealth, Edwards believed, "in the service of the community, and avoid cheating, bribery, gambling, speculation, indebtedness, usury, and other vices."[33] Reg-ulated by the individual pursuit of private gain, free markets promoted self-interest over the public good, which was destructive of the corporate welfare and contrary to the will of God. "When a people grow very corrupt," Edwards comments in a sermon on Proverbs 14:34, "[m]en look every one at his own separate interest," and regard "only their own wealth and their own honor"; they disregard "common justice and honesty" and act "like wolves to one another." The "rich" particularly "give themselves up to an indolent and use-less way of living" and "spend their whole time eating and drinking, and sleeping and visiting, and taking their ease and pleasure."[34] At the height of the awakening, Edwards led members of his congregation to promise, as part of a covenant renewal ceremony, to renounce these economic vices. They vowed not to "overreach or defraud our neighbor in any matter," and if "we have by any means wronged any of our neighbors in their outward estate," they pledged to "not rest till we have made that restitution, or given that satisfaction, which the rules of moral equity require."[35] A saint's desire to place God first in the affections kept the profit motive, Edwards reasoned, in its proper subordinate place. Wealth, like power, was used justly only by the redeemed.

The eighteenth century was also a period of changing gender relations in New England society. The construction of gender in Puritan communities began at home. The family was the foundational social institution, the model for both church and state. All persons were members of families, and laws prohibiting adults from living alone reinforced this corporate element of personal identity. Gender images of both men and women were, therefore, defined primarily by their distinct but complementary roles in the family. An adult man was a household head, who by virtue of his superior rationality and self-control ruled over and provided for the dependent members of his household, including his wife, children, and servants. An adult woman was a wife; her weak and passionate nature required a man's guidance, and she lovingly submitted to her husband's headship. Woman's subordination was, however, mitigated by several factors. Drawing on Genesis 2:18, in which "God said, It is not good that the man should be alone; I will make him an help meet for him," Puritans identified woman's proper role in the house-hold as companion, not subject. As two halves of a complementary pair, husband and wife were expected to love and respect one another in a rela-tion that was, according to Amanda Porterfield, "simultaneously hierarchical and affectionate."[36] The man's authority as family head had limits; the law prohibited wife abuse and mandated provision of adequate food, clothing, and shelter. Marriages straying too far from the ideal type could, furthermore, be terminated by divorce.

Women's integral role in the domestic economy also promoted gen-der parity. "Almost any man's strategy for becoming an economically inde-pendent householder," Anne Lombard explains, "explicitly included find-ing a partner able to provide the female labor needed for successful housekeeping."[37] As her husband's helpmeet, a wife provided the skilled labor necessary for such essential domestic activities as cooking, dairy-ing, clothes making, and child-rearing. And given the overlapping of male and female space in the household, there were few gender-specific tasks.

A colonial wife often functioned as a "deputy-husband" when her mate was absent. "Almost any task," Laurel Thatcher Ulrich observes, "was suitable for a woman as long as it furthered the good of the family and was acceptable to her husband."[38] This fluidity of gender roles was, furthermore, reinforced by the spiritual equality of men and women before God. According to the Calvinist Christianity of the Puritans, men and women were both sinful and were both in need of salvation through God's irresistible grace. Although women could not be ordained or vote in church matters, they met the rigorous qualifications for church membership more frequently than men and after the founding generation constituted the majority of the members in all New England's Congregational churches. Spiritual equality was not social equality, but because marriage was itself a spiritual union, women's religious authority permeated the domestic sphere.

The breakdown of these settled images of manliness and femininity was part of the general transformation of eighteenth-century New England society. New gender constructs began to emerge that would, by the beginning of the next century, revolutionize domestic roles for both men and women. Economic change gradually fragmented the unified household sphere that had supported the hierarchical interdependency of husbands and wives. The middle-class home became a private female space separate from the public male space of work and politics. In addition to the traditional subordinate role of wife and mother, women acquired a new identity as guardians of the home, responsible for creating a domestic refuge of piety, harmony, and nurture to which their husbands could retreat to escape the pressures of a competitive and amoral workplace. Corresponding to this separation of home and workplace into two gendered spheres was the emergence of a double standard regulating moral and sexual behavior. As Cornelia Hughes Dayton has shown, seventeenth-century Puritans judged both men and women by a single standard of virtue, which required chastity outside marriage, public confession of sin, and equal punishment of offenders of both sexes. But in the eighteenth century, even as premarital pregnancy rates rose, men increasingly fought paternity claims and refused to marry their pregnant lovers. Women continued to be presented in court for fornication, while the prosecution of men declined. With the restructuring of the gender system, chastity became an exclusively female virtue, leaving men free to pursue a more profligate course of behavior.[39]

While Jonathan Edwards occupied the Northampton pulpit, the older hierarchical model of gender relations and the emerging oppositional model competed for dominance in New England society. This lack of a settled gender ideology shaped both his theology and his ministry. In neither his writings nor his pastoral work did he consistently align himself with either construction, at times anticipating the ideology of separate spheres while at others resisting it. Although Edwards wrote little about the proper relations between husbands and wives, his support of the family structure that defined traditional Puritan communities is clearly seen in his use of domestic images to depict the relation between Christ and the church. Paternal and even maternal metaphors are both found in his writings, but he considered the marital union to be the most comprehensive type of the believer's union with God. This spousal imagery had biblical roots in the erotic love poetry of Canticles, which Puritan divines such as Edwards interpreted as a spiritual affirmation of ordinary domestic relations. It elevated the religious significance of marriage and made the union between husband and wife the primary referent for the Christian's experience of grace.

One of Edwards's most thorough explorations of the typological relation between marriage and the religious life is found in a sermon on Matthew 25:1. From this text Edwards draws the doctrine, "The church is espoused to the Lord Jesus Christ," and he develops this doctrine with frequent reference to the social norms regulating both betrothal and marriage in colonial New England. In every particular, Edwards argues, Christ makes a most excellent match. First, he is a most attractive suitor. In comparison with him, all other lovers "are base and vile in their nature." Although these rivals have a "seeming beauty and loveliness," it is only "a mask that they put on." Christ is also a most "profitable" suitor. "This glorious person that seeks your love and invites you to a spiritual espousal to him," Edwards notes, "is one that is of unsearchable riches." He has a substantial estate from his Father, who "is the great possessor of heaven and earth, and if you will yield to his suit and your soul becomes his spouse, his riches shall be yours." Consequently, he has the "wherewithal to feed you," and will "feast you and satisfy your soul." He has "wherewithal to cloth you"; if you marry him, he will adorn you in "glorious robes." His rivals, however, will leave you "in rags and nakedness as you are."[40]

Once by faith and through grace the divine match is made, Edwards describes the union between Christ and his betrothed spouse as the perfect likeness of the Puritan marital ideal. This spiritual marriage is a relation of mutual love and companionship. "The love of Christ to his church is that which transcends all the love of earthly lovers," Edwards writes. He "promises forever to cleave to her" and to "take care of her and be her everlasting friend and portion." Like ordinary domestic relations, this union is one of "mutual communion, cohabitation and enjoyment as friends and companions," but it is not the love of equals. Christ is united to the church, Edwards explains, "as her friend and companion, yet she is subject to him as Lord." Christ condescends to accept "a little feeble poor insect to be his bride," and she responds by depending upon him "for guidance, protection, and provision." And as Puritans expected marriage to include sexual passion, this simultaneously affectionate and hierarchical union also has an erotic dimension. On the wedding night, "a truly believing soul" will "be received into the arm of Christ as his bride, to go home to him to dwell with him in his house." And there the "King shall bring her into his chamber," Edwards writes, paraphrasing Canticles, "to behold his glory and to enjoy his love forever and to enjoy the most free and intimate converse with [him]." Edwards represents Christ, therefore, as both the head and the attractive, loving, and passionate companion of his spouse. To "reject so honorable a match," Edwards warns his congregation, as if he were a father admonishing his reluctant daughter, "will end in everlasting disgrace and contempt."[41]

Espousal theology, like that used by Edwards in this sermon, permeated Puritan understanding of both marriage and the religious life. The spiritual marriage between Christ and the church was the model earthly couples strove to emulate in their own marriages, and through their own domestic relations couples learned the meaning of the Christian life. Spousal metaphors, therefore, feminized the posture of genuine faith. When Edwards exhorts his congregation "to harken to the invitations of Jesus Christ" to make "an espousal with him," he figures both men and women as wives. In their devotional lives, all persons were prospective brides of Christ who should adopt the passive and subordinate posture best expressed by the feminine virtues of humility, submission, and obedience. This ideal of "female piety," according to Porterfield, "functioned similarly for both men and women by representing the loving disposition and deference to authority that all Puritans associated with grace." And it elevated the status of women, making godly housewives models of true Christian faith.[42]

Throughout his life, Edwards's own household was filled with multiple exemplars of female piety. Not only was he the only boy in a family of eleven children, but of his own eleven children eight were girls. And from the earliest days of their courtship, he represents Sarah Pierpont, whom he would marry in 1727, as a vision of holiness. When she was a girl of thirteen, he composed a lyrical description of a "young lady . . . who is beloved of that almighty Being, who made and rules the world," which he apparently copied onto the flyleaf of a book and presented to her as a gift. In "certain seasons," he writes, God "comes to her and fills her mind with exceeding sweet delight." Unconcerned with earthly pleasures, she looks forward to the time when she will "be raised out of the world and caught up into heaven," where she will "dwell with" Christ and "be ravished with his love, favor and delight, forever."[43] And in his 1742 treatise defending the evangelical revival then sweeping New England, Edwards included an extended narrative of his wife's religious experiences. Without revealing Sarah's identity in the text, he observes that the Holy Spirit gave this paradigm of heartfelt religion a "clear and lively view or sense of the infinite beauty and amiableness of Christ's person" that continued "for five or six hours together, without any interruption." Her "extraordinary views of divine things" were "attended with very great effects on the body," such as a "fainting with the love of Christ," or "an unavoidable leaping for joy," and "an increase of a spirit of humility and meekness." If such experiences are "the fruits of a distempered brain," he exclaims, "let my brain be evermore possessed of that happy distemper!"[44]

This ideal of female piety reflects the more fluid construction of gender of Puritan New England, in which men and women occupied a unified domestic sphere, performed at times interchangeable functions, and were judged by the same standard of virtue. That Edwards chose to depict conversion and the religious life through the experiences of women also displays, however, a movement toward the gendered construction of virtue that characterized the nineteenth-century ideology of separate spheres. The narratives of Phebe Bartlett and Abigail Hutchinson are examples not only of the young people's leadership in Northampton's revivals; when viewed in conjunction with Sarah Edwards's narrative, these three accounts suggest, as Julie Ellison observes, a "tacit recognition of a uniquely feminine form of piety."[45] As Ruth Bloch similarly concludes, "In his depiction of female exemplars of piety, Edwards took measured steps in the direction of upholding a female standard of virtue."[46] These narratives, therefore, figure godly women both as models of Christian piety and as models of feminine virtue. This ambiguity is an apt reflection of the transitional moment in which Edwards lived, allowing him to appeal to both sides of the gender conflict in eighteenth-century New England. But in his pastoral ministry, he frequently took sides, clearly revealing his support for the gender construction of his Puritan forebears.

Congregational churches were gathered both to promote their members' piety and to police their moral conduct. When Edwards used the powers of his office to discipline wayward congregants for their moral indiscretions, he was following a longstanding conception of ministerial duty. Nevertheless, in the post-awakening years, his surveillance of the boundary separating licit from illicit sex was a source of constant conflict in Northampton. During this time period, four controversial church discipline cases can be identified: the so called "bad book affair" of 1744, in which Edwards disciplined several young men in his congregation for reading illicit books and harassing young women, and three fornication cases. The church censured Samuel Danks in 1743, Thomas Wait in 1747, and Elisha Hawley in 1748, each for his persistent refusal to confess to a charge of fornication and for his contempt for the authority of the church. In each of these cases, Edwards's aim was clear. To remain within the fellowship of the church, the offending young men should with contrition and humility accept responsibility for their transgressions. But none willingly embraced the Puritan model of the real Christian man, choosing instead to deny responsibility for their sins. In each case, although Edwards's attempt to apply the traditional single standard of virtue was generally supported by the church brethren, it aroused opposition in the larger community. This conflict was a symptom of growing sympathy for what Dayton has called the sexual "double standard," which excused male sexual license with a sly wink and nod.[47] Although a growing number of Northampton's middling and elite families objected to the public scrutiny of their sons' moral failings, Edwards's opposition to this new ethic of privacy persisted. The young people, who had headed his exhortations during times of revival, ultimately failed to follow his lead, choosing instead to support the efforts of Northampton's older establishment to dismiss Edwards from his pastorate.[48]

Edwards's ministry in Northampton was deeply embedded in the social relations that defined life in colonial New England. The eighteenth-century was, however, a time of change. For social historians, the principal question is how Edwards interacted with these forces of change. As the preceding analysis suggests, he often resisted the new and criticized emerging constructions of class, gender, and the economy. In their homogeneous yet hierarchical communities, Puritan men and women had formed a godly society; change, therefore, was not progress but declension, the triumph of sin over holiness. But there was one new development that Edwards enthusiastically embraced. The wave of evangelical pietism that swept the colonies in the eighteenth century transformed New England Congregationalism and conferred upon Edwards himself international fame. It also promoted a spiritual elitism that had the potential to subvert both the older hierarchy of birth and the newer aristocracy of wealth and talent. From the divine perspective, the only viewpoint that ultimately mattered, only two classes of people existed: the saved and the damned. A member of any race, class, or gender could, through the power of the Holy Spirit, become one of the spiritual elite, acquiring power and authority over all who refused to accept the gospel, no matter their social location. During the revivals, for example, Edwards undercut the traditional deference accorded to age by elevating the spiritual status of the youth in his congregation, and throughout his ministry he used this aristocracy of grace to challenge the wealthy and powerful. Edwards's evangelicalism, therefore, tempered his antimodernist views and complicated his conviction that the "beauty of order in society" manifests itself when "everyone keeps his place and continues in his proper business."[49] For Edwards, only holiness was truly beautiful.

Edwards's understanding of the conflict between evangelical empowerment and worldly submission is clearly displayed in the case of Bathsheba Kingsley. Kingsley, a member of the church in Westfield, Massachusetts, began during the awakening to act contrary to her role as goodwife. Thinking that she had knowledge "very eminent and superior to that of others" and convinced she was called "for some great thing in the church of God," she began to exhort the local population. For over two years she wandered "about from house to house, and very frequently to other towns, under a notion of doing Christ's work and delivering his messages," even at times taking her husband's or a neighbor's horse for transportation. In her travels she proclaimed the "vileness and wickedness" of her neighbors and denounced her own minister; she also "talked against her husband" in front of the family. Despite "harsh words" and "blows," she would not obey his demand to stay at home. The Westfield church was similarly unsuccessful in their disciplinary actions, and it finally called a council of ministers, of which Jonathan Edwards was a member, to consider her case. This council strongly condemned Kingsley's unwomanly behavior. "[S]he has neglected her proper business and gone quite out of her place to promote religion," Edwards noted in his copy of the council's judgment, "and has of late cast off that modesty, and sobriety, and meekness, diligence and submission, that becomes a Christian woman in her place." But the ministers were unwilling to curtail her religious activity entirely. Although she should "submit to her husband in meekness and modesty" and "keep chiefly at home," he should give her "reasonable liberty to go to religious meetings in this town and to lectures in other towns." Nor should he prohibit her from "visiting Christian neighbors and brethren for mutual edification" or speaking with "Christian friends" who came to their home. He should treat her "with love and tenderness," and should even submit to her reproofs if given in a "humble, submissive, and loving manner." So long as Kingsley did not neglect her domestic duties, the council reasoned, she should be encouraged in her religious calling.[50]

Evangelicals were similarly willing to grant a measure of religious equality to African slaves. Believing the aristocracy of grace transcended racial division, Edwards, for example, preached to persons of all races and reported in *A Faithful Narrative* that "several Negroes . . . appear to have been truly born again in the late remarkable season."[51] He baptized black children of God as well as white and admitted all qualified candidates to full membership in the Northampton church. According to Kenneth P. Minkema, he was the first of the town's ministers to recognize the spiritual equality of black Christians, but other of his actions expose the limited ability of grace to challenge the status quo.[52] Edwards's seating of slaves in a segregated area of the church gallery, for example, compromised his commitment to equality, as did his conviction that blacks, who he believed were innately inferior to whites in their mental abilities, could legally be enslaved.[53] Edwards did foresee a time when "many of the Negroes and Indians will be divines," and when "excellent books will be published in Africa, in Ethiopia, in Turkey." Short of the millennium, however, when the wide diffusion of knowledge will enlighten even African intellects, slavery will remain "part of the fallen world's order."[54] In his time, ownership of slaves was not sinful, but an affirmation of a divinely ordained racial hierarchy.

Edwards bought an African slave not long after his ordination. To mark this new social status, he traveled to Newport, Rhode Island, the center of the New England slave trade, and purchased a fourteen-year-old African girl named Venus for eighty pounds. For a man of means to acquire a slave for domestic labor was in New England both legal and socially sanctioned. Edwards's father was a slaveowner, as were several members of the Northampton aristocracy. And Venus was the first of several slaves Edwards himself bought and sold during his lifetime, the last being a "Negro boy named Titus" who was valued at thirty pounds in the inventory of his estate.[55] This record clearly indicates Edwards never questioned the justice of slavery as an institution. Christian masters, he maintained, should educate their slaves in the truths of the gospel and refrain from the cruelty and brutality common among slaveowners, but he never called slavery itself a sin nor identified slaveowning as contrary to the gospel.[56] In his one extant writing on the topic, Edwards unapologetically defended the right of a neighboring minister to possess slaves. When Benjamin Doolittle's Northfield parishioners criticized him for slaveowning, Edwards drafted a defense of the practice for the Hampshire County Ministerial Association. While condemning the overseas slave trade as unjust and contrary to the evangelization of Africa, he used both reason and Scripture to justify the continuing enslavement of the descendants of African captives living in American colonies.[57] New Divinity theologians, such as Joseph Bellamy, Jonathan Edwards, Jr., and Samuel Hopkins, found in their mentor's ethical writings the seeds of their radical abolitionism, but Edwards himself never preached from his pulpit such revolutionary views.[58]

More than the medicinal rattlesnake he sent to his daughter Esther, Edwards's ownership of slaves forcibly locates him in the social context of eighteenth-century New England. His treatment of women was often surprisingly evenhanded. Puritan New England's ideology of gender subordinated women to men in their natures, intellects, and capacities, but in many ways allowed women greater freedom and equality than the ideology of separate spheres that superseded it. Edwards's advocacy of this outmoded construction of gender, together with his conviction that all persons were equal in Christ, complicates the representation of masculinity and femininity in his theology and pastoral ministry. But the spiritual equality he accorded slaves did little to mitigate the depth of their oppression. Abolitionism was really not a live option for Edwards or his contemporaries, for no antislavery movement of any size existed in New England until well after his death. His proslavery views, however, remain a disturbing but necessary reminder that even this precocious student of Newton and Locke was in significant ways a man of his times.

Notes

1. Laurel Thatcher Ulrich, *Good Wives: Image and Reality in the Lives of Women in Northern New England, 1650–1750* (1991; reprint, New York: Vintage Books, 1982), 154.
2. Letter to Esther Edwards Burr, WJE, 16:576–8.
3. Ibid., 576–7.
4. Ibid., 577–8.
5. David D. Hall, *"Worlds of Wonder, Days of Judgment": Popular Religious Belief in Early New England* (Cambridge, MA: Harvard University Press, 1990), 197.
6. "Let it be considered," Cotton Mather writes in *The Christian Philosopher*, "that the venomous Creatures have their great medicinal uses; . . . the Viper's Flesh cures Leprosies, and obstinate Maladies. The Gall of a Rattle-snake (which we take out of him in the more early Months of his yearly appearance, and work into Troches with Chalk or Meal) is a rich Cordial and Anodyne, for which purpose I have often taken it, and given it: it invigorates the Blood into a mighty Circulation, when fatal Suppressions are upon it; it is highly alexipharmick [capable of counteracting the effects of poison], and cures Quartan-Auges [malaria]" (reprint; Winton U. Solberg, ed. [Urbana, IL: University of Illinois Press, 1994], 180).
7. Jon Butler, *Awash in a Sea of Faith: Christianizing the American People* (Cambridge: Harvard University Press, 1990), 83–97.
8. WJE, 16:577–8.
9. Charles E. Hambrick-Stowe, *The Practice of Piety: Puritan Devotional Disciplines in Seventeenth Century New England* (Chapel Hill, NC: University of North Carolina Press, 1982), 4.
10. WJE, 16:577.
11. In his preface to *Errand into the Wilderness*, Miller famously pronounced, "I am the last to decry monographs on stoves and bathtubs, or tax laws, banks, the conduct of presidential elections, or even inventories of artifacts. . . . [H]owever valuable as documentation might be the mass of work being accomplished by those I may call 'social' historians, they [are] not," he writes, "getting . . . anywhere near *the* fundamental theme" of American history (*Errand into the Wilderness*, [Cambridge, MA: Harvard University Press, 1956], vii–viii).

12. Perry Miller, *Jonathan Edwards* (1949; reprint, Amherst: University of Massachusetts Press, 1981), 127, 260.

13. WJE, 6:164; 22:411–12.

14. Miller, *Jonathan Edwards*, 147–8.

15. Patricia Tracy, *Jonathan Edwards, Pastor: Religion and Society in Eighteenth-Century Northampton* (New York: Hill and Wang, 1979), 41, 87, 94–7. In this groundbreaking book, Tracy employs a community study approach, the foundational methodology of early American social history, to contextualize Edwards's pastorate in Northampton. The only book-length study of its kind, its conclusions inform many aspects of this chapter.

16. Ibid., 95–6, 100.

17. WJE, 4:146–8.

18. Letter to Thomas Prince, Dec. 12, 1743, WJE, 16:116.

19. WJE, 4:191–205.

20. *Some Thoughts Concerning the Present Revival of Religion,* WJE, 4:394. For a full analysis of the implications of this passage, see Catherine A. Brekus, "Children of Wrath, Children of Grace: Jonathan Edwards and the Puritan Culture of Child Rearing," in Marcia J. Bunge, ed., *The Child in Christian Thought* (Grand Rapids: Eerdmans, 2001), 300–28; idem, "Remembering Jonathan Edwards's Ministry to Children," in David W. Kling and Douglas A. Sweeney eds., *Jonathan Edwards at Home and Abroad: Historical Memories, Cultural Movements, Global Horizons* (Columbia: University of South Carolina Press, 2003), 40–60.

21. Brekus, "Children of Wrath," 301, 317–18.

22. *A Strong Rod Broken and Withered* (Boston, 1748), 12.

23. WJE, 14:276.

24. Ibid., 10:446–7.

25. Ibid., 4:158.

26. This summary of Edwards's ministry to the elderly is taken from Kenneth P. Minkema, "Old Age and Religion in the Writings and Life of Jonathan Edwards," *Church History* 70 (Dec. 2001): 674–87.

27. Letter to Thomas Gillespie, July 1, 1751, WJE, 16:382.

28. "Miscell." 864, WJE, 20:99–100.

29. Gerald R. McDermott, *One Holy and Happy Society: The Public Theology of Jonathan Edwards* (University Park: Pennsylvania State University Press, 1992), 120–1.

30. WJE, 17:359–60.

31. Mark Valeri, "The Economic Thought of Jonathan Edwards," *Church History*, 60 (March 1991): 40. See also idem, "Jonathan Edwards, the Edwardsians, and the Sacred Cause of Free Trade," in Kling and Sweeney, eds., *Jonathan Edwards at Home and Abroad*, 85–100.

32. Tracy, *Jonathan Edwards, Pastor*, 126.

33. Valeri, "Economic Thought," 41.

34. WJE, 14:493–5.

35. Ibid., 4:551.

36. Amanda Porterfield, *Female Piety in Puritan New England: The Emergence of Religious Humanism* (New York: Oxford University Press, 1992), 20.

37. Anne S. Lombard, *Making Manhood: Growing Up Male in Colonial New England* (Cambridge, MA: Harvard University Press, 2003), 100.

38. Ulrich, *Goodwives*, 36–8.

39. Cornelia Hughes Dayton, *Women before the Bar: Gender, Law, and Society in Connecticut, 1639–1789* (Chapel Hill: University of North Carolina Press, 1995, 157–230.

40. Sermon on Matthew 25:1 (Nov. 1737), Beinecke Rare Book and Manuscript Library, Yale University, New Haven. This sermon is the introduction to a nineteen-unit sermon series that Edwards preached in the winter of 1737–8 on the parable of the wise and foolish virgins.

41. Ibid.

42. Porterfield, *Female Piety*, 6–7, 9.

43. WJE, 16:789–90.

44. Ibid., 4:332–3, 335, 341.

45. Julie Ellison, "The Sociology of 'Holy Indifference': Sarah Edwards' Narrative," *American Literature* 56 (Dec. 1984): 490.

46. Ruth Bloch, "Women, Love, and Virtue in the Thought of Edwards and Franklin," in Barbara B. Oberg and Harry S. Stout, eds., *Benjamin Franklin, Jonathan Edwards, and the Representation of American Culture* (New York: Oxford University Press, 1993), 147.

47. Dayton, *Women before the Bar*, 159.

48. See Ava Chamberlain, "Bad Books and Bad Boys: The Transformation of Gender in Eighteenth-Century Northampton, Massachusetts," *New England Quarterly* 75 (June 2002): 179–203.

49. WJE, 8:568.

50. "Advice to Mr. and Mrs. Kingsley," Trask Library, Andover Newton Theological School, Newton Center, Mass. Transcription supplied by the Works of Jonathan Edwards, Yale University. See also Catherine Brekus's discussion of the Kingsley case in *Strangers and Pilgrims: Female Preaching in America, 1740–1845* (Chapel Hill: University of North Carolina Press, 1988), 23–6.

51. WJE, 4:159.

52. Kenneth P. Minkema, "Jonathan Edwards's Defense of Slavery," *Massachusetts Historical Review* 4 (2002): 34.

53. Ibid., 35; Kenneth P. Minkema and Harry S. Stout, "The Edwardsean Tradition and the Antislavery Debate, 1740–1865," *Journal of American History* 92 (June 2005): 49–50.

54. *A History of the Work of Redemption,* WJE, 9:480; Kenneth P. Minkema, "Jonathan Edwards on Slavery and the Slave Trade," *William and Mary Quarterly* 54 (Oct. 1997): 828.

55. On Edwards's ownership of slaves, see Minkema, "Edwards's Defense."

56. Minkema and Stout, "The Edwardsean Tradition and the Antislavery Debate," 50.

57. Minkema, "Edwards's Defense," 32–8.

58. Minkema and Stout, "The Edwardsean Tradition and the Antislavery Debate," 49–61.

The Works of Jonathan Edwards
Yale University Press Edition

Vol. 1   *Freedom of the Will*, Paul Ramsey, ed.
Vol. 2   *Religious Affections*, John E. Smith, ed.
Vol. 3   *Original Sin*, Clyde A. Holbrook, ed.
Vol. 4   *The Great Awakening*, C. C. Goen, ed.
     A Faithful Narrative
     The Distinguishing Marks
     Some Thoughts Concerning the Revival
     Preface to True Religion by Joseph Bellamy
Vol. 5   *Apocalyptic Writings*, Stephen J. Stein, ed.
     Notes on the Apocalypse
     An Humble Attempt
Vol. 6   *Scientific and Philosophical Writings*, Wallace E. Anderson, ed.
     The "Spider" Papers
     Natural Philosophy
     The Mind
     Short Scientific and Philosophical Papers
Vol. 7   *The Life of David Brainerd*, Norman Pettit, ed.
Vol. 8   *Ethical Writings*, Paul Ramsey, ed.
     Charity and Its Fruits
     Concerning the End for Which God Created the World
     The Nature of True Virtue
Vol. 9   *A History of the Work of Redemption*, John F. Wilson, ed.
Vol. 10   *Sermons and Discourses, 1720–1723*, Wilson H. Kimnach, ed.
Vol. 11   *Typological Writings*, Wallace E. Anderson and Mason I. Lowance, eds.
     Images of Divine Things
     Types
     Types of the Messiah
Vol. 12   *Ecclesiastical Writings*, David D. Hall, ed.
     A Letter to the Author of an Answer to the Hampshire Narrative
     An Humble Inquiry

Further Readings

Biographical Studies

Aldridge, Alfred Owen. *Jonathan Edwards.* New York: Washington Square Press, 1964.

Allen, Alexander V. G. *Jonathan Edwards.* Boston: Houghton Mifflin, 1890.

Davidson, Edward H. *Jonathan Edwards: The Narrative of a Puritan Mind.* Boston: Houghton Mifflin, 1966.

Dodds, Elisabeth D. *Marriage to a Difficult Man: The "Uncommon Union" of Jonathan and Sarah Edwards.* Philadelphia: Westminster Press, 1971.

Dwight, Sereno Edwards. *The Life of President Edwards.* New York: G. & C. & H. Carvill, 1830.

Griffin, Edward M. *Jonathan Edwards.* Minneapolis: University of Minnesota Press, 1971.

Gura, Philip F. *Jonathan Edwards: America's Evangelical.* New York: Hill and Wang, 2005.

Hopkins, Samuel. *The Life and Character of the Late Reverend, Learned, and Pious Mr. Jonathan Edwards, President of the College of New-Jersey.* Boston: S. Kneeland, 1765.

Jenson, Robert W. *America's Theologian: A Recommendation of Jonathan Edwards.* New York: Oxford University Press, 1988.

Lesser, M. X. *Jonathan Edwards.* Boston: Twayne, 1988.

Marsden, George M. *Jonathan Edwards: A Life.* New Haven: Yale University Press, 2003.

McGiffert, Arthur Cushman, Jr. *Jonathan Edwards.* New York: Harper and Brothers, 1932.

Miller, Perry. *Jonathan Edwards.* New York: W. Sloane Associates, 1949.

Morris, William Sparkes. *The Young Jonathan Edwards: A Reconstruction.* Brooklyn: Carlson, 1991.

Murray, Iain H. *Jonathan Edwards: A New Biography.* Edinburgh: Banner of Truth Trust, 1987.

Parkes, Henry Bamford. *Jonathan Edwards, the Fiery Puritan.* New York: Minton, Balch, 1930.

Simonson, Harold P. *Jonathan Edwards: Theologian of the Heart.* Grand Rapids: Eerdmans, 1974.

Smith, John E. *Jonathan Edwards: Puritan, Preacher, Philosopher.* Notre Dame: University of Notre Dame Press, 1992.

Tracy, Patricia J. *Jonathan Edwards, Pastor: Religion and Society in Eighteenth-Century Northampton.* New York: Hill and Wang, 1979.

Winslow, Ola Elizabeth. *Jonathan Edwards, 1703–1758: A Biography*. New York: Macmillan, 1940.

Historical Context

Axtell, James. *The Invasion Within: The Contest of Cultures in Colonial North America*. New York: Oxford University Press, 1985.

Bercovitch Sacvan. *Typology and Early American Literature*. Amherst: University of Massachusetts Press, 1972.

———. *The Puritan Origins of the American Self*. New Haven: Yale University Press, 1975.

Bloch, Ruth. *Visionary Republic: Millennial Themes in American Thought, 1756–1800*. Cambridge: Cambridge University Press, 1985.

Bonomi, Patricia U. *Under the Cope of Heaven: Religion, Society, and Politics in Colonial America*. New York: Oxford University Press, 1986.

Brekus, Catherine A. *Strangers and Pilgrims: Female Preaching in America, 1740–1845*. Chapel Hill: University of North Carolina Press, 1998.

Brooke, John H. *Science and Religion*. Cambridge: Cambridge University Press, 1991.

Butler, Jon. *Awash in a Sea of Faith: Christianizing the American People*. Cambridge, MA: Harvard University Press, 1990.

Caldwell, Patricia. *The Puritan Conversion Narrative: The Beginnings of American Expression*. Cambridge: Cambridge University Press, 1993.

Cassirer, Ernst. *The Philosophy of the Enlightenment*. Boston: Beacon Press, 1962.

Castillo, Susan and Schweitzer, Ivy, eds. *The Literatures of Colonial America*. Oxford: Blackwell, 2001.

Cooper, James F., Jr. *Tenacious of Their Liberties: The Congregationalists in Colonial Massachusetts*. New York: Oxford University Press, 1999.

Crawford, Michael J. *Seasons of Grace: Colonial New England's Revival Tradition in Its British Context*. New York: Oxford University Press, 1991.

Davidson, James West. *The Logic of Millennial Thought: Eighteenth-Century New England*. New Haven: Yale University Press, 1977.

Elliott, Emory, ed. *Puritan Influences in American Literature*. Urbana: University of Illinois Press, 1979.

Foster, Frank Hugh. *A Genetic History of New England Theology*. Chicago: University of Chicago Press, 1907.

Foster, Stephen. *The Long Argument: English Puritanism and the Shaping of New England Culture, 1570–1700*. Chapel Hill: University of North Carolina Press, 1991.

Frazier, Patrick. *The Mohicans of Stockbridge*. Lincoln: University of Nebraska Press, 1992.

Gaustad, Edwin S. *The Great Awakening in New England*. New York: Harper, 1957.

Gay, Peter. *The Enlightenment: The Science of Freedom*. New York: W. W. Norton, 1977.

Grasso, Christopher. *A Speaking Aristocracy: Transforming Public Discourse in Eighteenth-Century Connecticut*. Chapel Hill: University of North Carolina Press, 1999.

Greene, Jack P. *Pursuits of Happiness: The Social Development of Early Modern British Colonies and the Formation of American Culture*. Chapel Hill: University of North Carolina Press, 1988.

Greene, Jack P. and Pole, J. R. *Colonial British America: Essays in the New History of the Early Modern Era*. Baltimore: Johns Hopkins University Press, 1984.

Greven, Philip J. *The Protestant Temperament: Patterns of Child-Rearing, Religious Experience, and the Self in Early America*. New York: Knopf, 1977.

Haefeli, Evan and Sweeney, Kevin. *Captors and Captives: The 1704 French and Indian Raid on Deerfield*. Amherst: University of Massachusetts Press, 2003.

Hall, David D. *The Faithful Shepherd: A History of the New England Ministry in the Seventeenth Century*. Chapel Hill: University of North Carolina Press, 1972.

Hall, Timothy D. *Contested Boundaries: Itinerancy and the Reshaping of the Colonial American Religious World*. Durham: Duke University Press, 1994.

Hambrick-Stowe, Charles E. *The Practice of Piety: Puritan Devotional Disciplines in Seventeenth-Century New England*. Chapel Hill: University of North Carolina Press, 1982.

Heimert, Alan. *Religion and the American Mind: From the Great Awakening to the Revolution*. Cambridge, MA: Harvard University Press, 1966.

Holifield, E. Brooks. *Theology in America: Christian Thought from the Age of the Puritans to the Civil War*. New Haven: Yale University Press, 2003.

Juster, Susan. *Disorderly Women: Sexual Politics and Evangelicalism in Revolutionary New England*. Ithaca, NY: Cornell University Press, 1994.

Karlsen, Carol and Crumpacker, Laurie, eds. *The Journal of Esther Edwards Burr, 1754–57*. New Haven: Yale University Press, 1984.

Knight, Janice. *Orthodoxies in Massachusetts: Rereading American Puritanism*. Cambridge, MA: Harvard University Press, 1994.

Kuklick, Bruce. *Churchmen and Philosophers: From Jonathan Edwards to John Dewey*. New Haven: Yale University Press, 1985.

———. *A History of Philosophy in America*. New York: Oxford University Press, 2001.

Lambert, Frank. *Pedlar in Divinity: George Whitefield and the Transatlantic Revivals, 1737–1770*. Princeton: Princeton University Press, 1994.

———. *Inventing the "Great Awakening."* Princeton: Princeton University Press, 1999.

Lombard, Anne S. *Making Manhood: Growing Up Male in Colonial New England*. Cambridge, MA: Harvard University Press, 2003.

Lovejoy, David S. *Religious Enthusiasm in the New World: Heresy to Revolution*. Cambridge, MA: Harvard University Press, 1985.

Lucas, Paul R. *Valley of Discord: Church and Society along the Connecticut River, 1636–1725*. Hanover, NH: University Press of New England, 1976.

Main, Gloria L. *Peoples of a Spacious Land: Families and Cultures in Colonial New England*. Cambridge, MA: Harvard University Press, 2001.

May, Henry F. *The Enlightenment in America*. New York: Oxford University Press, 1976.

Miller, Perry. *Errand into the Wilderness*. Cambridge, MA: Harvard University Press, 1956.

Munk, Linda. *The Devil's Mousetrap: Redemption and Colonial American Literature*. New York: Oxford University Press, 1997.

Nichols, Stephen. *Jonathan Edwards: A Guided Tour of His Life and Thought.* Philipsburg, NJ: P &R, 2001.

Niebuhr, H. Richard. *The Kingdom of God in America.* New York: Harper and Brothers, 1937.

Noll, Mark A. *America's God: From Jonathan Edwards to Abraham Lincoln.* New York: Oxford University Press, 2002.

Noll, Mark A., Bebbington, David W. and Rawlyk, George A., eds. *Evangelicalism: Comparative Studies of Popular Protestantism in North America, the British Isles, and Beyond 1700–1990.* New York: Oxford University Press, 1994.

Osler, Margaret J., ed. *Rethinking the Scientific Revolution.* Cambridge, MA: Cambridge University Press, 2000.

Parrington, Vernon Louis. *Main Currents in American Thought.* 3 vols. New York: Harcourt, Brace, 1930.

Peterson, Mark A. *The Price of Redemption: The Spiritual Economy of Puritan New England.* Stanford: Stanford University Press, 1997.

Pope, Robert G. *The Half-Way Covenant: Church Membership in Puritan New England.* New Haven: Yale University Press, 1969.

Seeman, Erik R. *Pious Persuasions: Laity and Clergy in Eighteenth-Century New England.* Baltimore: Johns Hopkins University Press, 1999.

Shea, Daniel B., Jr. *Spiritual Autobiography in Early America.* Princeton: Princeton University Press, 1968.

Spiller, Robert E. et al., eds. *Literary History of the United States.* 3 vols. New York: Macmillan, 1948.

Stevens, Laura M. *The Poor Indians: British Missionaries, Native Americans, and Colonial Sensibility.* Philadelphia: University of Pennsylvania Press, 2004.

Taves, Ann. *Fits, Trances, and Visions: Experiencing Religion and Explaining Experience from Wesley to James.* Princeton: Princeton University Press, 1999.

Ulrich, Laurel Thatcher. *Goodwives: Image and Reality in the Lives of Women in Northern New England, 1650–1750.* New York: Vintage, 1980.

Warch, Richard. *School of the Prophets: Yale College 1701–1740.* New Haven: Yale University Press, 1973.

Winship, Michael P. *Seers of God: Puritan Providentialism in the Restoration and Early Enlightenment.* Baltimore: Johns Hopkins University Press, 1996.

Youngs, J. William T., Jr. *God's Messengers: Religious Leadership in Colonial New England, 1700–1750.* Baltimore: Johns Hopkins University Press, 1976.

Intellectual and Theological Studies

Brown, Robert E. *Jonathan Edwards and the Bible.* Bloomington: Indiana University Press, 2002.

Carse, James. *Jonathan Edwards and the Visibility of God.* New York: Charles Scribner's Sons, 1967.

Chai, Leon. *Jonathan Edwards and the Limits of Enlightenment Philosophy.* New York: Oxford University Press, 1998.

Cherry, C. Conrad. *The Theology of Jonathan Edwards: A Reappraisal.* Garden City, NY: Doubleday, 1966.

———. *Nature and Religious Imagination: From Edwards to Bushnell.* Philadelphia: Fortress Press, 1980.

Conforti, Joseph A. *Samuel Hopkins and the New Divinity Movement: Calvinism, the Congregational Ministry, and Reform in New England between the Great Awakenings.* Grand Rapids: Christian University Press, 1981.

———. *Jonathan Edwards, Religious Tradition, & American Culture.* Chapel Hill: University of North Carolina Press, 1995.

Cooey, Paula M. *Jonathan Edwards on Nature and Destiny: A Systematic Analysis.* Lewiston, NY: Edwin Mellen Press, 1985.

Danaher, William J., Jr. *The Trinitarian Ethics of Jonathan Edwards.* Louisville: Westminster John Knox Press, 2004.

Daniel, Stephen H. *The Philosophy of Jonathan Edwards.* Bloomington, IN: Indiana University Press, 1994.

De Jong, J. A. *As the Waters Cover the Sea: Millennial Expectations in the Rise of Anglo-American Missions.* Kampen: J. H. Kok, 1970.

Delattre, Roland André. *Beauty and Sensibility in the Thought of Jonathan Edwards: An Essay in Aesthetics and Theological Ethics.* New Haven: Yale University Press, 1968.

De Prospo, R. C. *Theism in the Discourse of Jonathan Edwards.* Newark: University of Delaware Press, 1985.

Elwood, Douglas J. *The Philosophical Theology of Jonathan Edwards.* New York: Columbia University Press, 1960.

Erdt, Terrence. *Jonathan Edwards: Art and the Sense of the Heart.* Amherst: University of Massachusetts Press, 1980.

Fiering Norman. *Jonathan Edwards's Moral Thought and Its British Context.* Chapel Hill: University of North Carolina Press, 1981.

Gerstner, John H. *Steps to Salvation: The Evangelistic Message of Jonathan Edwards.* Philadelphia: Westminster Press, 1959.

———. *The Rational Biblical Theology of Jonathan Edwards.* 3 vols. Powhatan, VA: Berea, 1991–3.

Gildrie, Richard P. *The Profane, the Civil, and the Godly: The Reformation of Manners in Orthodox New England, 1679–1749.* University Park: Pennsylvania State University Press, 1994.

Guelzo, Allen C. *Edwards on the Will: A Century of American Theological Debate.* Middletown, CT: Wesleyan University Press, 1989.

Hall, David D. *Worlds of Wonder, Days of Judgment: Popular Religious Belief in Early New England.* New York: Knopf, 1989.

Hall, Richard A. S. *The Neglected Northampton Texts of Jonathan Edwards: Edwards on Society and Politics.* Lewiston, NY: Edwin Mellen Press, 1990.

Holbrook, Clyde A. *The Ethics of Jonathan Edwards: Morality and Aesthetics.* Ann Arbor: University of Michigan Press, 1973.

———. *Jonathan Edwards: The Valley and Nature: An Interpretive Essay.* Lewisburg: Bucknell University Press, 1987.

Holmes, Stephen R. *God of Grace and God of Glory: An Account of the Theology of Jonathan Edwards.* Grand Rapids: Eerdmans, 2000.

Kling, David W. *A Field of Divine Wonders: The New Divinity and Village Revivals in Northwestern Connecticut, 1792–1822.* University Park: Pennsylvania State University Press, 1993.

Kreider, Glenn R. *Jonathan Edwards's Interpretation of Revelation 4:1–8:1.* Lanham, MA: University Press of America, 2004.

Lee, Sang Hyun. *The Philosophical Theology of Jonathan Edwards.* Princeton: Princeton University Press, 1988.

Lovelace, Richard F. *The American Pietism of Cotton Mather: Origins of American Evangelicalism.* Grand Rapids: Christian University Press, 1979.

McClymond, Michael J. *Encounters with God: An Approach to the Theology of Jonathan Edwards.* New York: Oxford University Press, 1998.

McDermott, Gerald R. *One Holy and Happy Society: The Public Theology of Jonathan Edwards.* University Park: Pennsylvania State University Press, 1992.

———. *Jonathan Edwards Confronts the Gods: Christian Theology, Enlightenment Religion, and Non-Christian Faiths.* New York: Oxford University Press, 2000.

Miller, Perry. *The New England Mind: From Colony to Province.* Cambridge, MA: Harvard University Press, 1953.

Morimoto, Anri. *Jonathan Edwards and the Catholic Vision of Salvation.* University Park: Pennsylvania State University Press, 1995.

Noll, Mark A. *American Evangelical Christianity: An Introduction.* Malden, MA: Blackwell, 2001.

Opie, John. *Jonathan Edwards and the Enlightenment.* Lexington, MA: Heath, 1969.

Pauw, Amy Plantinga. *The Supreme Harmony of All: The Trinitarian Theology of Jonathan Edwards.* Grand Rapids: Eerdmans, 2002.

Peterson, Mark A. *The Price of Redemption: The Spiritual Economy of Puritan New England.* Stanford: Stanford University Press, 1997.

Pfisterer, Karl Dietrich. *The Prism of Scripture: Studies on History and Historicity in the Work of Jonathan Edwards.* Bern: Herbert Lang, 1975.

Piper, John. *A God Entranced Vision of All Things: The Legacy of Jonathan Edwards.* Wheaton, IL: Crossway, 2004.

Porterfield, Amanda. *Feminine Spirituality in America: From Sarah Edwards to Martha Graham.* Philadelphia: Temple University Press, 1980.

———. *Female Piety in Puritan New England: The Emergence of Religious Humanism.* New York: Oxford University Press, 1992.

Post, Stephen G. *Christian Love and Self-Denial: An Historical and Normative Study of Jonathan Edwards, Samuel Hopkins, and American Theological Ethics.* Lanham, MD: University Press of America, 1987.

Scheick, William J. *The Writings of Jonathan Edwards: Theme, Motif, and Style.* College Station: Texas A&M University Press, 1975.

Storms, C. Samuel. *Tragedy in Eden: Original Sin in the Theology of Jonathan Edwards.* Lanham, MD: University Press of America, 1985.

Stout, Harry S. *The New England Soul: Preaching and Religious Culture in Colonial New England.* New York: Oxford University Press, 1986.

Sweeney, Douglas A. *Nathaniel Taylor, New Haven Theology, and the Legacy of Jonathan Edwards.* New York: Oxford University Press, 2003.

———. *The American Evangelical Story: A History of the Movement.* Grand Rapids: Baker, 2005.

Sweeney, Douglas A. and Guelzo, Allen C., eds. *The New England Theology, 1734–1852: America's First Indigenous Theological Tradition, from Jonathan Edwards and the New Divinity to Edwards Amasa Park.* Grand Rapids, MI: Baker, 2006.

Turnbull, Ralph G. *Jonathan Edwards, The Preacher.* Grand Rapids: Baker, 1958.

Walton, Brad. *Religious Affections, and the Puritan Analysis of True Piety, Spiritual Sensations, and Heart Religion.* Lewiston, NY: Edwin Mellen Press, 2002.

Ward, W. R. *The Protestant Evangelical Awakening.* Cambridge: Cambridge University Press, 1992.

Westerkamp, Marilyn J. *Triumph of the Laity: Scots-Irish Piety and the Great Awakening, 1625–1760.* New York: Oxford University Press, 1988.

Westra, Helen. *The Minister's Task and Calling in the Sermons of Jonathan Edwards.* Lewiston, NY: Edwin Mellen Press, 1986.

Wilson, Robert J. *The Benevolent Deity: Ebenezer Gay and the Rise of Rational Religion in New England, 1696–1787.* Philadelphia: University of Pennsylvania Press, 1984.

Zakai, Avihu. *Jonathan Edwards's Philosophy of History: The Reenchantment of the World in the Age of Enlightenment.* Princeton: Princeton University Press, 2003.

Collections of Essays on Edwards

Angoff, Charles, ed. *Jonathan Edwards: His Life and Influence.* Cranbury, NJ: Associated University Presses, 1975.

Hart, D. G., Lucas, Sean Michael and Nichols, Stephen J., eds. *American Religion and the Evangelical Tradition.* Grand Rapids: Baker Academic, 2003.

Hatch, Nathan O. and Stout, Harry S., eds. *Jonathan Edwards and the American Experience.* New York: Oxford University Press, 1988.

Helm, Paul and Crisp, Oliver, eds. *Jonathan Edwards: Philosophical Theologian.* Aldershot, UK: Ashgate, 2003.

Kling, David W. and Sweeney, Douglas A., eds. *Jonathan Edwards at Home and Abroad: Historical Memories, Cultural Movements, Global Horizons.* Columbia: University of South Carolina Press, 2003.

Lee, Sang Hyun, ed. *The Princeton Companion to Jonathan Edwards.* Princeton, NJ: Princeton University Press, 2005.

Lee, Sang Hyun and Guelzo, Allen C., eds. *Edwards in Our Time: Jonathan Edwards and the Shaping of American Religion.* Grand Rapids: Eerdmans, 1999.

Oberg, Barbara B. and Stout, Harry S., eds. *Benjamin Franklin, Jonathan Edwards, and the Representation of American Culture.* New York: Oxford University Press, 1993.

Scheick, William J., ed. *Critical Essays on Jonathan Edwards.* Boston: G. K. Hall, 1980.

Stein, Stephen J., ed. *Jonathan Edwards's Writings: Text, Context, Interpretation.* Bloomington: Indiana University Press, 1996.

Stout, Harry S., Minkema, Kenneth P. and Maskell, Caleb J. D., eds. *Jonathan Edwards at 300: Essays on the Tercentenary of His Birth.* Lanham, MD: University Press of America, 2005.

Collections of Primary Texts

Bailey, Richard A. and Wills, Gregory A., eds. *The Salvation of Soul: Nine Previously Unpublished Sermons on the Call of Ministry and the Gospel by Jonathan Edwards.* Wheaton, IL: Crossway, 2002.

Faust, Clarence H. and Johnson, Thomas H., eds. *Jonathan Edwards: Representative Selections, with Introduction, Bibliography, and Notes.* 2nd ed., New York: Hill and Wang, 1962.

Ferm, Vergilius. *Puritan Sage: Collected Writings of Jonathan Edwards.* New York: Library Publishers, 1953.

Karlsen, Carol F. and Crumpacker, Laurie, eds. *The Journal of Esther Edwards Burr 1754–1757.* New Haven: Yale University Press, 1984.

Kimnach, Wilson H., Minkema, Kenneth P. and Sweeney, Douglas A., eds. *The Sermons of Jonathan Edwards: A Reader.* New Haven: Yale University Press, 1999.

Levin, David, ed. *Jonathan Edwards: A Profile.* New York: Hill and Wang, 1969.

McMullen, Michael D., ed. *The Blessing of God: Previously Unpublished Sermons of Jonathan Edwards.* Nashville, TN: Broadman and Holman, 2003.

Smith, John E., Stout, Harry S. and Minkema, Kenneth P., eds. *A Jonathan Edwards Reader.* New Haven: Yale University Press, 1995.

Townsend, Harvey, ed. *The Philosophy of Jonathan Edwards from His Private Notebooks.* Eugene: University of Oregon Press, 1955.

Van Doren, Carl, ed. *Benjamin Franklin and Jonathan Edwards: Selections from Their Writings.* New York: Charles Scribner's Sons, 1920.

Winslow, Ola Elizabeth, ed. *Jonathan Edwards: Basic Writings.* New York: New American Library, 1966.

Bibliographical Aids

Johnson, Thomas H. *The Printed Writings of Jonathan Edwards, 1703–1758: A Bibliography.* New York: B. Franklin, 1970 [c. 1940].

Lesser, M. X. *Jonathan Edwards: A Reference Guide.* Boston: G. K. Hall, 1981.

———. *Jonathan Edwards: An Annotated Bibliography, 1979–1993.* Westport, CT: Greenwood Press, 1994.

———. *The Printed Writings of Jonathan Edwards, 1703–1758* (rev. ed.) Princeton: Princeton Theological Seminary, 2003.

Manspeaker, Nancy. *Jonathan Edwards: Bibliographical Synopses.* New York: Edwin Mellen Press, 1981.

Index

Other titles in the series (*continued from page iii*)